Political Succession in the Arab World

Political succession is a key issue in the contemporary Middle East. In this new study the author examines the process and shows how respect for those in authority and tribal codes of loyalty have been far more influential in maintaining regimes than security institutions and political repression.

The Arab world is faced by political turmoil and demands for reform. Many of the problems of the region are attributed to the form of leadership that dominates the area – leadership that is authoritarian and focused on regime survival rather than political change. This book highlights the ways in which family loyalties pervade political, economic and social life and how constitutions are being used to consolidate the power of ruling families in republics and monarchies.

This volume explores the notion that the region's rulers, monarchic and republican, are inclined to pass their power on to their sons, and evaluates the use they make of familial and tribal networks to maintain their power. The work seeks to demonstrate that, despite economic and social problems, Arabs value stability and prefer an authoritarian family-based regime over a government run by Islamist groups.

Providing new insights into the influences on political succession in the Middle East, this work will be of great interest to scholars of Middle East studies, history and international relations.

Anthony Billingsley is a lecturer at the University of New South Wales in Australia, having spent many years in the diplomatic and intelligence areas. His areas of interest include the politics of the Middle East, especially the Gulf region, as well as international and constitutional law.

Routledge Studies in Middle Eastern Politics

1. Algeria in Transition
Reforms and development prospects
Ahmed Aghrout with Redha M. Bougherira

2. Palestinian Refugee Repatriation
Global perspectives
Edited by Michael Dumper

3. The International Politics of the Persian Gulf
A cultural genealogy
Arshin Adib-Moghaddam

4. Israeli Politics and the First Palestinian Intifada
Political opportunities, framing processes and contentious politics
Eitan Y. Alimi

5. Democratization in Morocco
The political elite and struggles for power in the post-independence state
Lise Storm

6. Secular and Islamic Politics in Turkey
The making of the justice and development party
Ümit Cizre

7. The United States and Iran
Sanctions, wars and the policy of dual containment
Sasan Fayazmanesh

8. Civil Society in Algeria
The political functions of associational life
Andrea Liverani

9. Jordanian-Israeli Relations
The peacebuilding experience
Mutayyam al O'ran

10. Kemalism in Turkish Politics
The Republican People's Party, secularism and nationalism
Sinan Ciddi

11. Islamism, Democracy and Liberalism in Turkey
The case of the AKP
William Hale and Ergun Özbudun

12. Politics and Violence in Israel/Palestine
Democracy versus military rule
Lev Luis Grinberg

13. Intra-Jewish Conflict in Israel
White Jews, Black Jews
Sami Shalom Chetrit

14. Holy Places in the Israeli-Palestinian Conflict
Confrontation and co-existence
Edited by Marshall J. Breger, Yitzhak Reiter and Leonard Hammer

15. Plurality and Citizenship in Israel
Moving beyond the Jewish/Palestinian civil divide
Edited by Dan Avnon and Yotam Benziman

16. Ethnic Politics in Israel
The margins and the Ashkenasi Center
As'ad Ghanem

17. Islamists and Secularists in Egypt
Opposition, conflict and cooperation
Dina Shehata

18. Political Succession in the Arab World
Constitutions, family loyalties and Islam
Anthony Billingsley

Political Succession in the Arab World

Constitutions, family loyalties and Islam

Anthony Billingsley

Routledge
Taylor & Francis Group
LONDON AND NEW YORK

First published 2010
by Routledge
2 Park Square, Milton Park, Abingdon, Oxon OX14 4RN

Simultaneously published in the USA and Canada
by Routledge
270 Madison Ave, New York, NY 10016

Routledge is an imprint of the Taylor & Francis Group, an informa business

Typeset in Times New Roman
by Keystroke, Tettenhall, Wolverhampton
Printed and bound in Great Britain
by CPI Antony Rowe, Chippenham, Wiltshire

British Library Cataloguing in Publication Data
A catalogue record for this book is available
from the British Library

Library of Congress Cataloging in Publication Data
Billingsley, Anthony.
Political succession in the Arab world : constitutions, family loyalties, and Islam / Anthony Billingsley.
p. cm. – (Routledge studies in Middle Eastern politics ; 18)
Includes bibliographical references and index.
1. Heads of state–Succession–Arab countries. 2. Arab countries–Politics and government. I. Title.
JQ1850.A58B55 2009
352.230917′4927–dc22
2009025651

ISBN10: 0–415–49536–9 (hbk)
ISBN10: 0–203–86282–1 (ebk)

ISBN13: 978–0–415–49536–3 (hbk)
ISBN13: 978–0–203–86282–7 (ebk)

Contents

Acknowledgements

In writing this book I have received the assistance of numerous people who have provided guidance, support and encouragement. In particular I wish to thank my wife, Brenda, whose patience and drive were vital to my maintaining momentum throughout the project. I also must express my deep appreciation to Emma White, who provided support with editing and comments which greatly improved the end product.

To my children, Andrew, Cameron and Owen, and to Lucie Willink, I wish also to say thank you for your help and understanding.

Figures A5.1 and A5.2 in Appendix 5 are from *Arab Elites: Negotiating the Politics of Change* edited by Volker Perthes. Copyright © 2004 by Lynne Rienner Publishers, Inc. Used with permission of the publisher.

Note on transliteration

This book does not attempt strictly to follow a formal method of transliteration such as that employed by major publications such as the *International Journal of Middle East Studies* (based on the Encyclopaedia of Islam system). Diacritical marks have not been used, except for the mark ` to indicate the *ein* in certain instances, for example, 'Shi`a' but not '`Abdallah', '`Ali' or 'Mu`awiya'.

The transliteration attempts to approximate the Arabic to the extent possible. For example the spelling 'Quran' is used rather than 'Koran'. Otherwise, transliteration generally follows common practice, such as 'caliph' rather than 'khalifa'.

Spellings and interpretations are based on Wehr, Hans, *A Dictionary of Modern Written Arabic*, Cowan, J. Milton (ed.) (Wiesbaden: Otto Harrassowitz, London: George Allen and Unwin Ltd., 1971), and Middle East Centre for Arab Studies, *A Selected Word List of Modern Literary Arabic* (Beirut: Khayats, 1969).

Introduction

> No question in Islam is more fundamental and shaping than this one, a source of political instability and violent dispute from the beginning, as it remains to this day. Who could, after all, succeed a prophet who was also a dominant statesman? In this highly contested succession lie the origins of many of the major shapes and terms of Islam . . . Shiites, and Sunnis, caliphs and emirs, Umayyads and Abbasids, all of these crucial internal divisions.[1]

The Arab world is a unique political system. It is a region of dramatic political contrasts with dynamic forces challenging the structure of the region's state system and authoritarian governments attempting to contain demands for political change. It is a new system, having achieved independence from foreign rule only in the past 100 years. But it is also a system with a long tradition reaching back to a tribal past and reflecting the revolutionary impact of the Prophet Mohammed in the seventh century AD. It is also the inheritor of a memory of Moslem greatness inspired by the achievements of the Ottoman Empire over hundreds of years.

To a great extent, the Arab political system is still developing and establishing its own particular identity. Major features of the system have not yet acquired established status. Even the state system itself remains a tentative response to the collapse of the Ottoman Empire and there are numerous forces competing with the state for the loyalty of its citizens. In that context, the governments of the Arab world are operating in a state of crisis. Every Arab government is confronted by major challenges to its power. The response to this environment has been to focus on survival and consolidation. It is in the response to the challenges confronting the region's governments that the shape and nature of the Arab political tradition can be discerned.

The behaviour of Arab regimes is particularly affected by the dramatic economic, social and political change that has been sweeping through the Arab world over the past few generations. The challenges of the modern period have been particularly demanding of the Arab world, with its growing populations and faltering economies, as well as its central importance to the world economy. Demands for political reform can be heard around the region. Arab regimes are responding to these demands, but their response has been to follow a course consistent with the Arab tradition rather than to imitate the liberal democratic ideal favoured by the West. They are operating within a tradition which is resilient and creates a major filter through which new ideas need to be fed if they are to take root. The response of Arab governments to calls for change has been to attempt to modernise – not to promote democracy, but to consolidate their hold on power in the new environment. Governments in the region are determined not to surrender executive power in the name of greater openness and liberalisation. This is not to suggest that all Arab regimes are necessarily opposed to the idea of greater democracy, liberalisation and participation or that concepts like the rule of law have no future among the region's states.[2] Rather the suggestion is that Arab regimes are still engaged in the nation-building project. They are still trying to establish themselves, and the challenges they are facing are immense. This is also to suggest that the governments in place in the Arab world are going through a major transition phase which will see them become more sophisticated in their approach to government. In response to the increased complexity of the world in which they exist, Arab governments are increasingly turning to the 'mechanisms of state', including the rule of law, to achieve recognition and acceptance of their legitimacy.

One of the most notable and important characteristics of the Arab world is the way in which the region has come to be dominated by long-serving rulers who are committed to dynastic or family rule. Regardless of whether they are rulers of republics or of monarchies, there is a tendency on the part of Arab leaders to want to pass on power to their sons. Formal Western models of governance, with their institutional mechanisms for the transfer of power, are in place in most Arab countries. The impact of these models is, however, restricted and the predilection to dynastic rule suggests something deeper and more enduring in the Arab world's approach to politics, an indication of the imprint of the Arabs' tribal and patriarchal origins, of the complex heritage of Islam and of the lessons learnt from generations of exposure to the ideas of outsiders.

Critics and analysts interpret the failure of the Arab world to develop along liberal democratic lines as a fundamental flaw in the region's social and political structures,[3] and that out of this flaw emerge political instability and violent resistance which spills out into the wider international community. It is argued that the way to overcome the region's weaknesses is to improve the economic and governmental performance of the region and that the path to this end is through the process of democratisation. The problems of the region, however, do not necessarily reflect popular rejection of the region's governments for all their failings. Instead, Arab regimes enjoy a significant level of legitimacy, without which they would not survive. Arabs have a deep aversion to political instability and, partly with this in mind, they have traditionally tolerated autocratic rule. They are also familiar with the complex network of patrimonial relations that Arab regimes have established in their societies. As a result, significant sectors of Arab societies have a vested interest in the survival of the regimes and the stability those regimes provide. The result is a precarious legitimacy, but one that has endured over generations.

With this in mind, this book examines the background of the Arab political tradition to highlight a number of aspects that explain the appeal and the tenacity of the dynastic approach to political succession. The first of these aspects, tribal and family loyalties and attitudes, is central to the issue and derives from the tribal past. Loyalty to the family and the tribe permeates Arab societies and has considerable implications for the broad sweep of Arab politics. Despite suggestions from some observers that urbanisation and the power of the modern state have destroyed the traditional tribal way of life, the persistence of the attitudes associated with tribal and especially family loyalties is a key to understanding the way in which Arab governments and populations behave. The second great historic force working on the Arab political tradition is Islam. A movement that revolutionised the world of the Arabs in the seventh century, the religion affects most aspects of Arab life, including the political. Taken together, these two characteristics contribute to a political tradition in which the idea of dynastic succession has been a constant and central element throughout the tumultuous years since the death of the Prophet Mohammed in 632 AD. In some respects, the impact of Islam was incomplete and Arabs were forced to augment the teachings of the Prophet Mohammed with the older traditions of the tribe. The issues of political succession and the nature of leadership are two areas where that resort to the past for values and rules was necessary. The result has been a tension over the extent to which dynastic succession is an acceptable part of the Arab political tradition.

Despite this tension, the practice of dynastic succession exerts a strong appeal among the political elite throughout the region. In almost every country of the Arab world the ruling groups believe that sovereign power should be closely held within a family group. Moreover, whilst dynastic succession has widespread support among the Arab ruling elites, there is also significant support for or, at least, acceptance of the practice among the general population in Arab countries. Indeed, dynasticism and family solidarity are pervasive features of Arab society and can be identified as underpinning many aspects of Arab political, social and commercial behaviour. To that extent, dynastic succession reflects mainstream Arab attitudes. Moreover, it is striking that the urge to dynastic rule is common to both monarchies and republics. The logical incongruity of dynastic succession in republics and the difficulty in institutionalising such an approach are obvious, even to Arab rulers themselves. Nevertheless, republican regimes appear determined to try to maintain family rule. Their strongly felt need to regularise and systematise the practice represents a challenge to all Arab republican governments.

Military force has been a characteristic of the political process in the post-independence era in the Arab world. Arab governments have begun to try to break their reliance on force and are attempting to diversify their methods of control. This includes a focus on political mechanisms to consolidate their dominant positions. To this end, Arab regimes are turning to the constitution as a potential source of legitimacy. While they have no real precedent in the Arab political tradition, written constitutions and legislative frameworks are becoming increasingly important ways of regularising, systematising and legitimising the practice of governance in the region. Constitutions are being adopted by all Arab governments as a way of clarifying, consolidating and legitimising the governmental structure of the state, including the process of succession. As one generation of leaders gives way to the next, constitutions are being seen as an important way of establishing a set of rules for government which will consolidate their dominant positions and provide a framework within which responses to the new international environment can be developed. The rulers of the Arab world believe that a constitutional structure will relieve or divert some of the pressure for change and give their rule added legitimacy. In this pursuit of constitutional justification Arab elites see, in what is essentially a European idea, an opportunity to reinforce the tribal underpinnings of their societies and the perpetuation of their rule.[4]

It is possible that, over time, constitutions will develop from a device for regime survival into an important factor in the evolution of the Arab political tradition. While the various regimes see their constitutions as political processes to be exploited, the constitutions also represent vital elements in the political process. Constitutions are the embodiment of political compromises between competing groups. The stability of states depends on the maintenance of such agreements. Once the deals have been agreed and incorporated into a formal document, they give that instrument a certain authority which cannot be ignored or defied without endangering the regime's hold on power. Over time, the Arab constitutions may well play a part in guiding and promoting the cultural shift that will be necessary if Arab political systems are to adapt effectively to changing circumstances. Among other things, they may come to facilitate change in the political process towards a more open and representative system.

A central feature of the new Arab constitutions is their treatment of political succession. The monarchic governments have reasonably clearly spelt out the way in which power is to be passed from one generation to the next. The fact that the process is spelt out in clear, public terms is intended to minimise the possibility of challenging the arrangements. For republican governments the task is more complex as it is not possible to specify dynastic succession in the constitution of a republic. Nevertheless, the constitution is seen as an important instrument which has a role in legitimising the transfer of power from fathers to their sons.

Methodology

To address all these dimensions of political succession in Arab monarchies and republics properly, extensive use has been made of written sources, including primary and secondary Arabic- and English-language materials. This book also draws on an extensive series of interviews conducted over a period of years, mainly in the Middle East. The interviews were conducted with a range of people, including senior members of the Jordanian and Emirati royal families, current and former cabinet ministers in a number of countries, government and semi-government officials in Egypt, dissidents in Syria, academics and media experts. Interviews were also conducted with people in a number of countries who were in no way involved with politics. The intent was to develop a picture of Arab attitudes to key issues of relevance to this book from as diverse a group of people as possible. Other material is based on informal conversations with friends and contacts in the region. These relationships were built up over many years, including the experience of having lived and worked in a number of Middle Eastern countries between 1972 and 2001.

Not all countries of the Arab world are dealt with in this book. The focus is on those Arab states that have developed out of the great Arab waves of conquest and integration of the seventh and eighth centuries AD. These are the 17 states stretching from the Euphrates to the Atlas.[5] They are states whose orientations are largely Mediterranean and west Asian. Countries like Somalia, Sudan, Mauritania and the Comoros are not addressed as they are not significant elements in the Arab political system and they have a strong African influence alongside their Arab heritage. While geographically and historically rooted in the Middle East region, Iran and Turkey are not Arab countries and are not dealt with, except in addressing the important historic political and social influences of the two former empires on Arab governing practices. Similarly, Israel is not an Arab country and is not be included, despite its constant presence in the considerations of many Arab leaders.

The particular focus is on succession in republican Egypt, Libya, Syria and Yemen on one hand and on monarchic Jordan, Morocco and the Arabian Peninsula states on the other hand. It is possible to extrapolate from the experiences of these countries to much, if not all, the Arab world. The states selected have been chosen because they demonstrate different aspects of the dilemmas facing Arab regimes. Syria is a republic where a dynastic succession has already taken place. Egypt and Yemen have not yet taken that step, but there is persistent speculation that the sons of President Mubarak in Egypt and President Saleh in Yemen are being prepared to take over in due course. In both cases succession is confronted by significant obstacles, some of which are bound up in the countries' constitutions. The other example that is drawn on, Libya, is also facing the prospect of dynastic succession. Libya perhaps does not have the constitutional inhibitions that complicate the other examples, but it is nonetheless fraught with political challenge.

For the monarchies, the issue is ostensibly simpler to the extent that dynastic succession is a feature of monarchies wherever they are in place. The challenge for this group is to be found, at least in part, in the impact of the form of the succession arrangements in place on the monarchies' ability to survive. The nature of the succession mechanism, especially the issue of primogeniture,[6] is thought to influence the degree to which a monarchy is stable and secure. Jordan and Morocco represent the primogeniture model, while the states of the Arabian Peninsula have a different, more tribal-based approach.

Discussion of some key terms

Several important concepts throughout this book need to be addressed. While this discussion is not about democracy per se, much of the criticism of the region, its leadership and succession practices and performance is conducted in the context of

Western views of the efficacy of democracy as an ordering system. In this context, a useful definition of democracy is given by Lipset:

> 'Democracy' in a complex society may be defined as a political system which supplies regular constitutional opportunities for changing the governing officials, and a social mechanism which permits the largest possible part of the population to influence major decisions by choosing among contenders for political office.
>
> This definition, . . . implies a number of specific conditions: (1) a 'political formula' or body of beliefs specifying which institutions – political parties, a free press, and so forth – are legitimate (accepted as proper by all); (2) one set of political leaders in office; and one or more sets of recognised leaders attempting to gain office.[7]

Arab political systems reflect some of these characteristics to varying degrees, including where elements of traditional practices have survived. There was, for example, a basic democratic element in the working of the Arab tribe, including tribal assemblies. Watt notes, however, that this element has not been sufficient to provoke the development of institutions of representative government associated with Western democracies. He speculates that this might reflect the persisting personal element of Arab politics as reflected in the tribal *majlis* and the tendency towards the personalisation of loyalties. Watt also stresses the Moslem emphasis on the rules of God rather than the rights of man.[8]

Another term is 'patrimonialism' which, in the Islamic and Arab contexts, is seen by Black as a:

> . . . system of government in which the ruler is permitted to regard the state as his and his family's benefice (from on high), and the people are regarded as clients under his protective and distributive patronage. His powers are subject not to the intervention of others (far less constitutional rules) but to the unwritten obligations of fatherly beneficence. This includes the duty-right to manage the economy for the benefit of the people ('estate-type domination').[9]

Black observes that this relationship between ruler and subject has been constantly in conflict with attempts by succeeding dynasties to enforce religious rectitude as ways of strengthening their hold on power. He also identifies as a 'striking feature in the history of Islamic political thought' the continuous dialectic between neo-tribalism and patrimonialism. He argues that this dialectic continues to the modern day and, to an extent, drives the relationship between religion and politics.[10]

Yet another term is 'tribalism'. Tapper notes the great difficulty associated with the development of an acceptable definition of the term.[11] However, it is a necessary task because of the way in which tribalism and patrimonialism together have reinforced the importance of heredity, especially as an indicator of religious and leadership worth, as well as social standing. Therefore, Arab tribalism is being taken as representing a persistent form of social organisation and behaviour throughout the Arab world which is expressed in the continuing importance of family and clan and tribal and dynastic connections. The form this organisation takes has changed dramatically over time and varies across the countries of the Arab world. What is important in this discussion of succession in the Arab world, however, is not so much the tribal structure and the power they can exert within a particular society. Rather the focus is on attitudes which have derived from older forms of tribal and familial organisation and which have crossed into modern society. This importance is particularly reflected in an exclusivist attitude towards outsiders and a focus on kinship and personal relationships. A popular manifestation of these personal relationships is contained in the term '*wasta*', a term that means intercession or mediation, but also has the connotations of influence. Arabs will seek the benefits of *wasta* from people in authority or in positions of power. Rather than pursue an interest or issue through formal bureaucratic channels, tribal and familial connections will be exploited. For those in power, the ability to intercede on behalf of tribe or family members is an important indication of their power and a reinforcement of their patrimonial standing.

The final term to be dealt with is 'primogeniture'. This is a controversial term that is important in understanding the processes of succession in force in a number of Arab monarchies. 'Primogeniture' is defined in the Chambers Dictionary as 'the principle or right of inheritance of the first born'. In the Arab world the principle is applied in a number of monarchies. Article 28 of the Jordanian constitution states:

> The Throne of the Hashemite Kingdom of Jordan is hereditary to the dynasty of King Abdullah Ibn Al-Hussein in a direct line through his male heirs as provided hereinafter:
>
> (a) The Royal title shall pass from the holder of the Throne to his eldest son and to the eldest son of that son and in linear succession by a similar process thereafter. Should the eldest son die before the Throne devolves upon him, his eldest son shall inherit the Throne, despite the existence of brothers to the deceased son.

The Moroccan and Bahraini constitutions contain similar provisions. They also, however, all provide provision for the king to break with this structure should he so desire. The following completes Article 28 (a) of the Jordanian constitution:

> The King may, however, select one of his brothers as heir apparent. In this event, title to the Throne shall pass to him from the holder of the Throne.

In many instances, it is sufficient to refer to family rule or dynasticism. The practice in some of the Gulf states, for example, is unclear. The succession in Abu Dhabi went from Sheikh Zayed to his oldest son, but there is no indication whether that was on the basis of primogeniture or other considerations. There are, however, occasions when a degree of precision is helpful as it bears on relationships within ruling families. It is also important to the extent that a number of rulers of countries where primogeniture does not apply appear to be drawn to the concept.

Outline of chapters

The book is broken up into chapters which address the most important influences on the issue of succession and Arab leaders' attempts to use constitutions to consolidate their power. Chapter 1, 'The Arab political tradition', sets the context in which Arab governments are operating and the dramas of political succession are being played out. The chapter highlights the intense domestic and international criticism of the way in which Arab politics are conducted. It also provides some explanation of the factors that drive Arab leaders.

Chapter 2, 'Competing influences: Tribalism, Islam and outsiders in the Arab world', provides background to the Arabs' traditional approach to succession. It looks at those forces that have contributed to the development of the Arab political tradition and, in particular, attitudes that encourage the idea of dynastic succession. In particular, the chapter considers the nature and the persistence through history of tribal and family loyalties, which have a significant impact on attitudes to leadership and succession throughout the region. The other great influence on Arab thought, Islam, is also considered, particularly in the context of the degree of guidance the religion provides Arabs in their attempts to come to terms with leadership and succession. The other major influence on the Arab political tradition considered is that exerted by the various peoples that were conquered by or who ruled over the Arabs. These include the Byzantine Greeks, the Persians, various Turkic groups culminating in the Ottomans and, finally, the West.

Chapter 3, 'The just prince: Leadership and legitimacy in the Arab world', examines the nature of Arab leadership, including the various influences on the way in which leadership is exercised in the Arab world. In particular the chapter analyses the nature and the sources of legitimacy from which Arab leaders derive their authority. Whereas the Western liberal tradition sees legitimacy as deriving from the concept of 'the people', Arab leaders throughout history have established their authority on a different basis. Leadership in the Arab world has tended to be a top–down process, where the obligation of the population is to accept those in power as long as they adhere to certain conditions. At the same time, public acquiescence or support is not an irrelevant issue and it is argued that Arab leaders enjoy greater legitimacy than critics in the West acknowledge.

Chapter 4, 'Family first: Arab succession and dynasticism', looks at a fundamental issue of this book: the question of political succession. It examines how leaders in the modern Arab monarchy and republic have tended to pass on power to their own family members, and how this practice enjoys a significant degree of support in Arab society. The problems facing succession in monarchic and republican systems are considered in the light of some of the issues raised earlier, such as the stress on the family and tribe and the desire for stability in the Arab polity.

Chapter 5, 'Constitutionalism and constitutions: The challenge of succession', examines the origins of constitutions in the region and the attitudes that Arabs have towards them. In the course of this analysis, the chapter considers the legal basis of Arab political systems and highlights some of the major divisions in Arab thinking, such as the different schools of Sunni and Shi`a Islam. These differences are particularly important when it comes to the handling of the issue of succession. The chapter also contains a brief comparison of the state of constitutionalism in the Arab world with the situation in Tudor and Stuart England and with current practices in some countries identified with constitutionalism. The intention is to highlight the importance of evolution in the development of respect for constitutionalism. Attention is paid to the implications of the inclusion in constitutions of agreements between contending groups which relate to the fundamental principles on which societies are run.

Chapter 6, 'Back to the future: Arab monarchies', looks at the way in which tribalism and Islam influence the way in which the Arab monarchies operate. The chapter looks at a number of monarchies, examining the nature of their power and the reasons for their survival. The main focus of the chapter is Jordan and Morocco, as examples of the practice of dynastic rule based on primogeniture, and the tribal monarchies of the Arabian Peninsula, which rule within a dynastic framework. The chapter examines the relative strengths of these two approaches to hereditary rule.

Chapter 7, 'Hybrids: Monarchic republics of the Arab world', looks at the republican model and analyses the approaches to succession of Egypt, Syria, Yemen and Libya. These are systems where the issue of dynastic succession is being played out and where governments are attempting to come to terms with the logical and political conundrum of seeking to hold power in family hands in the context of a republican system. As with the monarchies, the constitutions of the Arab republics are coming to play an important role in the way in which republican leaders exercise their power and are providing a basis on which the nature of republican power is changing.

Chapter 8, 'Tradition versus change: The challenge of dynasticism in the Arab political tradition', sums up the evidence gathered to demonstrate the importance of the dynastic impulse in all types of Arab political systems. It also highlights the growing reliance on constitutional measures by Arab rulers. The chapter also provides some tentative suggestions about how this trend might develop over time.

1 The Arab political tradition

> In the light of on-going events, it appears that the Arab psychology has become addicted to the dictatorial model of life. Indeed, all the Arab peoples – all of them – have become completely addicted to dictatorship, oppression, and regimes that beat (the people) on their heads with their shoes and hit them below the belt . . . I do not exaggerate by saying this because, within each of us, there is a little dictator who feels gratification when he is repressed by those stronger and more brutal than he and who, at the same time, does not refrain from acting this same way, in his milieu, towards those weaker and inferior in status.[1]

The Arab region represents one of the world's most important geo-political units. It occupies a crucial position in the international system, where contests between the world's major powers have historically been pursued. The region contains a large and rapidly growing population and, of course, vital economic resources on which the world is deeply dependent. The Arab world is described as inherently authoritarian and oppressive, features that are seen as being responsible for major social and economic problems. These problems are inextricably linked to some of the great challenges confronting the international community. What follows is an attempt to understand some of the bases of these criticisms and to place Arab political behaviour in the context of an Arab political tradition with its own unique characteristics and values.

The Arab world has been going through a dramatic transition from the era of Ottoman dominance through the tumult of the colonial and early independence periods to the post-Cold War age of uncertainty. After considerable nation-building progress in the early days after independence, Arab countries have failed to keep up with the development of the rest of the world, despite the region's economic potential. International organisations such as the World Bank and the United Nations Development Programme (UNDP) have highlighted the way economic growth in the region has failed to keep pace with the increase of population.[2] Instead, in the past 20 years, the region has been marked by high birth rates, struggling economies, growing social inequality, environmental degradation and significant political unrest.

In the period since the end of the Cold War the problems of economic stagnation and social dislocation have come to be attributed largely to the authoritarian nature of Arab politics. Criticism has focused on the failure of governments to adapt to the times and to develop responsible, accessible and representative governance practices. The Arab approach to political succession and the ways in which regimes regenerate and maintain themselves have been identified as among the most intractable elements of this failure, with particular attention focused on the informal, closed and undemocratic nature of this process in most countries of the region. Arab succession practices are seen as inconsistent with the democratisation that is being promoted by the West and by some in the Arab world itself. Current practices are, however, deeply ingrained with strong Islamic and historical underpinnings. They also reflect the fractious and unstable nature of Arab societies. Change, even when possible, is not easy.

It is a characteristic of the Arab world, with its high degree of repression of domestic debate and dissent, that much of the criticism of Arab political processes is being driven from outside. Outsiders argue that change is overdue, especially as regimes age and new cohorts among Arab populations demand to be heard. Modern, invigorated, inclusive and efficient Arab governments are represented by the West as the most effective antidote to economic stagnation and Islamic extremism. There is a danger, however, that attempts by outsiders to promote change in their own image will be unsuccessful and will instead provoke greater unrest and authoritarianism. One of the results of the 2003 invasion of Iraq, for example, has been the degree to which the overthrow of Saddam Hussein released sectarian and tribal forces that are potentially antipathetic to the West's stated goals of change.

Demands for change from both within and outside the Arab world include the issue of the rule of law. Indeed, real reform will never occur without a radical change to the way in which Arabs regard the nature of power and the roles of their heads of state and government. Governments need to operate within transparent and predictable guidelines which limit government discretion and share power more evenly throughout the community. This is, however, a fundamental issue within the developing Arab political system and one of the most intractable practical issues confronting Arab political leaders today.

The Arab world is, *inter alia*, a manifestation of a people's yearning for a united or single identity in the face of the reality of 22 separate states, which are the members of the Arab League (see Appendix 2).[3] From the early days of independence from the Ottomans and the Europeans, the idea of a united Arab nation has beguiled ordinary Arabs. There are, however, distinct differences that divide the people of the region and lend a certain logic to the continuing existence of those states, including linguistic, cultural and historical variations. Arabic, for example, is, together with Islam, a common thread that runs throughout the region. At the same time, variations between the Arabic spoken on a day-to-day basis in different Arab countries can be considerable. And Islam itself is marked by the great schism between the Sunni and Shi`a branches, which are themselves divided by numerous smaller offshoots. There are differences between Arab countries that draw on their nomadic origins and those that have had more settled histories. Significant variations of outlook exist between those states that have formed part of the Mediterranean civilization and those that have existed on the periphery of that experience. Countries with a long national and cultural history, such as Egypt, display characteristics that are quite different from those of countries with short formal histories as states, such as the countries of the Gulf region.

Despite these differences, the states of the Arab world also reflect shared historical experiences and cultural influences that have resulted in a considerable degree of common identity. On the basis of this identity, it is possible to discern among members of the Arab world clear patterns of similar political and cultural behaviour and attitude from which significant inferences can be drawn. This is a political tradition of considerable coherence and uniformity, making possible meaningful analysis and generalisation of the region.

A system under fire: criticisms of the Arab political system

The reasons for the perceived shortcomings of the Arab world are inevitably diverse. Arab political systems and the tradition on which they are based have been in a state of crisis since the countries of the region achieved independence in the twentieth century. The crisis has been provoked by a number of factors, many of which are exogenous to the region. These include the creation of Israel and the wars that have ensued from that event. Of particular importance, however, has been the impact of Western (and Soviet) interference in the region's affairs. Brown, for instance, describes the Middle East as 'the most penetrated international relations sub-system in today's world' and suggests that the boundaries between local, national, regional and international politics have become so blurred that the politics of the region cannot be understood without reference to the West.[4] Lustick comes to a similar conclusion in his analysis of the treatment of Western attitudes to Mohammed Ali and Nasser of Egypt and Saddam Hussein of Iraq. Lustick concludes that the West was determined not to permit a regional hegemon to develop in the Arab world.[5]

It is, of course, possible that much of the problem lies closer to home in the outmoded and authoritarian nature of Arab governments and a range of endogenous factors. Arab governments have concentrated on regime survival over other goals. This has led to an inability or at times a reluctance to respond flexibly to changing circumstances and to accommodate popular demands for greater access to national spoils. Regimes fail to operate with the necessary level of transparency that would encourage economic growth and give their citizens a sense of identity and involvement in the well-being of their own countries. The result of these factors has been great pressure on the ruling elites throughout the whole region and a perceptible closing of ranks in the face of criticism.

The lack of democracy in the region, despite the formal trappings of the democratic process (i.e. constitutions, elections, political parties and parliaments), has been a direct focus of major criticism. *The Arab Human Development Report, 2002* ranked the Arab world as the least free of all the world's regions based on a range of indicators, including the political process, civil liberties, political rights and the independence of the media.[6] The World Bank has criticised the governments of the Arab world on the basis of their lack of inclusiveness and accountability and argues that weaknesses in governance in the region have been a major factor in the region's poor economic performance since the early 1980s.

This is not to suggest that there is no desire for democracy throughout the Arab world. Public opinion survey results reported over a number of years by various survey organisations suggest that the concept is alive and well throughout much of the Arab world.[7] It is not clear, however, how Arabs perceive democracy in their region and what they expect to derive from it. The enthusiasm for democracy identified by the surveys should perhaps be qualified by recognition that Arabs' idea of democracy is relatively vague and varies from country to country and in response to differing experiences. It is possible that Arabs tend to think about democracy as a step towards reviving Arab military and economic greatness and promoting personal economic advantage rather than from the more philosophical or ideological perspective of votes, open debate, the rule of law and individual rights. Arabs' concern for stability may also condition any enthusiasm for democracy in the region. People of the region highly value political stability and are deeply concerned by the dangers of challenging the established order. In many cases, an attempt to challenge the government is regarded as tantamount to committing a sin.

Regardless of the reasons, it is this lack of a democratic environment within the Arab political system that has been seized upon by critics, both from outside and within the Arab world. The system is accused of being dominated by and even breeding governments that are undemocratic, nepotistic, unaccountable, brutal, corrupt, inflexible and inefficient. Some of the criticisms imply that, for various reasons, Arabs are inherently incapable of organising themselves to run adaptable, efficient and legitimate political systems. Much of the blame for the perceived Arab malaise has been assigned both to Arab culture and to Islam, with its alleged anti-democratic nature. Some Western analysts argue that Western democracy is inconsistent with the Arab and Islamic traditions of the region. Huntington, for example, suggests that the failure of liberal democracy to take hold in Moslem societies is partly a result of the nature of Islam,[8] while the historian Bernard Lewis is equally convinced about the congenital hostility of the Arab world to Western style democracy. Lewis argues that the basic manifestations of democracy, including elections, did not have a place in the development of Islamic political practice and theory, with the result that Islamic states have, over history, been characterised by autocracy. Obedience to the Moslem ruler became a religious duty and disobedience was a crime but also a sin under Islam.[9]

This form of criticism has also been taken up by some Arab commentators. Abdallah Rashid laments the dictatorial impulse of the Arab people, arguing that despotism and oppression have become a central element of the Arab approach to politics.[10] In commenting on the way in which Arab regimes manipulate the political system, Rami Khouri makes the observation that there is a certain predictability surrounding Arab elections with those gaining most in elections comprising largely representatives of Islamist movements, incumbent regimes and allied parties, as well as centrist tribal groups who are close to the regimes.[11]

As if to confirm the critics' concerns, some on the Islamist right tend to portray liberal democracy as an anti-Islamic, anti-Arab, Western intrusion. Influential writers like Sayed Qutb consistently pursue the line that Western imports are detrimental to the interests of Moslems. The deputy leader of the Algerian Islamic Salvation Front, Ali Belhadj, welcomed the Algerian Government's announcement that it was to hold general elections in early 1992. He declared that, having won power, the Front would not be holding any more elections. Belhadj suggested the idea of popular elections was inconsistent with Shari`a law.[12] He argued that once an Islamic government had been achieved, by definition there would be no further need for elections. This prompted the cancellation of national elections by the Algerian government and a famous comment by a former American diplomat, Edward Djerejian, that, while the West supported the idea of 'one man, one vote', it nevertheless opposed an alternative that boiled down to 'one man, one vote, one time'.[13]

Such a response highlights the region's concern about a potential descent into Islamic totalitarianism that has not been isolated to Algeria. In the 1950s and 1960s, Egypt's President Nasser and King Feisal of Saudi Arabia both considered introducing measures that would have led to a degree of democratisation in their countries. Initially they envisaged that they would be able to control or manage the change, but increasingly public responses to the proposed measures came to be seen as opportunities for opposition to their governments. Both came to fear a descent into chaos as radical elements, especially the Moslem Brotherhood, sought to take advantage of any weaknesses exposed by liberalising changes introduced to impose their own dictatorships. Nasser's and Feisal's responses were retreats from their democratisation goals towards more authoritarian approaches.[14]

An important element of the various criticisms is the issue of whether there is, in fact, a cause and effect relationship between the nature of Arab governments and the persistence of widespread problems in the Arab world, including poverty, social and economic rigidity, terrorism, instability and religious fundamentalism. Arab power structures clearly have an impact on national development and regional stability. The tendency for power to be exercised by a small group means that government is not accessible to the majority of citizens, does not tolerate criticism and diversity of opinion and, therefore, does not respond efficiently to the demands of a rapidly changing political, social and economic environment. A key question underlying the nature of power in the Arab world is how legitimacy is achieved in such a political system. The Western liberal tradition is relatively clear and united on the role of government and its sources of legitimacy. Liberalism follows Aristotle's dictum that the state's reason for existence is to promote the public good. It also is concerned with the excessive accumulation of power in a small number hands, which it sees as an opportunity for tyranny. Finally, liberalism is holds that governments must not only make and enforce the law, but also abide by it.

By these measures, Arab governments have never satisfied the liberal criteria. This has only become an international concern over the final quarter of the twentieth century. In the early years after independence, many Arab governments and their populations were carried along in post-colonial enthusiasms for independence and nation building. Economic growth was generally strong and social change was rapid. Discontent was ignored or firmly repressed. During the Cold War, the shortcomings of any pro-Western government were ignored or camouflaged by the exigencies of the all-important need to confront the Soviet Union. Repressive and autocratic rule was seen as acceptable by the West provided it was anti-Communist.[15] Indeed, Western powers worked to thwart popular movements in a number of Arab countries, such as Algeria and Egypt, in favour of autocratic rulers who were sympathetic to Western interests. The end of the Cold War and the collapse of the Soviet Union, however, released huge pressures on Arab governments from many directions. The sweeping and indiscriminate effects of globalisation (including its pressure towards economic and social openness and the rule of law) and the sudden disappearance of the super power patronage system that provided Arab countries with financial, military and political support threw the underlying challenges to Arab political systems into stark relief.

While offending Western ideals of governance and legitimacy, and despite the massive problems confronting the region, the governments now in place in most Arab countries do meet certain levels of legitimacy, especially when the difficult political, social and economic circumstances are taken into account. It is missing the point to claim that the Arabs' failure to develop Western constitutional processes and procedures to regulate political power within their deeply divided and stressed societies is necessarily evidence that the governments of these societies lack legitimacy. Some of the autocratic measures adopted by Arab governments are, in fact, accepted by their populations as necessary responses to serious problems.

The dramatically changed circumstances in which Arab regimes find themselves reinforce the trend towards dynastic rule and the importance of securing effective succession arrangements. In contrast to the region's early reputation for instability and the rapid turnover of regimes, the Arab world now features many Arab rulers who are been notable for their longevity (see Appendix 3). There appears to be a correlation between this longevity and the strength of the dynastic impulse in Arab republics. The four republics where dynastic succession is most talked about – Syria, Egypt, Libya and Yemen (and Iraq before the American invasion) – have all experienced long-serving rulers. This longevity has coincided with a degree of political stability in those countries. The stability that has been achieved has arguably been a mixed blessing. By putting personal and regime survival first, Arab leaders have failed to pursue the goals of development, growth and inclusiveness. This has, in fact, undermined their attempts to establish themselves and their regimes with any degree of permanency.

A problem for Arabs is that they have found themselves ruled by men who, in many cases, have achieved power on the shoulders of the armed forces and whose attitude to government has been affected by that fact. Such a context encourages Arab governments to operate on an arbitrary basis in which the rule of law has no place. Moreover, instability of the states of the region and the vulnerability of the people in power has been aggravated by the lack of legitimate succession practices.

This has been one of the dominant issues in Arab politics since the independence process began. Peterson considers that 'Succession is a problem faced by nearly all Arab states, regardless of the type of political system'.[16] He further maintains that '(t)he lack of established rules for succession can lead to uncertainty or even political malaise, which stifles political initiative.'[17]

Arab governments have been responding to the demands of the outside world in ways that they regard as appropriate. New constitutions have been adopted in a number of countries. Elections to public office have been organised, in some cases for the first time. (Saudi Arabia conducted its first elections [limited to the municipal level] in February, 2005.) The terms 'democracy' and 'participation' are commonly heard in speeches by Arab leaders. There remains, however, a certain reticence on the part of many Arabs and their leaders about how relevant a lot of the measures being suggested are to the Arab circumstance. Many people in the region see Western measures and concepts as means to further Western domination of the region. Many of the imports are considered to be alien to the Arab experience and to the Arab political tradition. Certainly, there is a strong body of opinion that is sceptical about the commitment of Arab ruling groups to progressive change. Ottaway, for example, argues that, without this commitment, 'Governments will introduce some reforms as long as they can do so without undermining their own power and exposing themselves to real competition'.[18] A central focus of this book is on constitutions as one of the more important manifestations of Western political influence. This book's objective is to demonstrate how Arab regimes have been attempting to make constitutions fit the Arab political tradition especially as it relates to the key issues of leadership selection and succession.

While addressing some of the underlying legal, religious and social principles of political life in the Arab world, it is important to keep in mind the Arab political tradition in a broader context and to see how it bears upon Arab political life. The tradition underpins and deeply influences Arab political life, including political succession, in most Arab countries and is, to an extent, reflected in the constitutions of Arab monarchies and republics. The significance of the existence of this tradition lies in the ways in which the countries of the Arab world will develop in the future and, specifically, in how these countries will respond to Western pressure to change in particular directions. The success of Western pressure may depend on the durability of this political tradition and its compatibility with the Western ideals.

The Arab political tradition

The Arab political tradition, like any belief system, is a dynamic and complex framework of ideas, not all of which are internally consistent. The tradition is particularly complex because of the region's domination by outsiders for the past two millennia and the influence of those outsiders on Arab thinking and attitudes. Contrary to the image spread by fundamentalist Islam, especially the Salafi-Wahhabi variety,[19] Arabs have historically been open to new ideas and practices.

The impact of foreign rulers and ideas has led to major adaptations and borrowings in Arab political and religious thinking. The sources of these ideas include the Classical and Byzantine Greeks, the Romans, Christianity and Judaism, the Persians (including Zoroastrian and Sassanian ideas), the Mamluks, the Seljuk and Ottoman Turks and the Western colonial and neo-colonial powers.

One of the most important pillars of the Arab political tradition is Islam, and this absorptive capacity can be found in the emergence and development of Islam itself. While based on ideas specific to the experience of pagan Arab tribes and town dwellers of seventh-century Arabia, Islam clearly and deliberately took on many of the features of the other two monotheistic religions among which it developed, namely Christianity and Judaism. Over the centuries, Islam also adapted in response to the new circumstances in which it found itself: as ruler of a major empire, as a religion of widely differing peoples in widely differing circumstances and, importantly, in response to the ideas of Classical Greece and Rome with which it came into contact throughout the mediaeval period. This adaptive capacity was particularly apparent in the context of the law. Given the all-encompassing nature of Islam as a philosophy and guide to life, it is, at least theoretically, impossible to separate its role in secular and religious life. Nevertheless, Islamic law was required to deal with issues that were not contemplated when the religion first appeared. Mallat highlights the centrality of the legal manifestation of Islam, Shari`a law, when he likens it to Common Law to the extent that it is the dominant common legal tradition throughout the Middle East.[20]

All these influences have made their mark on the Arab psyche and on Arabs' attitudes to leadership, democracy, order and the state. Arabs are, however, not merely synthesisers and borrowers of other people's ideas. Their political tradition is not simply the sum of other's ideas. Arabs have learnt from their experiences of the Crusades, the Mongol invasions, their subjection by the Ottomans and Western colonialism in responding to the reality around them. They have also combined these memories with the rules of Islam to develop a deep and lasting edifice of political thought and practice.

There are two important modern manifestations of the Arab political tradition. First, tribalism,[21] which spread from the Arabian Peninsula in the Arab eruption of the seventh and eighth centuries to establish itself throughout the southern and eastern Mediterranean world, served as both a transmitter and preserver of ideas. Second, Arab nationalism emerged hesitantly from the unrest accompanying the decline of the Ottoman Empire in the mid-nineteenth century and advent of the Arab state in the twentieth century.[22] As noted earlier, the resulting political tradition is not necessarily a seamlessly unified whole. The concept of unity, which is central to Islam, the racial and linguistic particularity of Arab nationalism and the focus on blood relationships of tribalism[23] do not fit together comfortably. Indeed, the relationship between these elements of the tradition is still being worked out. Instead these elements create a system of different and competing pressures on the modern Arab state. Kedourie highlights one aspect of this problem when he remarks that:

> . . . there was potential divergence and conflict between the customary norms of the tribes and the legal norms of the state. In other words, private property, the foundation of modern constitutional government and indispensable safeguard against despotism, was in a fluctuating state, imperfectly established and easily disputed.[24]

Political succession is one area where harmonising the different approaches has proven to be particularly difficult, just as it has in the Western and other traditions. Arab rulers have tried to address this challenge, increasingly through constitutional measures through which they intend to regulate and formalise their approach to the process. The relative success of Arab monarchies in establishing their form of succession generally influences Arab attitudes to the issue. The various measures adopted to regulate succession may be driven largely by necessity, but they are inevitably predicated on the presumption that the power of the ruling family or elite, be it monarchy or republic, should not be weakened as a result. Even those regimes that are ideologically committed to the welfare of their populations have no interest in relinquishing their power (and the benefits that power brings). In both republics and monarchies the state is seen as a device for the promotion of the rulers' personal and family interests based on dynastic principles. And the stagnation of the Arab state system has meant that personal and private motives routinely take priority over national and social objectives. It does not matter if the state is inclined to republicanism or an established monarchy; the formal mechanisms of government serve either to further the rulers' goals or as facades behind which rulers wield great power and the general public has no role.[25]

A major challenge for Arab regimes will be to consolidate their power and to secure for the constitutional and political structures that they develop a significant degree of legitimacy. This will call for a greater degree of identification with the state as a valued institution by both the ruler and the ruled. The (often grudging) tolerance of Arab regimes by their citizens will have to be converted to loyalty to the state over and above their allegiance to the ruling group. A major test of the strength of the ability of regimes to make this change has already commenced with the departure of one dominant generation, begun by the deaths of leaders such as King Hussein of Jordan, Hafez Al Assad of Syria and Sheikh Zayed Al Nahayan of the United Arab Emirates. Their successors will inevitably lack their predecessors' stature and, possibly, their political skills, but they will be called upon to respond to demands of dramatic change and uncertainty of an economic, social and political nature.

It is, however, precisely this development that may contain the seeds of a resolution of Arab problems over succession. There are indications that constitutions are gradually becoming more important in Arab political systems as the embodiment, guardian and expression of fundamental political deals and understandings on which political systems are based. This development might expose the challenge facing monarchies and republics alike. If Western experience provides any guide, and interesting parallels do exist between European and Arab experiences, then it might be predicted that constitutionalism will take a greater hold on the attitudes and behaviour of both the rulers and the ruled in the Arab world. The modern Arab dilemma has echoes of the mediaeval and early modern English experience, when absolute monarchs traded certain powers for greater access to national resources and ultimately suffered a change in the balance of power in favour of the parliament. It also contains a potential lesson as when, in the case of James II, the monarch tried to overturn the political compact embodied in constitutional rules but failed in his attempt.[26]

Of course, predictions on such a basis are extremely hazardous and the process of employing parallels between the Arab present and the European past should be conducted with great care. There are many significant differences between the emergence of the European state structure and the history of that which exists in the non-Western world. Attempts to introduce Western concepts such as constitutions and constitutionalism, republic, monarchy, democracy and parliament to the Arab world will be complicated by the various experiences and expectations that different people bring to the issue. The process may also be heavily influenced by the unique meanings that Arabs attach to such concepts, many of which have no basis in Arabic. Ayalon suggests, for example, that the Arabic word for 'republic' is '*jumhuriya*', a modern construct which took over 100 years to develop its modern meaning. From Napoleon's invasion of Egypt in 1798, various Arabic words were used to convey the unfamiliar concept of republic, and these often conveyed a range of other ideas, from anarchy to rule by notables. *Jumhuriya* itself carried a variety of meanings into the modern day, including an arrangement understood to be similar to European republics, the republic inspired by the Soviet Union and an Islamic republic.[27] There are no Islamic republics in the Arab world, but the intimate involvement of Shari`a law in Arab constitutions represents an example of how the concept has been incorporated into the political tradition. The result is considerable diversity of constitutional form among Arab republics. In fact, the republican structures of Egypt, Lebanon and Yemen differ so markedly from each other that one of their few uniting features is their professed non-hereditary structure.

The same problem can be observed with the other Western political and legal models that have been introduced into Arab political systems in a context of the Arab tradition. The meaning attributed to such models will vary according to experience and will be coloured by the broad political tradition, especially its tribal and Islamic elements. Even the broad concept of law itself has different connotations in the Arab world than in the West. Zahraa comments that 'Islamic law seems to constitute a unique legal system which is simply different from pure rule-law, instance-law, the common law system and the civil law system'.[28]

Political succession takes place in the context of widespread questioning of the legitimacy of the Arab state system. Almost as soon as the colonial powers withdrew, a pattern began to emerge of rejection by significant forces throughout the region of the structures that those colonial powers had left behind. The states of the region have tended to portray themselves as part of a broader Arab nation rather than on the basis of the European idea of sovereignty. Even the great Egyptian nationalist Gamal Abdul Nasser presented himself as the champion of

Aran unity. He continually sought to turn that ideology into reality. Article 1(2) of the Syrian constitution reflects this attitude: 'The Syrian Arab region is a part of the Arab homeland'. Article 1 of the Egyptian constitution contains a similar sentiment: 'The Arab Republic of Egypt is a democratic state based on citizenship. The Egyptian people are part of the Arab nation and work for the realization of its comprehensive unity'.[29]

The political and economic sectors in the Middle East are intimately related. In Lebanon, for example, the distinction between government and business became particularly blurred while Rafiq Hariri was Prime Minister. Hariri was accused of having exploited his political office to promote his business interests. While in office, Hariri passed day-to-day control of his business interests to his oldest son, Sa'ad. On Hariri's death, Sa'ad also took over his father's political activities. Tunisia is another example of the way in which the political and economic systems come together. There has been no suggestion so far that the President, Zine Al-Abdine ben Ali, intends to keep the presidency within his immediate family despite his having been in office since November 1987. The relative youth of his son might be an immediate problem for such succession planning. Nevertheless, there is no reason to expect him to be the exception to the rule.

The emphasis on the family in ben Ali's regime is striking. Faced with economic crises, the ruling regimes across the region have sought new sources of revenue by allowing indigenous capitalists to become junior members of the ruling elite. Tunisia has been prominent in this development, but the regime has kept close control over the process. It has only allowed a small number of groups based on powerful families, usually with close ties to the ruling elite, to gain significant power within the economy. For example, in Tunisia today, two organizations claim to represent the private sector. First, the Union of Industry, Commerce and Artisans is generally seen as a state body and is run by a wealthy textile manufacturer and relation of the President. Second, the Arab Institute of Business Leaders is led by Chakib Nouira, the son of a former Prime Minister and CEO of the main private bank. The Institute is open only to large companies and the large-scale entrepreneurs who dominate the Tunisian economy. These people owe their existence to the regime and rely on the state for their prosperity. In effect, the regime of ben Ali maintains close family-based control over the economy and continues to exercise a controlling influence over the state and society, as Tunisian governments have been doing since the nineteenth century. His government continues to apply long-established patterns of social interaction and elite maintenance and renewal, including masterminding, orchestrating and implementing the direction, pace and scope of change in society. Importantly, the regime also restricts access to the core elite of the society and economy to members of the political elite, who are largely ben Ali's close family.[30]

The important thing is that the process or mechanism of control developed by ben Ali reflects the dynastic principle that is apparent at the political level in Syria and those republics that are on the cusp of a dynastic transfer of power. Political structures are largely patriarchal in those republics, with the ruling group maintaining its control and legitimacy through a pattern of relationships based on widening circles of patron–client relationships, extending to a significant proportion of the population.

The monarchies are also deeply involved in their economies. King Mohammed of Morocco and his family have been criticised for their extensive direct involvement in the economy. The Jordanian royal family has a similarly extensive stake in the economy. In the Gulf, most royal families dominate their economies. The term 'Dubai Inc.' is commonly used to refer to the all-encompassing activities of the Dubai royal family, the Maktoums. The business interests of the House of Saud are extensive and the Saudi economy seems to be structured to favour members of the royal family and their clients.[31]

2 Competing influences

Tribalism, Islam and outsiders in the Arab world

> Twentieth-century states in the Muslim world differ, broadly speaking, from Western states in the strength of traditional networks throughout the 'civil society' over which they rule. Social membership and obligation run in family clans, sects large and small, Muslim, and non-Muslim, local districts and tribes.[1]

Political succession is closely connected to the nature of leadership and to the range of social and political factors that cause leaders to think and act as they do. With this in mind, this chapter sets out to examine some of the key factors that influence the behaviour of Arab leaders in the context of political succession and the rule of law.

This chapter is specifically directed at an examination of three of the most important underpinnings of the Arab political system. It includes a discussion of the role of tribal and family loyalty in the Arab world, the extent of Islam's influence on the Arab tribal tradition and the impact of outside ideas and practices on the region's political traditions. It is intended to show how these elements and their interactions fundamentally influence the way Arab leaders operate and the way the people of the Arab world perceive the political process. The impact of these forces is controversial and often mutually inconsistent, but taken as whole they make up much of the Arab political tradition. It is demonstrated, in particular, how much influence the Arab tribal tradition exerts on the central focus of this book: the handling of political succession.

It is not intended that the impact of these three forces be portrayed in a deterministic way. Nor is it intended to deny the importance of the impact of structural factors and constraints, such as class and state formation on political behaviour. Khaddar warns of how:

> . . . politicians and specialists alike, often mystified by the state, became accustomed to stressing the role of Islam, tribalism, sects, national character and principles at the expense of other considerations related to social stratification, power struggle, state formation and the impact of world capitalism.[2]

It is also not intended to suggest that these forces are necessarily unique to the Arab world. Family loyalties exist to varying extents and in differing manifestations in most societies of the world. On the other hand, it will be argued that tribal and family attitudes and Islam are tenacious in their influence over Arab leaders and pervasive in the attitudes of much of the populations of the countries of the Arab world. These forces have influenced and shaped the impact of influences from outside, especially the West. The chapter will contain an analysis of how these, at times, inconsistent and competing forces affect the decisions that Arab leaders take, especially in the context of political succession. The important and frequently conflict-ridden interplay between tribalism and Islam and the extent to which outside ideas, especially Western concepts of constitutionalism, have been incorporated into the tradition is an important part of this consideration.

A significant amount of the research into the nature of Arab political and social systems has identified patrimonialism as being of central importance. Black describes 'the continuous dialectic between neo-tribalism and patrimonialism' as one of the most striking features of Islamic political thought.[3] Given the importance of patrimonialism, Weber's discussion of the subject and of the charismatic, traditional and bureaucratic or legal bases of legitimacy provides a useful framework for an analysis of the way in which tribalism and Islam influence the Arab political tradition.[4]

Families and tribes: the spirit of the Arab world

In the mosaic of relatively self-contained but potentially competitive families, clans, villages, tribes and sects that characterise the Middle East, the two basic forms of social organisation, the tribe and the family, are among the most politically important and enduring aspects of Arab political life. Tribalism can be broadly defined as the range of loyalties and attitudes based on family, clan, tribe ('*qawm*' or '*qabila*') and tribal confederation. Underpinning the tribe is '*asabiya*', or small group identity based on blood ties, which is regarded as the central basis upon which Arab relationships depend. It is at the heart of the small group relationships, especially the immediate and extended family. According to Ibn Khaldun, *asabiya* is more important in the Arab political culture than elements such as royal authority and religious merit.[5] The significance of this characteristic varies from country to country across the region but, importantly, the importance of blood relationships does not depend on whether a country is monarchic or republican. Despite the effects of modernity, urbanisation and the intrusiveness of the security state, some of the most fundamental decisions taken by Arab rulers, be they monarchs or presidents, are deeply influenced by considerations of family and tribal loyalty and cohesion. This applies especially in the area of leadership succession and has a marked impact on Arab leaders' attitudes to the rule of law.

It is not possible to undertake an anthropological discussion about tribes and tribalism, although the literature addressing this issue as it relates to the Arab world is considerable and much of it bears on the focus of this book. It is important, however, to develop some broad assessments from a light survey of relevant literature that is relevant to the subject. Springborg, for example, notes that tribes in the Arab world are an heterogeneous phenomenon. Their nature and behaviour are not static and vary from country to country across the Arab world.[6] There are, for example, Arab and Berber tribes across the Maghreb as well as tribes that result from a melding of those two ethnic groups. There are tribes in Iraq that cut across religious divisions, with even Saddam Hussein having claimed Sunni and Shi`a branches in his tribe.[7] More generally, tribes are not immutable institutions. Instead, mergers and break-ups, especially of the larger groupings, have occurred frequently throughout history. Hourani provides a useful working definition of the concept of tribe in Middle Eastern society, when he describes two forms of the phenomenon. The first form is based on actual kinship and comprises a relatively restricted form of relationship which closely resembles the concept of the extended family. The second form is a broader construct based on some kind of elusive but, nonetheless, omnipresent and potentially effective form of solidarity. Usually the solidarity is drawn from a shared myth of a common ancestor and is recognisable through adherence to a common name.[8]

To an extent, family and tribal loyalty are facets of the same phenomenon and both play central roles in regime maintenance and survival. As discussed below, however, family solidarity represents perhaps the most fundamental basis of Arab loyalty and identity. It is to the family which Arab leaders turn for help in resolving the most important issues, such as political succession. It is the family, of all the traditional forms of social identity, that has most effectively survived the rapid and extensive urbanisation that has taken place in the Arab world over the second half of the twentieth century. Libya's Colonel Qaddafi described the family in a way that would resonate with many people in the Arab world today: 'To the individual man, the family is of more importance than the state . . . Mankind, as a matter of fact, is the individual and the family, not the state'.[9]

The influence of tribalism on Arab political systems is a matter of some controversy throughout the Arab world. Many people tend to view tribalism as a sign of backwardness, a primitive residue of the forces of reaction and a trait that is incompatible with a modern political system. It is not uncommon for Arabs to play down the impact of tribalism, especially when talking to outsiders. Even in some of the more obviously 'tribal' states of the Gulf, it is not uncommon for sheikhs to modernise the English form of their names by removing some of the tribal identifiers in their names. Others, particularly tribal leaders themselves, are proud of their heritage and will often seek to dramatise the role of their tribes in their political system. Paul McGeough provides a number of accounts where tribal leaders have claimed considerable power, including the ability to end the Iraqi insurrection against American occupation.[10] The decision of the American military authorities in Iraq in 2007 to accept the support of tribal forces to suppress radical resistance groups is credited with playing a significant role in reducing the level of violence in that country. The result would appear to reinforce arguments about the potential power of the tribes.

There are two broad lines of argument taken by those who are sceptical about (or possibly embarrassed by) the idea that the family and the tribe retain significance in the Arab world. Some reject or downplay tribalism based on normative or ideological considerations. The tribes are seen as inherently unruly, unreliable and potentially subversive, a possibility of which Arab nation-builders have been acutely aware and which they have struggled to address with varying degrees of success. In part, this interpretation emerges out of the traditional hostility between the 'desert and the sown', the mutual contempt felt between the Bedu and the city dweller (*hadar*).[11] For city dwellers, continued ties to a tribal past and excessive reliance on family are regarded as incompatible with a modern and developing society. They regard the tribes as reluctant to respect the authority of the state and its borders. Indeed, even in the days of the *Rashidun*, the Rightly-Guided caliphs,[12] tribalism was seen as a problem of government. 'Under the caliphate of Othman, the 'tribal factor' continued to destabilise the *Umma*,[13] and now from its very core'.[14] In the modern day, tribalism is seen as incompatible with the state system and inimical to the development of national sentiment. The tribes' loyalty to the family and their own particular world view is seen as more important than their loyalty to the state, and this attitude can lead to civil unrest and resistance to state power. Tibi, for example, suggests that Shi`a hostility to the Iraqi state under the Ba`ath Party cannot be understood just in terms of sectarian tensions. He considers that the tribe–state dimension must also be taken into account.[15] This ambiguity of tribal loyalties can even be said to apply to Islam itself. As Batatu observes, the tribes have traditionally 'not been known for the vigour of their religion' and Fandy suggests that 'When Islam and the tribe face off in Arab politics, it is almost inevitably the tribe that wins'.[16]

The tribes and their values are seen as antipathetic to the values that many modern reformers have been seeking to embed in the Arab political culture. Reformers have tended to see tribalism as something of a hangover from older, undesirable forms of government, focused on narrow interests rather than on the wider national project. In a number of Arab countries where revolutionary movements took over government, destroying tribalism was one of the new regimes' most urgent priorities. In Iraq, for example, the Ba`ath Party specifically rejected tribalism and, from its seizure of power, set out to eradicate the power of the tribes. The Party's Communiqué Number One described tribalism as a 'remnant of colonialism'.[17] Similarly, Libya's constitutional instrument, the Preamble of the Declaration of the Establishment of the Authority of the People, adopted in 1977, declares the country's opposition to 'all forms of traditional instruments of government, be they individual, family, tribe, sect, class, representative, party or group of parties'.

The persistence of tribalism and the problems associated with it in the modern context are points that have also been picked up by outside observers, many of whom are looking for causes for the failure of liberal democracy to take root in the Arab world. Kalb suggests that tribalism as a global phenomenon is the result of the end of the Cold War and the loss of certainty that followed:

> The end of the Cold War has given us the New World Order but also made manifest the tendency of the modern world towards tribalism. The tendency

> runs deep. Man forms tribes because he knows what he is by contrast with what he is not, and because a single worldwide society is far too vast for feelings of participation and loyalty.[18]

Ronfeldt goes so far as to suggest that tribalism, with its primitive, backward connotations, is the root of all evil. He argues that modern terrorism has its roots not in radical Islam but in 'extreme tribalism'.[19]

Another way in which opposition to the influence of family and tribal loyalties is expressed is to deny the potency of the ideas themselves. The rapid move towards urbanisation in the Arab world and the huge pressure on nomadic groups to adopt sedentary lifestyles, the force of modern communications and the all-powerful nature of the modern state are said to have reduced traditional ways of life and loyalties to little more than an irrelevance, at best a concept with mythical quality. Manea, for example, argues that, despite their reputation, the tribes in Yemen 'have only limited influence in the political decision-making process in Yemen today'.[20] Abukhalil sees a need for studies that will 'challenge the classic cliché about the family as the primary source of identification and loyalty'.[21] Such arguments have particular resonance in the context of Arab republics, such as Iraq, where governments have specifically set out to restructure 'backward' societies. The evidence from a number of Arab countries, however, is that, while the state ultimately has the capacity to impose its will on the tribes, the structure has so far resisted its destruction and has managed to maintain its hold on Arab attitudes.

One of the reasons people are inclined to dismiss or bemoan the strength and importance of tribalism and family solidarity in the Arab world is because this form of social identity is regarded as a feudal characteristic of a time best forgotten. Elements of European feudalism were introduced into the Middle East first by the Crusades and elaborated later by Mohammed Ali, the ruler of Egypt in the early nineteenth century. There is, for example, evidence that a form of serfdom was alive and well in Egypt until the mid-nineteenth century and in Syria-Palestine until the early twentieth century. Nevertheless, the system that operated under the Ottomans displayed marked differences from the feudal system of Europe, with a different relationship to the land among the most important differences.[22] Before turning to those differences, it is useful to consider some of the similarities.

Among the most important parallels between the Arab condition and that of feudal Europe involves the strength of ties of blood (*asabiya*):

> A legal document of the eleventh century originating from the Ile de France enumerates them (kinfolk) thus: 'His friends, that is to say his mother, his brothers, his sisters and his other relatives by blood or by marriage' . . . The general assumption seems to have been that there was no real friendship save between persons united by blood.[23]

There are, however, numerous other areas where similarities are apparent. Military and mercantile leaders in mediaeval Europe, for example, were deeply dependant on their kinsfolk for success and issues of family honour were characterised by the vendetta or family feud. Such characteristics, to the extent they can be related to the Arab world, are important in the context of settled society. Nomadic Arab society had its own set of rules, many of which were similar to those described above, and these worked their way into urban Arab society. It is of note that numerous Arab cities, including Cairo, developed from the Arab military camps in the early days of the great Arab expansion. These camps were dominated by tribesmen and the forms of organisation of these tribesmen persisted, albeit in modified form, in the new cities. 'As Weber rightly observed, the continuity of clan and tribal organisation within the city context imported rival feuding arrangements into urban life.'[24]

That such attitudes should have persisted over time should not be surprising. Even with the effects of the Industrial Revolution on Europe, an examination of European countries shows how strong loyalties to family units have persisted in many areas, most notably in the Mediterranean region. This evidence generally underlines the extent of continuity in the human experience. It also specifically highlights how throughout Arab history the political, commercial and social systems of the Arab world have been characterised by enduring social structures operating under periodic dynastic political change. The evidence indicates that neither the modern Arab leadership nor the populations of the region have significantly broken with the past in this respect. Given the pressure for change and the demands being placed on Arab social and political structures, however, it helps to understand the full significance of these attitudes by looking at older Western ideas of society and to examine the development of the role of family and tribal ties without prejudice.

Egypt is the one Arab country where tribalism is not regarded as an important characteristic of political life. The historically centralised nature of Egyptian civilisation marks the country off from its Arab neighbours. The sedentary nature of life along the Nile valley has long highlighted the gap between settled and nomadic societies there. Nevertheless, even in Egypt tribal factors can be seen to play a role. Tribes are active in the south of the country, in the Sinai and in the western and northern desert areas, especially around Siwa and the western oases and Mersa Matrouh near the Libyan border. Their direct role in the county's political life may be limited, but they have been involved in much of the unrest that has been affecting the country, including terrorist attacks over the past 20 to 30 years, and this has had implications for political life more generally. Egyptian tribes in the Mersa Matrouh area showed themselves to be vulnerable to the influence of Colonel Qaddafi of Libya during his attempts to undermine the regime of Anwar Sadat during the 1970s.[25] Moreover, the urge towards family solidarity in the political sphere, especially in the context of the presidential succession, is as strong today in Egypt as it is elsewhere.

Tribalism: accommodating change

It is clear that the nature of tribes in the Arab world and their role in the Arab political system have changed considerably over time, especially in the post-Ottoman period. Urbanisation has had a major impact on the lifestyle of the tribes across the region. Whereas once the tribes were the essence of the urban–rural divide, now this distinction is losing its importance. Other pressures and attractions have challenged Arab loyalties. The great power of the modern state now bears heavily on the independence of the tribes. In the United Arab Emirates, for example, nomadic tribes are being forced into permanent housing and their children are being required to undergo schooling and then enter the workforce.

The influence of tribes and families varies in its nature and degree from country to country and it is generally true that the tribes do not normally represent a direct challenge to the supremacy of the state. In a direct confrontation with a government that is in control, a tribal group would be unlikely to prevail. For example, while he was in control of Iraq, Saddam Hussein set out to subdue the tribes using a mixture of overt force and incentives to comply. He was sufficiently dominant to be able to remove tribal sheikhs at will and to replace them with compliant leaders and to reward those who conformed to his agenda. As his power slipped in the 1990s, Saddam sought to co-opt the tribes in his support, but it was only after government collapsed in 2003 that the tribes were able to assert a degree of independence. Even the Saudi regime, whose origins lie in the tribal system of the Arabian Peninsula, has been able to subordinate tribal interests to the interests of the family-based structure of the regime. This ability of the modern Arab state to generally control the tribes is not in doubt.

Nevertheless, while a government can physically overwhelm tribal resistance, it struggles to destroy the tribal sentiment and attitude of large sectors of the population. This became apparent in the lead-up to the American invasion of Iraq in 2003, when many urban Iraqis sought sanctuary in their tribal areas. It was claimed by one tribal leader that as many as 90 per cent of Iraqis had retained a connection with their tribal roots, a factor which would have facilitated this reaction.[26] In similar vein, Qaddafi's attempts in his early years in power to abolish the tribes were not successful despite his dominance of the Libyan political system.

This tenacity of tribalism suggests that there is considerably more to the phenomenon than the superficial image suggests. Baram has written about 'neo-tribalism' as a way of acknowledging the great changes that have affected tribalism over time, while emphasising the persistence of many of the traditional practices and ways of thinking into the modern day.[27] His remarks about the persistence of tribalism are addressed specifically at Iraq, however, they have a wider applicability. The weight of the evidence supports the view that loyalty to families and tribes continues to play an important role in the political systems of all Arab countries, from Morocco in the west to Iraq and the Gulf countries in the east. This importance, moreover, does not necessarily detract from the social and political modernity of the countries of the region. Iraq, for example, was, until the imposition of United Nations sanctions in the early 1990s, one of the most advanced countries of the region in terms of education, health care, social services and the level of training of the workforce. Nevertheless, Iraq is regarded as a highly tribal society. At the other end of the scale, Libya, whose educated and trained population was effectively wiped out during the Italian colonial period, is also regarded as highly tribal.

The tribal legend

Tribalism maintains a hold over the Arab imagination in much the same way as national myths influence other cultures. For example, the late nineteenth century and early twentieth century values of Australian pastoralists pervaded Australian literature to create a national ethos, an Australian legend, which had little to do with the reality of Australia but nevertheless summed up an Australian self-image and aspiration. At the same time as denying the political strength or relevance of tribalism, even urbanised Arabs retain and often reveal a certain pride in their tribal, familial or geographic roots. One interlocutor, a tribal sheikh and modernising government minister, sought to downplay the tribal origins of the people of his country while regularly conducting the tribal *majlis*, the forum where members of his tribe could seek redress for ills, pursue favours or simply keep up with the gossip and maintain their tribal links. Anderson describes the level of ambiguity in the attitude to tribalism of Libya's Colonel Qaddafi:

> Early on he made it clear that he was simultaneously opposed to tribalism as a principle of political organisation and proud of his own origins in a saintly, though not noble or wealthy tribe, the Qadadfa.[28]

There is, moreover, evidence that this emotional attachment to tribe and family is deeply rooted and long lasting in the thinking of people of the region. Tribal and family-based relations persist among Arabs despite assumptions that modernisation and urbanisation leads to their demise or weakening. Al Thakeb discusses a number of studies that suggest that Kuwaiti families maintain strong relations with their wider family groupings regardless of whether their background is urban or rural. These studies indicate that modernisation has had little if any impact on the functioning of the nuclear family.[29] Joseph makes a similar finding in the context of Lebanon. He suggests that the ruler of the state has become effectively the head of the national family, the senior patriarch in an order of patriarchs created out of class and tribal systems.[30] This applies in the commercial context, where major Lebanese enterprises are largely in the hands of family groups, which value employees who are driven by a sense of family loyalty rather than simply rewards. These groups regard the environment outside the confines of the family as inherently hostile.

The relationship can even survive migration to the other side of the world. Speaking at a conference in Sydney, Australia, about the strong Islamic and Lebanese influence on his Sydney electorate, an Australian federal politician remarked that his Lebanese constituents had been bringing their family and village loyalties with them from Lebanon when they migrated to Australia. He observed how buildings throughout his electorate were being purchased on a village basis so that people who had migrated from the same village could continue to live together.[31] A similar observation was made by Massingnon, who noted how Algerian migrants to Paris settled in specific parts of the city where their relations or people from the same districts had settled so as to preserve a kind of tribal identity.[32]

The attitudes, thinking and strategies of Arab leaders are of particular importance to the way in which the tribal legend works on the Arab political system. To an extent and importantly, these attitudes reflect the ambiguity of the broader Arab populations noted above. Arab leaders are pragmatic and even cynical in their treatment of tribes, reflecting an attitude that sees the tribes almost in ideological terms whereby they are to be saluted but also exploited and that there is nothing sacrosanct about them. This attitude can be seen in Saddam Hussein's handling of Iraq's tribes over the term of his rule. After initially setting out to destroy the tribes, Saddam's policies began to change until he announced in 1991 that 'the Ba`ath is the tribe of all tribes'. Baram suggests that, while Saddam may have begun his presidency sharing the general Ba`athist hostility towards the tribes of Iraq, he quickly realised their value and the need for a new approach. Saddam's change of heart reflected strong pragmatic considerations. The Ba`ath Party was struggling to maintain support in rural areas and Saddam needed to find a way to ensure the survival of the regime. He decided to adopt the tribes as tools of the regime and even substitutes for Ba`ath Party rule. This decision was a major factor in his ability to survive in power so long.

The policy change was, however, not just an act of political expediency. It also underlined the importance and persistence of those Iraqi traditions that are the reality of tribal ties and family solidarity. These traditions are culturally important to all Iraqis, including the leadership, and Saddam was no exception in this. His policy of favouring his immediate family and the group of tribes covered by the broad label of 'Tikriti' was given public expression in 1991 when Saddam declared in a speech: 'Therefore, . . . no one should be allowed to emerge in the . . . leadership in the Ba`ath Party if . . . [he does not] come from a good origin . . . [a good] family background'.[33] Such an attitude can be found among most leaders across the Arab world. Even Khaled Bakdash, the leader of the Syrian Communist Party from 1936–95, fell into the family-first approach to party leadership, seeking to keep the leadership of the Party in his family's hands after his death.[34]

It is significant that Arab constitutions, even those of ostensibly revolutionary and republican impulses, reflect a commitment to the family, if not the tribe. Such references can, to a point, be interpreted as indications of the attitudes of the elite, given their role in the development of Arab constitutions. While some constitutional instruments, such as the Libyan Declaration on the Establishment of the Authority of the People and the Iraqi Ba`ath Party's first policy statement, condemn tribalism, most constitutions, republican and monarchic, contain prominent reference to the family and its place in society. The family is variously described as 'the basis of society' (Bahrain, Article 5(a), Egypt, Article 9 and Oman Article 12), the 'foundation of national unity' (Libya, Article 3) and 'the corner-stone of society' (Kuwait, Article 9). In another context, such references might be relatively innocuous but in the context of societies where family loyalty is an important social and political issue, they take on an added significance.

Tribal loyalty: a basic support

Important in attitudes to tribal and family loyalty are the ideas of membership and obligation. Tribalism is much more than just part of the Arab legend, the complex of issues that make up Arabs' self-image. Experience in Arab countries, especially, but not exclusively, in the 'states of exception' (see Chapter 5), such as Syria and Egypt, has taught people not to trust anyone from outside their particular religious sect, ethnic group, social class, tribe or family. This applies at the individual and at governmental levels. In the light of this general absence of community trust, the existence of family and tribal units provides Arab leaders with sources of support upon which they can rely and from which they can draw people to fill the key positions in their governments. Rulers place their family and tribal allies in key military and security positions from which the survival of the regime can best be promoted. According to Brinkerhoff and Goldsmith:

> One of the best ways for a political leader or agency manager to stay in control is to be surrounded by loyal people. He or she may calculate that some inefficiency is a small price to pay for loyalty. Patronage allows leaders to build a temporary team of public managers who share the leaders' policy agenda and who can be counted on not to sabotage or delay important programs . . . [35]

This is a significant consideration for regimes based on minority groups, such as Syria and Bahrain, but is more generally applicable given the segmented nature of Arab societies over history. This practice can be seen in every Arab government, regardless of whether it is republican or monarchic. According to Quinlivan: 'The use of special loyalties as a central support of these regimes (Syria, Iraq and Saudi Arabia) is real and not fully understood'.[36] In Jordan there is an informal practice of filling key government positions with tribal representatives. For example, the head of one of the major Jordanian security agencies is regularly drawn from one of the southern tribes of Syria. The Saudi National Guard, which has the responsibility for protecting the royal family, exclusively comprises members of tribes from the family's heartland, the Najd region. The kings of Morocco have, for many years, maintained a process of regular consultation with Berber tribes and have established the practice whereby senior members of the royal family marry Berber women in order to strengthen support for the monarchy in the Berber community. Under Hafez Al Assad, the Syrian ruling elite consisted of like-minded family members and careful structuring of the military establishment to ensure that loyal members of the Alawite community were in key positions to prevent action against the regime.

While it is generally true that the tribes lack the capacity to challenge a determined and united government, they do have a significant latent power that might prove to be decisive under certain circumstances. The power of the tribes tends to grow in response to internal problems. When the government and society are divided, the potential for tribes and family groups to play a more direct and forthright role is considerable. This power becomes especially formidable when harnessed by or used in support of the state, and it can become a central element in the ability of governments to survive. This latent power can be seen in times of national stress, such as in Iraq when central order almost broke down in 1991 after the American attacks and United Nations sanctions were imposed. The role of the tribes became important again in 2003 when Iraq fell under American control. It was evident in Jordan at the time of the fighting in September 1970 between the government and the Palestine Liberation Organisation (PLO). King Hussein called on the Jordanian tribes to help him and even brought in tribes from Syria to assist him against the Palestinians and the Syrian armed forces. It could be seen in Libya where Colonel Qaddafi fell back on tribal units in an attempt to control the People's Committees he had created. Finally, the power of the tribes was on display in post-independence Syria. The country in the 1950s was a society in great turmoil and was deeply divided. As Tibi notes, such a situation made it possible for such small groups to seize control:

> When sub-ethnic tribes like the Alawite Matawira in Syria are capable of obtaining control of the state, not only do underdogs become topdogs but they also instrumentalise their pre-national tribal ties to maintain their control.[37]

More generally, having the support of the tribes or, at least, their acquiescence can be vital to the maintenance of a regime and to the standing of individuals within the regime. The Jordanian example is particularly pertinent. A senior member of the Jordanian royal family explained to this writer how King Hussein had worked diligently with the tribes over the duration of his reign to ensure their continued support. Another interlocutor observed that the King's brother, Prince Hassan, had pursued the same policy in recognition of the tribes' central role in the survival of the Hashemite monarchy. It has, however, also been suggested that Prince Hassan failed to win the support of the tribes and that this was a fatal political weakness which undermined his chance of becoming king. The tribes could neither trust him nor identify with him. Ironically, it is also possible that these considerations were involved in the downfall of Prince Hamza, a younger son of King Hussein who had been nominated as crown prince by the late King. Hamza was, however, quickly demoted from this position by the new King, Abdallah, who replaced him with his own son. It is possible that Hamza's popularity with the tribes represented a potential threat to Abdallah, who is regarded as being 'detribalised' (his mother is English and his education is foreign), and who therefore lacks deep tribal support. Abdallah was understood to fear that Hamza might have used his tribal base against him.[38]

Another idea associated with tribal and family solidarity, namely, obligation, has important implications for Arab leaders' relations with their family and tribal supporters and for their personal legitimacy. It is here where the clientalist nature of the patrimonial Arab political system becomes particularly evident. While Arab leaders lean on their tribal and family members to help preserve their regimes, the strength and reliability of this relationship is dependent on the idea of mutual obligation. Tribal and family allies are expected to support the regime whenever called on to do so. Regime leaders are expected to ensure the flow of liberal rewards to their followers as evidence that they deserve their support.

This practice can also extend to a regime's dealings with its potential opponents. When living in Syria in the 1970s, this writer was able to observe the close clientalist relationship between the Alawite regime and the Sunni merchants of Damascus. Ba`athist ideology was not sympathetic to private enterprise and there was little mutual respect between the Alawites and the Damascenes. Nevertheless, the government was able to keep Damascus quiescent, despite the city's reputation as a particularly fractious place to govern. This was pursued through the distribution of positions in the economic area to leading Damascenes through the toleration of an active black market in which the merchants were involved. They made a determined effort to control extremist religious elements. In part this was an attempt to hold together a system marked by deep divisions and it formed an important part of Hafez Al Assad's set of policy tools. Hafez was able to buy the neutrality of the Sunni establishment and to gain a degree of legitimacy in the process. Assad's practices were not new. They reflected those pursued throughout Arab history, including in pre-colonial Egypt and Syria. Kettering notes that the existence of well-established clientalist structures in the early Middle East was a way of strengthening the central government:

> They distributed royal patronage to secure provincial loyalty and support. . . . In this way the crown was able to secure the cooperation of important members of the regional ruling elites. And in this way too, regional elites were introduced into the national political arena, and their regional resources were mobilised on behalf of the national government.[39]

Patronage is essential in holding together an alliance of even family and tribe members. Allegiances within the family or tribe are not immutable and can change from one member of the family or tribe to another unless the leader is able to continue to meet expectations of rewards and personal gain. This is a striking characteristic of Bedouin behaviour, but it can be seen to apply in urban societies in the Middle East as well. The competitive tension that Saddam Hussein maintained between his sons, Uday and Qusay, the tensions that have existed in the Assad family over the succession, even when Hafez Al Assad was alive, and the reports of family discontent over the right of Ahmed Saleh to replace his father, Ali Abdallah Saleh, as President of Yemen all suggest that, even for the most entrenched leader, there is pressure to continue to provide the benefits associated with incumbency.

The dynastic steps being taken by Arab leaders could be approached from a different angle. It could be argued, for example, that the appointment of Bashar Al Assad to the Syrian presidency was an indication of the strength of family loyalty. It also indicated that Bashar was bound to honour his family obligation by accepting his father's summons to assume the role of heir apparent on the death of his older brother, Basil. Bashar was unprepared, not obviously equipped and possibly reluctant to take on such a difficult challenge, and he was surrounded by established politicians of his father's era.[40] It is significant that the manner of Bashar's ascension to the highest office has left him apparently struggling to take advantage of the aspect of obligation that was so important in his father's case. The relationship of mutual obligation between Bashar and the surviving members of his father's regime is not as strong as that between his father and those who had been part of Hafez' regime for a generation. Assuming the presidency as his father's heir, he had to rely on his father's circle for support, and the people in this circle were not wholehearted in ceding real power to the new incumbent. He is seen as not being in full control of the Syrian government largely because his own power base of supporters who are bound to him by mutual bonds of obligation is still not fully established. He has introduced some of his own supporters throughout the government apparatus and has removed some members of the old guard, but the entrenched power of those who were put in place by his father remains a constraint on his ability to make change. This predicament has been aggravated by the persistent challenges facing Syria from outside its borders.

The situation in Jordan is similar to a point. Again reflecting the power of family solidarity, King Hussein changed the succession arrangements to ensure his oldest son, Abdallah, became king, replacing his brother, Hassan, who had been Crown Prince for about 35 years. As with Bashar Al Assad, Abdallah is faced by the problem of not having any network of obligation in place upon which to consolidate his rule. Indeed, he would be aware that his uncle, Hassan, and his brother, Hamza, and others were not completely convinced of his claim to rule. In Hamza's case, the feeling might be sharpened by the knowledge that King Hussein had appointed him Crown Prince and had expressed the hope that he would eventually rule. Abdallah's advantage over Bashar is in large part a function of the difference between a hereditary monarchy and a republic, insofar as Abdallah can inherit his father's structural networks and expect them to operate, at least in the early stages of his reign. Bashar Al Assad could make no such assumptions. Despite his election as president, Bashar's power is greatly dependent on informal, political factors. The republican institutional framework provides limited legitimacy for him.

These examples highlight, among other things, the fluid nature of the family and tribal structure of loyalty. Every new ruler, be he republican or monarchic, must establish a new basis of family rule upon which his regime is to survive. It is just this fluidity and unpredictability that Arab leaders are seeking to resolve, including through their constitutional structures.

Islam and tribalism

Arab family and tribal traditions set many of the criteria that have guided the behaviour of Arab leaders over time and continue to mould Arab attitudes. Islam has also played a crucial role in the formation of Arab attitudes to leadership, especially concerning the issue of legitimacy, the development of the political succession process and the role of law in the Arab world. These two forces of religion and *asabiya* have had a complex and often uncomfortable relationship over the centuries. Their interaction has itself been a characteristic influence on Arab leaders and their regimes. Islam itself emerged out of a tribal society. As a member of the leading tribe of Mecca, the Quraysh, the Prophet Mohammed was very much part of tribal society. Islamic doctrine also drew heavily on the tribal framework in which it developed, especially in the political context. The impact of tribal traditions in areas such as leadership and succession can clearly be seen as Islam developed over the centuries. As Berkey notes:

> The political structure of Mohammed's *Umma* as reflected in the 'Constitution of Medina' and in other sources owed a good deal to traditional Arabian practice and values. . . . the tribal factor continued to play an important and destabilising role in the development of what would come to be identified as the Islamic polity.[41]

Mohammed can be seen as a revolutionary leader at a time when Arabia, in particular, Mecca and Yathrib (Medina), were ready for reform. Resolving the ills of those societies was among the more important of his objectives. In many respects, the direction provided by the new religion marked a significant break with the past and the Islamic revolution swept away much of the social malaise of the *Jahiliyya* (the period of ignorance or darkness before Islam) and provided the basis for a new and better society. In some areas, however, the revolution was incomplete when Mohammed died and specific guidance on important questions regarding leadership and succession had not been developed. Some writers, such as Abd Al Raziq (1888–1924), argue that the Prophet never intended to set out specific rules for the establishment and operation of a political system. Whatever the Prophet's intention may have been, his silence in such key areas raised many immediate problems for the growing society.

In the political context, Islam promoted certain general principles, such as justice, freedom, human dignity and equality, and the rule of law. The interpretation of these principles has, however, not necessarily been the same as that adopted in the West. In some of these areas, such as individual equality, the Islamic interpretation can be traced to tribal ideas of kinship and egalitarian democracy.[42] One area where there was insufficient guidance for the community from the Prophet was political succession. It was an area that quickly developed into one of the most problematic aspects of the Islamic structure. The Prophet's death, without clear provisions on how succession was to be organised and how leaders were to be legitimised, left a vacuum in Arab political practice and thinking. Where the Quran and legitimate *Hadiths* were silent or ambiguous, tribal attitudes and practices filled the void. Many of these were firmly established in Arab political thinking. None of these solutions, however, provided a satisfactory and lasting answer to the issues of leadership, succession and legitimacy.

In the period immediately after Mohammed's death, his closest followers, the Companions,[43] selected his successor as ruler of the *Umma*, or Islamic community, from among their group. There were four *Rashidun* or Rightly Guided companions, who became Caliph in turn: Abu Bakar, Omar, Othman and Ali, Mohammed's cousin and son-in-law. With the exception of Ali, their selection was loosely based on the tribal process of election or endorsement by their peers. This process could not, however, survive the first major challenge to the new community. The unity of the community collapsed in the face of Ali's claim to a hereditary right to rule as caliph. Ali claimed the right by virtue of his relationship to the Prophet. His opponents argued roughly along lines developed from the tribal experience that the leader of the community should be the most fit person to rule and should be chosen by consensus, initially at least, from the tribe of Quraysh. Over time that debate developed doctrinal dimensions, but tribalism remained an underlying characteristic of the dispute. The followers of Ali (to become known as the Shi'a) maintained that sovereignty should follow the family line of Ali (and, therefore, of Mohammed himself) rather than the broader tribal line (which became the Sunni branch of Islam), an argument that has some echoes of the Western feudal approach. There is some evidence to support the view that the Prophet himself favoured the hereditary principle. Aisha, the Prophet's favourite wife, is reported as having declared about Mohammed's adopted son, Zayed:

> It never happened that the Holy Prophet included Zayd in the army going to battle but not as its commander, Had he been alive at the time of the Prophet's death, he would have been selected by the Holy Prophet as his Caliph.[44]

By the start of the rule of Muawiya ibn Abi Safyan and the beginning of the Umayyad Empire in 661, the Sunni tribal view had clearly prevailed. The deaths of Ali and his son Hussein and the general endorsement of the claim of Muawiya removed any serious challenge to the Sunni and traditional approach. At the same time, a broader interpretation of eligibility to rule began to develop. Muawiya was from the Umayya, an establishment Meccan family within the Quraysh, and therefore represented continuity from traditional tribal custom through Islam. It was, however, a political system with a difference, for while leadership was to be drawn exclusively from the Umayya, some of the more important tribal practices, such as the quasi-democratic tradition of consultation, lost their force.

In the area of succession, Muawiya displayed what has become commonplace in modern Arab societies: a determination on the part of political leaders to keep power within their own families. In a revolutionary move, Muawiya nominated his son as his successor, but he sought approval of the nomination by means of the traditional tribal declaration of allegiance to his heir. Like many of the other concepts or principles that emerged from the tumult of the early days of Islam, this particular idea has survived to the present day. This precedent has been followed, for example, by King Hussein of Jordan, King Hassan of Morocco and the Saudi royal family and has been incorporated into a number of modern Arab constitutions. The constitutions of Bahrain (Article 1 (b)), Kuwait (Article 4 (2)), and Qatar (Article 8) specify that the heir to the throne must be appointed quickly after the ruler's ascension to the throne. Article 5(c) of the Saudi Basic Law stipulates that the newly nominated heir must be endorsed by the traditional pledge of allegiance. The precedent could also be said to have been followed by Syria's Hafez Al Assad. Hafez did not issue a public proclamation or seek to secure formal constitutional endorsement. This would have been inconsistent with the country's republicanism and would have flown in the face of the Syrian political ethos. Years before his death, however, Assad made it clear that he wanted first his oldest son, Basil, and on Basil's death, a younger son, Bashar, to succeed him. This decision was endorsed by the Parliament's oath of allegiance. At some point, Hosni Mubarak, Ali Abdallah Saleh and Muammar Qaddafi are expected to make similar nominations on behalf of their sons, although this might take the form of the father acceding to the (well-orchestrated) demands of the public.

The governance model that began with Muawiya retained, as noted, the Arabs' close links with their tribal past. Over time, however, significantly different foreign political systems and practices infiltrated Moslem practice to the point where the features' origins became lost and they became an integral part of Moslem practice. Many of the foreign introductions were responses to perceived weaknesses in the ability of the existing Arab legal and political framework to deal with the huge empire that the Arabs had conquered. Over time, with the loss of Arab control over the empire, the foreign influences, especially those of Persia and Turkic-speaking nomads, became more pronounced. The issue of succession and legitimacy was one area where these influences could be seen. Approaches to who should rule and the process of determining succession were dominated at the state level by outsiders – the Persians, Turks, Mamluks and others – while traditional Arab family and tribal practices continued at levels below the state. Despite their dominance in some areas of Arab political thinking, none of these alien rulers introduced rules for succession that took root in the region. Even Muawiya's initiation of the practice of dynastic succession was never wholeheartedly endorsed by the community. According to Lewis:

> . . . the succession became in fact, though never in principle, dynastic, and remained within the house of Umayya. There was no rule or right of succession – indeed, later Moslem dynasties, no doubt inhibited by the strongly anti-monarchical attitude expressed in the Quran and in the oldest traditions, did not accept a fixed rule of succession, by primogeniture or otherwise.[45]

As such, the tension expressed by this question typified the problems Arabs have always had in harmonising their nomadic, tribal traditions and the foreign influences imported by their conquerors over the generations. The problem in its modern guise is very specific. The lack of rules, such as those of primogeniture, meant that succession under Islam was always going to be a major challenge to the political system and its leaders. The effects of this problem on modern Arab political culture and practice can be felt in the difficulties faced in achieving a peaceful transfer of power and the intense personalisation of the political process. Western liberal democracy attaches authority to offices rather than to individuals, but in Islamic society, there was no attempt, until sustained Western pressure began in the nineteenth century, to replace personal rule with institutions such as the constitutional monarchy or the republic.

At the same time, however, a number of Moslem scholars acknowledged the principle that 'might is right' and denounced civil disobedience even when the political authority could not claim to be constituted according to accepted principles. This development, highlighting the region's historic focus on order and stability, underlined a major problem with Islamic law: its authority depended not so much on the degree to which it was observed as on the arguments of scholars as to why it should be observed. Under both the Umayyads and the Abbasids (the first and second Moslem empires) the state was structured in such a way that there was no clear distinction between the executive and judicial functions, leaving supreme power in the hands of the Caliph. It was assumed that the Caliph would be suitably qualified for the role, but there was no mechanism, such as an independent judiciary or an independent electoral process, to ensure that this was so.[46] Abbasid theory supported the idea that the Caliph was the servant of the law and that legal authority was vested in the scholar-jurist, not the political master. In practice, however, the Caliphs moved to control the legal scholars and to use them to further the power of the political leader.

The impact from outside the tent

We have been discussing, in general terms, significant influences on the Arab political tradition that originated outside the Arab world. In this, the Arab political tradition is much like any other political system. The foreign influences that have imposed themselves on the Arab world range from classical Greece, Rome and Byzantium to Marx, Nietzsche and Stalin,[47] from pre-Islamic Persia to the Mongol and Turkish tribalism of the steppes. These diverse influences are, moreover, not necessarily compatible, and the synthesis that emerges is generally the result of, at times, painful, even violent, experience. This has been particularly the case in the Arab world, given the way in which the Arab experience has unfolded. From small-scale and introverted tribal societies to an extensive and complex empire and civilization, through a thousand years of domination by outsiders punctuated by occasional violent invasion to tumultuous independence, the Arab political system has had to deal with dramatic change and challenge. Throughout all this turmoil, traditional attitudes and practices have persisted with surprising tenacity. This process of adapting to or rejecting foreign influences can be seen at work today as the region attempts to come to terms with the impact of Western dominance. Much of the adaptation process has been felt in the areas of rulers' rights and responsibilities and in their selection and replacement.

The Umayyads' approach to ruling a great empire exposed major deficiencies in their tribe-based practices, but also highlighted the Arabs' long-term receptiveness to the example of other models.[48] Tribal leadership was generally determined on the basis of a form of election. The result of the election was, however, heavily qualified. Regardless of how strong a person the head sheikh might be, he could not interfere with the entrenched rights and customs of the families of the tribe. A tribal sheikh lacked the power of enforcement of duties or punishment, instead operating more as an arbitrator than a ruler. Moreover, the rules and values for which he bore some responsibility applied only to members of the tribe. The sheikh's election was by senior members of the tribe making him something of a *primus inter pares*. These senior tribe members also comprised the *majlis*, the tribal advisory body, which has developed into a rudimentary parliament in some countries. The candidate for sheikh tended to be drawn from a single family within the tribe, known as the *ahl al beit* or the people of the house, but other families also regarded themselves as enjoying elevated status within their tribe and, therefore, as a certain right to rule if the dominant family were to fail in its responsibilities. Even the power of the Prophet himself was limited. Turner observes that while Mohammed gained great power among the tribes at Medina as a result of his military successes, he never achieved the position of an arbitrary patrimonial leader.[49]

The tribal election process was intended to ensure that 'the fittest' person should rule. Initially the idea of 'the fittest' related to the understanding that a tribe's very survival in the difficult environment of Arabia depended on effective leadership. With the advent of Islam, however, the term gradually acquired broader implications to incorporate Moslem standards of behaviour. In effect, this idea of the fittest has come to form an important criterion for guiding dynastic succession. In the modern era, it has been expressed in some constitutional documents, such as the Saudi Basic Law (Article 5(b)).

In the response to the various shortcomings of Arab political practices, Greek thinking and practice established an important influence on the first Umayyad caliph, Muawiya. At the time of the Arab conquest, Damascus, Muawiya's capital, was a largely Christian city and Byzantine practices, procedures and attitudes permeated Arab rule for much of the life of the Umayyad dynasty. It was in the practices and attitudes of the Christians employed by Muawiya and his successors that the Umayyads found many of the measures they adopted in response to the growing challenges of running their rapidly expanding empire, including patriarchalism, dynastic rule and kingship. The development was also arguably to be expected in the context of Weber's idea of the progression of political systems from one form of governance to another, more sophisticated system. From Muawiya on, there was a gradual progression from the charismatic leadership provided by the *Rashidun* and Muawiya himself and the tribal systems on which the empire was originally based towards patrimonial and bureaucratic domination.[50] In its predictability and rule-based framework, the development of dynastic rule in the Arab empire was arguably one manifestation of such a move towards bureaucratic or legal authority.

Another outside source of influence on the Arab political system was the largely tribal Mongol and Turkic-speaking invaders who made such a significant impact on the Arab world. These groups' ideas on leadership and succession had much in common with Arab tribalism and were incorporated with relative ease into the Arab tradition. One effect of their influence was, therefore, the reinforcement of tribalism as an underlying factor in Arab attitudes. These steppe invaders, however, also added to ideas supporting dynasticism and the powerful ruler, in contrast to the more democratic principles underlying the traditional Arab approach.

Classical Greek ideas were an important influence on many of the major thinkers of the Islamic empire. They were studied in the context of the consolidation of Islam, which created a rough framework in which Greek principles had to fit. Discussion of the ideas of Aristotle and Plato was particularly prominent in the writings of men like Ibn Khaldun (1332–1406) and Al Farabi (870–950), who looked for ethical structures that might guide rulers in their jobs. Plato's concept of the philosopher-king carried great appeal to Shiite thinkers who found in it support for their view of the correct succession to the Prophet Mohammed and the concept of Imami rule (effectively rule by a strong leader).[51]

The influence of Persia, in particular pre-Islamic Persia, is probably the most important of all the foreign cultures that pressed upon the Arab world, at least until the modern era. As with Greece, Persia was an early influence on Arab tradition, with the first Umayyad and Abbasid caliphs employing many people imbued with the Persian administrative culture. An early mark of this influence was the increasing remoteness of the caliph and the decline in the influence of the traditional Arab tribal chieftains. Persian and Greek influences were probably adopted with ease as they were regarded as sharing much of the Arab approach to governance and as being part of the same broad cultural heritage. Of course, by the time the Arab empire was beginning to take shape, Persia was also Moslem, which added to its acceptability. Black notes that support for patrimonial monarchy was a persistent feature of Persian influence and the concept developed in the direction of the idea of 'divine right' with the claim that a king possessed the 'divine effulgence', 'the sacred element of fire or light in the person of the rightful ruler'. In this context, Persian and Shiite writers even sought to elevate Alexander the Great to a model of an enlightened imperialist ruler, and upon this built arguments that had the effect of strengthening the power of the caliph.[52] Assimilation of influences even from these sources, however, was rarely a simple matter and, indeed, often became a point of great division, as Muawiya's resort to the kingship and inherited succession demonstrated. A major problem for this dynasticism was the strong philosophical aversion of early Arab tribalism to kingship and hereditary entitlements. Black suggests that an important effect of the Persian influence was to enable Arabs to explain away much of this aversion. 'The heritage of pre-Islamic Iran provided a language and images by which Islamic Commanders-cum-tribal chiefs could justify their ascent into absolute monarchy'.[53]

Western influence and pressure is still unfolding and has been particularly divisive and disruptive to the Arab region. A significant feature of the response of Middle Eastern leaders to the challenge from the West has been to attempt to shore up their power by means of a retreat into politics with a strong Islamic flavour. For example, the Ottomans, while always conscious of their central role in Islam, pursued a relatively tolerant attitude to non-Moslems in their midst for centuries. As pressure increased from the West for the Porte to provide trade concessions and to allow Western access to parts of the empire and the government was faced with pressure from within to modernise the empire, the government reacted by developing a pan-Islamic policy designed to attract the support of the peoples of the empire and to appeal to Moslems in lands ruled by the European states. Subsequently, writers like Rashid Rida (1865–1935) and Hassan Al Banna (1906–49) employed Islam as the unifying foundation of their resistance to European domination. The strong emphasis on Islam and Islamic symbolism in the various declarations by the Al Qa'ida leadership could be similarly interpreted as an attempt to employ religion in support of the organisation's largely secular objectives.[54]

Resistance has been a prominent feature of the Arab response to Western influence. Adoption and adaptation have, however, also been significant. As Antonius makes clear, the early leaders of Arab nationalism were heavily influenced by the West. They acquired ideas of nationalism, in which they saw a useful measure to promote anti-colonialism, democracy, totalitarianism and socialism.[55] Many of these reformers welcomed Western influence because they 'recognised the fundamental dualism of temporal and religious law in the system of public law under which they were living'.[56] This dualism was essential if their modernisation programmes were to be carried out. In many cases, however, these ideas were adopted without a real appreciation of their implications. For example, the Ottomans, in their attempt to respond to demands that they modernise in the face of the Western challenge, adopted a number of measures, including the constitution of 1876, which reflected significant Western influences. The Ottoman rulers had no intention, however, of allowing the constitution to change Ottoman rule or to restrict their power in any way. In this the rulers in Constantinople set an example that has been followed by many rulers throughout the Arab world.

The Arab political tradition which has emerged in the twentieth century is an amalgam of many diverse influences, which have been integrated to varying degrees according to the nature of the challenges facing the Arab world and their mutual compatibility. To an extent, those that were able to take root compensated for deficiencies in the native Arab system. Traditional tribalism, for example, had strong democratic elements, but it was too personal, fractious and based on small communities to provide an adequate foundation for an advanced political system. In the early days of Islamic civilization, the ongoing conflict with Byzantium and the challenge of running an extensive and complicated empire required firmer, more cohesive and long-term leadership than the Arabs' traditional form of governance could provide. Persian and other models offered various solutions to the Arabs' problems – solutions that often promoted authoritarianism and dynasticism. The modern variants of these solutions have tended to be sceptical of constitutional and law-based methods of government, including the idea of checks and balances. As a result, a system ultimately founded on tribal, Islamic and authoritarian central Asian practices and theory has emerged as the dominant political influence on Arab societies.

Much of the discussion so far has had a significant historical focus. This is because, perhaps more than any other advanced political tradition, the forces of history remain an important part of the modern Arab tradition. The experience of generations under foreign rule, the importance of tribal traditions and the centrality of the framework established by the Prophet Mohammed have meant that Arabs are inclined to look to the past for guidance and solutions. This is not unique to the Arab world. Americans regularly resort to their two hundred year old constitution to resolve political issues. The British have their reliance on tradition and precedent in their political and legal spheres. The French are still engaged in resolving issues that were provoked by the Revolution. For Arabs, however, there is the added complication of the intense external pressure, which seeks to influence the way they deal with basic political challenges. As noted above, this reinforces an instinctive reaction to fall back on the past and seek comfort on sureties in history.

Throughout all this turmoil, the attitudes of the tribal ethos have remained potent influences on the way Arabs look at the world – and political systems – around them. The most important of these influences is the desire to promote the family and the view that the family remains, in all the tumult, the one source of reliable support and the main focus of loyalty. This attitude is a major influence on the way Arab leaders approach their roles today.

3 The just prince

Leadership and legitimacy in the Arab world

> Who has become rich through pillage shall waste away; who rules by treachery shall be expelled; the army of the unrighteous shall be defeated and the noose of tyranny shall be broken.[1]

In any political system the nature of leadership and governance is a matter of fundamental, long-term and wide-reaching implications. In the Arab world, where authoritarian governance is the norm, this issue is seen by many as being at the centre of a crisis of legitimacy. Arab regimes are regarded as narrowly based and dependant on force and the threat of force to maintain their control over their societies. Their willingness to use violence against their own citizens has earned them the reputation of being world leaders in the 'industry of repression'.[2] An important related issue is that, perhaps more explicitly than in Western systems, Arab regimes tend to be the agents of specific interests, be they the family, the tribe, the military or a particular religious sect, rather than attempting to represent some broader view of the national interest. Indeed, the concept of the state as an institution has, to some extent, failed to take root in the region. Instead, tribal, confessional and even regional loyalties assume greater importance to Arabs than their state, especially when the state is under pressure. According to Palmer:

> Family loyalties continue to compete with loyalty to the state and it is probably safe to assume that most residents of the Middle East place the interests of the extended family far above the interests of the state.[3]

A number of factors is involved in explaining why the Arab state may have failed to attract the loyalty of its citizens, including the persistence of family and tribal loyalties, the appeal of the Islamic community of believers (*Umma*) and the chimera of Arab unity. Arab regimes emerging from foreign control paid great attention to the establishment of formal state structures, which, in the West, have served as a focus of the loyalty of citizens. In the Arab world, these structures have survived and have provided the reinforcing framework of the region's state system and set the parameters within which the various member states operate. Nevertheless, the structure and its component states lack full legitimacy because of the persistence of the rival ideals which undermine popular loyalty and provide a basis on which opponents of the different regimes can operate. Because of this uncertain and potentially fluid situation and the failure of modern political structures to take root and develop an institutionalised legitimacy of their own, individual leaders have stepped in to fill the void and to secure public support for their highly personalised regimes. Charismatic rulers, like Egypt's Gamal Abdul Nasser and Tunisia's Habib Bourguiba, dominated their countries and held together their political systems. Even less commanding leaders elsewhere in the region have similarly provided much of the legitimacy that their states enjoy.

Traditionally, Arabs have tended to resolve their problems through negotiation with the goal of ensuring that all parties to an issue are satisfied with the outcome. At the level of the modern state, however, Arab politics have come to operate on a zero-sum basis.[4] Therefore, the question of who secures and holds the highest political office has a significant impact on which groups and interests will be the major beneficiaries of the political system and which interests will largely miss out. Membership of the ruling family or its clientalist network has always been one of the main ways of acquiring wealth in the Arab world and it is, perhaps, the starkest expression of Harold Lasswell's famous definition of politics as the art and science of determining who gets what, when and how.[5] The stakes in Arab politics are, therefore, high, but the processes for determining how a ruler rules, how power is exercised and how resources are allocated are generally immature and unpredictable.

Arab leadership: developing legitimacy under stress

The situation in which Arab leaders find themselves stands in marked contrast to the Western experience. Western countries have spent hundreds of years developing rules, checks and balances intended to limit the power of the leadership. These measures have focused on a number of key areas such as responsibility, accessibility and representativeness, all structured within the sovereignty of the people. The processes have been institutionalised through constitutional sanction, be it statute-based or reflecting powerful quasi-constitutional convention. As a result, the Western approach has developed a certain robustness and an aura of legitimacy in the face of the inevitable inclination of those in office to seek to accumulate and to abuse power. The idea that power should be limited enjoys widespread support and it is this consensus that underpins the whole framework. Should the consensus break down, however, even a mature system is vulnerable to abuse, as could be seen in the extreme in the Nazi experiment in Germany. Less dramatic examples can also be seen in the Iran-Contra scandal and the more recent controversy over former United States' President George W. Bush's use of Presidential Signing Statements.[6]

In contrast to such an established structure, in the relatively short period since independence, the Arab world has been struggling with the question of the correct role of leaders. The region's leaders and people have been wrestling with problems similar to those encountered throughout Western constitutional history, such as separation of powers, accountability, the role of religion and dynasticism. Moreover, Arabs are attempting to resolve these issues under intense external and domestic pressure as Western powers seek to influence the nature of Arab governments and regime opponents seek change ranging from democratisation to revolutionary overthrow. In considering the causes of instability in the Middle East, Perry draws attention to the 'decisive' impact of outside influences on political development in the Arab world:

> The failure of such regimes in the Arab world, notably that of Egypt, to democratise during the 'third wave' – at a time when democratisation, at least in a superficial manner, has been seriously pushed in other parts of the world – may be seen in large part as a function of Washington's need for allies in the area.[7]

The domestic threats are no less burdensome. Most Arab states have been threatened by major domestic challenges. While the Moslem Brotherhood insurrection against the Syrian government in Hama in 1982 could be regarded as an extreme example of such a challenge to the regime, it encapsulated the nature and the gravity of the problems facing most regimes from their own populations. Seale described the final phase of the Brotherhood insurrection as a 'last-ditch battle which one side or the other had to win and which one way or another, would decide the fate of the country'.[8] The Algerian civil war of the 1990s was a similarly existential challenge to an Arab state. Put together, such concerns might be extended and applied to the problems the Arabs are encountering in resolving their domestic political and constitutional problems, including leadership and the exercise of power.

Developing leadership in an emerging system

This chapter sets out to examine in this context how the Arabs look at leadership. It considers some of the major influences on the practice of leadership in the Arab world and assesses how they affect Arab rulers' legitimacy. In particular, the chapter addresses the appeal to almost all Arab leaders of tradition, with its deep roots in tribalism. A major feature of this issue is the persistence into the modern day of the legacy of the difficulties faced by the young Arab empire at the time of the Rightly Guided Caliphs and the Umayyad and Abbasid dynasties. The empire needed to develop an effective and adaptable method of governance that would enjoy broad legitimacy across generations. It is this legacy that has, in large part, provoked frustration among observers of the Arab world and has maintained conditions which cause domestic unrest. A major focus of the chapter is on how today's Arab leaders attempt to achieve lasting legitimacy for their regimes and the degree to which they are successful. Despite the resort to arbitrary repression by Arab regimes, it is argued that the regimes and their individual leaders are proving remarkably resilient and have established a considerable degree of legitimacy, especially among key elements of Arab society. These include the private sector, which sees the regimes as necessary, if at times unpalatable, defenders of their interests.

Max Weber's work on authority and legitimacy and his ideas on the charismatic, traditional and legal bases of leadership provide a framework that helps in understanding the nature of the forces that work on modern Arab leadership and in appreciating the rules behind who gets what, when and how in the Arab world. Weber defines authority as power exercised with legitimacy and as having three possible manifestations: the rational, which is based on a belief that power is wielded in a way that is legal; the charismatic, reflecting devotion to an individual of perceived exceptional personal qualities or achievement; and the traditional, an established belief in the sanctity of immemorial traditions. To this definition Weber adds the idea that the regime is legitimate if the population believes that the system will endure and that resistance to its will is futile, that its hold on power is unassailable.[9] According to Seymour Martin Lipset:

> Legitimacy involves the capacity of the system to engender and maintain the belief that the existing political institutions are the most appropriate ones for the society . . . Groups regard a political system as legitimate or illegitimate according to the way in which its values fit with theirs . . . Legitimacy, in and of itself, may be associated with many forms of political organisation, including oppressive ones.[10]

An important symptom of a regime's legitimacy, therefore, is the existence of a minimal level of order in the state, akin to Rousseau's social contract. It is inevitable that states will resort to the use of force, or at least the credible threat of force, in order to achieve this necessary level of security. In the case of the Arab states, this requirement is perhaps more evident and the willingness to use force plays a prominent role in the achievement of legitimacy and in regime maintenance.

Force does not exist as an option in isolation in the Arab world. As a general principle, modern Arab rulers operate according to the same laws of nature as those in any other country insofar as their behaviour is influenced by the complex elements of their beliefs and the culture of the political system in which they are involved. Variables such as age, social class, history, political ideology and the political environment will have a major impact on the way Arab political leaders respond to the challenges facing them.[11] As discussed in Chapter 2, the origins and the parameters of modern Arab leaders' practices can be found to a great extent in the Arabs' ancient tribal traditions. They are also evident in the peoples' experience since the advent of Islam and in the political and social structures that have built up over time under those influences. The impact of outsiders on Arab leaders has been considerable. For much of their history, the Arabs have been ruled by others. The Mamluks, the Crusaders, the Persians, various Turkic-speaking groups, the Ottomans and finally the Western powers built empires on Arab lands where matters of leadership were resolved in anything but a systematic, law-based way. There was little or no Arab input and limited reference was made to Arab concerns, traditions and attitudes. The experience of Western rule was not any more agreeable than its predecessors, and the West's realist approach during colonial rule and since independence has done little to endear Western ideas of governance to many of the people of the region.

Arab political processes and practices can give the impression of having been frozen in time for 1,500 years, until the modern era and independence. It is an impression reinforced by the regular reference back to the days of the Prophet and the *Rashidun* by Islamic conservatives and Arab nationalists alike. During the period of foreign domination, however, there were periods of great intellectual debate about the major issues of political organisation. These included the need to establish criteria to identify the characteristics of a good ruler and a whole genre of writing developed based on providing advice to leaders on how to rule (Counsel for Kings or *nasihat al-muluk*).[12] This genre had its roots in pre-Islamic notions of justice, service (especially to religion) and the welfare of the people. The Arabs derived from this debate a number of ideas, including a great appreciation of the power of force, which is something that resonated with tribal concerns, and of the evils of instability. There was, however, no opportunity until the twentieth century for Arabs to assimilate these ideas into their own traditions and practices. There was also no opportunity for traditional leadership to mature and to be modified by experience in the way in which European practices developed. As a result, some of the weaknesses of the early days of the Arab empire proved to be of fundamental importance to the development of Arab politics in the modern era.

The caliphate and leadership: an uncertain model

Among the major and lasting problems that emerged from the early days of the empire was the Arabs' difficulty in agreeing on the exact nature of leadership. The questions of who was to rule and what was to be the nature of rule were a continuation of the challenges the Prophet Mohammed faced in his relations with the populations of Medina and especially Mecca. They were unresolved at his death and the consequences were momentous. The succession to Mohammed shook the unity of Islam more severely than any other event in the history of that religion. The questions of who is to rule, how is the ruler to be chosen, what is his role, what are the limits of his power, can he be replaced and who is to succeed him, all emerged to create the division which was to shatter the unity of the *Umma* and to permanently and deeply divide the Sunnis and the Shi'a. The issue of how the *Umma* was to be ruled was, initially, more than a matter of religious doctrine. Mohammed was, after all, a hugely important political and military leader, and his actions and sayings (the *Hadith*) constitute an important part of Islamic and Arab political precedent. Leadership of the Islamic community developed in the context of hundreds of these *Hadith*, which have been reported, codified and, inevitably, embellished over time. His silence on the issue of succession left a vacuum. His example as a leader coupled with his religious stature created standards of behaviour and expectations of achievement that no future leader could hope to meet.

The dominant Sunni attitude to leadership of the Islamic community developed, therefore, in the context of Mohammed's immense standing as a political and religious leader, his death and his silence on the issue of succession. In the absence of guidance from the Prophet, the traditional, tribal approaches, which were based on merit and a form of election but which also contained the possibility of dynastic succession, survived the general impact of the Prophet's teaching. By contrast, the approach to leadership among the Shi`a branch of Islam was deeply influenced by the nature of the deaths of Ali, Mohammed's cousin and son-in-law, and Ali's son, Hussein, as well as their claims to hereditary leadership. As a result, the nature of leadership was caught up with succession, forming the defining political feature of the emerging Islamic civilization. It reflected raw power politics and ancient tribal and family rivalries, especially involving Mohammed's tribe, the Quraysh.[13]

The challenges facing the Caliphate which succeeded the Prophet were considerable. The Prophet's replacement as the supreme sovereign leader of the Islamic world was expected to meet a complicated set of criteria. The term 'caliph' combined the ideas of deputy and successor. It was also a term that combined the secular and religious. The Caliph had to maintain order and security and ensure the conditions under which people would be able to lead the good Moslem life. The Caliph was, however, faced with an impossible situation. Many of Mohammed's successors possessed considerable personal and leadership qualities. The second Caliph, Omar, for example, is to this day regarded as the epitome of the just ruler. These men could not, however, hope to replace the Prophet, whose position was unique. They had to accept a lesser role, which was to act as his deputy and to uphold and protect the faith. The Caliph's duties were, moreover, not clearly set out, leaving its role to be determined largely by the abilities and the attitudes of the occupant of the position. This meant that the authority of the successor to the Prophet would always be vulnerable to challenge.

In its early stages, the position of caliph 'was still conceived of in terms appropriate to the chief of a nomadic tribe'.[14] This provided little guidance, however, when the heirs of the Prophet were required to deal with a rapidly developing and expanding political system of greater complexity than anything that confronted Mohammed. Inevitably, new situations arose which provoked new questions and demands on the Islamic structure. Without the guidance of the Prophet, however, these questions and demands proved difficult to resolve. As the task of running the empire became more complicated and the responsibilities of the position became more difficult, the position assumed a more forceful role and a process of specialisation developed. At the same time, however, the shortcomings of the arrangement were exposed. In particular, to the extent that the caliphate began life as a reflection of the tribal system, it was inadequate as a leadership model for something as complex as the empire became under Muawiya, the first Umayyad Caliph, and his successors.

Muawiya exploited the vagueness and ambiguity of the Caliph's role to expand his and his family's power. Under both the Umayyad and Abbasid empires, therefore, increasingly sophisticated practices developed, reflecting a progression from charismatic and traditional rule towards patrimonial, bureaucratic processes and dynastic rule. The system developed from that of the days of tribal experience, the rule of Mohammed and the *Rashidun*, to an elaborate rule-based process under the dynasties and their successors. The Umayyads' involvement in this development provoked great hostility, especially from Sunni tribal groups. Much of the criticism, especially during the Abbasid period, was based on the way in which the Umayyads were seen as converting the caliphate into a family kingdom (*mulk*). Persian and Byzantine influences could be seen in the way in which Muawiya and his heirs ruled. Their support for the idea of kingship and pre-determined dynastic succession challenged the familiar tribal model. Muawiya's innovations were, however, consistent with what might be anticipated through a Weberian interpretation. From Muawiya on, there was a gradual progression from the charismatic and traditional leadership provided by the *Rashidun* and Muawiya himself towards patrimonial and bureaucratic domination. Turner comments on this interaction between tribalism and the new ideas:

> Whereas the first four 'rightly guided' Caliphs did not form dynasties, Muawiya nominated his son Yazid as his successor and became the founder of a dynasty (mulk). The hereditary principle in both Umayyad and Abbasid dynasties was never fully abandoned, but this was accompanied by a fictional appeal to the traditional norm of acclamation (*baya*).[15]

Islamic regimes such as the Ottomans and the Persians developed answers to these questions over time. Most of the answers reflected a bias towards authoritarianism, drawing on pre-Islamic Persian and central Asian practices. They are questions, however, that the Arabs are still wrestling with. They are questions that must be addressed in the context of the mixing and clashing of the Arabs' historical experiences. In particular, the influence of foreign ideas that penetrated Middle Eastern thinking from the Umayyad Empire to the twentieth century, their tribal traditions and the incomplete synthesis of tribalism and Islam must bear upon analysis of Arab attitudes to leadership and succession.

The passage of time and the expansion of the Arab empire saw the breakdown of the unity of the Prophet's immediate followers and a confusion of attitudes to leadership replace the pattern set by Mohammed. Arab family and tribal traditions set many of the criteria that guided the behaviour of Arab leaders into the new era of empire and continue to mould Arab attitudes. Islam has also played a central role in the formation of Arab attitudes to leadership, especially concerning the issue of legitimacy. For some, the Quran, with its emphasis on obedience, can be seen as the final defeat of the tribal Arab by the city dweller. In many respects, the direction provided by the new religion marked a significant break with the past. Mohammed's relationship with the Bedouin was complex. As Watt notes, the people of Mecca and Medina were 'descendants of nomads and still retained many of the desert-born habits of their ancestors'.[16] Mohammed, nevertheless, had urban origins, and, as might be expected, sought to apply a concept of social order and discipline on the Bedu. Once the Prophet had left the scene, however, Arab tribes began to resent the authority and discipline of the new Islamic empire. They objected to the way in which the new order intruded into difficult traditional areas such as revenge and blood feuds and, in so doing, challenged the tribes' role as the bearers of Arab ethical values. This resentment contributed to the events that resulted in the murder of Othman, the third Caliph.

At the same time, Islamic doctrine itself drew heavily on the tribal framework in which it developed. This was made necessary by the failure of the Prophet to provide the guidance on a number of key issues that the new community would need to survive. The *Umma* was confronted by immediate problems of political practice and theory, and it should be no surprise that the solutions were often sought in tribal practices. Moslem leaders consciously sought in tribal precedence legitimacy for their authority. This was natural given the close integration of Islamic and tribal arrangements and the fact that most members of the new *Umma* remained committed members of tribes. In the context of leadership and legitimacy, therefore, the idea of Islam as representing a sweeping revolution in the Arab world needs to be qualified. The picture that emerges involves a complex and unresolved relationship between Islam and tribalism and a constant tension between these two forces.

Tribalism's triumph: a flawed victory

Some observers consider that the relevance of tribal and family loyalties (*asabiya*) has been overwhelmed by the complexity of the nation state and the twentieth century's enhancement of the power of central government. Leadership in the Arab world is, however, still strongly influenced by factors and attitudes that, in essence, date back to pre-Islamic times. There is considerable evidence that tribal attitudes have remained strong and continue to exert a major influence on Arab leaders' approaches, raising issues such as the concern for regime survival, family and tribal advancement and the retention of power in the family and tribe to the front rank of regime priorities.

It is true that Islam and other influences have dramatically modified aspects of tribal society[17] and that tribes are no match for the state in material terms (see Chapter 2). Today we are obviously not seeing behaviour that was prevalent at the time of the Prophet Mohammed or even at the time of Mohammed Ali (the modernising leader of Egypt from 1805–48). Tribal behaviour and loyalty to the tribe and the family must be significantly different from what it was only a century ago. Nevertheless, there still exists a deep, if at times subliminal, impact of attitudes associated with tribe and family on political and other issues. The phenomenon is real and pervasive and bears heavily on the workings of Arab political systems. Tribal and family attitudes and loyalties remain a central determinant of the behaviour and attitudes of Arab leaders. Significantly, they are forces that tend to complicate and even undermine the process of state building throughout the region.

An understanding of the development of these attitudes is helpful in appreciating their impact in the modern Arab political system. Tribal values survived the challenge of Islam in modified form and even infiltrated urban society. They permeated the Arab political system at the beginning of the Islamic era under Mohammed, the *Rashidun* and for much of the Umayyad Empire. They persisted over the ensuing centuries, often at the expense of stability and order. Modern Arab attitudes to leadership continue to reflect this influence while, at the same time, revealing the ongoing tension between the attitudes of nomadic and settled Arabs. This tension was given a new life in the early independence struggle. T. E. Lawrence notes, in *Seven Pillars of Wisdom*, the decision of the leaders of the Arab revolt to abolish the Turkish civil code:

> . . . a return to the old religious law, the undiluted Koranic procedure of the Arab Kadi. . . . Meanwhile, of course, what townsmen lost by the abolition of the civil law, the Bedouins gained. Sherif Hussein had silently sanctioned the restoration of the old tribal order.[18]

It is this widespread persistence of tribal values and their continued strength and appeal that drive Arab leaders today to heavily rely on traditional ideas of authority for their legitimacy. The problem for modern Arab leaders is that, as a basis for legitimacy, tribal practices are inherently unstable and inadequate for the modern world. Most Middle Eastern dynasties have been shaken by succession struggles involving tribal competition. For example, the overthrow of the Umayyads by the Abbasids was, in large part, a tribal conflict between the Qays and Yemen tribal confederations.[19] In more recent times, the Hashemite rivalry with the Al-Saud tribe resulted in the Hashemites' expulsion from their homeland in the Hejaz. Ultimately, the durability of tribal values in the modern era has ensured that Arab politics will continue to be greatly influenced by issues such as the role of the family and tribe as a focus of loyalty and the question of obedience to established rule. This will remain a constant question mark over the legitimacy of Arab leaders. They are issues that affect the modernising republics as much as the more traditional monarchies.

The tensions between Islam and tribalism in the context of leadership had very personal origins. The issue focused on a debate over a pragmatic form of governance against a strict adherence to the Quran. It came to a head early in the Islamic era with the role of the leader of the *Umma* being a central issue of concern. Two men, Ali ibn Abi Talib, the fourth Caliph, and Muawiya ibn Abi Sufyan, the founder of the Umayyad dynasty, personified this dispute and the breakup of the *Umma*. As he has been throughout the history of Islam, Ali has been the focus of controversy and division. He has been at the heart of disputes over the nature of leadership and the process of succession that have been particular features of the relationship between Sunni and Shi`a Islam. Over time, Ali came to be seen, especially by the non-Arab subjects of the empire, as a selfless and devout follower of the Prophet who, by virtue of his family relationship, possessed some of Mohammed's special qualities.[20] The contrast to the establishment-supported, pragmatic and tolerant Muawiya was dramatic and helped impel the religious aspect of a ruler's responsibilities to the front of those issues on which a ruler was potentially open to criticism.

The followers of Ali maintained that leadership was directly a matter of divine right and the ruler under Shi`a Islam derived 'his authority from the hereditary transmission of divine inspiration along the line of the Prophet's descendants'.[21] Within that framework the sole requisites for rule were piety and competence. The three main branches of Shi`a thought – the Zaidites, the Isma'ili and the Imamites – are agreed on this centrality of the family line of Ali and on the role of the whole community in electing, monitoring and deposing the political leadership. In the face of perceived Sunni impiety and immorality, the Shi`a maintained the view that their Imamate was absolutely vital to Islamic belief and behaviour. This principle became the basis on which the Shi`a assumed the role of permanent opposition to Sunni dominance throughout the centuries. Some groups have taken a more radical tack. For example, the Zaydi of Yemen, a Shi`a sect claiming descent from the Prophet Mohammed, adhere to a concept of just rule which includes the possibility of the overthrow of an unjust ruler. These groups claim legitimacy for their view from several *Hadith* associated with the Prophet, one of which states that:

> The Muslim is required to hear and obey in that which he likes and dislikes, unless he was commanded to sin. When he is commanded with sin, then there is no hearing or obeying.[22]

This *Hadith* is taken to mean not just that a Moslem is entitled to reject the sinful dictates of his or her ruler, but that there is a Moslem duty to do so. This approach has specific implications for the Saleh regime in Yemen, but it could also be adopted by regime opponents in other countries.

In contrast, Muawiya was a pragmatist faced with the task of running a complex, multi-cultural empire. His relaxed attitude to religion, his reliance on non-Moslems in his army and bureaucracy and the tribal nature of his regime contributed to the buildup of resentments that led to a series of revolts, political schisms and civil war (known as *al fitna al kubra*, the great sedition), which permanently split the *Umma*. Muawiya was essentially an Arab tribal ruler who tried to adjust the approach with which he was familiar to a complex situation. A basis of the hostility to Muawiya's rule was partly that he favoured one tribal group over another, but also that his system of government reflected Arab ideas, not Islamic ways of thinking. The manner of Muawiya's accession to the caliphate was another important factor in the controversy. Muawiya had risen to supreme power as a result of the split among the faithful. The split began as a political dispute over Ali's right to rule as Caliph. While the schism gradually developed doctrinal dimensions, it remained a political dispute over succession and, increasingly, over the nature of leadership and legitimacy.

Some of the practices introduced by Muawiya and his successors drew on foreign ideas in response to perceived weaknesses in the ability of the existing legal and political framework to deal with the huge empire that the Arabs were in the process of conquering. The issue of leadership was a particular area where these influences could be seen. Part of the response by Muawiya and his successors to these weaknesses was to establish a dynastic and monarchic form of rule, a structure which, incidentally, anticipated some of the features of the Western notion of divine right of kings. The governance model that began with Muawiya retained the Arabs' close links with their tribal past. Dynastic rule, for example, was consistent with the traditional tribal practice of keeping rule within the one family. At the same time, by openly promoting monarchic rule and anointing his successor, Muawiya reflected ideas and practices of the defeated Sassanian Empire. These further manifested themselves in the emphasis on authoritarianism and the formal rituals of rule. Such practices stood in marked contrast to the democratic informality that still characterises many an Arab tribal *majlis*.

These developments also reflected the change in the nature of the empire from helter-skelter conquest and expansion to consolidation and reorganisation. In its growing predictability and reliance on a rule-based approach, the Umayyads' dynastic rule is arguably one manifestation of the move towards Weber's bureaucratic or legal authority. The Umayyads' adoption of kingship was never wholeheartedly endorsed by the Arab part of the *Umma*, which persisted with traditional Arab family and tribal practices. Ultimately, this half-way house between tribalism and oriental despotism proved to be an inadequate basis for the dynasty's legitimacy.

As in the relationship of the caliph and the sultan, the unresolved tension between tribalism and Islam is part of what is behind the approach of today's Arab leaders to their jobs. While the modern Arab state is very different from anything the Arabs experienced before independence, some of the same challenges and pressures that existed in the early days of Islam continue. The strong compulsion towards dynasticism and the search for legitimacy continue to influence the thinking of Arab leaders in modern Arab political systems, just as they did at the time of the Umayyads and their successors. And the search continues in tribal precedent.

Duty to obey or rule by the most 'fit'

The search for an adequate basis for lasting legitimacy is at the heart of the strategies of modern Arab leaders. Hudson observes that:

> The central problem of government in the Arab world today is political legitimacy. The shortage of this indispensable political resource largely accounts for the volatile nature of Arab politics and the autocratic, unstable character of all the present Arab governments.[23]

Again this highlights the crucial nature of the coming together of succession, which is discussed in Chapter 4, and leadership as fundamental challenges in the Arab political system. The means by which a leader achieves power will have major implications for his legitimacy and his ability to carry out political and economic programmes. If the succession is not regarded as legitimate, the leader's power will be impeded and his attention will have to be focused on survival above all else. For example, Bashar Al Assad of Syria was made President at his father's wish and was understood to have been committed to a range of modernising and liberalising measures. Bashar's survival in the role, however, is largely dependent on his ability to free himself from the influence of the old guard of Syrian politics that came to power with his father in the early 1970s.[24] Until he does so, Bashar's authority will be limited and his ability to pursue his reforming initiatives and regime consolidation will be severely constrained.

There are various routes to the nirvana of legitimacy, and the military path has been the dominant route in the Arab world in the period since independence. According to Weber, one way leaders might achieve legitimacy is through effective domination. The perception of strength in a leader is a central attribute of legitimacy in traditional, charismatic and bureaucratising regimes, including in the Arab world. Put another way, Seale writes of Syria's President Hafez Al Assad, 'in accordance with Machiavelli's dictum that to lead men you must turn your back on them, he made remoteness a principle of government'.[25] Such notions can be traced not so much to tribal traditions as to the Persian idea that power itself and its effective exercise was a basis for rule.

The idea that effective domination implied legitimacy was developed by a number of Moslem scholars who found in the Quran and *Hadith* support for the principle that might is right and that civil disobedience (*fitna*) is a sin. This applied even when the political authority could not claim to be constituted properly or when the ruler was guilty of inappropriate behaviour. The approach maintains that Islam requires almost unquestioning obedience of the ruled and that having gained power, a ruler is legitimate as long as he meets minimal standards set by Islam, that is, as long as he does not impede a Moslem's ability to practice his or her religion. This is predominantly a Sunni perspective, which began to develop in the early years of the Abbasid caliphate. The Shi`a approach, which developed as a defence of a persecuted minority, tends to be more exacting in its criteria for legitimacy and obedience. It also carries certain traces of European thinking. According to Tierney, there was some resonance in Shi`a thinking of Augustine's[26] argument that:

> . . . the discipline that even bad rulers imposed provided a partial remedy for sin in that it restrained men from indulging to the full the criminal proclivities of fallen nature.[27]

The other strain of thought in Islam stresses that the obedience of the citizen must be balanced by the responsibility of the leader and that the leader must be the most fit to rule. Over history, many Moslem thinkers have accepted that great power in the hands of rulers will inevitably lead to their great corruption. In his major work, *The Muqaddimah*, ibn Khaldun writes extensively on the natural life spans of dynasties and on the gradual corruption of dynasties leading to their eventual demise.[28] Numerous writers attempt to devise ways of dealing with the problem. While noting the prevalence over time of autocratic rule in the Moslem world, Lewis stresses that 'Islamic tradition strongly disapproves of arbitrary rule' and notes the bonds of mutual obligation that exist under Islam between ruler and the ruled.[29] Abu Nasser Al Farabi, perhaps the earliest Moslem political scientist whose writings have survived (died 950 AD), provides, through a synthesis of Platonic and Islamic concepts, a description of the ideal leader as someone who is at once a prophet, lawgiver and imam. This is an idea that has reappeared in other writers over the years, including Ibn Sina (Avicenna), Ibn Bajja (Avempace) and Ibn Rushd (Averroes). The work of these writers reflects an ongoing search for the 'just prince'[30] and for principles to help Moslem rulers strive for the primary goal of Islamic politics, namely, good governance through justice and peace. This goal remains an important feature of contemporary Arab political thought.

Unquestioning loyalty to the leader is a particularly significant concept in the context of the Arab world, where the regimes upon which individual leaders build their control are not democratic and, therefore, in the eyes of Western politicians and commentators, lack legitimacy. Such an attitude is not necessarily supported by people in the region. There is no shortage of people in the Arab world who promote democracy. As noted in Chapter 1, the *World Values Survey* finds that Arabs support democracy as the best form of government as enthusiastically as people in any other part of the world, including the West. Nevertheless, the people of the region retain serious reservations about the applicability of democratic systems to the Arab world at this stage in its political development and there appears to be no support for the idea among Arab elites.

This attitude is driven, in part, by the strong emphasis on stability and unity in Islamic and Arab thought. Citizens will lament a regime's lack of accessibility, accountability and responsiveness to their demands, but they will continue to accept a ruler's legitimacy. The issue for Arabs is one of priorities. Democracy, however the term is interpreted in the region, is highly desirable but order, stability and predictability are foremost among people's concerns. According to an Arab maxim, 'Better sixty years of tyranny than one day of anarchy'. This is a view shared by people in the business sector as well as in the social context.

There may also be an element of fatalism involved. The tolerance of people for authoritarian government, especially in the states of exception of Syria and Egypt, may in fact be a reflection of their assumptions that totalitarian regimes are so powerful as to make real change impossible and that they have no choice but to accept things as they are. This interpretation is consistent with Weber's category of legitimacy based on social action as 'zweck-rational' or 'purpose rational' action.[31] Finally, there is a strong religious element involved in some people's approach to leadership. Important justification for authoritarian rule can readily be found in several passages the Quran. The most notable and widely quoted passage (Sura 4, Aya 59) reads: 'Believers, obey God and obey the Prophet and those in authority among you.' This passage is widely seen as approving obedience of the ruler for the sake of stability and cohesion over resistance to unjust rule.

From Western liberalism to authoritarianism

The Arab nationalists who championed the independence of their countries tended to be steeped in Western concepts. The republican inspiration was largely the

French model, while the monarchies drew support from the British example. Even the adoption of the term 'king', with its traditionally negative connotations in the tribal mind, was intended to help regimes like that of Jordan claim some sort of affinity with the British monarchy. The Arab systems, therefore, began life as European transplants, but modifications, some of which were significant, started to appear early on. Paul Salem comments that as soon as the Arabs succeeded in gaining independence, the Western-inspired liberal politics and laissez-faire economic outlook began to lose its appeal, and in its place was offered authoritarianism and a form of socialism in the context of pan-Arab nationalism.[32]

Such a process is hardly surprising given the Arabs' history. The Western idea of the separation of powers, for example, has never enjoyed support in Islamic political thought. The Caliph inherited from Mohammed the role of the community's leader in religion and war and the status of the superior legal authority. In the modern context, likewise, the separation of powers has no meaning and all arms of government are directed at promoting the interests of the regime. Bromley suggests that the 'dependent development' process through which Middle Eastern economies emerged acted as a 'powerful stimulus to authoritarian rule'.[33] To that should be added the influence of the long period under authoritarian rule by outsiders, especially the Ottomans. It is often overlooked that until the Young Turks began a programme of discrimination against the Arabs, most Arab members of the Empire were content to live under Ottoman rule and proud of what it represented.[34] Authoritarianism was an accepted part of that package.

Support for authoritarian rule can often be found among the many minority groups scattered throughout the Arab world. Under the Ottomans and even in the early post-independence stage, minorities enjoyed a considerable degree of security, which only started to weaken in the context of the reaction to growing Western activity in the region. Ideas of Arab nationalism and a growing assertiveness of Islamic groups led to concerns about the tyranny of the majority. These concerns were sharpened by the weakness of constitutional and legal protections in place. Most of the Arabs' constitutions make no provision for the protection of minorities, but they do speak of equality within an Islamic society. For example, Algeria's constitution (Articles 29 and 36) specifies that:

> All citizens are equal before the law. No discrimination shall prevail because of kind, race, sex, opinion or any other personal or social condition or circumstance – and:
>
> Freedom of creed and opinion is inviolable.

On the other hand, the Preamble of the constitution defines the country as being based on Islam and Arabism and Article Three declares Arabic to be the official and national language. The constitution is silent on the important Arab–Berber division in society. Similarly, Morocco, another country with a large Berber minority, is defined in its constitution's Preamble as Arab.

The situation of minorities is perhaps most secure under the harsher authoritarian regimes such as Syria and, until the American invasion, Iraq. Syria's constitution highlights the Arab nature of the state (Preamble) but acknowledges the major divisions in the country based on religion:

(1) Freedom of faith is guaranteed. The state respects all religions.
(2) The state guarantees the freedom to hold any religious rites, provided they do not disturb the public order (Article 35).

The 1990 interim constitution of Iraq attempted to address the major ethnic division in the country in the context of the Ba`ath Party's pan-Arabism:

(a) Iraq is a part of the Arab Nation.
(b) The Iraqi People are composed of two principal nationalisms: Arab Nationalism and Kurdish Nationalism.
(c) This Constitution acknowledges the national rights of the Kurdish People and the legitimate rights of all minorities within the Iraqi unity (Article 5).

The constitution of Iraq also provided protections for the country's various languages (Article 4). In practice, and with the significant exception of the Kurds, minorities in these countries have benefited from the approach outlined in their constitutions.

The prevalence of authoritarian rule is also unsurprising in the security context in which modern rulers find themselves. Pillai, Scandura and Williams report evidence suggesting the potency of authoritarian styles of leadership during periods of political stress.[35] This is pertinent to the Arab situation as there is no Arab country that is not faced by either a domestic or an external security threat. Such an environment creates the opportunity and the incentive for leaders to justify the maintenance of authoritarian rule in some form or other. To this end, a number of Arab countries justify continued use of emergency powers that effectively subvert their constitutional arrangements. Egypt, for example, has had an emergency law that undermines its constitution's human rights provisions in place since the assassination of Anwar Sadat in 1981. The retention of this law is justified on the basis of a severe internal security threat (see Chapter 7).

Leadership priorities: survival not justice

A feature of today's Arab republican and monarchic rulers is that they reflect a combination of Weber's charismatic and traditional leadership rather than the rule-based form of leadership. Instead of a Platonic just prince, the Arab world has a group of leaders who are more interested in survival than excellence and in securing obedience than demonstrating responsibility. These leaders' methods of rule are effective rather than ethical. These are not professional middle-class politicians, but men whose origins are generally rural. They are often from groups whose home lives have been disrupted by war or industrialisation. They tended to be men who have learnt their skills in the armed forces or a revolutionary political party and who have risen to power in the dramas of national creation and consolidation. They tend also to be members of the second wave of national leaders, stripped of much of the (largely European) liberal or even socialist ideologies of those who led their nations to independence. Instead they are focused more on the hard realities of their new states and are influenced more by traditional Arab attitudes and approaches and less by Western ideas. They have generally been confronted by difficult international and regional environments and by the existential challenge of consolidating their nation states in the face of the siren calls of Arab unity and Islamic comprehensiveness.[36]

Theories of political power and legitimacy in the Middle East context have traditionally been derived from a combination of conquest and religious sources. The Ottomans pursued territorial expansion in the name of Islam. For the past 200 years, however, this pattern has been reversed in the face of Western pressures. This period has instead witnessed what has seemed to be an irreversible disintegration of the traditional equilibrium of government and its accompanying socio-economic structures. Leaders have sought to use traditional structures, such as the consultative councils (*Majlis al Shura*), to counter this decline and to reinforce their authority and legitimacy. This does not mean, however, that Arab leaders have felt the need to subject themselves to any process of accountability and these councils have been without legislative or executive capacity. Force and the control of the mechanisms of force – the armed forces and security and intelligence agencies – have underpinned all Arab regimes for the past decades regardless of whether they are traditional or charismatic in nature. Arab leaders have shown themselves to be willing to supplement their charisma or traditional appeal with force to the degree necessary to maintain their authority. The nature of Arab regimes has meant that a successful leader has seized power and then consolidated his position through a mix of overt force and terror and the threat of such tactics. Opposition has, to a great extent, been cowed into acquiescence. Writing about Saddam Hussein, Samir Al Khalil observes:

> To be such a Leader (as Saddam Hussein), the part must be well acted out. Authority is not in the form of 'pure' Weberian charisma, rooted in personal attributes like extraordinary heroism or revelatory powers, it is rehearsed, staged and elaborately organised. Charisma is indissolubly bound up with bureaucratic organisation. The Leader's image must be at least as ubiquitous as his secret police, but in contrast to the hidden presence of agents and informers, it must be visible, solid and overpowering.[37]

All Arab leaders also resort to force with varying degrees of enthusiasm to accompany their use of patron–client networks. This is consistent with Weber's concept of domination. It has been suggested that Arab leaders work on the principles that it is better to be feared than to be popular and that a firm hand is the only way to maintain order in such fractious societies. From the violent suppression of the Moslem Brotherhood insurrection in Syria from 1980 to 1982 by Hafez Al Assad and the defeat of the PLO by Jordan's King Hussein in 1970 to the responses by the Saudi government to Islamist attacks on the regime in 2003, Arab leaders have not hesitated to resort to violent measures should they assess that their hold on power is in danger. Having demonstrated a willingness to use force ruthlessly, the credibility of the Arab regimes' threat of force and the arbitrary nature of the state security apparatus go a long way to enforcing compliance.

Despite the considerable coercive powers at their disposal, Arab leaders have always recognised that force is not sufficient to gain legitimacy. Even in the regimes where force or its shadow is most evident, the rulers have tended to regard force as a last resort. For example, where possible, the Saudi regime applies a process of re-education of people accused of terrorist activities directed at the overthrow of the Al Saud monarchy instead of imprisonment or even execution, which might provoke further resistance. According to his biographer, Hafez Al Assad reluctantly resorted to force to suppress the Moslem Brotherhood insurrection in Hama in 1982. Assad

> . . . did not revel in killing but resorted to it only for raisons d'etat or what might laxly be called self-defence. . . . Assad was by nature solitary and authoritarian. These aspects of his temperament now became more pronounced. In 1970 he was popular, by 1982 he was feared.[38]

But even at this time of crisis, Assad took care also to obtain political support, in the form of the Federation of Syrian Chambers of Commerce, for his action from the Sunni majority of Syria. Despite his need to resort to the most violent measures, Assad recognised that his legitimacy derived from more than force.

While the resort to force has always been a feature of political control in the Arab world, its weakness as a source of legitimacy has also been recognised. This is perhaps epitomised by Mamluk rule in Egypt. According to Al Ghazali, writing in the twelfth century:

> Government in these days, is a consequence solely of military power, and whosoever he may be to whom the possessor of military power gives his allegiance, that person is the Caliph.[39]

Such arrangements were inevitably unstable. It is in the prevalence of military-based or military-reliant regimes throughout the modern Arab world that many have tended to see the region's problems. From one perspective, such a basis for a regime lacks legitimacy and is inevitably unstable. This is a point stressed by Sharabi, who argues that:

> Political stability itself was damaged primarily by the rise of army-dominated regimes, which undermined the foundations of legitimacy and radically changed political attitudes and habits.[40]

This assessment is supported by the experience of most Arab regimes which have had to endure at least one serious challenge to their rule since independence. For example, post-independence Syria experienced three military coups in the nine months from March to December, 1949. Iraq also experienced a number of violent military coups.

In response to this environment, it is through the images, ideals and beliefs associated with both charismatic and traditional leadership that Arab rulers have sought to establish legitimacy for their long-term hold on power. The monarchies have tended to largely rely on traditional claims, such as descent from the Prophet (Jordan and Morocco) and tribal roots (the Gulf). The republics began with an emphasis on their 'charisma' as leaders of the fight for independence (Bourghiba), the overthrow of corrupt regimes and defeat of outsiders (Nasser), resistance to outside enemies or internal subversion (Assad) or their effective use of force in defence of their group (Saddam Hussein who, in the last years of his regime, also uncovered a family connection with the Prophet). Despite the differences in tactics of the various regimes, their approaches in fact represent a degree of consistency with the past. As Turner observes:

> The prophet, who was for Weber the epitome of charismatic leadership, based his message on an appeal to an idealised past in order to break with a corrupt present. Charisma may, therefore, be based on traditional norms rather than representing a distinct break with them.[41]

Put in Weber's terms, Arab leadership style is influenced by the nature of the basis of their rule. The ruler of a monarchy draws more directly on traditional principles for his legitimacy. His style will be different from one whose position reflects a charismatic basis, such as Nasser. Republics have tended to operate largely on the basis of what Weber would describe as charismatic domination and a degree of bureaucratisation of the process, at least while the first and second generations of post-independence leaders are still in control. However, even monarchies have relied on an element of charismatic authority for their legitimacy. Kings Hussein and Hassan, for example, played a similar role to the nation-building presidents, although they were also part of an established traditional dynasty and sought to add to their stature by emphasising their links to the family of the Prophet.

Survival and legitimacy: the uncertain status of the rule of law

The appeal of charismatic authority is likely to be strong for young leaders attempting to reform their societies. Leaders who have been in power for some time, however, will be appreciative of Weber's comment that charismatic leadership is precarious and short lived. The task for Arab leaders has been particularly complex given the significant and rapid breaks with tradition that they have attempted, such as trying to limit the influence of Islam, controlling or even destroying the tribes, re-shaping social structures and modernising economies. Even the monarchies, with their more conservative agendas, have had to deal with the collapse of the Ottoman Empire and the subsequent abolition of the caliphate, the colonial period and, in most cases, the need to develop functioning states almost from scratch.

Pursuing charismatic legitimacy in such a context has created a range of expectations. Initially, the new republican leaders conveyed an image of almost puritanic austerity and personal rectitude. People like Nasser and Ben Bella sought no personal financial benefits and did not promote family interests. Their example forced the monarchies, including Saudis, to try to present a less self-aggrandising image. Such personal propriety has been important in justifying the overthrowing of old rules. Weber suggests that charismatic authority is essentially unconstrained by rules of behaviour and that, consistent with their revolutionary approach to governance, charismatic leaders are intent on cutting through old habits and values.[42] While ostensibly maintaining the Western ideas and constitutional structures of the early years of independence, the current Arab leaders have regarded the parliaments and elections as impediments to their nation-building programmes. A law-based, nationally-structured system does not sit comfortably with the revolutionary approach with which many Arab leaders began their rule. Interestingly, the charismatic rejection of rules is consistent with the traditional tribal approach with its emphasis on survival, honour and group exclusivity. While living by a complex code of honour, Arab tribal attitudes do not easily accept the constraints of the modern rule-based state. The persistence of group feeling (*asabiya*) has weakened Arab leaders' willingness to allow the law to provide a framework for the work of government.

Importantly, in the face of the persistence and strength of regime opponents, the idea of due process and rule of law came to represent potential weakness. The violent actions into which Hafez Al Assad was drawn in 1982 convinced him that only force could contain his opponents and save his regime. According to Seale: 'this slide into brutality swept aside any semblance of the due process of law'.[43] King Hussein of Jordan was convinced of the value of constitutional government for his country and tended to respect it except in dealing with matters affecting the royal family or major threats to the regime. On several occasions, he experimented with the routinising of government, involving attempts at parliamentary government. In the face of the uncooperative response of his opponents, however, he felt constrained to abandon these experiments. The concern about the potential for opposition groups to seize upon elections as a point of weakness circumstances can also be seen at the beginning of the Algerian civil war. The military terminated the electoral experiment in 1991 because of their concern that opposition groups would abuse the rule of law to establish a theocratic dictatorship.

These problems underline a major problem with the place of law within Islam. Under the Umayyads and the Abbasids, the state was structured in such a way that there was no clear distinction between the executive and judicial functions. This left supreme secular and religious power in the hands of the caliph. Abbasid theory supported the idea that the caliph was the servant of the law and that legal authority was vested in the scholar-jurist, not the political master. In practice, the caliphs moved to control the legal scholars and to use them to further the power of the political leader.[44] It was assumed that the caliph would be suitably qualified for the role, but there was no mechanism, such as an independent judiciary or an authentic electoral process, to ensure this. The only real mechanism was military force, a factor that became increasingly important from the declining years of the Abbasid dynasty to the present.

Presidents and kings: in the same boat

The constitutional division of the modern Arab world into monarchies and republics and the ideological frameworks that have been built up around a number of nation-building projects tend to obscure the underlying unity of the region's political systems that has been implicit in this book. The differences between and within these two models are obviously significant. The monarchies have relied more deliberately on traditional authority to promote their legitimacy. This has enabled them to attempt to modulate change by working through established, if tightly controlled, elite structures and to limit the unrest that change inevitably provokes. Republics have pursued radical and rapid change, which included the overthrow of traditional elites, economic nationalism, social modernisation and the secularisation of public life. As Arab society has changed over time, however, so have the political systems of the Arab world and their ruling elites. Throughout the region, the individual leader has emerged as the personification and dominant feature of the regimes, whether monarchic or republican. This has made possible a change in the tactics employed. The republican regimes, in particular, have altered the mix of their legitimacy formula. Charisma remains important, but traditional factors, such as the family and the role of Islam, have become increasingly significant in reinforcing their legitimacy. Dogan and Pelassy maintain that 'There is no rational authority that is not also founded on tradition . . . '[45] and in all the states of the region, tribal considerations are among the most important of the traditions to which the elites have turned. According to a member of the Abu Dhabi royal house,

> Moslem legitimacy, certainly in the Arab Gulf region, was – and remains – deeply rooted in tribal customs. . . . Their pertinence to local tradition was and is self-evident to its inhabitants.[46]

Rulers of Arab monarchies and republics face many common challenges as they seek to exercise power. They share the same broad political tradition and increasingly employ similar tactics and practices to consolidate and legitimise their power. For example, Morocco's King Mohammed, like his father, Hassan, before him, rules through an informal patrimonial system (*makhzen*), in which clientalism is an important part. Similar networks are also relied upon by republican rulers. These are networks that Richards and Waterbury describe as 'another manifestation of small group genes'.[47]

Part of the reason for the increasing symmetry in approach is that Arab monarchies and republics share many of the same goals. They are both attempting to modernise highly traditional societies at a time of immense social change. They focus on centralisation to allow for quick and coherent decisions, to control dissent and, generally, to assist in regime consolidation. Regimes in both systems have at times considered greater social and political openness, as well as economic modernisation and industrialisation. Increasingly, however, the various regimes have shown a lack of tolerance of opposition after the failure of their initial attempts at pluralism and rule of law.

Weber would anticipate the traditional and charismatic style of leadership of this post-independence generation of Arab leaders to give way to routinisation or bureaucratisation under their sons. The sons, who lack the same heroic context, are looking for another basis upon which to establish and justify their power. It is interesting, therefore, that we might indeed be seeing such a shift towards the bureaucratic and legal form of authority. The long-standing Arab rulers are coming to the end of their lives and are looking for routinised ways in which to justify their families' continued hold on power and to legitimise their dynastic intent. They are also tyring to block others from replacing them by the same methods they themselves used to gain power. After years of disregarding legal processes and institutional mechanisms, these leaders' ambitions are being manifested in the development of constitutions and other formal mechanisms which set out the means by which they will maintain their hold on power (see Chapter 4).

There is a 'catch-22' at work in Arab political systems. In the name of survival and stability, regimes fall back on those they can trust: their family and tribal networks. In doing so, they are narrowing their support base and potentially making it harder to strengthen their legitimacy. As the support base of the regime narrows, opposition develops and a degree of repression is likely to become necessary. The narrowing of regimes' core support is, in turn, largely a symptom of what is driving these leaders to hold power at all costs and to seek to pass that power on to their families. This driving force is the enduring ability of the family and the tribe to maintain a grip on Arab loyalties and to provide a degree of legitimacy to Arab regimes. Arabs expect individuals to be loyal to their families, clans and tribes, and these relationships are extended to people in positions of power. To an extent, the obverse is also an important factor. The more a leader concentrates on the support of his family and tribe, the more likely he is to suspect other families and tribes and be distrusted by them in return.

The instability that Sharabi associated with Arab regimes has changed into a form of stability that verges on stagnation, at least if measured by the longevity of their leaders. The second cadre of Arab leaders has survived in power for more than a generation (see Appendix 3). The picture to emerge is one of rulers whose tenure is longer than their counterparts in almost any other part of the world. Such a development is at first glance surprising, given the contracting nature of the Arab regimes' support bases, which might be expected to promote instability. It might be expected, for example, that such a development would require ever greater reliance on force to preserve the regime. Instead, regime legitimacy has been achieved in part by a move away from the military focus. Quinlivan outlines in detail how Arab leaders are increasing their control over their security and military forces by creating competing centres of power in those organisations. Military and security forces are still in control of key security positions in the various regimes, but their ability to play 'king-maker' has been undermined.[48] In Saudi Arabia, for example, the various arms of the security forces have been divided among the senior members of the royal family. King Abdallah runs the National Guard, Crown Prince Sultan is Minister of Defence and runs the Air Force and Crown Prince Naif is in command of the interior forces. This serves the dual purpose of ensuring that the armed forces are not able to attempt a coup by themselves, as occurred in 1969, when the Air Force attempted to overthrow the monarchy, and that none of the princes alone is strong enough to be able to mount a coup.

Domination should, Weber says, not be based solely on force. The reliance on force does appear to be declining in its appeal among Arab leaders and their potential successors, who are attempting to pursue legitimacy by a variety of means, including political processes. Egypt's President Mubarak, Yemen's President Saleh and other republican leaders throughout the region can be likened to Weber's plebiscitary leader who formally derives his legitimacy from the affirmation of the ruled. These leaders have subjected themselves and their governments to superficially competitive but carefully controlled election tests throughout their presidencies. This electoral endorsement of the president could be equated to the traditional tribal declaration of allegiance (*bay'a*). Arab monarchies rely even more directly on the traditional form of *bay'a* to bolster their claims which are consistent with their more overt appeal to tradition, but they also rely on an indirect electoral process to bolster their position. Whilst there is nothing democratic about such processes, they do provide an opportunity for rulers to reduce their reliance on overt coercion.

Another important element influencing Arab rulers in their attempts to reinforce their legitimacy is the economic power structures that operate throughout the Arab world. Under the Ottomans, the commercial sector was largely unregulated and left to local leaders to control. In the modern Arab state, the central government has assumed a more assertive role, undertaking major nation-building projects and controlling economic life more generally. Many of the old structures, the guild-based artisans and craftsmen, remain, leaving much of the new economy to the rulers who have made themselves and their families *de facto* owners of their countries' wealth. The ruling families have used the revenues not only for their personal aggrandisement, but also in the traditional Arab manner of ensuring loyalty through the distribution of largesse. This approach has often avoided the need for direct taxation, an attractive measure from a business perspective. However, it also means that popular identification with the state and participation in the decision-making process has been limited and has, in cases such as Libya, produced an attitude of apathy and dependence in the population.[49]

An additional factor behind this change in approach to legitimacy is to be found in the role of the military itself, which has been changing in response to changes in society. Increasingly, people who started their careers as military men have expanded their activities into business and now dominate large sectors of the economies of many of the countries of the Arab world. The more resources a regime controls and the more independent a country's elite is from other socio-economic groups, the more likely it is that an authoritarian regime will establish itself.[50] There are other reasons for the military's involvement in the economy. Personal greed is, of course, a powerful incentive. In countries such as Egypt, however, the military's status helps to drive this process of economic involvement. The Egyptian military's share of the national budget has been declining in real terms by around 50 per cent over the past few decades. This has not been compensated for by American military aid, which has also been declining in real terms. Whatever their motivation, the new cadres of military leaders have become diverted from their original objective or those of their fathers. They still have great potential power, but their inclinations appear to be moving towards non-military solutions to issues. This involvement of the military and senior regime members in the region's economies is an important element in maintaining regime solidarity and is unlikely to encourage Arab regimes to undertake real economic liberalisation.

Weber notes that reliance on military force may be effective in maintaining stability over a limited period, but not over the longer term. No system could remain stable as long as these Arab regimes have 'if it was based merely on physical compulsion or mere expediency'.[51] For these regimes to have survived for so long, their legitimacy must be more broadly based. Important in that process is ensuring that there is no one in a position from which he might launch a challenge to a ruler or who might be used as a figurehead to lead a challenge. In 1954, the Egyptian leader, Nasser, became concerned that General Mohammed Neguib, the figurehead of the Revolutionary Command Council, which overthrew the monarchy, had began to develop ideas about playing a more active role in the new government. Nasser was determined to ensure that Neguib did not gain real power, and he forced Neguib's resignation and eventual retirement from public life. Similarly, the current President of Egypt, Hosni Mubarak, drove one of the few serious potential challengers to his rule, the Minister of Defence, Field Marshal Abu Ghazala, from public life in a series of demotions over a number of years. Mubarak has gone one step further and left the formal succession process in limbo by refusing to nominate a vice president. In doing so he is seeking to ensure that no one is in a position to threaten his rule or his son's succession. More generally, Arab leaders are working to reduce their reliance on their original power base (generally the military or a political party, such as the Ba`ath) and intensifying their reliance on their families, tribes and client networks.

Ideology: an empty barrel?

Yet another factor with the potential to legitimise a regime (and, if necessary, delegitimise its predecessor) is ideology. Salem suggests that in the Arab world ideology has had less impact than might be the case in other regions. He maintains that on the whole the resort to ideology by various movements in the Arab world has failed to achieve a level of legitimacy that would promote stability within Arab political systems.[52] At its height under Nasser, the ideology of Arab nationalism gained great support among the people of the Arab world and posed a major challenge to the region's state system. It was, however, seriously undermined by a number of events, such as the failure of the United Arab Republic,[53] the Arab-Israeli war (June 1967) and the Egyptian–Israeli peace treaty (1979). These developments allowed the traditional forces of tribalism and Islam to resurface as major expressions of the values of Arabs. The dominant ideological forces contributing to legitimacy in the post-independence Arab world are thereby contained in Weber's idea of traditional and charismatic legitimacy.

Monarchies and republics seek to create the impression of a distance between the process of government and the person who rules. Prime ministers and their cabinets carry responsibility for failed or unpopular policies, while the rulers claim credit for success. Turner observes that: 'One prominent method of preserving the insecurity of official appointments is to use administrative staff as scapegoats for mass dissatisfaction'.[54] This is a common practice in the Arab world today. In Jordan, Morocco and Yemen, for example, the rulers have regularly resorted to the sacking of prime ministers and their governments in response to public dissatisfaction over government policies – policies that might well have been imposed on the government by the king or president. Generally, dismissal carries no long-term penalty as the countries' ministers have been regularly re-cycled in subsequent governments. An alternative approach was pursued by the late King Hassan of Morocco. In response to widespread concern about public sector corruption involving some of his most senior officials, Hassan submitted legislation to Parliament to improve the management of public enterprises, thereby diverting attention from the issue of political accountability that underpinned the scandals.[55]

Legitimacy through solidarity

Legitimacy depends greatly on group solidarity. The stronger a group's solidarity, the less likely the authority of that group is to be challenged. Solidarity has been a feature of the successful Arab regimes, which have paid great attention to ensuring it has been maintained. This aspect is coming under great pressure as the regimes move to address generational change. The first of the established regimes to be forced to deal with this particular problem has been Syria, and the emerging challenges have been significant.

Reflecting Weber's approach and his discussion of charismatic and traditional power, the focus of much analysis of Arab regimes has tended to be on the individual at the top (e.g. Nasser, Qaddafi and Hussein) and only occasionally the wider ruling group. Despite the understandable focus on the individual, however, it is clear that Arab regimes are more complex structures than simply charismatic dictatorships. Arab political systems have developed since independence into what Mosca would describe as oligarchies. In this system, minorities combined into a coherent force, presenting a united front to other forces in society.[56] Marr comments that even in the absolute dictatorship of Saddam Hussein, there was a political elite 'of people who make decisions on national policy'.[57] Such a situation promotes regime solidarity, which benefits the ruler but also gives group members a degree of influence. All the people who have committed themselves to the successful party, leader or clique can be said to form part of the regime's clientalist structure and to act as a support for and an influence on the ability of the person or people at the top to rule. Mosca outlines this process in the following terms:

> Below the highest stratum in the ruling class there is always . . . another that is more numerous and comprises all the capacities for leadership (advisers, administrators, propagandists, police) in the country. Without such a class, any sort of social organisation would be impossible.[58]

The key areas of the system are occupied by reliable members of the regime or its clientalist network. It is through this process that the regime ensures that decisions taken by the elite are implemented throughout society and that potential regime threats are anticipated and counteracted. This framework encourages the broadly based acquiescence throughout the population, without which no leadership would be able to function.

This aspect of leadership has particular resonance in the Arab context where so many countries are ruled by minority groups. Syria is controlled by the Alawites, who make up less than ten per cent of the population. Yemen's presidential and ruling family are Zaidi Shi'a, representing about a fifth of the population. Bahrain's ruling family is Sunni, but the majority of Bahrainis are Shi'a. Before the American invasion, Saddam Hussein's regime was in a similar situation. In such a context, the implications of a change of government could include the loss of power and privileges and even the violent settling of scores.

Fragile legitimacy

Arab regimes are confronted by great problems and Arab leadership is widely seen as potentially brittle. However, Arab rulers have displayed great durability over the past 30 or so years, and this apparent brittleness should not be taken as a sign that leaders lack legitimacy. Nor, however, should the longevity of leaders be taken of an indication of profound legitimacy. Arab rulers operate in a volatile, contended environment where consensus over some of the basic ordering principles of the state is rejected by significant elements of society. Under such conditions, Arab leaders have increasingly fallen back on traditional bases of support, which ultimately means reliance on the control of force by the family and the tribe.

Arab leaders have been successful in protecting their hold on power. They have gained public acceptance for their provision of stability and predictability. Even those who do not support their rule often accept the regime on the basis that nothing can be done to change the situation. In addition, the regimes' reliance on family and tribe make sense to the rest of the population. It is consistent with society's expectations, which centre on the family. The regimes have established the loyalty and solidarity of important groups in society, giving them a critical mass of public support. Finally, these regimes have begun to adopt more sophisticated and political means of retaining and exercising power. This is, in part, a necessary response to changing circumstances, but also a sign of greater confidence in the stability of their systems. It also means that regimes enjoy a significant degree of legitimacy, albeit precarious in the long run.

4 Family first

Arab succession and dynasticism

> The absence of rules such as primogeniture made succession problematic under Islam. This affects political culture and practice today, making a peaceful transfer of power and the introduction of new blood through elections very difficult. Electoral democracy presupposes the authority of offices rather than individuals. In Islamic society, there was no attempt, prior to sustained Western influence, to replace Imamate or Sultanate with constitutional monarchy or a republic.[1]

Having looked at the most significant formative influences on the development of the Arab political tradition and the attitudes and practices of Arab leaders, this chapter turns to the fundamental issue of political succession in the Arab world. It examines how the countries of the Arab region have struggled to develop institutionalised mechanisms for the transfer of power from one ruler to another and how they have sought legitimacy on the basis of a range of measures, including traditional practices. Driving the practices of Arab regimes is the motivation of dynastic succession.

Arab monarchies have been ostensibly more successful at managing the challenge of succession than have the republics, in part because their approach to governance is closer to traditional tribal practices and family rule is, therefore, easier to justify. Despite this, the urge towards dynastic rule is increasingly apparent among the republics where most leaders are intent on passing on power to their immediate family members. This attitude enjoys a considerable degree of popular support, or at least acceptance, in Arab society, in part because the underlying attitude of family permeates many levels of political, economic and social activity in the Arab world. Even government opponents are often more intent on replacing one family elite with their own than with a programme of major structural reform.

The practices of political succession in monarchic and republican systems and the challenges raised by those practices are considered in the light of some of the issues raised in earlier chapters, such as the centrality of the family and tribe and the paramount desire for stability in the Arab polity. It is also noted that, while the dynastic impulse is perhaps dominant throughout the Arab world, there is also considerable opposition to the practice. There are significant forces in the Arab world that argue that dynastic succession is not acceptable. Some of these follow what might be seen as the Western path, pressing for electoral and constitutional reform as part of a campaign for greater democracy in the region. Others, largely conservative elements, maintain that the tribal or Islamic system is the correct basis on which to determine succession.

The centrality of succession

The effective management of political succession is a vitally important part of any political system. Political systems are dynamic and, if they are to survive, governments need to adapt to change. Changing balances of power, societal developments and generational change demand responses and competing ideas demand the chance to be heard. The external environment continually poses new challenges to any government. Leadership is a crucial element of a society's ability to adapt. Leaders, however, be they democrats or autocrats, tend to lose their dynamism over time. They lose the ability to be responsive to changes in their social and political environments. Governments become tired. Syria in the 1990s, for example, experienced a period of political and economic stagnation as President Hafez Al Assad lost the physical capacity and the will to maintain the initiative in the Syrian political system and adopted a policy based essentially on maintaining the status quo.[2] Those around him responded by jockeying for position for when the impending succession took place, rather than pursuing their governmental responsibilities. The result was stalemate in the system and increased vulnerability of the regime. Conversely, the capacity of a political system to develop legitimate procedures for political succession enhances its ability to deal with challenges effectively. This in turn contributes to political and social cohesion and stability and the efficient government of a state.

Importantly, effective succession procedures contribute to the stable operation of a political system in part because they contribute to the legitimacy of a regime. The prospect that a regime is able to negotiate the interests of different groups at a time of leadership change encourages citizens to abide by the rules and to accord the system legitimacy with all the advantages that entails. Legitimacy enables a regime to exercise its authority with less attention to survival and the use of force. Legitimate governments, which do not need to spend as much time and effort defending their hold on power, can pay greater attention to bread and butter issues. For example, General Abdel Karim Qassem's overthrow of the Hashemite monarchy in Iraq in 1958 enjoyed considerable popular support. He was able to take advantage of that support to initiate a range of reforms, such as the nationalisation of the British-owned Iraq Petroleum Company and significant land redistribution. In the period from 1960 to 1963, however, he found himself losing credibility among the populace and support among his allies. He lost legitimacy and, in response, had to focus more of his energies on survival and less on reform. As Palmer notes, this fundamentally changed the nature of Qassem's regime:

> To safeguard his power, Qassem turned on his former allies and forged a new alliance with anti-communist officers in the security forces . . . The remainder of Qassem's reign was preoccupied with the task of survival.[3]

By contrast, in the aftermath of the Arabs' comprehensive defeat by the Israelis in 1967, Egypt's President Nasser announced his resignation from the presidency. Massive public demonstrations of support, however, enabled him to hold on to power.[4] Despite the disaster of his policies towards Israel, Nasser had retained much of his charisma and his legitimacy.

Western succession procedures create limits to the maintenance and the use of power. Even the most successful Western leadership group understands that its time in office is limited and that a rival group will gain power in due course. The implications of such a prospect – the risk of suffering some form of retribution as a result of a government's misrule – are a potent factor inhibiting the misuse of power. In Arab countries such as Syria, the same concerns or considerations have led to the opposite conclusion. Members of the minority Alawite regime assess that they must retain power to ensure that the community is not subjected to retribution. It is hard not to see the developments in Iraq after the American invasion, including the circumstances surrounding the execution of Saddam Hussein and reports of Shi`a death squads, as evidence to support the Alawis' concerns.

Leadership changes are both a necessary and inevitable fact of life in any political system. With this in mind, it is evident that central features of political systems that are seen to have legitimacy are the existence of generally accepted procedures for accommodating the various pressures for change and the transferring of power from one leader or leadership group to another. This applies regardless of whether the political system is liberal democratic or based on some other form of political organisation. The viability of a politician's leadership will be influenced by the level of public support for the process by which they succeeded. In the United States, there was considerable disquiet about the legitimacy of the election of George W. Bush to the presidency in 2000 as a result of the disputed conduct of the elections in Florida. That disquiet might have hamstrung Bush's presidency but for the attacks of 11 September 2001. In the Middle East, where succession practices lack institutional transparency, this issue is more overt and has been subject to close scrutiny with the deaths of the long-term rulers of Jordan, Syria and Morocco and the succession to power of their children.

The Arab approach to succession effectively means the likely domination of countries of the region by individual families. In the monarchies, the principle of dynastic succession has been generally accepted, although the right of particular families to monopolise power is often challenged. Attempts in republics to develop a national consensus in favour of any systematic process of succession have failed to secure a sufficient degree of public support, thereby weakening the legitimacy of successions. The determination of republican regimes to pursue their dynastic ambitions risks creating pressure for violent or extra constitutional measures among those seeking change. This problem has been manifest throughout Arab history. Lacking legitimate and institutionalised succession procedures, Middle Eastern regimes were noted for violent bloodletting as putative heirs to the throne sought to defend their position by removing their brothers or other possible rivals. The experience of the Ottomans and Mamluk rule in Egypt was characterised by bloodthirsty regime change and an absence of popular endorsement.[5]

Succession in general is a difficult issue to address to the extent that it is often decided on the basis of informal, political considerations. The long-term, relatively smooth operation of the process and the separation of powers in liberal democracies have meant that succession is not even regarded as a subject worthy of study and many writers on politics ignore it. Succession is not dealt with in a formal way in many countries. There is, for example, no reference to succession in the Australian, the Canadian or the German constitutions. The issue of who is to be chosen through these various arrangements is left to the political process to resolve. In most Western countries great emphasis is placed on the separation of powers where sovereignty is divided between different arms of government. In Westminster-based systems, for example, a clear distinction has developed between the formal and symbolic role of the head of state, who reigns, and the executive, which rules. This Western approach has emerged out of papal thinking of the Middle Ages, where the separation of the office and the individual was of fundamental importance.[6]

The situation in the Arab world is markedly different and succession is a major, almost existential issue. The processes in place to deal with it operate under great political pressure. It is one of the major focal points of interest for all actors in the system largely because of the tendency of Arabs to identify or equate their leaders with the state itself. Whereas in Western countries, leaders come and go without major impact on the political system, for Arabs, especially in the republics, the leader assumes a central importance as 'the guarantor of the sovereignty of the state and the distribution of power and resources'.[7] The Lebanese constitution, for example, describes the president as 'the symbol of the nation's unity. He shall safeguard the constitution and Lebanon's independence, unity and territorial integrity' (Article 49(1)). Tunisia's constitution describes the president as 'the guarantor of national independence, of the integrity of its territory and of respect for the constitution and the laws' (Article 41). The Algerian constitution declares that 'The President of the Republic, the Head of State, embodies the unity of the nation' (Article 70(1)). At the political level, the late President of the United Arab Emirates, Sheikh Zayed Al Nahayan, was regularly described in such terms as 'the father of the nation'. His death was dreaded by many, given Zayed's central role in establishing the country and holding it together. When asked by a journalist about the Tunisian political system, President Bourghiba once famously replied: 'System? What system? I am the system'.[8]

This phenomenon can be seen as an example of Weber's 'routinisation of charisma', where charismatic authority becomes 'encrusted in sacred values', which govern its allocation, as in the procedure for resolving the problem of succession. The sacred values elevate the charismatic leader above mundane matters such as law and procedure.[9] Moreover, the experience of the Algerian and

Lebanese civil wars and of the Moslem Brotherhood uprising in Syria have worked to reinforce the established view that the security of the state, even its survival, is wrapped up in the individual or group of individuals in power. This perception applies regardless of the shortcomings of the regimes. Anyone attempting to change the political order is threatening the long-term viability of the state.

Succession in the Arab world is, therefore, more than just an issue of transition from one generational cohort to the next or from one political party to another. It is not about providing an opportunity for the other side to have a go. Indeed, in keeping with the region's tribal traditions and the zero-sum nature of Arab politics, the other side is to be kept out of power to the greatest possible extent. Over history, dynasties have experienced the gaining of power (*dawla*) usually by force, which is endorsed by God.[10] The challenge is to maintain this blessing so that the regime can cross the generations, in line with families' dynastic ambitions. The reluctance of families to share power and the controversies over succession in the Arab world have exposed the fragility of the region's institutions and practices and highlight the authoritarian and tribal aspects of the region's traditions.

The issue typifies the problems Arabs have always had in coming to terms with the influences of their nomadic, tribal traditions, the revolutionary impact of Islam and imported foreign influences over the generations. The problem in its modern guise is very specific. Black comments that the absence of accepted rules for succession under Islam affects modern political behaviour. It makes the peaceful transfer of political power particularly difficult and encourages the personalisation of the system. It was not until Western ideas began to make inroads on Arab thinking that concepts such as constitutionally-based political systems and rule-based political behaviour began to have an impact.[11]

Throughout their history, the people of the Arab world have been living with the consequences of this lack of consensus over how to deal with the problem of political succession. As noted earlier, during the long periods under non-Arab rule, Arab traditions were largely irrelevant and succession was resolved among the foreign ruling groups. Independence, however, released the Arabs to address their political systems as they choose. What this has done, however, has been to expose the historic lack of consensus, in particular, the tension between tribal concepts and the Persian influence on Islamic political thought. The disagreement between those who support a form of democratic transition and those inspired by more authoritarian examples is fundamental to the way politics is conducted in the region.

Ancient parallels?

The Arab succession dilemma is, of course, nothing new, nor is it unique to the Arab world. There are many examples throughout history where political systems have operated on the assumption that state survival is dependent on continued family rule. At least superficially, the succession practices of the Arab world contain elements in common with aspects of the European experience. In mediaeval and early modern Europe, dynastic issues were resolved by both force of arms and appeals to constitutional legitimacy. Similarly, in the modern Arab world some regimes have resorted to force to support their claims, while others have attempted to enshrine their dominant status in national constitutions. As Elton makes clear with regard to the Tudors of England, regime survival depended on 'the presence of an effective king' and succession provisions, even for a powerful and feared monarch such as Henry VIII, were difficult to enforce from the grave.[12] Keir notes that 'possession was nine-tenths of a law of succession, which was exceedingly indefinite and uncertain'.[13] It took the English generations to resolve the issue, in part by ending the identification of the future of the state with the person or dynasty in power. As a result, while the British monarch can be seen as the embodiment of the nation, effective power lies elsewhere. It could be argued that even the British process is not complete, with the monarchy retaining residual powers. These were on display in the Australian constitutional crisis of 1975 when the monarch's representative removed the elected Prime Minister from office.[14] The nations of the Arab world are just setting out on this process. The approach they are taking can be seen by the steps taken by some Arab governments, for example, Jordan and Morocco and most of the Gulf countries, to incorporate in their constitutions succession provisions that are specifically designed to promote the continued dominance of the ruling dynasties.

This historical model often appears to have a certain resonance to the modern day experience. For example, Louis XIV of France and the Stuarts of England claimed their right to rule on hereditary grounds which were founded in a hierarchical structure ordained by God.[15] This justification had been anticipated by the Umayyad and Abbasid dynasties and later by the Ottomans to justify their claims to power.[16] In these instances, there was a strong element of tradition and legal argumentation involved. By the fifteenth century, the four recognised schools of jurisprudence in Sunni Islam, the Hanafi, Malaki, Shaf'i and Hanbali, all agreed on the right process of political succession. According to Coulson:

> Their doctrine of the Caliphate, of which the central feature is that the office belongs to a member of the tribe of Quraysh upon election by the qualified representatives of the community, is based on their recognition of the authority of the Medinan, Umayyad and Abbasid Caliphs.[17]

These doctrines were never able to develop into an integrated part of the Arab political tradition. They were attempts to justify and legitimise widespread practice, but there was too much opposition to the practice for their proponents to be able to claim that a consensus existed. As a result, Moslem dynasties that came after the Umayyads avoided developing a fixed rule of succession. This meant that the transfer of power was frequently based on the exercise of naked force. As noted, the period of Mamluk rule in Egypt from 1250 to 1517 was dominated by the violent overthrow of rulers by military usurpers. Over this period, the average term for a Mamluk ruler was seven years. In modern times, the 'succession' from the Hashemite monarchy to the republic in Iraq in 1958 was a particularly violent affair.

In the case of the early Moslem empires, especially the Umayyads and the Abbasids, political succession was limited in its impact, involving only a relatively minor change of personnel. This was partly because the new rulers lacked the necessary resources for administration. The rapid and continued expansion of the empire exposed the lack of trained Arabs needed to run the non-military aspects of government. Consequently, they were forced to rely on existing structures and conquered populations. The Arab conquerors, therefore, ruled but left the routine business of government to those they had conquered. One ruler would succeed another but continue to rely on his predecessor's advisers and ministers. The Abbasid caliphs even recruited advisers who had worked for the hated Umayyads because of their need for experience and skills. In the modern day, this pattern has been reflected in the ascension to power of Syria's Bashar Al Assad, Jordan's King Abdallah and Morocco's King Mohammed, all of whom have depended on broadly the same personnel employed by their fathers. The goal is not to initiate significant political or economic reform so much as to hold the ruling group together and thereby protect the family's position.[18]

There have, of course, been exceptions, such as when ideologically-driven groups overthrew the existing order and removed the agents of that regime. Nasser in Egypt, Qaddafi in Libya, the Ba`athists' seizure of power in Syria in 1963 and the Iraqi regime changes in the 1960s and 1970s involved 'an almost complete turn-over of high-level government personnel'.[19] In the Syrian and Iraqi cases, this was at once necessitated and made possible by a formal party structure supporting the new government and accompanied by supporters who needed to be accommodated.

Tribal succession: family rule

Despite the failure to institutionalise succession, tribal values have informally guided rulers' handling of succession. The transfer of power-based ideas that can be traced to traditional tribal concepts has been an underlying feature of politics throughout the Arab world despite often revolutionary rhetoric. Given the long-term foreign dominance of the region's political system, the tribes tended to be the focus of Arab politics, a factor that has helped to preserve the relevance of tribal values in the modern day. The Arab tribal approach to succession is a mix of the dynastic and the democratic. The tribes themselves have tended to be non-hierarchical in their ethos, with members presuming and demanding equality with their fellow tribesmen. One can still see this democratic or egalitarian approach on display in the tribal *majlis* in some Arab countries. Moreover, tribal succession is circumscribed by certain rules or codes. The concept of kingship has tenuous and ambiguous standing in tribal society and dynastic rule is theoretically unacceptable. As Hitti observes:

> Before his death, Umar is represented as having nominated a board of six electors . . . with the stipulation that his own son not be elected to succeed him. The constitution of this board called al-Shura (consultation), including the oldest and most distinguished companions surviving, showed that the ancient Arabian idea of a tribal chief has triumphed over that of the hereditary monarch.[20]

Nevertheless, a form of dynastic rule became established over time. The leader, the sheikh, would secure the leadership often on the basis of a form of election involving senior tribal members and would be endorsed by the tribe's offering of the *bay'a* or oath of allegiance. Hudson stresses the importance of personal qualities in this process. 'The leader must demonstrate his personal competence if he is to earn the traditional oath of allegiance'.[21] Having achieved leadership, the sheikh holds power on the basis of his ability to maintain his followers' support. Until relatively recently, this was achieved by the sheikh's ability to lead his followers on raids against neighbours in search of booty and honour through battle. Nowadays, it is effected more through the distribution of largesse. In theory, permanent leadership of the tribe is difficult to maintain, as Weber notes:

> It (a tribe) has a permanent leader only when a man, through feats of warfare or judicial wisdom, has gained such distinction that, by virtue of his charisma, he is recognised as a sayyed . . . His example and verdict will be honoured by the sibs only so long as he proves his charisma.[22]

There was a good practical reason why dynastic succession should retain a degree of flexibility among the tribal Arabs. A tribe's continued existence might depend on the effectiveness of its leadership. Arabs tended to believe that the noble qualities needed to rule a tribe successfully were passed on in families on a hereditary basis. It was natural, then, that the right to rule would be accepted as residing in a particular family. In this context, however, in the event of the death of a chief, the decision as to which member of that family was to succeed would be made by the adult males of the tribe on the basis of who was best qualified or most fit.[23] This is an important feature of the rule of succession and it means that tribal and Islamic law do not allow an individual to nominate his specific successor. In practice, however, the succession process tends to favour the established family. A powerful sheikh has generally been in a good position to promote the interests of his favoured successor and, provided that choice demonstrates noble qualities, the tribal assembly is likely to accept the succession.

The pattern whereby Arab tribal leaders have tended to be drawn from the same families was established by the Quraysh tribe, which dominated Mecca at the time of the Prophet Mohammed. The practice has survived to the modern day, where the decision on who is to succeed as ruler is often made only by the family or extended family of the leader, effectively usurping the traditional role of the tribe. For example, when the Ruler of Abu Dhabi, Sheikh Shakbut, was replaced by his brother, Sheikh Zayed, in 1966, and when the Ruler of Qatar, Sheikh Khalifa, was replaced by his son, Sheikh Hamad, in 1995, only the inner circles of the families were involved in the process. The rest of the members of their tribes were left to accept the decisions and to offer *bay'a* to the new ruler. A similar process was involved in republican Syria where President Hafez Al Assad sought the agreement of key members of his family to his choice of successor.

The founder of the Umayyad dynasty, Muawiya, and his successors operated on the basis of a dynastic form of succession. This precedent was rejected by those that came after the Umayyads, but the spirit of this innovation persists to this day. Muawiya set one important and lasting precedent that was taken up by the Umayyads' successor dynasty, the Abbasids, and which was intended to overcome the tribal resistance to inherited rule. He nominated his son as his successor and sought the tribal *bay'a* while he was still alive, which was in effect pre-emptive action to secure legitimacy for the succession. Like many of the other concepts or principles that emerged from the tumult of the early days of Islam, this particular idea has been revived in modern Arab states. This precedent was followed, for example, by King Hussein of Jordan, King Hassan of Morocco and the Saudi royal family and has been incorporated into a number of modern Arab constitutions (Bahrain Article 1(b), Kuwait Article 4(2), and Qatar Article 8). It was also followed by Syria's Hafez Al Assad. Hafez did not issue a public proclamation, which would have been inconsistent with the country's constitution and would have flown in the face of the Syrian political ethos. He made it clear, however, that he wanted his son, Bashar, to succeed him. In that case, *bay'a* could be said to have been offered in the form of the overwhelming parliamentary endorsement Bashar received on his accession to power.[24] Hosni Mubarak of Egypt, Ali Abdallah Saleh of Yemen and Muammar Qaddafi of Libya have all hinted at their similar intentions for their sons, and are helping their sons to develop support for their claims.

It is, moreover, common that the dominant families' roles extend beyond simply endorsing the decision on who is to succeed to the leadership. Importantly, the family is often actively involved in the decision that a change of leader is necessary.[25] Often, this has involved negotiating extensive compromise within the family, given the competing claims of various family members. The complexity of the process of compromise is becoming increasingly apparent in the case of the Saudi leadership with different branches of the family positioning themselves for the succession as the next generation takes over. The announcement in October 2006, that an Allegiance Committee (*Al Hayaat Al Bay'a*) had been created to manage the Saudi succession is an indication of the depth of the problem.[26] In similar vein, in 2003 a *coup d'état* was staged in Ras Al Khaimah, one of the emirates that make up the United Arab Emirates. The coup was conducted by Sheikh Sultan bin Saqr Al Qassimi, a younger son of the Ruler, against his older brother, the Crown Prince and Regent. The action was legitimised by the ruling family. No legal or formal process was involved. There was simply an announcement issued in the name of the Ruler, advising that the change had taken place. The federal government in Abu Dhabi supported the action with the deployment of tanks and troops, suggesting it did not object to this somewhat arbitrary process of leadership succession.[27]

The ladies of the house

One issue that attracts little public attention because of its secretive and sensitive nature is the role of leaders' wives and mothers in the succession process. While the issue is never discussed in public, it is clear that women are a significant political factor in Arab politics. The status of the different female members of the family, which carries with it the political and economic interests of different tribes and families, reflects important political balances and understandings. Political stability and the ruling family's ability to rule may depend on the alliances personified by women in the family. Within the family, senior women of strong character can play an important active part in affairs of Arab regimes, especially in mediating family relations. They can also be a factor in creating or aggravating internal family divisions. This is, of course, a tradition that goes back to the household of the Prophet himself.[28] The rivalry of the different wives of rulers on behalf of their children is a significant feature of Arab politics and can be a source of great friction in both monarchies and republics. Such rivalry appears to have been a major issue in the period preceding the death of Sheikh Zayed of the United Arab Emirates. It was also an issue with the succession to King Hussein of Jordan and is the basis for the most important schism in the Saudi royal family.

The impact of Islam

Islam is a major factor in the Arab approach to succession, although there is a tendency to overstate the extent to which it has supplanted tribal attitudes and practices. It is a factor that has certainly complicated the Arab response to leadership selection by introducing an added tier of demands on rulers to those of tribal society. The tribal requirement that the leader be the most fit in a military and political sense took on the added connotation of being the most devout. This was an important element in the claim made by Ali's supporters that he and his descendants were the appropriate successors of the Prophet. The Shi`i argued that Ali was the most fit Moslem, especially in comparison with the lax Muawiya.

Islam's influence has, however, been limited. In the early days of the Islamic era, the issue of succession was a relatively simple one to address. Mohammed had left no guidance on how the succession was to be treated. This may have been because, despite his immense status in the community, the Prophet wanted to leave the decision on his replacement to the traditional tribal processes. As a result, the Caliphs of the *Rashidun* period were selected according to tribal processes of election to the satisfaction of most. Even in this context, however, the old rivalries between the people of Mecca and Medina and wider tribal hostilities challenged the unity that Mohammed had brought to the community. The third Caliph, Othman, was assassinated by a group who championed the succession of Ali as the sole successor to the Prophet in direct defiance of the dominance of the Quraysh of Mecca. As time passed and the Arab empire expanded, non-Arabs were absorbed into the *Umma* and the unity of the Companions that enabled the election of the leadership was lost, as was, along with it, any hope of an agreed and uniform process of succession.

What became the Sunni and Shi`a split began as a highly personal dispute involving Ali and the group around the Prophet. His ambitions were contested by Aisha, one of the Prophet's wives, and the other *Rashidun*. The dispute also had important tribal and family dimensions. Ali's claim to the right to succeed Mohammed was based on his family relationship to the Prophet. His opponents argued roughly along lines developed from the tribal experience that the leader of the community should be the most fit person to rule and should be chosen by consensus from the tribe of Quraysh. Over time, that dispute developed doctrinal religious dimensions, but succession remained a fundamental underpinning of the debate. Supporters of Ali's succession asserted the highly contested claim that Ali had been specifically identified by the Prophet as his chosen successor. They further maintained that sovereignty should follow the line of Ali (and, therefore, of Mohammed himself).

From Muawiya to statehood

The problems of succession in the early days of Islam have persisted into the present day. While the Quraysh have lost their status, several Sunni ruling houses (Morocco, Jordan) attempt to augment their legitimacy through their claim of descent from the family of the Prophet, and the claims of Ali continue to resonate among the Shi'a.

Modern Arab succession practices are part of and highlight the legitimacy problems that are associated with the Arab political system as a whole. The absence of consensus over the nature of government was reflected in the intense instability affecting the area in the years after independence. In the early years of independence, the crisis of legitimacy facing Arab governments was thrown into relief by the way in which the military coup became a regular feature of the succession process in republics and monarchies. Most Arab countries experienced coups and many governments were overthrown, often violently. Some, like Syria and Iraq in the 1950s and 1960s, experienced so many coups that they became synonymous with chronic instability and violence. According to one count, there were as many as 32 successful *coups d'état* in the Arab world from 1949 to 1966.[29] Most of these were not about fundamental issues of social and economic reform, but about who rules, that is, whose family or tribal group was to dominate. This era of the forceful succession process culminated in Hafez Al Assad's coup in 1970 and Saddam Hussein's seizure of the Iraqi presidency in 1979. In such an environment, it is not surprising that survival became a major preoccupation of Arab regimes and that, out of this, should emerge the focus on succession and dynastic rule.

Nowadays, despite this reputation for political instability, a common criticism of Arab countries is not that they are unstable, but that have known too much political stability. The critics argue that Arab states have fallen out of step with economic and political developments in the rest of the world and have become stultified and incapable of responding to the demands of the modern world.[30] This changed reputation is largely a function of the fact that many Arab rulers have been in power for long periods (see Appendix 3), surviving by crushing and suppressing opposition but, in doing so, stifling the momentum for and possibility of change.

Since independence, Arab countries have experienced a succession of rulers who have retained power for over 25, 30 and even 40 years. It is expected that, with the exception of Saddam Hussein, most of these rulers will be succeeded by their sons, at least in the short term. It is, perhaps, the longevity of these leaders that has made it possible for them and their families to entertain ideas of fulfilling their instincts for dynastic rule. Rulers' longevity eases concerns about coups and, therefore, succession, allowing the regime to consolidate its hold on power. It also makes possible the rulers' increasing dominance of their original power bases, generally the armed forces, and the corresponding increasing importance of tribal and, especially, family affiliations. On the basis of this level of control, leaders are able to prepare the ground for the inevitable need to address succession as they approach the end of their lives.

A major claim to legitimacy by Arab rulers is based on their ability to provide stability for their populations. It is difficult for an outsider to appreciate the depth of the desire for stability among people of the Arab world. All manner of ruthlessness is endured or excused by this need, as is the steady retreat from promises of modernisation and reform. Succession is also part of the argument insofar as the passing of an established ruler is a time of high vulnerability for a regime, carrying with it the danger of the breakdown of order. A smooth transfer of power from one member of the established elite to another helps to limit the prospects for instability. It should be noted, however, that this argument does not accord with predictions by Betts and Huntington, who maintain that 'the level of instability in the years after a leader's death is strongly associated with the number of years he has been in power'. They suggest that:

> Prolonged duration of the leader in power indicates political rigidity and the absence of reform and policy adaptation to socio-economic changes and hence is likely to lead to intense political demands and significant political upheaval after the leader's death.[31]

So far, experience does not support the argument of Betts and Huntington. Arab leaders have provided a high degree of stability over their rule and the five successions that have taken place over the past few years (Syria, Jordan, Morocco, Saudi Arabia and the United Arab Emirates/Abu Dhabi) have been accompanied by limited unrest.

This capacity to survive and the apparent success of their succession plans have not necessarily brought with them the benefits of lasting legitimacy for Arab leaders. The causes of this problem are deeply rooted in the Arab experience. According to Anderson, the succession challenge facing governments in the Arab world is probably terminal. The monarchies face the problem of developing a modern justification for the continued existence of the institution of the monarchy. The republics face the even more daunting task of justifying dynastic succession in a republican context. The result is a continued personalisation of Arab politics with all the dangers associated with systems reliant on the personal skills and characters of individual rulers.[32]

As far as establishing legitimacy for the succession process is concerned, the monarchies seem to be making a better fist of the problem than the republics. Part of their strength is that, regardless of the nature of the regimes themselves, their succession arrangements are set out in some detail and clarity in their constitutions and these reflect actual practice. Constitutions of the monarchies make clear that the kings are to be drawn from the current ruling families. For example, the Saudi Basic Law (Article 5) states:

a) The system of government in the Kingdom of Saudi Arabia is that of a monarchy.
b) Rule passes to the sons of the founding King, Abd Al-Aziz Al Saud, and to their children's children. The most upright among them is to receive allegiance in accordance with the principles of the Holy Quran and the Tradition of the Venerable Prophet.
c) The King chooses the Heir Apparent and relieves him of his duties by royal order.

The public nature of these arrangements enables the broad process to be understood by the population and encourages acceptance. Those kings who have recently acceded to power from their fathers, Abdallah II of Jordan and Mohammed VI of Morocco, have settled reasonably securely into their thrones.

The succession provisions in republican constitutions are either not so explicit or have been shown by the behaviour of republican rulers to mean little as a guide to their intentions. Provisions for the election of the president will not be allowed to stand in the way of the urge to family rule. The result of this approach, however, has been a degree of continued uncertainty, which plagues the ruler long after his installation as President. Bashar Al Assad, for example, is considered still to be attempting to establish his power over the old guard and the military. His main claim to legitimacy is his relationship to his father, but it would seem evident that his father's endorsement can only carry him so far.

As far as the Arab monarchies are concerned, the image of legitimate orderliness promoted by the succession practices of the Arab monarchies is potentially misleading. The Arab monarchy with the deepest historical roots is perhaps the Alawite regime in Morocco. The dynasty has ruled Morocco since 1649, allowing for a period of French colonial rule from 1912 to 1956. Since then, power has progressed along the family line from Mohammed V to Hassan II and now to Mohammed VI. That progress, however, has not been all smooth. Hassan survived numerous assassination attempts, including one from within the military, which constituted a major threat to the regime.[33] King Abdallah II of Jordan, a more recent and less established political system, is the latest of a line of monarchs whose fortunes have tested the dynasty's legitimacy greatly. The founding King, Abdallah I, was assassinated. His successor, Talal, was found to be suffering from schizophrenia. Talal's replacement, Hussein, was the target of numerous assassination attempts, including one occasion involving the Syrian Air Force, and of the attempted coup by the PLO in September 1970. It is true that assassination does not constitute a test of legitimacy per se and the attempts on the lives of Hassan and Hussein were inspired by a range of motives, including outside attempts to overthrow the monarchy. Nevertheless, Salibi's comments with regard to Jordan could also apply to the Moroccan regime:

> There were many people inside Jordan who felt hostile enough towards the regime, for one reason or another, to attempt acts of sabotage or terrorism either on their own initiative or prompted by the political parties to which they adhered.[34]

In addition, anti-regime Islamist groups such as the Moslem Brotherhood (*Ikhwan Al Muslimeen*) have been active in most of the monarchies of the region. The Ikhwan appears to have abandoned violence, but the thrust of its political activities is to question the regime's legitimacy.

The appeal of family rule

There have been many serious challenges to the royal families of the Arab world and their long-term succession plans. The monarchies have, however, demonstrated considerable capacity to keep these various challenges in check and they seem to be reasonably secure, at least when seen in the light of the general Arab experience since independence. In particular, those countries, Bahrain, Jordan and Morocco, that have written dynastic succession into their constitutions appear to be particularly stable and secure. This is, in part, because their approach to succession is generally understood and widely accepted or tolerated amongst their populations.

The Arab attitude to the dynastic principle and hereditary succession has been contradictory. The practice clearly has had a powerful, deep-rooted and widespread impact on the Arab world, including among the Bedouin tribes. It is, however, a break with Arab tradition. Watt observes that the European practice of primogeniture[35] achieved even less acceptance among Arabs than dynastic succession, if only because of difficulties in establishing relative ages and the importance of matrilineal lineage.[36] In particular, the practice of primogeniture in the Arab world sits uncomfortably with the tribal focus on the most fit as the basis for succession. This highlights the need to be particularly careful in drawing parallels between aspects of the Arab political tradition and late mediaeval to early modern Europe. Some of these parallels have been noted above, such as the nomination of the heir by the monarch and the development of constitutionalism.

Nevertheless, the influence of primogeniture can be seen at work on the broad practice of political succession in the Arab world, especially, but not exclusively, in the monarchies. This influence can be seen in the Jordanian succession process. Prince Hassan, the brother of the late King Hussein of Jordan, had served as the country's Crown Prince for 35 years. He was dumped unceremoniously just before the King died in favour of the Hussein's oldest son, Abdallah. Several years later, the new King did the same thing to his younger brother, Hamza, who had been nominated as Crown Prince by King Hussein. Prince Hassan was bitter about the circumstances of both events, but claimed to have no argument in principle about the right of Abdallah, as Hussein's oldest son, to be the king or about Abdallah's right to nominate his eldest son to be the next in line. Indeed, Prince Hassan has criticised a constitutional provision introduced by King Hussein that made possible the appointment of a crown prince other than the oldest son of the king. While the constitution does specify primogeniture as the mechanism for succession (Article 28(a)), Prince Hassan is understood to consider that the provision in the same article enabling the king to 'select one of his brothers as heir apparent' to the throne weakens the focus on primogeniture.

Opinion about the appropriateness of this approach is varied. On one hand, there is the argument that primogeniture contributes to political stability and security by introducing an important element of certainty and predictability into the succession process. Rivalry between brothers (and other family members) is limited. The oldest son can be prepared throughout his life for the responsibilities of the office and has the time to establish his own power and legitimacy before assuming office. On the other hand, primogeniture is criticised as possessing a number of potentially negative implications for the survival of regimes. Indeed, it is regarded by some writers as a system that is inherently flawed and as having contributed to the disappearance of monarchies in the region and beyond.[37] It has, for example, created the situation where, should the throne be inherited by an underage son, the establishment of regency arrangements would be still necessary. Rousseau provides a rather jaundiced view of the process:

> What has been done to prevent this evil? Thrones have been made hereditary in certain families, and an order of succession thus set up, to prevent any dispute on the death of the king – that is to say, by substituting for the disadvantages of elections, the disadvantages of regencies, apparent peace has been preferred to wise administration, and the risk of having children or monsters or imbeciles as rulers preferred to having to dispute the choice of a good king.[38]

Primogeniture has served to limit the expectations of other members of the ruling family, thereby making the ruler and his or her successor more secure. The practice could, however, detract from family support for a regime, especially if it is highly personalised, such as in Jordan. King Hussein's regency council served him well and the other members of the family supported his accession. This need not, however, necessarily be the norm. There have been numerous instances of rule by regency in Europe to support Rousseau's argument, and there is no reason to expect the Arab world to be any different. Members of the ruling house may decide that, as they have no prospect of becoming ruler, there is no real personal benefit to be gained from the arrangement and they may even consider their ambitions to be constrained by the relatively rigid structure in place. They may, as a result, perceive fewer reasons to support a regime's continuation and even work towards its demise.

In addition, primogeniture can, as Rousseau suggests, throw up monarchs who are unfit to rule. Europe has had a number of instances of this sort of problem, such as Christian VII of Denmark, who was probably a schizophrenic, and Afonso VI of Portugal, who was regarded as severely retarded. This was an issue also faced by the Hashemite family in Jordan. In 1952, while Hussein was still a minor, his father, King Talal, was found to be suffering schizophrenia. The royal family was, however, able to deal with that problem. Talal was declared unfit to rule and deposed and a regency council ruled on Hussein's behalf until 1953, when he reached 18 years of age and was crowned King. The Jordanian constitution now contains provisions specifically designed to handle such an eventuality (Article 28(e)). It is ironic that the tribal yardstick of fitness to rule should be used to support a system based on primogeniture.

Not all Arab monarchies rely on primogeniture as the basis for their dynastic rule. Instead they treat the issue of succession as something to be resolved by the family each time a king dies. None, however, goes so far as to follow the Ottoman policy of judicial royal fratricide.[39] In a number of countries, especially those of the highly tribal Arabian Peninsula, succession is drawn from the ruling family, broadly defined, not necessarily from the sons of the ruler. In such countries succession is potentially more complicated and fraught.

Saudi Arabia is the most important example of this practice. The kingdom is still ruled by the sons of the kingdom's founder, Abd Al-Aziz Al Saud. Most of that generation are reaching the end of their lives, but they still dominate the political process. According to the Saudi Basic Law, anyone of the 36 sons could become the king as the Basic Law requires only that the succession pass through 'the sons of Abd Al-Aziz'. Another requirement is that the king must be the most 'fit', in a religious and tribal sense (Article 5(b)). In reality, most of the sons accept that they are not in the running to become king and only the most senior can contend for that role. Over the years, the succession has broadly but not rigidly followed the line of seniority.[40]

A problem with the Saudi arrangement is that, given the advanced ages of the sons and even the grandsons of Abd Al-Aziz, the country is facing a dramatic generational change and the Basic Law is not clear about how the next wave of successions is to be managed. Article 5(b) states that 'Rule passes to the sons of the founding King, Abd Al-Aziz bin Abd Al-Rahman Al-Feisal Al-Saud, and to their children's children'. There is limited guidance about the basis for selection among the following generations. Article 5 also specifies that the 'most fit' will accede, but no definition of the term is provided, leaving the outcome to be decided on the basis of tribal negotiations. There is no reference to seniority despite that having been the effective basis for succession so far. Competition over who is to succeed the current cohort has raised speculation that a number of the senior Saudis, including King Abdallah, are interested in the idea of keeping the succession within their immediate family.

Solidarity is as important for Arab monarchies as it is for the region's republics, and there is concern that rivalry within the Saudi royal family has the capacity to affect its cohesion and its ability to rule effectively. The immediate effect appears to have been that attempts at serious economic and political reform have been blocked for reasons of family politics. In an attempt to address both current tensions and the likelihood of problems among future generations, King Abdallah has decreed the establishment of the 'Allegiance Committee', which will seek to resolve family disputes over future successions. While it is too early to see how the Committee will operate, the new body seems to reflect a combination of tribal democracy and authoritarianism. Theoretically, the king's choice of successor can be overruled by a vote of the Committee, in line with traditional tribal practices. The practice will probably reflect the degree of authority exercised by the king.

The succession in the United Arab Emirates emirate of Abu Dhabi reflects a combination of primogeniture and family-based arrangements. The former ruler, Sheikh Zayed, who was not faced by the need to conform to a constitution, had almost complete power to decide on his successor. The emirate is run effectively as the personal property of the Ruler and only the inner family is consulted on matters of this nature. When Zayed himself came to power in Abu Dhabi in 1966, the decision was made by the family in line with tribal practices. However, following the precedent set by Muawiya, Zayed announced that his oldest son, Khalifa, would succeed him. He also appointed Khalifa to senior governmental positions in the federal and Abu Dhabi governments, including as Crown Prince of Abu Dhabi. Despite Zayed's immense authority, the succession was still accompanied by considerable uncertainty, with widespread rumours of family disputes over the decision. It is believed that the ruling families of the Emirates kept the news of Zayed's death quiet for some weeks until negotiations within Zayed's family and between the Abu Dhabi and Dubai ruling families could be completed.

A problem with the tribal approach to succession, as with primogeniture, is that so much hinges on the quality of leaders. Given the stakes and the nature of the regimes, the process of removing poor leaders can be difficult. To the extent possible, Arab regimes have sought to resolve their leadership succession issues under a cloak of apparent unity. There have been several examples of poor leaders turning up in the Arab world. Some, such as Shakbut in Abu Dhabi, were dealt with smoothly by the family, and political life in the emirate continued largely uninterrupted. Others, like the succession of Feisal Al Saud in Saudi Arabia, were handled within the family, but not without difficulty. In Feisal's case, family tension became severe, even entering the public domain with all the potential dangers for political stability of such a development.[41]

Republics: Western institutions, Arab traditions

A major complication in the Arabs' attempts to resolve the problem of unacceptable leaders is the incompatibility between tribal and Islamic practices and the Western institutions and processes adopted on independence. The leaders at Arab independence generally promoted a range of Western political mechanisms such as universal suffrage, parliamentary supremacy, direct presidential elections and even constitutional monarchy. In the longer term, however, none of these mechanisms was fully incorporated into the Arab political tradition in any Arab country. Instead, traditional attitudes, forces and problems persisted and reasserted themselves as the enthusiasm for independence met the challenges of the day and conservative elements began to challenge the proponents of change.

The interaction of traditional and Western models of political succession has played itself out at the level of Arab constitutions, as discussed in Chapter 5. Most republican constitutions are, on the surface, based on similar principles to those that underpin Western instruments. In particular, the constitutions provide for leaders to be selected on the basis of democratic election and there is the potential for ruling groups peacefully to alternate in power. Such a prospect, however, is inconsistent with Arab history, with the family-based nature of Arab society and the winner-take-all character of Arab politics. It is also inconsistent with the intent of these constitutions. In Arab politics, the only way in which leaders have come to power has been by force or inheritance. Constitutions have been structured to ensure that the spoils gained in such ways are not lost in the ballot box. Restricted candidature slates and election by subservient parliaments are common devices written into Arab constitutions to ensure that ruling groups maintain control over the succession process.[42]

The preferred method of political succession in Arab republics has been the military coup, accompanied by varying degrees of violence. The coups have initially not reflected any family dimension. Nasser, for example, never contemplated introducing his family into the ruling Revolutionary Command Council. The republics have, however, shared certain characteristics with the monarchies. The overthrow of the Hashemite monarchy in Iraq was organised by a small, close-knit group of military officers among whom solidarity was regarded as vital to their success and survival. (Qassem's troubles noted above began when that solidarity started to weaken and members of the Ba`ath Party began to question his right to rule.[43]) The coups staged by Nasser and Qaddafi were similarly based on small groups of military people. The nature of the Ba`athist coups in Syria and Iraq was similar, but with the Party playing a central role in the plotting. In all these examples, a single individual is generally formally identifiable as the instigator of the change of power. But close behind the coup leader will be the family members, power brokers, advisers and others, who will flesh out the regime and consolidate its seizure of power. Over time, as suggested, the family moves closer to the controlling centre of the political system at the expense of other interests. Carapico explains that:

> In a successful succession, so to speak, the larger ruling coalition around the absolute leader remains intact. The legacy of the last coup, some 20, 30 or more years ago, is institutionalised beyond the personal rule of its leader, though still in the form of personal rule. . . . When personal rule becomes family rule, power monopolies endure or even solidify across generations.[44]

A difficulty for succession in republics is that no state has a meaningful process of determining succession in a way that is predictable and is accepted as legitimate. The monarchies can claim legitimacy on various traditional or charismatic bases, such as descent from the Prophet (Morocco, Jordan) or tribal identification with the territory of the state (the Gulf states). The republican leaders, however, have all come to power on the shoulders of the armed forces, including General Emile Lahoud, the President of Lebanon from 1998 to 2007 and his successor, General Michel Suleiman. As discussed in Chapter 3, this is not an adequate foundation for legitimacy. The republics' constitutions have detailed provisions outlining how a president is to be elected, his responsibilities and the constraints on his power. They contain specific provisions on the replacement of heads of state, with most countries having direct, popular election of the president. Almost all have specific provisions that give the incumbent great power to control who stands for election and the results. Tunisia, for example, requires candidates to obtain approval by a presidential election commission in which the sitting president is directly involved (Article 40(3)). Others, such as Syria, give the parliament a direct role in approving the candidates (Article 84), while Lebanon selects the president through a parliamentary vote based on the informal confessional understanding that has been in place since independence.

Despite these elaborate constitutional arrangements, the appeal of dynastic rule persists in the republican part of the Arab world as well as in the monarchies. Republican rulers generally seek to be seen to operate within the law but, just as Arab kings regard themselves as being ultimately above the law, so too do Arab republican rulers. Succession is regarded as too important to be left to the vagaries of popular election and constitutional constraints will be removed or ignored if necessary to ensure the regime's goals. For example, Article 83 of the Syrian constitution specified that a candidate for the presidency must be over 40 years of age. That provision was amended to allow Bashar Al Assad, who was 34 at the time, to succeed his father. Yemen's constitution was amended in 2005 to allow Ali Abdallah Saleh to serve an extra term as President, presumably to give his son more time to prepare. Tunisia's constitution was amended in 2004 to allow President Ben Ali to serve a fourth term. Lebanon's constitution has been regularly amended to permit incumbents to serve an extra term.

This reluctance to abide by a rule-driven process for political succession is matched by an unwillingness to allow a politically-driven selection process to develop. As noted above, many countries, especially in the West, have procedures to organise the process of leadership selection, but the formal aspect of these procedures is less important than what goes on in smoke-filled rooms away from the public eye. Instead they rely on the system producing the leader through various political steps. The leaders of Arab republics seek to ensure that no one else is able to disrupt their plans at the political level. They will resort to various tactics to prevent a potential rival from developing unwanted ambitions or establishing himself in a position from which he might challenge the incumbent.

President Mubarak of Egypt has ensured that the regime is fully in control of the succession process. Electoral law amendments adopted in 2005 were ostensibly designed to allow the direct and contested election of the president. They were, however, formulated in such a way as to ensure Mubarak's control over the process was not infringed upon.[45] Mubarak has also refused to appoint a Vice President, who would be the constitutional successor in the event of his retirement or death, for fear that the incumbent might use the position to challenge him. He has also removed any potential challengers to his son's succession from positions of power. In Syria, at the height of his concerns about a threat from his brother, Rifa'at, President Hafez Al-Assad appointed three Vice Presidents, including Rifa'at, as a way of weakening his brother's ties to his personal power base, the Defence Companies.[46] Towards the end of his life, Assad instigated a major anti-corruption drive, which had the effect of removing anyone who might have been a threat to the accession of his son, Bashar.

The latest cadre of leaders or potential leaders, Gamal Mubarak, Saif Al Islam, Ahmed Saleh and Bashar Al Assad, have been pursuing their succession largely in the context of the civilian political process rather than through the traditional military route. They are all are paying greater attention to rule-based political processes upon which to build their claims to power. None of these men has a substantial military background. This is a factor of the changed nature of the security threats and altered political environments to which all participants in the political system must adapt. In particular, it is, as Putnam observes, a reflection of how: 'Significant divergences among the outlooks of different generations . . . attitudes to democracy, to conflict, to opponents, and to style – compel attention to the nature of cultural change'.[47]

This does not necessarily mean that the new generation of younger, better-educated rulers is likely to be any less committed to the patrimonial form of governance introduced by their fathers. Family rule remains their goal, however, bureaucratic or legal measures are becoming a more important part of the mechanism for pursuing this goal and military approaches are becoming less pronounced. The experience of Morocco and Jordan would suggest that more enlightened rule is not on the way. For example, King Abdallah of Jordan is regarded as more authoritarian than his father. He is also less scrupulous in respecting the constitution and acknowledging the principle of cabinet government. Manipulation of the mechanisms of government is no less likely under the sons than it was under the fathers.

Public attitudes

The next few years are likely to present fundamental challenges to Arab leaders in many areas, not the least of which will be over succession. Part of the problem will be to maintain and strengthen the loyalty of members of the regimes themselves. Of equal importance, however, will be the task of addressing the attitude of Arabs to their states and to the regimes that run them. This is a significant issue as the success of dynastic rule depends on public support as much as it does on elite power. It has been a feature of political life throughout history that no ruler, no matter how tyrannical, can rule without a significant degree of public consent.[48] This rule applies in the Arab world as much as it does in any other country. There is considerable evidence of widespread support for democracy across the Arab region and considerable and serious opposition to many dynastic Arab regimes. Tessler, for example, reports that extensive survey material of Egyptian and other Arab attitudes indicates 'that most Egyptians favour democratic governance and second, that there is virtually no difference in the attitudes of more religious and less religious individuals' on this issue.[49] Arab thinkers have also pursued a more democratic and pluralist political system for the Arab world, but they have had to tread carefully so as not to challenge the idea of the unity of Islam. Reforming scholars such as Jamal Al-Din Al Afghani and Mohammed Abduh in the latter part of the nineteenth century and Rashid Rida and Abd Al-Raziq in the first half of the twentieth century promoted parliamentary constitutionalism as being consistent with the principles of the Quran. They also argued for recognition of the *de facto* separation between religion and politics that exists throughout most of the Arab world in order to accommodate democratic practices.[50] More recent writers, like Abdul Karim Soroush and Rachid Al Ghannouchi, have also championed pluralism and democracy in the Arab world.

Despite this evidence and the efforts of people like Rida and Al Ghannouchi, however, there remains a strong instinct among Arabs to support or at least tolerate any form of government, including dynastic government, provided it gives them stability and, at least, theoretically, promotes the unity of Islam. There is a strong basis in Islamic political thought for the view that any government, even bad government, is preferable to no government at all. This view has been reinforced in modern times by the disasters of the Lebanese, Algerian and Somali civil wars.[51] This almost fatalistic attitude is not necessarily inconsistent with the support for democracy among Arab people. Individual Arabs will support continued rule by a particular regime despite its shortcomings, in part because of their assumption that totalitarian regimes are too powerful for real change to be possible. In addition, Arabs are often fearful of what the democratic experience might release, given the powerful position of Islamist groups in many of the countries of the region. The general idea of democratic elections is appealing, but the prospect that a conservative religious government might result from such elections is less so. With such a possibility in prospect, people tend to fall back on the current regimes which offer order, stability, predictability, the rejection of religious extremism and, possibly, justice.

Arab regimes also benefit from the fact that dynasticism and the focus on family interests strike a resonant chord with many Arabs. These are more immediately real and of practical significance to them than the various debates of mediaeval Moslem scholars and polemicists. They are concepts that have deeply permeated Arab society and can routinely be found in many aspects of Arab civil society, including the business sector. Joseph, for example, observed in his study of Lebanon how deeply ingrained was support for the family basis of control of business enterprises.[52] There are, moreover, clear and close links between the political and the business sectors in the ruling structures and strategies of the families that rule most of the countries of the region. This includes that of President Ben Ali of Tunisia, where the dynastic impulse has not yet manifested itself.[53] A similar picture is evident in Lebanon where, before his assassination, the former Prime Minister, Rafiq Hariri, had passed control of many of his business interests to his son, Saad. On Rafiq's death, Saad also took over his father's political role, thereby merging the two processes.

Security and succession

Chapter 1 contains a discussion of the depth of the problems identified with the Arab political tradition and systems. As suggested, succession epitomises the problems highlighted by these criticisms, especially as it is the mechanism for the perpetuation of Arab systems of government, but also because, by extension, it is a symbol of a basic unresolved problem in Islam. The difficulty Arab regimes have encountered in developing legitimate succession management arrangements has wide-ranging and serious implications. As it is practiced, it has the potential to provide a degree of stability that is demanded by Arab populations. The centrality of stability as a political good and central objective in the Arab political system has been reinforced by experience and by authoritative interpretations of the Quran and various *Hadith*. This stability, however, comes at considerable cost to the region. The identification of the state, its security and its very survival with a particular ruler or family clique means that the survival of that individual and family becomes of central importance. As a result, the focus of government is on regime survival above all other considerations. This approach tends to breed a suspicion of all other groups that are not associated with the regime in some form of patrimonial or clientalist relationship and a reluctance to recognise or respond to the interests and demands of other groups. This includes an aversion to forms of economic and, especially, political liberalism. It is also reflected in an aversion to the idea of the rule of law. Issues that are central to Arabs, like justice, and to the West, like democracy, are sacrificed in the name of stability and family solidarity.

Regime survival has been achieved largely through a heavy emphasis on security, with the military and security agencies assuming vital roles in the process of governance in republics and monarchies. Arab regimes have presented themselves as threatened by domestic and outside forces. As long as they continue to make such claims, the military or security forces will be a factor in the succession process throughout the region. There are, however, emerging indications that the military's influence might be declining. From the champions of independence, nationalism and reform, the various armed forces throughout the Arab world have tended to degenerate into champions of the status quo and then into active players in their countries' economies, both in the official sector and the black market. The Egyptian military has, for example, been presented as an obstacle to Gamal Mubarak's ambitions to succeed his father as President of Egypt. Gamal's lack of military experience is portrayed as a fatal flaw in his campaign. One American observer remarked in 2003 on Gamal's prospects:

> . . . his chance of succeeding his father is nil. He has no military background. . . . It has been the case that the military makes the choice of the president and . . . I don't believe they will choose somebody who has no military credentials.[54]

Other observers, however, detect a lessening of the military's influence or interest to a point where the Arab military will increasingly adopt a role similar to that of the Turkish military, leaving political issues, such as succession, to be resolved by the political process and only intervening when a major challenge to national security has arisen. Gotowicki, for example, considers that Egyptian political institutions have become more mature and deeply involved in the country's political life. This means that the direct role played by the military as kingmaker has ended except in instances of severe national crisis.[55] There is also the possibility that Arab regimes across the region have managed to contain the ability of their militaries to threaten the civilian government. More generally, this retreat could be facilitated by the experience of relatively smooth transfers of power from one generation to the next. The military would also be comforted by the knowledge that the son is likely to pursue policies which are at least broadly consistent with those of his father and which, therefore, will generally be in line with the interests of the armed forces.

It is clear that weaknesses in Arab succession practices can have a destabilising impact on countries of the region. Paradoxically, however, the problems and the desire of regimes to legitimise their dominance might also help to encourage reform in some regimes. In the case of Saudi Arabia, there is a question of who will run the country when the end of the line of the sons of Abd Al-Aziz is reached. That time is not far off as King Abdallah and Crown Prince Sultan are well over 70 years of age. As noted earlier, the family has moved to develop a process that might reduce tensions within its ranks, which might, over time reduce the secretive, arbitrary nature of the process. In Oman, Sultan Qaboos has refused to nominate a successor and the arrangements for the selection of the next ruler that he has set in place leave room for considerable family dispute. Again, this might lead to more formal and transparent procedures to be developed. In Kuwait, the succession to Emir Jaber Al Ahmed Al Sabah and the Crown Prince, Sheikh Saad Al Abdallah Al Sabah, produced the remarkable (in the Middle East context) outcome of the parliament playing a major role in the decision of who was to become the next Emir. It may be that, in that one country at least, a precedent may have been set in this most sensitive of political areas. In many areas Kuwait is seen as something of a trendsetter and it is possible that these developments will have regional implications. The emergence in some countries of confident, strong, determined and better-educated young leaders, as in the case of Bahrain and Qatar, could also be the precursor of more widespread significant change and legitimising liberalisation.[56]

The development of these trends will depend on the diverse forces at play. There is the problem of simple sibling rivalry that can be found in any family. This is, moreover, accentuated by the peculiarities of Arab family structures, where a ruler may have or have had more than one wife. Succession then becomes a challenge for each wife to promote the interests of her favoured son over the children of another wife. In those polities where primogeniture has not been adopted, this sort of infighting can have serious effects. Despite such problems, the changes that emerge may result in a major process of reform throughout the Arab world. On one hand, it may be that the monarchies will handle these pressures better than the republics, given the logic of the different constitutional structures. On the other hand, there is no reason to expect that the result will be greater democracy, accessibility or responsible government. It may simply be a more efficient, effective version of the current arrangements.

On the positive side, as discussed above, well-managed father–son transitions in Arab countries might be preferable to what might arise under more democratic processes. Obviously, there is international and domestic concern about the possibility of extremist religious groups seizing power through a democratic opening. That such a development would be unsettling to all can be seen from the initial widespread support for the decision of the Algerian military to abort elections planned for early 1992 for fear of an Islamist victory. Similarly, the former United States Secretary of Defence, Rumsfeld, made it clear that the United States administration would not tolerate an Islamist government coming to power in Iraq by way of national elections planned for January 2005.[57]

There have been widespread domestic and international pressures on Arab countries to reform these aspects of their political systems. Some countries have made token responses. Egypt, for example, has amended its constitutional provisions dealing with the election of the president, ostensibly, to make the presidential election process more open and fair. None of these measures, however, including the Egyptian reforms, has made any impact on the powers of the leaders or created a process that might result in a democratically elected leadership.

The focus of this chapter has been on how Arab countries have struggled to develop institutionalised mechanisms for the management of their political succession. These arrangements include the reliance on traditional practices, at the heart of which is dynastic succession. Arab monarchies have been more successful at managing succession than the republics because their approach to governance is closer to traditional tribal practices in which dynasticism had some basis. This urge towards dynastic rule is, however, also increasingly apparent among the republics where most leaders are intent on passing on power to their own family members. This attitude enjoys support or at least acceptance in Arab society as a whole, in part because the underlying attitude of family permeates many levels of political and economic activity in the Arab world.

In the modern context, succession is tied up with regime type. While the similarities between the republican and monarchic systems have been stressed throughout, the fact remains that there is a fundamental, logical problem with a dynasty within a republican system. Moreover, the greater logic of the monarchic systems with regard to succession works to support those arrangements. The challenge for the republican systems will be to assimilate their powerful impulses to establish family rule in their countries with the constitutional arrangements in place.

5 Constitutionalism and constitutions

The challenge of succession

> But in the mind of every man, some determining rule or system – something like what in modern times is called a *constitution* – was indispensable to any Government entitled to be called legitimate, or capable of creating in the mind of a Greek a feeling of moral obligation to obey it.[1]

Max Weber observes that regimes that base their legitimacy and authority on charisma and tradition have little tolerance of the rule of law. He also argues, however, that regimes develop through the various stages of legitimacy, from the traditional and charismatic stages to the bureaucratic stage, where legitimacy is largely rule-based.[2] This chapter examines Arab approaches to constitutions and constitutionalism. It considers the possibility that Arab regimes are developing in a manner consistent with that suggested by Weber and that constitutions are becoming more significant as elements in Arab political systems.

It is widely contended that, while many Arab countries have impressive-reading constitutions, their political elites lack any real commitment those instruments. Instead of serving the tasks of Western constitutions – the limitation of power and the formalisation of the national compact – Arab constitutions are used to augment the political authority of those in power.[3] Of particular importance is the way in which Arab constitutions deal with the central challenge to regimes of political succession. There is an evident trend among Arab regimes to seek to sanctify their dynastic ambitions through the framework of a constitutional document. In so doing, regimes are turning their constitutions from a simple decorative device into the embodiment of deals and arrangements that may have lasting importance both to the regimes themselves and to other groups who have a stake in the deals reached.

This assessment rests, to a large extent, on the assumption that a nation's constitution can be an important element in its political system. It should, however, be acknowledged that many political scientists would challenge this assumption on the grounds that constitutions, especially written or codified constitutions, are not good indicators of how political systems actually operate. Constitutions, by their nature, lack flexibility and adaptability. Some, the Australian and the American, for example, appear to have reached a point where amendment is almost impossible and any flexibility can only be found in judicial interpretation. By contrast, political systems are dynamic and constantly adjusting to their changing environments.[4] Constitutions often do not address all the key features of a nation's political system. The lack of reference in the Australian constitution to political parties is a case in point. The Canadian constitution makes no mention of the position of Prime Minister. Most significant, in many countries, including in the Arab world, constitutions have limited political legitimacy and are regularly disregarded by ruler and ruled.

While these criticisms are valid to some degree, it is clear that constitutions do have an important role to play in countries' processes of governance. They are themselves highly political documents and are regularly invoked, resorted to or exploited by participants in the competition for power in nations. Acknowledging his debt to von Clausewitz, Baker describes constitutional law as 'a continuation of politics by other means'.[5] Powe argues that the constitution as an extension of politics was demonstrated when the Supreme Court under Chief Justice Warren worked with the Congress and was effectively an integral part of the Kennedy and Johnson programmes to promote the values of Cold War liberalism.[6]

The relevance and importance of constitutions is underscored by the fact that nearly every sovereign country in the world has felt the need to develop a constitutional framework. The constitution is the expression of a nation's most fundamental values through laws, and can only be changed by means of a relatively complicated amendment process that is intended to confirm society's consensus about the change. The existence of these amendment procedures is recognition that a community's basic needs and values will change over time. There are various approaches to amendment. The Australian procedure is, perhaps, an extreme example of a conservative amendment process. Other Western countries have less onerous provisions based on parliamentary action.[7] In Britain, Parliament's capacity to effect constitutional amendment is only subject to considerations such as the hierarchy of laws and the residual power of the monarch. While constitutional provisions normally take the form of a broad brush approach to fundamental issues, they are not simply generalisations remote from day-to-day politics. It is necessary only to look at the nature of cases before constitutional courts such as the Australian High Court or the American Supreme Court to see how comprehensively fundamental laws intrude into daily life. In the Arab world, the debate about whether Shari`a law should be incorporated into countries' constitutions as *a* or *the* principle source of legislation is a matter of considerable heat and concern.

Constitutions provide essential guides to the frameworks of governments. A constitution is, at its most basic level, a set of rules or norms that establishes, shapes and spells out the limitations on government and society's agreed expectations of government. It sums up the balance of power within society, especially within the broad elite. Magna Carta (1215) is a prime example of this feature. Put another way, a constitution is a set of enforceable norms that provide instructions for running a government or explanations of how that government works. As Mahler notes, often the constitution of a nation is the mechanism:

> . . . that shows us the political lay of the land and that describes the manner in which power is distributed among the many actors in the political environment. We look to the constitution for an explanation of who has the power to do what, what the limitations on power are in a given state, and what the relationships are between and among the many political actors we may find in a given state.[8]

This is a crucial function for a political system. Societies have become more complex and impersonal and 'competing narratives' have become harder to accommodate. The unity of society and the state has been split into what Unger describes as a 'sphere of social life that is sacred and untouchable and one that is subordinated to the sovereign's interests'. At the same time, the complexity of life is leading, in Unger's terms, to the 'disintegration of community', where accepted practices are increasingly open to challenge.[9] In such a context, the need for a negotiated explanation of the way societies and their political manifestations operate has become more important. Constitutions serve to provide that explanation.

Two broad types of constitution can be identified in use around the world. The first constitutional type, for example, the Australian constitution, is a functional or instrumental statement of understandings among elites which focuses on the distribution of power, on formal guidance or on containment of government action.[10] This type of constitution lacks any ringing symbolism and provides no endorsements of or appeals to such great issues as individual liberty and human rights. It provides a 'power map',[11] which is an outline of the structure of the state itself. This is an important issue for all nations and not just a problem facing new states. Canada is still wrestling with the appropriate allocation of powers between the different levels of government more than 140 years after confederation was achieved. In the Arab world, the emirates that make up the United Arab Emirates would never have been able to come together without a constitutional arrangement dealing with the distribution of powers. The Moroccan constitution and the Saudi Basic Law also bear some of the characteristics of this approach.

The second constitutional type goes beyond the functional approach of a power map to spell out society's ideology, its core beliefs, perhaps with an eye to the future. The French and the American constitutions are among the best-known examples of this approach, and many Arab constitutions contain similar formulations. Arab constitutions generally declare, for example, their countries' adherence to Islam and their membership of the Arab nation. They frequently outline what they see as key formative elements of their histories and set out broad objectives for their countries, such as development, freedom and Arab unity. This could be said to incorporate vital aspects of the concept of constitutionalism.

Among the most important roles of constitutions is that they serve to spell out, to give legal meaning to and to guarantee fundamental political arrangements that underpin the existence of the state, or at least the governmental system in a country. As noted above, the United Arab Emirates exists not as a result of military conquest or settlement, but as a result of political arrangements being given effect under the cover of a written constitution. This could be said about most, if not all,

Arab countries, where compromises and deals have been struck between competing elites over issues such as the extent of the influence of Islam on the political system and the matter of political succession. These deals and compromises have continuing relevance to the conduct of government in Arab countries and stability is, in part, dependent on adherence to them.

It has been observed that the fact that countries possess constitutions that have a certain level of significance in their political systems should not be taken as suggesting that they are necessarily driven by the force of constitutionalism.[12] 'Constitutionalism' is a term with significant ideological implications that are central to the Western liberal-democratic tradition. It contains within it the essence of that tradition, including such concepts as the importance of limiting the power of government, the centrality of the individual and the sovereignty of the people.[13] All these principles are to be defended through a commitment to the rule of law. It is on the basis of these principles that constitutions play such a central role in the conduct of Western government.

The focus of constitutionalism is on the codified American approach rather than the British model that Ackerman describes as reflecting 'their culture of self-government, their common sense and decency that distinguished their evolving commitment to democratic principles . . .'.[14] Indeed, the written constitution has become, in Ackerman's eyes, one of the most important factors of modern political development to the extent that it has gained almost universal appeal as a legal framework. According to the liberal democratic ideal, a constitution must address the relationship between government and the citizens of the state. Li regards the constitution as fundamental to the social contract and to the relationship between the state and the civil society'.[15]

Initially, the enthusiasm of liberals for the centrality of the constitution related to their concern about the dangers posed by the popular will to liberty and justice, or perhaps to their property and commercial interests. According to Unger, the 'law of privileges became the core of European constitutional law'.[16] In this respect, champions of constitutions were echoing some of the ideas of Aristotle and his suspicion of 'extreme democracy' and concern to balance 'quantity' with 'quality'. Subsequent writers, such as Kant, insist that the exercise of power must be constitutional if liberty and justice were to be safeguarded.[17]

The interest of early liberal writers in the control of the state or its exclusion from as much of daily life as possible could be seen as the promotion of a form of negative rights, the freedom from being compelled to suffer or to do something. This argument was developed by Isaiah Berlin, who suggested that negative rights represent a surer protection of the individual from state power.[18] Other writers have gone further, however, to promote constitutions as positive or prescriptive devices in the sense that they should actively protect and advance the rights of citizens. They achieve this in part by limiting the incursions of the state and the oppression of the minority in line with Aristotle's and Kant's ideas.[19] Western constitutions display considerable diversity in this respect. The United States constitution represents the most single-minded approach to individual freedoms. European countries tend to approach the issue from a perspective that includes a wider range of rights. Individual rights are accompanied by a range of other rights, especially of a social and economic kind, reflecting a more communitarian worldview.

History of constitutions in the Arab world

In their formal manifestations, Arab constitutions reflect many of these influences and considerations. Some have substantial histories, dating back to the nineteenth century. Tunisia's first written constitution was adopted in 1861. The origins of the Egyptian constitution date back to 1882. Others, however, are quite recent developments, even in terms of the existence of the states themselves. The United Arab Emirates adopted its first permanent constitution in 1996, 25 years after the federation was established. Qatar's first constitution was not adopted until 2003 and not promulgated until June 2005, 32 years after independence. Oman's constitution was adopted in 1996, 26 years after Qaboos became Sultan.[20]

The first example of an Arab constitution is the Constitution of Medina, which was developed by Mohammed around 622 AD (see Appendix 4). The document was intended to provide a basis for relations between different religious and tribal communities in the new Islamic order.[21] It did not address many of the technical or structural aspects of a modern constitution, but its purpose was consistent with modern expectations insofar as it was intended to serve as the constitutive document of the first Islamic state.[22] The Constitution of Medina also provides a model for aspects of constitutions to which modern Arab societies aspire and is invoked as a marker of the ideal Islamic society and an example of the Prophet's more democratic leanings.[23]

Since the death of Mohammed, Islamic scholars have developed constitutional principles affecting the governance of the *Umma* based on the Quran and the *Hadith* and reflecting a range of domestic, foreign and historical influences. According to Mallat, this system of rules could be described as the common law of the Middle East. That is, that Islamic law, the Shari`a, represents the dominant legal tradition of the Arab world.[24] The issue highlighted by Mallat is, in part, the central and unchanging relevance of Shari`a law to Arab states and the logical problems of change. As Gibb observes:

> . . . the law itself, the Sharia, defined once and for all the constitution of the Moslem community. The Sharia to the Moslem stands for all that the Constitution stands for to the United States of America and more. It established norms for all Moslem institutions and societies, which have ever since remained the sheet-anchor of Moslem culture through the many and terrible vicissitudes of later centuries . . .[25]

On the other hand, Shari`a law creates problems for the introduction of modern, Western-styled constitutions in the Arab world. While its divine origins derive from their transmission through the Prophet, Mohammed's death ended this connection to God, leaving the law perfect in expression, but unchangeable in principle and inadequate in practice. In 1978 Al Azhar University in Cairo attempted to develop a constitutional framework that would serve as a model for all Moslem states. The exercise failed partly because of the inability of Islamic texts and principles to meet all the complexities of a modern state within the confines of a single constitutional document. Coulson highlights the problems in applying Shari`a law to modern constitutional and political problems:

> Muslim jurisprudence, however, in its traditional form, provides a much more extreme example of a legal science divorced from historical considerations. Law, in classical Islamic theory, is the revealed will of God, a divinely ordained system preceding and not preceded by the Muslim state, controlling and not controlled by Muslim society. There can be no notion of the law itself evolving as an historical phenomenon closely tied with the progress of society.[26]

Such a notion would make governance in a dynamic world impossible. In practice, Shari`a law has, with difficulty, developed along with society. It has been assisted in this respect by the multitude of comments on the law attributed to the Prophet, many of which are apocryphal but convenient. Initially, Shari`a law reflected a merging of customary law and Islam through the works of Mohammed. Since then, this relationship between custom and the Quran has continued, especially in the area of family law, but also in constitutional areas. Over time, aspects of foreign legal systems, especially Sassanian/Persian, Roman/Byzantine and Western practices, have also augmented Moslem legal practice and merged into what is now recognised as Islamic jurisprudence.

Modern Arab constitutions bear the particular imprint of the Ottoman constitution, which was adopted in 1876 as part of the Empire's attempt to modernise. This constitution had many features of certain Western models, which were intended to strengthen the position of the monarch. For example, the French Constitutional Charter of 1814, the Belgian constitution of 1831 and the German constitution of 1871[27] were important influences on the Ottoman constitution.[28] Even such a mildly democratic constitution was resisted by Sultan Abdul Hamid (ruled 1876–1909), who rejected the extent to which it intruded into his prerogatives. Nevertheless, the constitution came to provide much of the framework for a number of the Arab constitutions that were developed around that time, and elements have appeared in constitutions developed subsequently.

An important feature of the 1876 constitution was the introduction, for the first time since Muawiya, of the idea of succession based on primogeniture. The constitution stated that:

> Ottoman sovereignty, which includes in the person of the Sovereign the Supreme Caliphate of Islam, belongs to the eldest Prince of the House of Osman, in accordance with the rules established *ab antique*.[29]

The constitutional amendments introduced by the Young Turks in 1909 contained a similar provision:

> The Imperial Ottoman sovereignty, which carries with it the Supreme Caliphate of Islam, falls to the eldest Prince of the House of Osman, according to the rule established *ab antiquo*. On his accession the Sultan shall swear before Parliament, or if Parliament is not sitting, at its first meeting, to respect the visions of the canon law and the Constitution, and to be loyal to the country and the nation.[30]

Today, all the countries of the Arab world have codified constitutional documents,[31] many of which reflect the influence of the Ottoman model. The acknowledgement of the separation of church and state in the phrase 'respect the visions of the canon law and the Constitution' has helped make possible the adoption of secular rules in an ostensibly non-secular world. Significantly, the Ottoman constitution's explicit reference to primogeniture has been adopted in a number of cases.

In the way that the Ottoman constitution made a lasting impact on the Arab world, the colonial era had a major impact on constitutions in the modern Arab world. Frameworks bequeathed by the outgoing rulers have been taken up by the post-colonial elites. The end product, however, has never been the result of simply the adoption of British or French models, but a function of the power of Western-oriented, modernising elites relative to the power of conservative, parochial and anti-secular groups. The modernising elites were inspired by what they saw as the benefits to be gained for their backward societies from the Western constitutional model, and the constitution became part of their revolutionary rhetoric. In Tunisia, one of the leaders in the struggle for independence from the French was the *Dustur* (constitution) Party. In Jordan, a popular newspaper is called *Al Dustur*. Even in Saudi Arabia, a Free Princes' Movement in the 1960s promoted the development of structures, including a Western-inspired constitution, which would have limited the power of the ruler.[32]

The opponents of the Westernisers, however, were always important in Arab society because of their power over the masses. In part this was because of tactical use rulers have made of such forces. Throughout modern Arab political history, rulers who have encountered serious challenges to their power from the modernising and democratising urges of the emerging elites have sought to counter that pressure by calling up the ginns[33] of Islamism. The government's tactic was frequently to attempt to crush the modernists, and then represent itself as the only bulwark against the excesses of Islamism. When the Ottoman Sultan Abdul Hamid was attempting to resist or reverse gains made by reformers at the end of the nineteenth century, he turned to conservative Islam for support.[34] In the late 1970s and early 1980s, President Sadat of Egypt attempted to bolster his legitimacy and to limit secularising and democratising pressures on his regime by similarly calling on Islam and tradition.[35] The effect, over time, has been for the Westernising elites to lose influence and for native-based groups that were bypassed by the colonial power to gain the ascendancy.[36]

These groups tend to have emerged out of rural and peripheral backgrounds. For example, Hafez Al Assad was from a poor village in north-west Syria. Libya's Colonel Qaddafi was from a peasant family from the desert region of Sirte. Not surprisingly, such leaders have less understanding of and sympathy for Western liberal concepts than their predecessors and are more deeply imbued with Arab and Islamic traditions. Their attitudes to constitutionalism are different, less reverential, than those of the older pro-Western elites. As these groups have risen to power, however, they have retained the form of the constitutions and the other Western structures bequeathed to them by their predecessors. Often they see in these legacies a potential asset in their pursuit of legitimacy.

The constitutions that have resulted from this tension between these groups and the modernisers look like Western constitutions to an extent. They contain guarantees of individual rights and protections, they also pay considerable attention to social and economic rights, such as the centrality of the family and the right to employment. The Preamble of the Tunisian constitution, for example, commits the country to 'assuring the protection of the family and guaranteeing to each citizen work, health and education'. Arab constitutions do, however, manifest significant differences from the European example. The constitutions are generally embedded in the process of nation building. Some, such as the Syrian constitution, contain measures to assist with the process of mobilisation of the masses as part of social change and economic development.[37] Most Arab constitutions will also contain specific provisions outlining the duties of citizens to their state, as well as their rights. Until amended in 2005, Egypt's constitution, for example, declared in Article 59 that 'safeguarding, consolidating and preserving the socialist gains are a national duty'. Article 65 of Algeria's constitution contains provisions dealing with citizens' responsibilities to look after the education of their children.

Constitutions in changing times

While such rights and responsibilities feature prominently in Arab constitutions, in practice, the focus is largely on the question of power and its allocation among competing groups. Brown observes that Arab constitutions seek: '. . . to render the political authority of the state more effective and secondarily to underscore state sovereignty and establish general ideological orientation'.[38]

It is important to bear in mind that Arab governments have enormous problems of practical governance to deal with. Constitutions have a valid role to play in that endeavour. While they may not seriously be intended to promote principles of liberal democracy, they nevertheless have a genuine normative or teleological role. They are frequently highly declarative instruments outlining the nature and the goals of the state and its adherence to Islam. The preamble of the Tunisian constitution, for example, begins:

> In the name of God, the Compassionate and Merciful, We, the representatives of the Tunisian people, meeting as members of the National Constituent

> Assembly, proclaim the will of this people, set free from foreign domination thanks to its powerful cohesion and to its struggle against tyranny, exploitation, and regression;
>
> . . . to consolidate national unity and to remain faithful to human values which constitute the common heritage of peoples attached to human dignity, justice, and liberty, and working for peace, progress, and free cooperation between nations;
>
> . . . to remain faithful to the teachings of Islam, to the unity of the Greater Maghreb, to its membership of the Arab family, to cooperation with the African peoples in building a better future, and with all peoples who are struggling for justice and liberty;

Similar provisions can be found in many other constitutions of the region.

The constitutions are attempts to address a number of major practical challenges that have faced Arab countries since independence. Arab ways of life have changed significantly over one or two generations. Population growth throughout the region is massive and, on the basis of current economic performance, unsustainable.[39] Even the rentier states of the Arabian Gulf have experienced periods when it has been difficult to provide the economic incentives that are seen as important if their citizens are to continue to support their regimes.[40] Traditional Arab political practices and institutions, especially the *majlis* (see Chapter 2), no longer fulfil the role they used to perform in simpler times. Arab leaders still hold their *majlis* sessions, but the rowdy democracy of earlier days has had to be contained because the increased population involved, the greater complexity of government and concerns about security.[41] In the light of such potentially destabilising changes, constitutions preserve traditions and provide a link between those traditions and modernity. Several constitutions maintain the language of the tribal past as well as the appearance of traditional institutions. They have, for example, established the Consultative Council (*Majlis Al Shura*), albeit without the power, the standing or the accessibility of the original idea. At the same time, they have set up a formal, bureaucratic structure to do the work of running the country.

A feature of the traditional model is the tribal ideal of inclusiveness and accountability. Any member of the tribe could approach his tribal chief in the *majlis* and demand redress, compensation or assistance. Some of the constitutions contain provisions designed to deal with Arab expectations of inclusion and accessibility. The Preamble of Algeria's constitution, for example, declares:

> Having fought and still fighting for freedom and democracy, the Algerian people, by this Constitution, decided to build constitutional institutions based on the participation of any Algerian, man and woman, in the management of public affairs; and on the ability to achieve social justice, equality and freedom for all.

And in Article 16 it states:

> The elected assembly represents the basis of decentralization and a place of the citizens' participation in the management of public affairs.

Article 10 of Oman's constitution sets the goal of:

> Laying suitable foundations for the establishment of the pillars of genuine Shura Consultation, based on the national heritage, its values and its Islamic Shari`a, and on pride in its history, while incorporating such contemporary manifestations as are appropriate.

These ideals have weakened throughout the region and clear distinctions have developed between the rulers and the ruled, even in the historically egalitarian countries of the Arabian Peninsula. Nevertheless, they reflect public expectations and are ignored at governments' peril.

The incorporation of traditional models into Arab countries' constitutions adds an element of familiarity with which populations might identify. The acknowledgement of tribalism is, however, a mixed blessing. As discussed in Chapter 2, the Arab tribes operate according to a code based on their ability to survive in an unordered environment. The rule of law, designed to facilitate life in more settled societies, is not consistent with this code. The pervasiveness of tribal attitudes and the traditional focus on the family and tribe work to undermine the status of constitutional frameworks in the eyes of populations and rulers alike.

Overwhelming all these issues is the constantly recurring problem that Arab regimes and nations are struggling to establish and maintain legitimacy (see Chapter 3). These are new countries, often reflecting in their political, economic and social arrangements the priorities of former colonial powers rather than the interests and traditions of their populations. They are societies where the concept of the nation state has to compete with family, tribal and religious loyalties to a much greater extent than in the West. Indeed, persistent ideals of an Arab nation and Islam's emphasis on (Arab and Moslem) communities probably carry greater emotive weight than the modern nation state. This fundamental tension is aggravated by the poor economic and military performance of the current state structures. The importance of these competing loyalties can be seen in the prominent treatment they receive in many Arab constitutions. With the exception of Lebanon, all stress the centrality of Islam in their political systems. All describe themselves as Arab nations or as part of the Arab nation.[42]

Arab rulers see their positions as dependent on the maintenance of national unity, and a major task of constitutions is to help these rulers promote this goal. To this end, they contain key concepts of liberal democracy, such as elections, individual rights and freedom from arbitrary treatment by the state. For example, Article 18 of Qatar's constitution states:

> The Qatari society is based on the values of justice, benevolence, freedom, equality, and high morals.

Articles 29 and 32 of the Algerian constitution declare:

> All citizens are equal before the law. No discrimination shall prevail because of kind, race, sex, opinion or any other personal or social condition or circumstance.
>
> Fundamental human and citizen's rights and liberties are guaranteed. They are a common heritage of all Algerians, men and women, whose duty is to transmit it from one generation to another in order to preserve it and keep it inviolable.

Complicating the development of a meaningful set of fundamental laws in Arab constitutions is the existence in most Arab states of important minorities that must be accommodated despite ambivalence on the part of the majority in many cases. Morocco and Algeria have large Berber populations. Sudan is divided between Arab and African. Syria and Iraq have significant Kurdish populations. Countries are also divided on religious grounds, with important Shi`a populations in the Eastern province of the predominantly Sunni Saudi Arabia and Shi`a majorities in Iraq and Bahrain. Lebanon's population is further divided between Sunni and Shi`a Moslems, various Christian groups and the Druze. In a number of cases, the minority is also the ruling group. Syria's rulers, the Alawites, make up around ten per cent of the population. Jordan's rulers, the Hashemites, are imposed foreigners, who are still seen as such by much of the population. Bahrain's ruling family is Sunni, who comprise only thirty per cent of the population. In the light of this diversity, the constitutions tend to serve to consolidate the dominance of a particular group. For example, many Arab constitutions specify that the king or president must be Moslem and Arab.

Among the most significant differences between Arab constitutions and their Western counterparts is the central place accorded religion. The pervasiveness and importance of Islam in the political systems of the Arab world is such that their constitutions must contain more than just a formal gesture to the central role of Shari`a law as a basis of constitutional law. This is a source of major contention in most Arab countries. The Tunisian constitution, one of the most secular of Arab constitutions, makes no specific reference to the role of Shari`a as a source of law. Nevertheless, the constitution still invokes the name of God and vows 'to remain faithful to the teachings of Islam' in the Preamble. It also contains in Article 1 a substantive provision that declares Islam to be the religion of the country. Other countries are more direct in according a central role for Islam in their constitutions. The Egyptian instrument declares in Article 2: 'Islam is the religion of the state and Arabic its official language. Islamic jurisprudence is the principle source of legislation'. Similarly, Article 7 of the constitution of the United Arab Emirates declares that the 'Islamic Shari`a shall be a main source of legislation in the Union.' Yemen's constitution describes Shari`a law as the source of all legislation (Article 3).

Some countries avoid describing their fundamental rules as constitutions. Saudi Arabia and Libya, for example, specify the Quran as their constitution and their

Basic Laws as simply power maps. Saudi Arabia's Basic Law states in Article 1 that 'God's Book and the Sunna of His Prophet . . . are its constitution'. Libya's 1977 Declaration on the Establishment of the Authority of the People states that 'The Holy Quran is the Constitution of the Socialist People's Libyan Arab Jamahiriya' (Article 2). Oman has a Basic Law which specifies the Shari`a as the basis of legislation (Article 2). The Omani and, especially, the Saudi Basic Laws present certain problems in this analysis. While they are not regarded as constitutions in those two states, the two Basic Laws contain some of the key features that might be expected in a constitutional instrument. They deal with general principles such as the flag, the divisions of authority in the kingdom and the issue of succession. However, the Saudi Basic Law, in particular, is not used in ways in which constitutions are used in other countries. For example, the courts do not refer to it for authoritative guidance in deciding cases and it is not employed by government ministries as a framework for policy directions and administrative guidance.[43] Saudi courts and judges operate on the basis of Islamic jurisprudence or legal theory (*fiqh*) of the Hanbali school of legal theory in Sunni Islam which, *inter alia*, maintains that all public authorities must be obeyed, provided their commands do not contradict the Shari`a or impede a Moslem's ability to practice his or her religion.[44] The model is not codified in any way. Instead it is left to the discretion and *ijtihad*[45] of the judges. In theory, senior *ulema*[46] control the development of *ijtihad* on the basis of what is required from new developments and cases. To an extent, this arrangement, devised by the Al Saud family and the Wahhabi movement, ensures regime legitimacy and protects it from pressures of modernisation, democracy and constitutionalism.

In the light of this approach to the Basic Law in the Saudi and Omani systems and the difficulty in treating them as superior law, the relevance of these instruments to the issues of the rule of law and constitutionalism is open to question. On one hand, they could be described as tentative steps in recognition of the need to develop a formal framework that will institutionalise the states' relationship with the increasingly complex societies of Saudi Arabia and Oman. On the other hand, these Basic Laws could be seen as a component of their constitutions, just as a number of basic documents might be described as forming the basis of the un-codified English constitution. The Basic Laws can then be regarded as providing precision and clarity to the underlying framework of the Quran and Shari`a law, and, taken together with these two fundamental elements, constitute the Saudi and the Omani constitutions.

The political forces behind these formulations are not necessarily opposed to the idea of modernisation or to the development of constitutions. Many have been happy to adopt modern ideas, provided those ideas can be shown to have been drawn from Islamic sources or to be consistent with Islamic criteria. Concepts such as individual rights and, especially, consultation, representation and responsibility have been justified by their compatibility with tribal concepts of *Shura* and *bay'a*.[47] In March 2004, the Moslem Brotherhood in Egypt presented a proposal for political reform, which contained a clear recognition of the value of a constitution. The proposal called for a 'republican, constitutional, parliamentary and democratic state that conforms to the principles of Islam'. The new state would replace the current political arrangements that the Brotherhood do not consider to derive from Islam. For many of these reforming conservatives, however, the processes involved are to be driven from the top down. The *sine qua non* of the arrangements to be adopted is that the successors of the Ottoman sultan-caliph should be in control of both secular and religious offices, and their powers should not be weakened by the modernisation process.[48]

Current practice in the Arab world

Before turning to Arab constitutions themselves and their treatment of the issue of succession, it is important to address the centrality of Arab constitutions to their political systems compared to Western countries. The relevance of provisions dealing with succession, for example, depends on the extent to which they are supreme manifestations of the rule of law or are in some way subordinate to the other institutions of state.

The approach of Arab governments to their constitutions is sufficiently divorced from the liberal-democratic norm that they are regularly dismissed when the idea of constitutionalism is considered. For example, Brown entitled his review of the constitutions of Arab political systems *Constitutions in a Non-constitutional World*.[49] There is popular agreement that the constitutions of Arab states play no significant part in the political process. Rather they are simply the trappings that a state must have if it is to claim to be modern and complete, but they are not something that should inhibit the activities of government. Another interpretation is that Arab constitutions are 'camouflage constitutions', intended to mask the reality of government along the lines of the Soviet Union's constitution under Stalin or the constitution of the German Democratic Republic.[50]

A widespread impression among Arab publics of their rulers since independence is that they have seized power and consolidated their power base, largely through the armed forces and the exercise of widespread repression and even terror. The rulers are now seeking to pass on their power to their sons or other family members. To the extent that it is seen by the public as playing a role, the constitution is used to facilitate this process. It may be amended or even redrafted to simply assist the ruler to consolidate and claim legitimacy for his power. The process is usually undertaken by a pliant parliament and without reference to the popular will. Plebiscites on amendments are generally not free or fair. People are often hardly aware that they had constitutions and certainly do not accord them the respect that someone from the West might. There is no trust in the idea that a constitution might serve to protect individual and civil rights. Instead, constitutions are seen as part of the range of mechanisms intended to increase the power of the rulers over the ruled.

In countries where the rule of law is beginning to take root, the constitution might be seen as playing an increasingly important role in certain areas of the daily life of ordinary people and in the business sector, but having no competence where ruling families and the broader ruling elite are concerned. In response to pressures in the

United Nations and the World Trade Organisation, some Arab countries are developing secular legal systems and structures and a growing body of secular law. One of the first major programmes introduced by King Mohammed VI of Morocco on his accession in 1999 was to begin the codification of the country's law. It is taken for granted, however, that presidents, sheikhs and princes are not bound by the law – a factor of considerable significance in a region where clientalism is a central feature of political life. Of particular importance is the fact that these people are often deeply involved in the economic life of their countries. In Morocco, for example, King Mohammed is one of the largest businessman in the country, but he is untouchable in a court of law. The economy of the emirate of Dubai is dominated by the ruling Maktoum family (Maktoum Inc. which directly owns key sectors of the economy, including in the tourism, construction and aviation sectors). At a relatively trivial but enlightening level, arrangements for enforcing speed limits on the roads in the United Arab Emirates had to be changed to ensure that the members of the families of leading sheikhs were not stopped for speeding. This is a pattern that can be found across the region and has a damaging impact on the attitudes of ordinary citizens towards their rulers' commitment to the rule of law.

A constitution's relevance and importance is measured by the degree to which the rule of law under a constitution is broadly respected and uniformly enforced. In this respect, Arab governments can safely be accused of contempt for constitutional processes. Examples of the lack of respect shown by Arab governments to the rule of law are routinely apparent from the actions of the governments. For example, Egypt's constitution (Article 41) states that:

> Individual freedom is a natural right and is inviolable. Except in cases of *flagrante delicto*, no person may be arrested, inspected, detained or his freedom restricted or prevented from free movement except by or as necessitated by investigations and preservation of the security of the society.

Under Egypt's state of emergency laws, however, this provision is regularly violated for political reasons.[51] Syria's constitution specifically forbids the resort to torture in Article 28(3), but there is extensive evidence to suggest that torture is conducted by government agencies for the Syrian and other governments.[52] Article 9(i) of the constitution of Jordan stipulates that: 'no Jordanian may be deported from the territory of the Kingdom'. In the late 1990s, however, the Jordanian government deported Khalid Mesha'al, a citizen suspected of membership of the Hamas organisation.[53] Similar examples of regimes ignoring the provisions of their constitutions are easily found for most, if not all, governments across the region.

There are more fundamental problems with Arab governments' approaches to the rule of law, which place them outside liberal-democratic constitutionalism. Arab constitutions regularly feature clauses that provide significant qualifications of their key provisions. For example, Article 45 of the Egyptian constitution states that:

> The law shall protect the inviolability of the private life of citizens. Correspondence, wires, telephone calls and other means of communication

> shall have their own sanctity and their secrecy shall be guaranteed. They may not be confiscated or monitored except by a causal judicial warrant and for a definite period and according to the provisions of the law.

The phrase 'according to the provisions of the law' provides considerable latitude to those seeking to work around the prohibition of intrusion into personal privacy. Similarly, Jordan's constitution (Article 15) guarantees that:

> Every Jordanian shall be free to express his opinion by speech, in writing, or by means of photographic representation and other forms of expression, provided that such does not violate the law.

Again, there is little to prevent censorship in this provision, given the open-ended nature of the proviso that the expression should not violate the law. It is an exception to which the Jordanian government resorts regularly.[54]

As far as the key issue of political succession is concerned, regime attitudes towards constitutions are ambiguous. Contempt for the constitution is exemplified by the process whereby Bashar Al Assad succeeded to the Syrian presidency on the death of his father, Hafez Al Assad. The constitution at the time of Hafez's death specified that the president must be 40 years of age. Bashar was only 34. According to Article 71 of the constitution, determining the presidential succession is the responsibility of the People's Assembly. In reality, the decision on succession is in the hands of the incumbent, with the support of key power groups. The People's Assembly has little more than a rubber-stamp role. Hafez Al Assad had made it clear that he wanted Bashar to succeed him, but he died before the preparations for the transfer were complete. To address this problem in June 2000 the major figures of the regime arranged for the constitution to be amended by the People's Assembly to make Bashar eligible for the presidency. This decision is clearly an example of the Syrian regime's lack of concern for the rule of law.[55] One interpretation of the action might be that it was *dajal* (deceit, pretending to be what you are not), part of, in Nenner's words, the 'oppression of the King's Subjects by Colour of Law', whereby the regime 'was pretending, and indeed seeming, to act in compliance with the law but in fact was not'.[56] Contemptuous or not, the fact remains that the government did feel a need to make the appointment constitutionally valid and it did follow due processes in securing the change. Parliament was convened and the amendment was adopted according to the provisions of the constitution (Article 49). Parliament then voted to elect Bashar as President, again according to the provisions of the constitution (Article 84). The issue of whether the hurdle set for amendment was as high as that in Australia, Britain or France is a separate one and is not necessarily grounds for criticism.

Similarly, the plans of the Egyptian President, Hosni Mubarak, for his son, Gamal, to succeed him appear to require a degree of constitutional cover. Gamal's route to the top is not following the path through the military followed by Nasser, Sadat and Mubarak himself. This means that the President must ensure that the various political elements, including the constitution, are aligned before the handover can occur. Mubarak is, however, confronted by a constitution of greater political importance than the Syrian document and constitutional provisions that make dynastic succession more difficult to manipulate. Article 76, which deals with the nomination process, and Article 189, which sets out the constitutional amendment provisions, are relatively onerous and politically difficult to ignore. In Palestine, despite or perhaps because of the difficult security situation facing the Palestinian Authority, the provisions of the provisional constitution relating to presidential succession were adhered to when Yasser Arafat died. His successor, Mahmoud Abbas, was anointed by the Americans and Israel, but still had to subject himself to a reasonably open election.

While Arab regimes can be criticised for their failure to comply with their constitutions, it is perhaps not surprising that Arab leaders might attempt to test their systems' tolerance and flexibility. This is not unique to the Arab world. The United States' constitution represents an example of the central role a constitution plays in underpinning, guiding and enforcing the rule of law. There are, however, numerous examples that suggest the commitment of American politicians to the centrality of the constitution might not be as wholehearted as might be expected and that they too are capable of testing the limits. The Watergate scandal and the Iran-Contra affair suggest that United States administrations have been willing to override or bypass the constitution in pursuit of a policy objective.[57] In July 2006, the American Bar Association issued a report on legislative 'signing statements' by President G. W. Bush in which it suggested that statements by the President that were at variance with the objectives of legislation before him were inconsistent with the constitution.[58]

Succession and the constitution

Political succession is a major focus of countries' constitutions because it directly relates to the distribution and exercise of power. This can be reflected in different ways. In Westminster-based systems, such as the United Kingdom, Australia and Canada, only residual power resides with the head of state. Actual power lies with the head of government. In France, the constitution of the Fifth Republic has created independent centres of power. One is based on a popularly elected head of state and the other on the head of government, elected from the parliament and drawing strength from his or her party's success in general elections. The French system has created the complex situation, which came to be known as 'cohabitation', whereby a president and a prime minister of different political persuasions are forced to moderate their differences and share power in the cause of effective government. Succession in the Arab world is very much about the power of the ruling family and not about the possibility of sharing it. The issue of how to maintain power in this context comes to a head in the area of succession. Arab constitutions are emerging as important factors in the management of this challenge.

From the perspective of the republican rulers in the Arab world, succession is bound up in their ability to maintain their possession of power. Republican leaders display a clear intention to make their possession permanent. It is notable that those republics where dynastic succession has become an issue – Syria, Egypt, Yemen and Libya – have experienced long periods of rule by a single man. The implication is that the longer a family holds onto power, the more the family is tempted by and attracted to a hereditary form of governance. The problem is how to ensure family control while promoting legitimacy by appearing to comply with the terms of the constitution.

Based on their constitutional provisions, the 22 members of the Arab League break down into 14 republics and eight monarchies (see Appendix 2). The 'monarchy' category includes four kingdoms (Saudi Arabia, Morocco, Jordan and Bahrain), an hereditary sultanate (Oman), two emirates (Kuwait and Qatar) and a republic (United Arab Emirates). The titles chosen by the rulers of these monarchies have some significance. The term 'sultan' is associated with authority and power, especially military power, and compares with the religio-moral-legal authority of the caliph.[59] The term 'emir' was originally a military commander and the early Caliphs incorporated it into their titles. 'Commander of the Faithful' (*Emir Al Mu'maneen*) is a term regularly used by the king of Morocco. The Arabic word for 'king' (*malik*) is derived from the word for 'possession' and contains the idea of power and dominion, knowledge and wisdom and was seen by some Islamic writers, such as Al Farabi, as suggesting a synthesis of the ideal Islamic ruler and Plato's philosopher king.[60] It has tended to be distrusted by Arabs, and this lingering distrust may account for the avoidance of the term by most monarchies in the Arab world. This writer was told that, in the case of the Gulf countries, the choice of title also reflected the relationship of the different countries with Saudi Arabia. Oman's choice of sultan, for example, suggested a degree of rivalry with the Saudi regime, while the choice of emir or ruler indicated a degree of acceptance of the leading role that Saudi Arabia has played in the area, at least until recently. In practical terms, however, there is no difference between the three titles, especially when it comes to political succession. All sultanates, emirates and kingdoms are based on heredity, with their constitutions specifying that succession is to be restricted to the families currently in power. Among these hereditary monarchies, primogeniture is arguably an appealing option to a number of rulers.

The United Arab Emirates stands out from its neighbours insofar as it has a president as head of state and its federal structure is designed on republican lines. The individual Rulers who control the seven emirates of the federation are, subject to the constitution's allocation of powers to the federal government, absolute monarchs in their own emirates (Article 3). While largely uncodified, succession is restricted to the ruling family and reflects the Saudi model, with a crown prince appointed early in a Ruler's reign. At the federal level, the most powerful emirates, Abu Dhabi and Dubai, have veto power over all federal legislation (Article 49). Succession to the leadership of the United Arab Emirates' President, Vice President and Prime Minister is formally determined on the basis of an election from the Supreme Council, an electoral college of the Rulers of the Emirates and the highest constitutional authority in the country (Article 46). Theoretically, the Ruler of any emirate could be elected to one of these senior offices but, in practice, this is inconceivable, given Abu Dhabi's power based on its great wealth, relatively large population and the dependence of the other emirates on it. An informal agreement provides for the ruler of Abu Dhabi to serve as President and the ruler of Dubai as Vice President and Prime Minister. This arrangement is likely to persist for the foreseeable future.

Among the 14 constitutional republics, succession is determined by direct popular election in 11 instances. The issue is determined by parliament in Lebanon (Article 49(2)) and by the Revolutionary Command Council in Libya (Article 19(1)). Yemen adopted direct popular election in 2006, however, as in Syria, the parliament retains a veto over the ability of people to stand for office (Articles 62 and 107). The Syrian case is complicated by the specific involvement of the Ba`ath Regional Command in the nomination process (Article 84).

While Arab constitutions outline the formal requirements for succession, those provisions can only go so far in regulating what is, essentially, a political issue. Reflecting this, Arab regimes rely on informal procedures within small ruling groups for the crucial decisions of who will succeed, and on what terms. The states of the Arabian Peninsula, for example, decide on succession among members of the ruling family behind closed doors. In Saudi Arabia, the Basic Law (Article 5(c)) provides that 'the King chooses the Heir Apparent and relieves him of his duties by Royal order'. In addition, the Basic Law states that:

> Rule passes to the sons of the founding King, Abd Al Aziz bin Abd Al Rahman Al Feisal Al Saud, and to their children's children. The most upright among them is to receive allegiance in accordance with the principles of the Holy Quran and the Tradition of the Venerable Prophet (Article 5(b)).

In practice, the decision on succession is entirely the prerogative of the inner circle of the ibn Saud family. This has been formalised to an extent by the establishment of the Allegiance Committee (*Al hayat al baya*). The Committee will comprise sons and grandsons of Abd Al-Aziz Al-Saud and will seek to smooth the succession process in the future. The Committee was established by a decree amending the Basic Law. While it is too early to see how the Committee will operate, it would appear to be a formalisation of the situation that exists now, with the senior members of the family deciding who is to be the next king. In the original arrangement, the king had the dominant role and it would seem likely that this will continue under the Allegiance Committee so that the Committee is unlikely to change the substance of the decision-making process. A feature of the new body is its tribal mix of democratic and authoritarian measures. The king's power remains considerable in the Committee, but should there be stalemate over the nomination of a crown prince, a vote will be taken (Article 7(b)). The Institution also seeks to address health problems the Saudi royal family has faced in the past, such as the long-term incapacity of King Fahd (Article 12) (see Chapter 6).

The process of succession devised by Oman's Sultan Qaboos is remarkable for the potential for dispute that it introduces. The constitution (Article 6(1)) specifies that a Ruling Family Council shall determine who is to succeed to the throne. In the event of a stalemate in the Council, however, the Council will resort to the Sultan's choice in an unopened letter he has written to the Ruling Family Council. Qaboos is reported to have hidden a number of copies of his letter around the country, and it is not hard to envisage disputes about the authenticity of any letter presented to support a particular claim to the throne.

In Arab countries, as in any other political system, it is not possible to determine simply from the terms of a country's constitution how committed that country is to constitutionalism and to the rule of law.[61] A constitution is, after all, part of a political process. On the basis of the discussions above, however, it would be difficult to suggest that Arab attitudes to the rule of law meet even the most basic of the criteria set by Locke, Montesquieu or modern analysts. In part this is because of these countries' limited experience of the concept. According to some observers, however, it reflects problems with Arab attitudes to governance. Garfinkle suggests that there are three prerequisites for democracy which are lacking in the Arab world. The first prerequisite is the liberal conviction that political authority derives from the people. For Moslems, authority derives from God. This creates problems for Arab acceptance of political pluralism and especially for the idea of a loyal opposition. The second prerequisite is the acceptance of the principle of majority rule and the commonly applied rule of winner take all in elections – ideas which clash with the Moslem preference of consensus being the basis for government decisions in the context of the Quran and the *Hadith*. The third prerequisite is the equality of all citizens before the law, a requirement which he claims is alien to traditional Islamic authority.[62] This is a particularly controversial argument which numerous writers have sought to challenge. Nasr, for example, insists that democracy and Islam are not incompatible and foresees a process whereby 'Moslem democrats' will begin overtly to integrate the values of Islam into the platforms of parties seeking to win elections by democratic means.[63]

Regardless of the strength of these arguments, however, there is evidence that Arab constitutions and the rule of law are playing a role of growing importance in Arab political systems. It is clear that Arab rulers are increasingly seeking legitimacy for their continued control and for the process of succession through constitutional processes. A significant related development is the growing recognition by ordinary citizens of the existence of constitutions and of the instruments' potential to further their interests. This is resulting in greater use being made of constitutions as part of the political process in a number of Arab countries.

In a number of Arab countries, the constitution is coming to be seen as a signpost or direction setter for the development of the economy and society and a support for regime legitimacy. In Egypt, the constitution enjoys a greater standing than in most other countries of the region. This can be attributed in part to a longer Egyptian experience of a constitution and a difficult domestic political balance, which is maintained in part by the existing document. Egypt's first constitution was promulgated in 1882, at the time of the Khedive Tawfiq, and was intended to introduce a range of constraints on royal power. A second and more important constitution, adopted in 1923, was closely modelled on a Western pattern, but with considerable potential for royal activism. A third constitution of 1930 was imposed rather than developed through consultation and debate and further strengthened the power of the king.[64] The Wafd, the dominant political movement of the monarchic period, attempted to exploit the latter two constitutions to limit royal power and to promote a limited degree of popular participation in the political process.[65] In the long run, the Wafd was discredited by its close association with the king and its willingness to reach compromises with him.

After Nasser's coup of 1952, the focus and objective of Egypt's constitution changed. It became an instrument for restructuring and reorienting the economy and society based on socialist principles. On his accession to the presidency, Anwar Sadat, added a series of amendments, which introduced new and incompatible principles into the document. Sadat's constitution was committed to the promotion of socialism, liberalism and Islamism. In Article 33, for example, it guarantees the 'sanctity of public ownership' and, in the following article, promotes private property. Egyptian leaders are aware of the problems with the constitution. Some believe that they can be resolved by means of a simple process of constitutional amendment. Others have been less confident, believing that certain articles cannot be touched for fear of releasing forces, such as Islamist pressures, which might prove difficult to control.

In many matters, the government has been able to sidestep the constitution through the continued imposition of emergency laws. In certain areas, however, this has been difficult. A feature of modern constitutionalism is the separation of powers doctrine, and Egypt is one of the few Arab countries where this doctrine has some effect. The government has had to come to terms with certain limits to its power imposed by the constitution. Egypt's constitution established a Supreme Constitutional Court (Articles 174–78), which has managed to inhibit the Government's actions in certain areas. Among the most significant of these areas has been the processes of reforming the constitution itself and amending the presidential succession provisions. This will be a concern for Mubarak if he is to facilitate his son's succession. Other Arab constitutions also contain Articles establishing constitutional courts. Algeria has a complex arrangement involving a High Court, Council of State and Tribunal of Conflicts (Article 152) that is intended to address issues of a constitutional nature. There is, however, no evidence that the arrangement operates with any independence from the executive. Bahrain has a constitutional court whose responsibility is to 'watch over the constitutionality of laws and statutes' (Article 106(1)). As its members are directly appointed by the king, the court's independence as a body of review is limited.

Another aspect of the constitutional issue is the relationship between the president, prime minister and parliament. Apart from the United Arab Emirates and Lebanon, no Arab state formally or effectively allocates real political power to the prime minister and parliament. Article 93 of Syria's constitution, for example, places political power firmly in the hands of the President, leaving the Prime Minister a largely administrative role. The United Arab Emirates and Lebanese exceptions reflect the need to balance long-standing rivalries and divisions in the two countries. In the United Arab Emirates, the ruling families in Abu Dhabi and

Dubai share power, reflecting their economic importance and their history of tribal warfare. In Lebanon, the confessional divisions are such that a formal sharing of power was felt necessary. Power is shared between a Christian president, a Sunni prime minister and a Shiite speaker of parliament. No other Arab state has such an arrangement, although the situation in Iraq might develop along similar lines.

Throughout the region, there are tentative but clear signs of change in the legal approach to succession. Regimes are no less determined to retain their control, but are resorting to different means of securing that control. From a constitutional point of view, a number of Gulf countries appear to be in the process of moving from the tribal system to be found, for example, in the United Arab Emirates, through the more mixed system of Saudi Arabia, towards the Jordanian/Moroccan structure. These two countries adhere to rules of agnatic primogeniture which are thought to provide greater predictability to succession and to reduce the incentive for palace coups.[66] A number of Gulf states, Bahrain, Qatar and Kuwait, in particular, have begun to experiment with a constitutional framework to manage their succession process. In February 2002, Bahrain, for example, upgraded its system from an emirate to a constitutional monarchy and introduced agnatic primogeniture as the basis for succession. Qatar has conducted qualified elections intended to promote the legitimacy of the ruling family. Oman has held limited elections.

The result of these experiments has not been encouraging, with the Kuwaiti constitution having been arbitrarily suspended on a number of occasions (1976–81 and 1986–92) and parliament having been dissolved frequently. The ruler of Bahrain, Sheikh Hamad bin Isa Al Khalifa, introduced a number of reforming measures in February 2002, but the measures, which included Hamad declaring himself King, gave the monarchy extensive powers as head of state, commander of the armed forces and head of the executive and judicial branches of government. The king appoints and dismisses ministers and senior officials and appoints the members of the parliament's upper house. The king can also amend the constitution and control the legislative agenda of the parliament (Article 33(d), (e) and (h)). Elections conducted under the new arrangements have had mixed results, with the majority Shi`a element of the population largely boycotting the process. The Qatari experiment has been too recent for any pattern of adherence to constitutional rule to be discernable. It is clear, however, that the whole drift of the constitution is designed to augment the ruler's power while creating the impression of greater popular participation in governance.[67]

The changes being introduced throughout the Arab world reflect a number of factors. The regimes are clearly under pressure from outside to do something to make them conform more to Western standards. At the same time, a number of the regimes are under pressure from domestic threats and from external rivals. Qatar's ruler, for example, needed to consolidate his coup against his father and to strengthen his hand against his rivals, the Saudis. There is also a generational change occurring throughout the region. The leaders of the post-independence years are leaving the scene. The emerging generation of leaders tends to be better educated, more knowledgeable of the outside world, especially the West, and generally more cosmopolitan than its parents. The new leaders assuming power throughout the region are looking to garner support from their cohort, which shares their life experiences and is less sympathetic of their parents' approach.

Historical parallels

In trying to work out how Arab constitutions might develop in the future, it is interesting to note some similarities between the constitutional process in the modern Arab world and the beginning of the modern era of constitutionalism, especially when it comes to succession. Berman remarks that:

> . . . in the West, modern times – not only modern legal institutions and modern legal values but also the modern state, the modern church, modern philosophy, the modern university, modern literature and much else that is modern – have their origin in the period 1050 to 1150 and not before.[68]

Berman is talking about a period of great political and social upheaval in Europe and the beginnings of what was to become the nation-state system. It was also a time of intimate connections between the West and Islam, with a steady flow of ideas, especially from Islam to Europe.[69] Based on this melding of ideas, it is not inappropriate to look for certain parallels between aspects of the development of the Arab world and Europe. Drawing on an analysis of the development of European constitutions, an argument could be made that the development of Arab constitutionalism will be influenced by similar forces to those that drove European constitutionalism – essentially power, with the related elements of centralisation and resistance. As with mediaeval Europe, the Arab world is characterised by civil unrest as rulers, who are inclined to absolute rule, attempt to extend their power over the whole of their societies.[70] It is also a time when, in the face of pressures on Arab regimes to democratise, some Arab rulers have shown an apparent willingness formally to concede certain powers or to make concessions in order to consolidate their overall hold on power. From such a perspective, it could be predicted that Arab constitutionalism might follow a similar path to that of Europe. The parallel with the Stuarts of England is interesting in this respect.

As with the first Ottoman constitution and the determination of Sultan Abdul Hamid to ensure that the document enhanced his power rather than constrained it,[71] so modern Arab rulers are attempting to augment their power through their constitutions. To this end, the constitutions of Bahrain (Article 1(a)) and Morocco (Article 1) describe the state as a 'constitutional monarchy.' The Saudi regime has allowed restricted elections at the municipal level and its consultative council, the *Majlis Al Shura*, is growing in importance and influence.[72] Other regimes are beginning to move tentatively in the direction of the rule of law, also seeking greater regime legitimacy and the regularisation and legitimisation of the succession process. These changes have been driven by and involve negotiations and compromises with the various elites of the societies.

The Tudor experience reveals some similarities with these developments. Keir notes that the first business of a new English ruling house was to consolidate its position.[73] The Tudors and, to an even greater extent, the Stuarts after them, entered into relationships with other centres of power in England, the feudal lords and Parliament. The monarchs were willing to trade apparently unimportant powers or rights in exchange for greater power in other areas. In other cases, the monarchy conceded powers as a reflection of its political weakness. In 1626, Charles I was forced to dissolve Parliament in an effort to avoid the impeachment of his minister, the Duke of Buckingham. A similar struggle can be witnessed in Kuwait, most recently in 2006 and 2009, when the emir felt obliged to dissolve parliament to prevent the Prime Minister, a member of the ruling family, from being interrogated by Members of Parliament. In part as a result of these struggles in England, civil war brought the republic and a repudiation of the concept of the divine right of kings – a repudiation that survived the Restoration of 1660. Similarly, Charles II was forced on a number of occasions, for example, the Dutch War of 1666–67, to concede various prerogatives to Parliament in an attempt to preserve other powers that he saw as crucial. These were all steps in the process that had the unintended consequence of the establishment of parliamentary sovereignty and a constitutional monarchy.[74]

It is, of course, a long way from Tudor or Stuart England to a presidential or royal palace in a Middle Eastern country, and any attractive parallels must be considered with considerable care. Nevertheless, it would not be unreasonable to suggest that the English experience noted above could recur in the Arab context with the possibility that concessions made with one end in mind might, over time, result in more significant changes in the balance of power in a political system. De Tocqueville's famous observation is also pertinent in this context:

> . . . experience suggests that the most dangerous moment for an evil government is usually when it begins to reform itself. Only great ingenuity can save a prince who undertakes to give relief to his subjects after long oppression. The sufferings that are endured patiently, as being inevitable, become intolerable the moment it appears that there might be an escape. Reform then only serves to reveal more clearly what still remains oppressive and now all the more unbearable.[75]

The concessions to constitutionalism made by Arab rulers may already have begun to promote change. Kuwait is unique in the Arab world to the extent that it tolerates a relatively independent-minded parliament. This represents a more even balance of power in Kuwait than in other Arab countries, enabling the parliament to make demands that would not be tolerated elsewhere in the region. For example, with the death of Emir Sheikh Jaber Al Sabah in January 2006, the ruling family was forced to negotiate the succession with the parliament in order to avoid a challenge to its choice of Jaber's successor and to later avoid what would have been a vote of no confidence in his Prime Minister, also a member of the royal family. Tétreault interprets this process as part of a transition to constitutional monarchy:

> On the surface, the brief succession crisis that gripped Kuwait in mid-January, 2006, merely saw the replacement of one member of the ruling Al Sabah family with another. But the crisis also saw the direct intervention of the Kuwaiti parliament to ensure that the succession proceeded according to the constitution. For the first time in an Arab monarchy, an elected body effectively deposed the monarch, without anyone firing a shot. In January, Kuwait really witnessed two transitions: one between emirs and another from a dynastic monarchy to a strengthened constitutional monarchy.[76]

There are other instances in the Arab world that indicate a degree of pressure on governments to comply with the law. Fundamental Arab legal instruments bearing many of, if not all, the characteristics of Western constitutions may be sufficiently important to provide a basis for a nascent form of constitutionalism, albeit with the emphasis on community, stability and order rather than human rights and individualism. Moreover, there is reason to expect that, as happened in the West, an evolutionary process will gradually impel Arab political systems in the direction of constitutionally-guided government. The resulting systems would reflect differing experiences, perspectives and political traditions. Nenner suggests of the English experience that, while the law was used to influence the way in which people regarded the constitution in England, the assumptions that underpinned that process were based on a cultural instinct. He adds that:

> Magna Carta meant more in the seventeenth century than it had in the thirteenth. King John's barons held the great Charter as a tenuous conveyance, but the whole English people, some four hundred years later, held it by inheritance as a secure and indefeasible estate.[77]

Perhaps the same sort of process, given time, will take place in Arabs' perceptions of their constitutions, and Arabs will look back at this period of constitution making as the beginning of the rule of law in their societies.

This chapter has examined the way in which Arab constitutions deal with political succession and a trend among Arab leaders to seek support in constitutions for their dynastic ambitions. It has also assessed the possibility that constitutions will become more significant elements in Arab political systems. Arab states are truly 'states of exception'.[78] Despite a considerable history of constitution making and the great depth of Islamic jurisprudence, constitutions in the Arab world lack the status and relevance that they enjoy in other parts of the world, especially the West. Nevertheless, there are indications that Arab regimes are resorting to constitutions as part of their efforts to promote their legitimacy and to consolidate their domination of their countries. In the process, the regimes are incorporating in their constitutions some of the important political compromises and concessions they have made to other power centres in their systems. Constitutions thereby become the expressions and guarantees of delicate balances of power and allocations of spoils. It is in this process that they are becoming more significant features of Arab political systems. The rule of law is likely to remain a vulnerable concept in the Arab world for the foreseeable future. The constitutions, however, will provide frameworks for political action and signposts of limits beyond which governments and their opponents will hesitate to go.

Arab constitutions are largely intended to promote the dominance of the ruling houses in the region. This does not mean that constitutional monarchy or constitutional republicanism is unlikely. The desire of Elizabeth Tudor and Charles II to preserve their families' dominant positions in English political life was no less than the desire of the Moroccan, Bahraini or Syrian ruling families to achieve the same end. However, their efforts still led to the development of effective constitutional controls on the powers of the head of state. There are many forces in play in the Arab world that are pushing in the same direction.

The constitutional challenge for monarchic and republican Arab rulers is to find a formula that will enjoy a degree of legitimacy and will endure across generations. In the short term, this will require some thoughtful and far-sighted strategies by the new leaders in the region. Anderson warns that the prospect of such an approach at the moment is not bright:

> Hidden among the heirs apparent, there may be a King Juan Carlos for the Arab world – someone whose profound democratic sentiments will become apparent only when he has a chance to move out of his predecessor's shadow. (Similarly, there might be a Nelson Mandela in the opposition, ready to spin democratic institutions out of thin air upon taking power.) But there is little in the education or experience of the new crop of rulers to equip them to think strategically about class alliances or democratic institutions.[79]

There are signs that some of the aspiring leaders are willing to look at new ways of establishing and consolidating their power, but their ultimate objectives remain the same and their means of exercising power are constrained by the divisions and weaknesses in their societies. In particular, as Bashar Al Assad is possibly finding, attempts at reform can be frustrated by the new rulers' inability to shake off the coalitions of power that developed under their fathers' rule. While clientalist structures depend greatly on the individual at the top, that leader is also reliant on those who depend on him.

6 Back to the future

Arab monarchies

> It has thus become clear that royal authority is a natural quality of man which is absolutely necessary to mankind.[1]

This chapter examines a number of Arab monarchies from the perspective of their constitutional arrangements, the impact of tribal values and their handling of political succession. Drawing from the more general preceding chapters, the chapter addresses the increasing importance of constitutions among the Arab monarchies and examines the nature of the commitment of Arab kings to their constitutions. The relevance of constitutions in monarchies' search for legitimacy and in their attempts to develop stable, predictable and legitimate succession arrangements will be considered. The importance of family and, to a lesser extent, tribe as influences on the behaviour of Arab monarchs is an important factor discussed in this chapter. The resort to family and other traditional factors, such as tribalism and Islam, to achieve legitimacy in their societies is a central element.

After inauspicious beginnings in the post-Ottoman period, Arab monarchies have developed into the more successful means of governance in the Arab region. This success can be attributed to a number of factors, including, in some cases, oil wealth as well as significant economic, political and military support from outside powers. The success is also attributable to the greater degree of affinity of monarchies to their peoples' political traditions, especially loyalty to family and to tribal attitudes.

The monarchies under consideration can be broken into two categories: those that apply primogeniture or a variation of that principle in their succession arrangements and those that, according to Black, are based in traditional Islamic practices whereby 'patrimony is divided equally among all sons'.[2] Herb has a slightly different categorisation of Arab monarchies. He proposes dividing the monarchies into those in which the ruling family plays a dominant and monopolistic role in government, the 'dynastic monarchies', and those in which the ruler governs alone.[3] There is merit in both approaches with Black's categorisation focusing on the structural element and Herb on the governing aspect. Both expose interesting aspects of the problem of succession in Arab monarchies. Some of Herb's latter group may rely on primogeniture as the basis of their power. A feature of this group is that the monarch:

> . . . has a wide latitude in his choice of lieutenants, who serve, in Machiavelli's phrase, 'by his grace and permission'. The irony of the situation of these kings is that while they enjoy more personal power, their regimes display far less stability. As Montesquieu noted, 'in proportion as the power of the monarch becomes boundless and immense, his security diminishes'.[4]

In a further irony, most of Herb's dynastic monarchies exhibit an inclination towards this second form of organisation.

The prominence of monarchies in the Arab world is an unusual characteristic of the region. In contrast to the experience in most of the rest of the world and despite the forecasts of many analysts, Arab monarchies have survived into the modern era. They are now regarded by many observers as the most successful form of governance in the Arab region. Indeed, the durability of this form of government stands in contrast to the considerable problems that republican systems of the region have been facing in establishing legitimacy among their populations (see Chapter 7).

There are good reasons for the monarchies' survival. While assessing Arab monarchies' long-term prospects as poor, Anderson suggests the success of monarchies can largely be attributed to their political succession arrangements. The relative clarity of monarchic succession procedures has worked in their favour.[5] Other analysts, however, go further to suggest that Arab monarchies are better placed than other systems of government to promote and carry out significant liberalising reforms in their societies.[6] This is an assessment taken up by Herb:

> . . . some forms of monarchism – even at the end of the twentieth century – display a remarkable vitality and resilience, and I argue that the survival of monarchism is not necessarily only a postponement of revolution, but instead offers the prospect of a gradual transition to a more liberal political order.[7]

This potential for flexibility in responding to changing circumstances is of considerable significance. Beyond their commitment to the continued dominance of their families and with the notable exception of Saudi Arabia with its Wahhabi ideology, the monarchies of the Arab world do not champion any particular ideological approach. While perhaps instinctively corporatist in their economic outlook, they are not tied, politically or constitutionally, to particular programmes of social engineering, nationalisation or the free market. The Moroccan constitution, for example, makes no reference to the economy, apart from a qualified guarantee of private property and free enterprise (Article 15) and the establishment of an advisory Economic and Social Council (Articles 93 and 94). The Bahraini constitution is similarly silent on the nature of the economy and, while it does describe the system of government as democratic (Article 1(d)), the associated civil rights are heavily qualified by resort to the inevitable 'saving clauses'.

> Ownership, capital and work, in accordance with the principles of Islamic justice, are basic constituents of the social structure of the State and the

national wealth. They are all individual rights with a social function regulated by law (Article 9(c)).

The Saudi exception is based on the compact between the ruling family and the Wahhabi clergy at the time of the establishment of the state.[8] That agreement led to clerical representatives assuming an important place in the Saudi political system, a status manifested in the Saudi Basic Law's heavy emphasis on the role of Islam in society. The Basic Law states that 'The family is the kernel of Saudi society and its members shall be brought up on the basis of the Islamic faith and loyalty and obedience to God.' (Article 9) It also declares that 'Education will aim at instilling the Islamic faith in the younger generation.' (Article 13)

This flexibility enables monarchies to respond to challenges with a degree of subtlety and pragmatism. They seem capable, for example, of allowing a degree of formal and public opposition, including, in Jordan's and Kuwait's cases, parliamentary debate which extends to challenges to government policies and personnel. This serves as a means of releasing political pressure and of assessing the nature and the strength of matters of public concern. This approach also enables the monarchs to create a distinction between their rule and their governments' activities. Kings Hussein and Hassan, for example, regularly dissociated themselves from any unpopular policies of their governments and presented themselves as the ultimate guardians of the public's interests by correcting the governments' mistakes. Another source of monarchic strength derives from the monarchies' training in the art of leadership and the considerable skills that a number of Arab monarchs, such as King Hussein of Jordan and Sheikh Zayed of the United Arab Emirates, have displayed over long periods. These skills have been crucial to regime survival and the development of regime legitimacy.

Perhaps the most important factor in this respect is raised by Adams who suggests, in the context of early modern Europe, that the rule of a king depended greatly on the regime's ability to establish in the minds of the population an identification between the monarchy and the state. Continuity and legitimacy depended on the maintenance of this identification.[9] Such an intimate identification between the monarch and the state appears to strike a responsive chord among significant proportions of Arab populations. Many regard the survival of the monarchy as a prerequisite for the continued existence of the state itself and, on that basis, regard the maintenance of stability and personal security in terms of the need to support the regime. This identification might be compared to the British approach to office – 'The King is dead. God save the King' – with the monarchy being seen as something larger than the individual.

Various expressions of this phenomenon of close royal family identification with their countries are apparent in the Arab world. The kingdom of Saudi Arabia is named after the individual who created it and after the family who, in a sense, own it. The Basic Law (Article 5) establishes the royal line based on the founder of the kingdom, Abd Al-Aziz. Jordan includes the family name in its title and, as with Saudi Arabia, the country has only existed under Hashemite family rule. The constitution similarly establishes the monarchy as being based on the founder,

Abdallah (Article 28). Morocco's history is more complex as the ruling family has been on the throne since before the French colonial period. Their role in the independence movement from France reinforces the identification of state and ruling family. There is, however, a strong personal element to the loyalty of Arab populations. This loyalty is directed at the monarch himself and is consistent with the tradition of Arab tribalism. One of the most evident emotions expressed at the time of the deaths of King Fahd of Saudi Arabia, Jordan's King Hussein and the United Arab Emirates's Sheikh Zayed was concern about what was to come next. There was concern that stability would be undermined by the succession of a lesser ruler.

Most important of all, the survival of these regimes has been contingent on their success in dealing with political succession in an unsettled environment. The importance of regime solidarity is recognised in the literature[10] and Arab monarchies have generally managed to maintain a united front in the face of a range of significant challenges. This has been particularly apparent at times of their greatest vulnerability, when going through a succession process. Moreover, the succession mechanisms adopted by the monarchies have, on the whole, been relatively refined and uncontested affairs, without bloodshed and with limited resort to measures such as exile or imprisonment.

What follows is an examination of Jordan and Morocco which, with Bahrain, represent the examples of primogeniture in Arab monarchies. The spirit of the idea is, however, also alive in some of the other monarchies as well as in some of the Arab republics. There is also be a discussion of some of the monarchies of the Arabian Peninsula, where any urge towards primogeniture is tempered by the traditional tribal approach to leadership and succession.

Jordan: a vulnerable child of colonialism

The Hashemite Kingdom of Jordan had a difficult birth. Transjordan, as it was originally known, was a consequence of the Arab revolt against the Ottomans, which had been almost exclusively a Hashemite affair. Other major tribal groups on the Arabian Peninsula remained largely aloof or, in the case of the Al-Saud family, were potentially hostile. There was also limited enthusiasm among the people of the Arab world more broadly for the project. For many Arabs, continued membership of a reformed Ottoman Empire offered greater potential for their interests to be met. Moreover, continued allegiance to the Ottomans meant continued membership of a great Islamic power. As Fromkin observes:

> . . . to the extent that it (the Moslem Middle East) was politically conscious, it was not willing to be ruled by non-Moslems. Behind the lines there were Moslems who were dissatisfied with the Young Turk government, but they proposed to replace it with a different Turkish government.[11]

Jordan was, in effect, a colonial convenience. Britain and France had colluded in the dismemberment of the Ottoman Empire and of historic Syria. Britain had also wanted access to the Mediterranean for Iraqi oil that did not rely on French benevolence. Britain simply took a piece of the Syrian Desert, which by-passed the French protectorate of Syria.[12] Britain's chosen ruler, Abdallah,[13] had been intended as a temporary measure to ensure this strip of territory did not become a problem with Zionist groups in Palestine and the French in Syria. Abdallah turned out to be a more tenacious and clever ruler of his temporary kingdom, if a rather less than scrupulous implementer of British policy.

The Hashemites were, therefore, an imposed, foreign regime[14] and they were seen by much of their population and the populations in other Arab countries in the context of Anglo-French colonial ambitions and the destruction of Arab rule in Syria. Abdallah's commitment to his Transjordanian kingdom was initially viewed with some scepticism by tribesmen who dominated the area. There are suggestions that the tribes of the region were concerned that Abdallah saw his rule in Transjordan as little more than a stepping stone for achieving his ambition of gaining control of Greater Syria.[15] His grandson, King Hussein, noted this concern in his forward to Abdallah's memoirs when he commented:

> King Abdallah Ibn Al-Husayn was particularly grieved by the partitioning of natural Syria, in consequence of the Sykes-Picot Agreement . . . King Abdallah's adversaries, in their relentless and unabashedly self-seeking efforts to abort his efforts towards restoring the God-created and timeless unity and territorial integrity of Syria, tried to denigrate his endeavours by distortive descriptions such as the 'Greater Syria Plan', to connote the idea of aggrandisement.[16]

In the event, however, suspicions of Abdallah's ambitions and the fact that the family did not originate in Transjordan have not proven to be insurmountable problems for the survival of the regime. The tribes of the area have always maintained extensive links with the Hejaz, Syria and Iraq. This meant that, while the Hashemites' Hejazi origins did complicate the family's efforts to develop firm roots in their new kingdom, the local tribes' familiarity with the family has provided a basis on which a cautious and pragmatic relationship has been constructed. Abdallah's effective exploitation of this potential and of the Hashemite family tree, with its claim of direct descent from the Prophet Mohammed, gave his family religious and political legitimacy among the Bedouin.[17]

The relationship with the Palestinians, however, has represented a major challenge to Hashemite rule. From the beginning, the regime's survival was deeply affected by events in Palestine, the creation of Israel and the controversy over the future of the remainder of Mandated Palestine. Palestinians had lived in the area that was to become Jordan under Ottoman and British rule, but the numbers were small and their role was apolitical. They were, to a point, one minority among many. The Israeli War of Independence of 1948, however, led to the arrival of huge numbers of refugees, who tripled Transjordan's population. The outlook of these refugees was dramatically different from that of the tribes, which had traditionally seen the area as their own. Their attitude to the Hashemites was not necessarily conducive to regime survival. Hinnebusch describes these arrivals as 'innately irredentist'.[18] From 1948, the Palestinians maintained their desire to cross from Jordan to Palestine and Israel, either to return to their homes or to strike at the Israeli state. They also tried to involve the Jordanian state in promoting their objectives against Israel. These constituted a constant challenge to Jordanian authority and security. This problem was aggravated when the 1967 debacle saw many thousands more Palestinians, including their political leadership, arrive in Jordan.

The threat from the Palestinians worked to promote a growing mutual dependence between the Hashemites and the tribes. The relationship that developed between the monarchy and its Transjordanian tribal supporters on one hand and the Palestinians on the other hand could be described as persistent ambiguity, especially on the part of the Palestinians. The Palestinians were asked to decide between their identity as Palestinians and their Jordanian nationality. Most tended to persist with their Palestinian identity in the hope of an eventual return home. They therefore resisted pressure to integrate into the new Jordanian state.

Both the Hashemites and their Palestinian citizens found themselves competing for the West Bank, which Jordan held from 1948 until 1967, and this competition has made it difficult over time to separate the fortunes of the Palestinians from those of the Hashemite regime. King Abdallah was assassinated by a Palestinian as part of a plot related to the status of Jerusalem. King Hussein escaped numerous assassination attempts, some of which were directly related to the problems of Palestine. The developments of 1967 to 1970, which culminated in the Black September conflict, represented a major threat to the survival of the regime. The Jordan-Israel peace treaty constitutes another significant threat to the regime as it remains deeply unpopular among Jordanians, be they Islamist or secular or of Transjordanian or Palestinian origin.[19]

Throughout these difficulties, the Jordanian monarchy has regularly been forced to rely on outside support, be it from Britain, the United States or Israel. The monarchy's connections with the West have been reinforced by the fact that the wives of many of the royal family are Western or have had extensive Western links. These factors have highlighted and reinforced perceptions of the foreign nature of the regime, and for much of the population, the Hashemite regime's commitment to Jordanian society remains suspect. It is still seen as a Hejazi import and as maintaining a lingering interest in Iraq and Saudi Arabia. These suspicions were given added life by rumours that Prince Hassan of Jordan was being considered by the Americans as a potential ruler of Iraq following Saddam Hussein's overthrow.[20]

The precarious legitimacy of the Hashemite regime has highlighted the reliance of the ruling family on two ultimate domestic sources of power: the security services (mainly the army) and the tribes. These elements serve more to balance the power of the Palestinian segment of the country than to protect the kingdom from external threat. It is in these two forces that the real basis of regime legitimacy lies, and the regime assiduously cultivates them. Great effort is put into ensuring the loyalty of the army and the tribes. Hussein and Abdallah II attended Sandhurst and regularly appear in military uniform. Equally, the regime's tribal origins permeate the style and approach of Jordan's royal family.

The potential of tribal loyalty to the Hashemite family has been useful in two ways. First, the Hashemites had to develop a state on the area offered to them by the British. This represented a significant challenge because, for most of the people of the Middle East, including the area of Transjordan, national structures, especially those imposed by foreign colonial powers, had little meaning. The tribes of the area had much stronger and deeper ties to the ungoverned area running from Mesopotamia through the Arabian Peninsula to Jordan and Syria. Abdallah I and Hussein did succeed, however, in co-opting the tribes into the nation-building project. Much as ibn Saud was able to develop a lasting alliance with the religious establishment of his new state, so Abdallah and his successors have maintained an alliance of mutual support based on a number of tribal groups.

Second, in return for the provision of benefits to the tribes and for the regime adopting an image that reflects the mores and symbols of tribal society, the tribes provide much of the non-commercial backbone of the new state. They make up the bulk of the Jordanian armed forces and have been prominent in major bureaucratic and security intelligence roles. This alliance is built on a number of core Jordanian groups, but it also reflects the older pattern of borderless Arabia insofar as other tribal groups can be involved if necessary. During the Black September struggle in 1970 between the government and the Palestinians, King Hussein brought in tribes from southern Syria to help. These tribes were happy to fight against the Palestinians (and potentially against the Syrian armed forces) in support of their tribal kinsmen. King Hussein also introduced people from southern Syrian tribes into the Jordanian security and intelligence services.

History of the Jordanian succession process

Jordan is based on a family whose roots lie in the region of Mecca, Medina in the Hejaz in what is now Saudi Arabia. Sharif Hussein, the great-great-grandfather of the current king, Abdallah II, ruled as Emir of Mecca and King of the Arabs and is the last of the Hashemite Sharifs that ruled the Hejaz from 1201 to 1925. Sharif Hussein's son, Abdallah, was installed by the British in 1920 as administrator and then in 1921 as the first King of Transjordan. The country was renamed Jordan in 1949 and Abdallah remained on the throne until his assassination in 1951.

Key among the many challenges to the survival of the Hashemite royal family has been the succession process. Any difficulties in settling the succession within the royal family could produce major problems more widely throughout a political system. It was, therefore, important that the process be robust and flexible. With this in mind, the generational succession of the leaders of Transjordan/Jordan has worked relatively smoothly, especially considering the less than benign circumstances in which the regime has found itself. Abdallah I survived questions about his performance by his British sponsors, the establishment of Israel, the loss of much of Palestine and the arrival of the first major wave of Palestinian refugees.

That he survived must be attributed in part to his own skills, notwithstanding British scepticism, to his careful identification with the tribes of the area and skilful use of their loyalty and, in no small part, to the presence of the British military in significant numbers. The success of the Jordanian succession process also reflects the broad understanding throughout the region of the tribal concept of family rule, despite Jordan's relatively short existence as a state. The hereditary principle has considerable support in Jordan because of its ancient and local lineage. Memories of even the distant past resonate strongly among people of the region and people will discuss the decision of Muawiya (the first Umayyad Caliph who ruled from 661 to 680 AD) to pass the monarchy on to his son as if it had happened only yesterday.[21]

There was never any question that Abdallah would seek to establish an hereditary monarchy in Jordan. He was simply carrying on his family's traditions, albeit in another place. The form that the hereditary process would take is of considerable interest. The principles on which the succession was based changed over time, but they have tended to rest broadly on primogeniture and on the centrality of the king in the political process. Abdallah had come to the throne of Transjordan/Jordan on the basis of the traditional Arab process. Whilst a son of the ruler of Hejaz, he had no particular claim to power. However, the circumstances of the time favoured his ambitions. Three of the four sons of Sherif Hussein secured parts of the old Ottoman Empire through a combination of family connections and personal qualities. By contrast, Talal, Abdallah's successor as King of Jordan (1951 to 1952), was Abdallah's oldest son and it was on this basis that he succeeded to the throne. This was a break with a basic characteristic of the tribal succession tradition and its requirement that the most fit be the leader. Given Talal's known bouts of schizophrenia, he could hardly be described as the fitter son to rule. He could only claim the throne on the basis of seniority. As such, Talal's ascension represents the beginning of the practice of primogeniture as the basis for succession in Jordan. Hussein (ruled from 1952 to 1999) also became King on the basis of seniority or primogeniture, and he maintained that principle in the context of his own succession. On Hussein's death, his oldest son, Abdallah, succeeded to the throne.

Despite this emerging pattern, Hussein appears to have had reservations about primogeniture, perhaps based on the experience of his father's illness. During his rule, Hussein introduced a number of modifications to the classical idea of primogeniture that reflected tribal practices. In 1965, he amended the constitution to allow the throne to go to the oldest of the king's sons or to one of his brothers.

> The Throne of the Hashemite Kingdom of Jordan is hereditary to the dynasty of King Abdullah Ibn Al-Hussein in a direct line through his male heirs as provided hereinafter:
>
> (a) The Royal title shall pass from the holder of the Throne to his eldest son, and to the eldest son of that son and in linear succession by a similar process thereafter. Should the eldest son die before the Throne devolves upon

> him, his eldest son shall inherit the Throne, despite the existence of brothers to the deceased son. The King may, however, select one of his brothers as heir apparent. In this event, title to the Throne shall pass to him from the holder of the Throne. (Article 28(a) amended 1965.)

This enabled him to appoint his younger brother, Hassan, as Crown Prince and heir to the throne, a position Hassan held for 35 years. This was a substantive position involving the crown prince serving as ruler in his brother's frequent absences, the last time being for over six months while the king was in the United States for cancer treatment.

In 1994, Hussein expressed the wish that a system other than primogeniture could be found to determine the succession. In 1998, he established a family council to resolve internal family disputes, including the succession. As his death approached, however, Hussein appears to have changed his mind in favour of primogeniture, culminating in his decision to replace Hassan with his eldest son, Abdallah. At the same time, he made it clear that he wanted Hamza, a younger son, to assume the role of Crown Prince, which is consistent with the 1965 amendment.[22] The council may have been an attempt by Hussein to prevent his succession plans being overturned by Hassan and to ensure the accession of Abdallah on his death. It was not until just before his death that Hussein gave effect to this change when he dismissed Hassan as Crown Prince and appointed Abdallah to the position, which he had held briefly as a child in the early 1960s. This was a reversion to the constitutional arrangement that existed before the 1965 amendment. It was a decision that created widespread comment in Jordan. Some observers expressed sympathy for the deposed Hassan but also welcomed the return to a stricter interpretation of the constitution. It was felt that it was appropriate and consistent with the principle of primogeniture in the constitution, and was therefore returning to its main thrust.

Abdallah II, for his part, has sought to consolidate this simpler pattern. Contrary to his father's wishes and the decision of the family council, he removed his younger half-brother, Hamza, from the post of Crown Prince, presumably with the intention of appointing his oldest son to the position when he comes of age.[23] It would appear that Hussein's (and Abdallah's) motives for these actions had little to do with matters of governance and everything to do with the more fundamental issue of blood and the desire that the king's direct descendants should continue to rule the country. According to Ryan, Hussein may have wanted to ensure that the succession remained within his immediate family line but became concerned that, given the opportunity, Hassan would appoint his own son as Crown Prince and by-pass Hussein's line. Certainly suspicion of Hassan appeared to be in Hussein's mind when he issued his letter of dismissal to his brother:

> We have differed, and we still do, over the succession, and who would succeed you. You were completely opposed to this until the time you would have assumed the Throne and decided who would have been your successor.[24]

The role of wives and mothers

An important feature of Hashemite family politics is the role of the royal wives, widows and mothers. This activity is generally conducted behind closed doors and attempting to understand its details and implications is, according to Ryan, the Jordanian equivalent of 'Kremlinology'.[25] It is nevertheless understood that in Jordan, as in most Arab systems, female members of the ruling family are routinely active in promoting their men's positions in the palace hierarchy. On occasion, when the stakes are high, this politicking can become intense, with the potential to threaten family unity. Media commentary, for example, reports that Queen Noor, Hussein's widow, played a major role in the removal of Prince Hassan from the line of succession and actively promoted the prospects of her son, Hamza.[26] Tensions between Noor and Hassan were also mentioned in Hussein's dismissal letter to Hassan.

There are dangers for the monarchy in the significance attached to the place of the wives in the Jordanian power structure. Abdallah's claim to the throne was originally questioned because his mother was English, a fact which was seen as undermining Abdallah's claim of descent from the Prophet Mohammed. There is also concern about the extent to which the wives are able to exercise power in secret and informal ways. It is understood that Abdallah's wife, Queen Rania, exerts great influence on the king and more broadly within the royal family. She is, however, unpopular among non-Palestinian Jordanians in particular, possibly because of the assumption of her power, but also because of her Palestinian origins. In this context, the family council may come to play an important part in mediating this sort of undercover politics and to assume a major role in the Jordanian political system, much as Cabinet developed under the Westminster system.

I am the state

What Hussein's and Abdallah's actions underline is the centrality of the king's power in the Jordanian system. There was some concern about the new king's ability and maturity. The succession process from Hussein to Abdallah was managed relatively smoothly, however, and Abdallah demonstrated considerable authority and confidence in overriding his father's wishes about the Crown Prince. Such a development is an indication of the importance of the king in Jordanian politics and the lack of real power in the hands of other members of the royal family. No other member of the royal family has access to real power, such as control of armed forces. Over the duration of Hussein's rule, only a small number of family members, including Prince Hassan, served in significant governmental positions. A major exception was Sherif Nasser, an uncle of King Hussein, who exerted great influence in the early years of Hussein's reign. He was allowed to establish an exclusively Bedouin unit, the Royal Guard, to protect the king. He also played a major role in raising the tribes and leading the assault on the PLO during the 1970 crisis.[27]

The potential for a member of the family to challenge the system should not, however, be completely ruled out. There was, for a time, concern that Prince Hassan would attempt to challenge his dumping as Crown Prince. Hassan's political position in Jordan is, however, generally seen as weak. For a while, he tried to improve his standing among the tribes, given their vital role in the political system and their lack of trust in him, and this was seen by some as evidence that he was preparing himself to challenge the new king. By contrast, Prince Hamza is regarded as being widely popular, as preferred by Hussein as his successor and as being very close to the tribes of Jordan. There was speculation that Hamza might serve as a rallying point for those discontented with the direction the regime was taking under the new king,[28] and this may have been a factor in King Abdallah's decision to remove him as crown prince. Abdallah has worked hard to improve his standing among the tribes of Jordan, and his move against his brother may indicate greater confidence on the king's part in his relations with the tribes.

Herb, among others, suggests that the problems associated with primogeniture outweigh its advantages and set Jordan at a disadvantage when compared with the succession practice to be found in the Gulf monarchies.[29] It certainly could be anticipated that the Jordanian monarchy would be likely to run into problems if its ruler were to prove to be incompetent, weak or simply lacking the charisma to inspire loyalty among the tribes. Competence and strength are highly prized attributes of leaders in tribal society, and were the tribes to detect weakness in the king, they could become susceptible to influence by his opponents.

The Hashemites have, however, already survived serious problems with the succession process. The first challenge was the assassination of the kingdom's founder, Abdallah. Salibi comments in reference to Abdallah's assassination that it was not so surprising that Abdallah should have been assassinated, but that his replacement – first by his son Talal and then by his grandson Hussein – should have been as orderly and constitutional as it turned out to be.[30] The second challenge confronting the Hashemite monarchy was the problem of the unfit monarch (i.e. the current king's grandfather, Talal). This again was dealt with effectively, albeit not without a degree of political unrest and family manoeuvring.[31] The family also had to address potential regime disloyalty at the time of King Hussein's death, and once more the family appears to have handled the problem successfully. With the exception of some frank public comments by Prince Hassan, the appearance of family unity has been maintained.

Contrary to Herb's suggestion above, the secret to this apparently effective formula may lie in the Jordanian monarchs' use of the broader political elite while by-passing the family. While the members of the royal family play little direct part in the exercise of power in the Jordanian political system, the king is not alone at the top. Susser suggests that the king is supported by a formidable coalition of forces drawn from the civilian and military elite. These are the king's men, who have motives of self-interest in supporting the existing regime. In addition, the king can rely on the loyalty of the armed forces and the internal security establishment and the support of foreign powers which see Jordan as playing a useful pro-Western role in the region.[32]

This is demonstrated in graphic form by Bank and Schlumberger in their depiction of the concentric rings of power in the Jordanian system. The central ring comprises military, security and intelligence heads, the head of the Royal Court, the Prime Minister, the Speaker of the Senate and a number of Royal Advisers (see Appendix 5).[33] None of the members of the royal family belongs to this central circle. Nevertheless, the loyalty of this group is possibly as dependable as the loyalty to be gained from a family group. No member of this elite can aspire to the top job and his position and power is always subject to the good will of the king. In turn, however, the king needs to be able to inspire his inner circle to a high degree of loyalty. There has been some concern that the current king's lack of his father's charm and experience will complicate his efforts to emerge from his father's shadow. Attempts by Abdallah to appear tough and in control run the risk of instead making him look aggressive and vulnerable. Without such soft power, Abdallah is forced to rely more on self-interest as the driving force of his inner circle's loyalty. Such a basis could be tested, however, should any of the main pillars of the regime's strength, regime's unity or tribal and army support start to weaken or any of Jordan's significant external allies withdraw their support. This could happen because of acute economic difficulties, deep social problems or yet another calamity in the Israel-Palestine issue. In such a context, another member of the family with a plausible claim might consider stepping forward.

Jordan and the constitution

Law and the constitution have played a prominent role since the creation of Transjordan. In 1928, an organic law, which set broad parameters for the new state, including the establishment of a parliament and the adoption of elections, was adopted. Given that the regime's power resided in traditional structures, the tribes and the army, the legal framework was largely intended to add legitimacy and gravitas to the new state. Over time, however, the constitutional framework began to assume a wider political role of contributing to the regime's efforts to deal with the problem of the Palestinians. It became the expression of the deal between the regime and the new arrivals, setting out restricted options for Palestinian involvement in Jordanian life, but also helping to promote Palestinian support for the monarchy.

As with other Arab countries, the role of the law and the promotion of the constitution is a top–down process. People outside the political elite often have a limited concept of a constitution, especially as something that might further their personal interests or their individual rights. Some Jordanians argue that people have no need for a constitution. They instinctively know the rules and stay within them. Others suggest that the general population would see no role whatsoever for the constitution in royal family matters such as succession, which is something that only the royal family could decide. The situation is different for some of the elements of the political elite, who might correspond with Bank and Schlumberger's outer ring of elite power. For these people (i.e. religious leaders, tribal chiefs, bureaucrats and academics), the constitution potentially provides a structure upon which they can base their challenges or resistance to regime policies, if not to the regime itself.

The law also has an increasing role to play in the context of the conduct of civil society. Commercial and criminal law tends to be respected and the parliament's role in the development of that law is honoured in general. The royal family has not, for example, sought to impose its public opposition to the practice of honour killings on a reluctant parliament. Instead, it has sought to convince the parliament that a replacement of the existing code would be appropriate.[34] It is when one examines the royal family's attitude to the constitution's applicability to itself that the weaknesses in the regime's attitude become clear. It is generally accepted as inconceivable that a member of the royal family could be subjected to legal action. Such an idea would be inconsistent with the special place in society that the royal family sees for itself.

Morocco: a monarchy with tradition

Morocco is, in Herb's terms, another non-dynastic monarchy where succession is based on primogeniture. Morocco's monarchy has many similarities to the Jordanian example. The Alawi family on which it is based traces its bloodline directly to the Prophet Mohammed. Whereas the Hashemites claim descent from the grandfather of Mohammed, the Alawi trace their origins to Ali, the cousin and son-in-law of the Prophet from whom the Shi`a branch of Islam derives. This claim of descent from the Prophet is routinely exploited to consolidate regime legitimacy and has been widely accepted throughout Moroccan society. The king is formally and constitutionally (Article 19) described as Commander of the Faithful (*Emir Al Mumaneen*), a term that adds to the regime's legitimacy through its links to the early caliphs in Islam.

Like Jordan, Morocco endured a period of colonial domination, although the Alawi owe nothing to French rule, having been in Morocco since the thirteenth century. Also like the Hashemites, the Moroccan ruling family has had to endure difficult times in the post-independence period, with numerous assassination attempts directed at the king. Both dynasties went through a succession process at the end of the 1990s after long periods of rule by King Hassan II in Morocco and King Hussein in Jordan. The domestic situations of the two monarchies also bear some resemblances, with Morocco having to deal with a significant Berber minority in its midst. This minority was exploited by the monarchy at one stage as a device to control the Arab majority but, under Hassan, the present king's father, a more subtle attempt at co-option was pursued. For example, senior members of the royal family have married Berber women. King Hassan established a pattern of annual levees where he would meet the leaders of the Berber tribes and listen to their problems and requests. That policy has been continued under his son, Mohammed.

Also like the Jordanian example, the Moroccan constitution does not forbid the involvement of royal family members in significant political or governmental positions. However, the practice has been for family members to not occupy key positions of power in Morocco. Zerhouni describes the core elite of the Moroccan political system as comprising a mix of individuals and organizations, such as the army, business groups and religious groups. This suggests that, as in Jordan, this elite is held together, at least in part, by economic self-interest.[35]

Article 20 of the Moroccan constitution specifies agnatic primogeniture as the process governing royal succession. It does, however, provide some flexibility should a monarch wish to deviate from the procedure:

> The Moroccan Crown and the constitutional rights thereof shall be hereditary and handed down, from father to son, to descendants in direct male line and by order of primogeniture among the offspring of His Majesty King Hassan II, unless the King should, during his lifetime, designate a successor among his sons apart from the eldest one. In case of failing descendants in direct male line, the right of succession to the Throne shall, under the same conditions, be invested in the closest male in the collateral consanguinity.

In practice, however, Moroccan monarchs since independence from France have pursued the classical agnatic primogeniture approach. The king at the time of independence was Mohammed V. He was succeeded by Hassan, his oldest son, and the current king, Mohammed, is the oldest son of Hassan. While a decision has not been made public, it is highly likely that the intention is that Mohammed's oldest child and only son, Crown Prince Moulay Hassan, will also succeed to the throne.

The success of the system practiced in Jordan and Morocco, both in terms of ensuring the succession of the oldest son of the king and in preserving the monarchy as an institution, depends on a range of factors. Both regimes have survived significant challenges and have displayed considerable political skills, but Herb, for example, would suggest that this has reflected a considerable degree of luck. He points out that had one of the many assassination attempts on King Hussein or King Hassan been successful, the regime may not have been able to manage the unrest and competition that the event might have released. Potential weaknesses of the succession process might have been exposed.[36]

The Gulf monarchies: responding to change

In contrast to the practice of primogeniture, the second form of monarchy in the Arab region is built on a broader family-based system of dynastic succession in which many, if not all, the members of the ruling family are directly involved in promoting their family's rule. These are monarchies whose demise was frequently predicted in the second half of the twentieth century. This was, in part, because of their pre-modern tribal structures and the huge challenges facing them from population growth, economic and social adjustment, domestic unrest and the external environment. Despite these forecasts, these regimes have shown considerable resilience and adaptability. This second part of the chapter, therefore, addresses, to the extent possible as a group, the various tribal monarchies of the

Arabian Peninsula whose succession practices are based on the principle of family rule or family-based succession (Herb's dynastic monarchies).[37] 'Family rule' means the process whereby succession is in practice not exclusively the preserve of the ruler, although a particularly respected ruler may exert considerable influence on the outcome. Succession is instead decided through a process of consultation among senior royal family members, which is a system with close parallels to traditional tribal succession practices. The regime also adheres to the practice of intimately involving royal family members in the day-to-day running of the state as government ministers and heads of government departments and in senior positions in the armed forces.

Before turning to the similarities, it is important to acknowledge the significant areas where the countries of the Arabian Peninsula differ. These are states that have been built on tribal traditions. They have been established either through force, as in the case of ibn Saud's unification of much of the Arabian Peninsula, through gradual encroachment, as with the Al Sabah of Kuwait, or on the basis of a pragmatic and self-interested decision that a unified state was in the ruling families' best interests, as in the United Arab Emirates. In part reflecting these different historical experiences, these monarchies display some diversity in the outward appearance of their political systems. At the constitutional level, the states are effectively monarchies, but different terms are used throughout the region to describe their governmental system.

Constitutionally, the United Arab Emirates is not part of this group of Gulf monarchies. It is a federal republic, presided over by a president and with a clear division of powers between the federal and the emirates' governments. The reality, however, is that power lies squarely in the hands of the individual emirates' royal families, especially those of Abu Dhabi and Dubai. As such, the United Arab Emirates' structure could be described as a republican monarchy and it could be compared to a tribal confederation where the paramount sheikh comes from one tribe or family but where other sheikhs retain considerable independence and status.

While most of the states of the Arabian Peninsula remain closely wedded to the traditional model of succession, there are other significant differences among the Gulf monarchies that shape their political systems and influence the ways in which the succession process is handled. Kuwait, for example, has a powerful merchant class, which, together with some Islamists and liberals, forms an important part of what might loosely be termed the Arab world's only 'loyal opposition'. Without attempting to undermine the overall dominance of the ruling family, this opposition has persistently promoted certain powers for the parliament. The death of the emir in early 2006 demonstrated the degree of the influence, if not power, of the parliament. At that time, members of the parliament, in particular the Speaker, demanded that the heir apparent, who was regarded as infirm and incapable of performing the job of Emir, be moved aside in favour of another member of the royal family. Such a development is inconceivable in the other countries of the Arabian Peninsula, even though many people in those countries look upon Kuwait with some admiration as a political trailblazer. None has a substantive parliamentary framework in which critics of a regime or its policies might be heard. The regional political culture, moreover, is such that political dissent is most unlikely to be manifested in public.

Stepping over these formal differences, it is clear that the countries of the region share many common and unifying attributes, such as the widespread family involvement in the running of their countries and a close connection to a tribal and traditional life. These similarities are apparent when the issue of succession is examined. The extent of these similarities makes it possible to draw certain conclusions about the succession processes in these countries.

Governance in the Gulf states is highly personal and the rulers of the Gulf monarchies represent something of a club, which has its formal manifestation in Heads of State meetings of the Gulf Cooperation Council. The informal manifestations of this phenomenon are, however, more significant. For example, in 1995, the current ruler of Qatar, Hamad bin Khalifa Al Thani, overthrew his father, Khalifa. The coup was reluctantly accepted by the other states of the region, in part because it was clear that the Al Thani family had approved Khalifa's removal. Nevertheless, the various rulers made clear their discomfort with what had happened. The idea that one of their group could be replaced in such as way would have been discomforting to them. Khalifa was given sanctuary in Abu Dhabi. It was made clear that the other states might insist on his reinstatement should the new regime adopt policies that were not broadly consistent with those of the rest of the region. Similarly, the ruler of Abu Dhabi has not hesitated to intervene in the affairs of other Emirates in the United Arab Emirates federation in support of rulers' wishes. In the family struggles at the time of federation of the United Arab Emirates, an arm of the ruling family of the emirate of Ras Al Khaimah that lost the struggle for power was given refuge in Abu Dhabi. A more recent power struggle in Ras Al Khaimah saw the losing element of the family being given sanctuary in Oman.

Among the most significant characteristics of the countries of the Arabian Peninsula are their strong links to their tribal past. Not all the people of the area have nomadic origins. In much of Yemen, Oman and small parts of the United Arab Emirates the populations have been sedentary for some time. Nevertheless, family and tribal allegiances are generally important and, significantly, very close to the experiences of many people. When working in the United Arab Emirates in the 1990s, this writer encountered students who had themselves or whose older brothers or sisters had been born into a semi-nomadic life. As Sheikh Zayed of the United Arab Emirates was approaching the end of his life, rumours spread on several occasions that he had died. These rumours were often accompanied by reports that people were gathering around their particular tribe or family patron in case unrest were to break out as a result of the President's death.

The growing population, rapid urbanisation and the greater access to the outside world has opened a gap between the ideal of tribal life and the reality of daily existence. Nevertheless, the images and ethos of tribalism maintain a strong influence over the thinking and practices of people of the area. The influence is to be seen in the governing structures established by the countries of the region. All pay considerable attention to ensuring that their tribal supporters are generally quiescent and content with the situation. This involves programmes to encourage the tribes to adopt sedentary lives in selected areas. Housing, education and other subsidies are provided. At the same time, the governments have had to be tolerant of a considerable degree of cross-border movement by the tribes, whose traditional lands and trade routes have often been divided by modern state boundaries. Abu Dhabi policemen and officials, for example, live in Oman and commute to work in the emirate without reference to border posts and other formalities. Most countries of the region, have established the consultative council (*majlis al shura*), which in name and in practice has some of the characteristics of the tribal practice. The United Arab Emirates has created a Federal National Council, which bears the tribal imprint in many respects. Kuwait has the National Assembly, which has substantive powers:

> No law may be promulgated unless it has been passed by the National Assembly and sanctioned by the Emir. (Article 79)
>
> Immediately upon its formation, every Cabinet presents its program to the National Assembly. The Assembly may make comments with regard to such a program. (Article 98)
>
> Every Minister is responsible to the National Assembly for the affairs of his ministry. If the Assembly passes a vote of no confidence against a Minister, he is considered to have resigned his office as from the date of the vote of no confidence and shall immediately submit his formal resignation. (Article 101)

Succession in the Gulf monarchies

Like the monarchies of Jordan and Morocco, the Arabian sheikhdoms were influenced by outsiders, especially Britain, in their formative years. As the colonial power, the British tended to leave existing ruling structures largely in place and to work through those structures. This is, of course, not to suggest that the British did not become directly involved in leadership struggles from time to time in those countries. For example, the British were involved in 1966, when the Al Nahayan family replaced the ruler of Abu Dhabi, Sheikh Shakbut, with his younger brother, Sheikh Zayed.[38] The result of this arrangement has been, however, that some of the ruling families of the political entities of the Arabian Peninsula can claim long periods of rule in their territories.

The system relies on family councils deciding who should be ruler with the wider families and the population at large accepting that decision. For much of their existence as identifiable units, these family-based succession systems have worked relatively well, containing within them the capacity for flexibility and for taking hard political decisions. In Abu Dhabi, the removal of Sheikh Shakbut was generally accepted by the family. Sons (who were not necessarily the oldest) replaced their fathers in Oman and Bahrain and twice in Qatar, and in all cases, the decision to make the change was reached by the family council and with consensus among the key members of the family. In Dubai, the deaths in 1990 of Sheikh Rashid, one of the founders of the United Arab Emirates, and his successor, Sheikh Maktoum, in 2006, were handled smoothly by the family through a sharing of responsibility and opportunity amongst the sons. In 2004, Sheikh Zayed of Abu Dhabi died, and again his sons were able to resolve what appears to have been some very difficult rivalries and to endorse the late ruler's choice of successor.

Public solidarity and mutual support are vital to the success of the system. There have, however, been some occasions when this solidarity has been lacking. The central figure in the history of modern Kuwait is Sheikh Mubarak al-Sabah al Sabah, who reigned from 1896 to 1915. Mubarak was convinced that the Ottomans planned to annex Kuwait and was dissatisfied with the way the ruler, a brother, was responding to the danger. Mubarak took a leaf out of the Ottomans' book and overthrew and then murdered the emir, did away with another brother and installed himself as ruler. He has come to be known as 'Mubarak the Great' to later generations of Kuwaitis. In the early 1960s, the Saudi Prince Talal broke with the family and issued a series of public calls for a democratic system for the country.[39] In June 2003, the Ruler of Ras Al Khaimah replaced his Crown Prince, his oldest son, Sheikh Khaled, who had been in the position since 1966, with a younger son, Sheikh Saud. The decision provoked an unusual public airing of the dispute, with Khaled disputing his father's right to make the change because he had not consulted the family council and calling on rulers of other emirates and neighbouring countries to help negotiate a resolution. The dispute provoked a surprising degree of public protest, to the extent that the federal government felt obliged to despatch tanks to the emirate to restore order. In Saudi Arabia, the Al Saud family encountered great difficulty dealing with internal tensions following the assassination of King Feisal in 1975. Disputes between different branches within the family broke out in public over issues as fundamental as the handling of opposition religious groups and the control of military forces by the different princes, exposing the serious potential divisions within the family.[40]

In principle, a ruler chosen under the family-based system remains ruler for life. This highlights the problem that the family-based system of rule is no better guarantee that the most fit leader will become king than those based on primogeniture. On a number of occasions since independence, states of the Gulf have had to deal with the problem of an unfit ruler and there have been instances where the system might have broken down in the face of family inability to find a solution. Among the more serious of these was the succession in Saudi Arabia from King Saud to his brother Feisal in 1964. Saud was deposed by the family, but not without the outbreak of acute family tension. The last ten years of the reign of King Fahd of Saudi Arabia were also a period of near crisis. This was a time of great domestic and international pressure on the Saudi state, but the king was incapacitated by a stroke in 1995 and decision making in the country was greatly impeded. Intense rivalry between the regent, Crown Prince Abdallah, and some of his half-brothers meant that no effective resolution of the king's inability to rule could be reached. Speaking of this period, Doran argued that the question of the succession affected the entire Saudi government process and neither Abdallah, nor his main rival, Prince Nayef, was powerful enough to bring the issue to a head.[41] The family attempted to work around the king and to govern through a sort of group leadership, but major decisions were regularly deferred through lack of consensus. On Fahd's death, this rivalry was put aside and Abdallah became King, perhaps deferring the hard decisions on succession to the next generation.

The family-based system was again severely tested by the Kuwait succession crisis in early 2006, when the two wings of the ruling Al Sabah family could not agree on how to deal with the incapacity of the crown prince to accede to the throne. The two groups operate on the basis of an unwritten agreement, whereby the position of Emir alternates between them. A solution was not reached until the Speaker of the Kuwaiti Parliament used his office and relevant provisions of the constitution to intervene and force the issue. The competing branches had to come to an agreement or face the choice of the decision being made for them by non-family members.[42]

Another challenge to the family-based system could emerge in Oman. There, Sultan Qaboos has refused to nominate a successor, a decision that may reflect his own decision to overthrow his father in 1970. Instead the Omani Basic Law requires the meeting of a Ruling Family Council comprising descendants of Said bin Sultan who ruled from 1806 to 1856 (Articles 5 and 6(1)) to determine the succession. As Qaboos has no children, the constitutional arrangement makes a degree of sense. It certainly reflects the traditional tribal approach to succession. The Basic Law contains, however, a measure which has the potential to unsettle relations within the ruling family. According to Article 6(2):

> If the Ruling Family Council does not agree upon a successor, the Defence Council shall confirm the appointment of the person designated by the Sultan in his letter to the Family Council.

This requirement that the Sultan lodge a letter with the Defence Council contains great potential for dispute. Qaboos is reported to have nominated two possible choices for his successor and to have hidden copies of the recommendations in different locations throughout the country. The nature of Qaboos's recommendations may have a disruptive effect, should one or both of those listed chose to insist that he was the sultan's chosen successor or should fraudulent letters begin to appear. In addition, there are rumours in the area that Qaboos has an illegitimate son by an Emirati woman, and that the son will be presented in due course. Such a development has potential to challenge the formal constitutional arrangements.

A major threat to regime solidarity is developing in all the countries of the Gulf with the growing numbers of the ruling families. Cordesman estimates that by 2020 there could be more than 20,000 members of the Saudi royal family, all of whom will be entitled to demand material benefits and political influence.[43] Putting aside the budgetary implications, which are considerable, this will impose great pressures on the Saudi system with princes who cannot be accommodated to the extent that they might expect becoming disillusioned with the system. The other countries of the region are facing, in relative terms, the same problem.

It is significant that even among these established family-based mechanisms, there are indications that the primogeniture-based approach has some appeal. When the Saudi kingdom was first created, the founding king, Abd Al-Aziz, sought to establish a succession process based on primogeniture. In 1933 he secured family support for his decision to appoint his oldest son as heir apparent rather than Feisal, who was recognised as more competent. It is of interest that the Wahhabi movement supported Abd Al-Aziz in this respect,[44] and the arrangement survived until the replacement of King Saud by King Feisal in 1964.[45] Such an approach, however, was not consistent with traditional tribal and Islamic processes, and pressure from those groups prevented the king from establishing the mechanism as a principle of the dynasty. In practice, however, a process of succession across the generation of Abd Al-Aziz's sons has prevailed in Saudi Arabia. Succession has passed from brother to brother roughly on the basis of age, a practice that was made official through a public announcement by the family in 1992 of the agreed sequence of succession. This would have been an important basis upon which Abdallah's rivals accepted his succession to the throne in 2005.[46]

Among the big debates in the modern Saudi context, however, is whose son is to succeed King Abdallah and on what basis will he be chosen. Abdallah appears to hope that his oldest son will succeed, if not immediately, then the next time the throne becomes vacant. Those interested in the outcome are attempting to position themselves or their sons to exploit the change when Abdallah dies. In the United Arab Emirates, Sheikh Zayed publicly selected his oldest son to succeed him. That selection was honoured despite considerable manoeuvring by the other contenders among Zayed's sons and wives. Sheikh Zayed's colleague in Dubai, Sheikh Rashid, was succeeded by his oldest son, Maktoum, although this did not continue after Maktoum's death, with his brother, Mohammed, taking over. Bahrain has primogeniture formally written into its constitution (Article 1(b)). Taken together, this suggests that the fundamental issue of blood and an innate desire that a ruler's direct descendants should continue to rule his country are strong factors in the thinking of rulers on the Arabian Peninsula.

Wives and mothers in the Gulf monarchies

As is the case in Jordan, the direct or indirect involvement of mothers and wives in the ambitions of members of the royal families is an issue in the Gulf states. Indeed, it has the potential to cause significant problems because it is not unusual for rulers to have more than one wife, many of whom represent important families or tribes in the various countries. The founder of Saudi Arabia, Abd Al-Aziz ibn Saud, took these Hapsburg dynastic practices to new heights by marrying as many as 22 women from different tribes around the country and fathering nearly a 100 children.

The maternal line represents one of the great potential schisms in the dynastic monarchies. The sons of Gulf rulers have often formed alliances based on their mothers and have cooperated to promote their mutual interests, if necessary, at the expense of sons of other mothers. Kechichian highlights this feature in the Saudi context when he notes:

> As important as seniority, the social standing of mothers and their tribal connections often determine the prominence of individual princes. In general terms, sons with mothers from prominent families, such as the Jiluwi or Sudayri, or important tribes, such as the Shammar, have stronger political credentials.[47]

The most notable example of this phenomenon is the Sudayri Seven in Saudi Arabia, the sons of Hassa bint Ahmed Al Sudayri. Their practice of working cooperatively to further their collective interests has posed the main challenge to King Abdallah and his plans for the succession. The mothers and wives are not passive foci of loyalty in this. As was noted above in the context of Jordanian palace intrigues, the activities of royal wives of the monarchies of the Arabian Peninsula tend to be conducted behind closed doors. Some royal wives are never even referred to in public. Others have public roles that are tightly constrained. Despite this isolation of the wives from the political process, they have to capacity to exercise considerable influence. The United Arab Emirates's succession process, for example, was seriously complicated by Sheikh Zayed's wives. It reached the point where judgements about who was most suited to succeed Zayed often became clouded by arguments about which of his wives was more powerful and therefore better equipped to promote her favoured son. Some of these problems may be moderating as the older, founding generations depart the scene and are replaced by younger men with different, more cosmopolitan and educated outlooks. Among the changes is the growing tendency for the new Gulf leaders to have only one wife. The effect of these changes will be to limit, but not eliminate, the degree of infighting among the ruler's sons.

Nelson describes the role of Sheikha Hussah bint al Murri, the wife of the leader of Dubai at the time of independence. The Sheikha, who used to hold her own public *majlis* for men:

> (P)layed a leading part in a political struggle that led to civil war, and the subsequent expulsion of the reformist party. On the other hand, she restored her husband's family fortunes by property development, trade, and, one gathers, that profitable but risky enterprise of Dubai, smuggling with Persia and India.[48]

This is an exceptional example, and most of the activity of the female members of the ruling families takes place out of the public view. Despite the impact of the modern world, the ability of the new generation's wives to play public roles is still restricted and actions by the wife of a member of a royal family that challenge traditional practices carry risks for her husband. The public support for women's rights espoused by the wife of the deposed Crown Prince of Ras Al Khaimah is given as one reason for the family agreeing to his removal. The Ruler of Qatar's wife is particularly active in her public activities and gives the impression of a person with considerable power. According to reports, however, her close involvement with Qatar's preparations for the Asian Games in December 2006, provoked great resentment among relevant ministers and heads of ministries, most of whom are members of the royal family.

Constitutional bases

There are many similarities between the position of the constitution in the family-based monarchies and those in Jordan, Morocco and Bahrain, especially in the attitudes of the ruling elites in both countries to their fundamental documents. A common view is that the constitution and the law do not apply to members of the ruling group. It is, in most of the countries, impossible to sue a member of the ruling family in the courts.[49] Members of the ruling elite make arbitrary decisions and expect their decisions to be carried out regardless of the legal (or financial) position. There is no real legislative or constitutional basis for this situation, simply a clear understanding in society that the law does not apply to the royal family and that the royal family must be obeyed. A formal expression of this attitude can be seen in Article 1(c) of the Bahraini constitution, which states:

> All provisions governing inheritance are regulated by a special Royal Decree that will have a constitutional character, and which can only be amended under the provisions of Article 120 of the Constitution.

The idea that a royal decree should have constitutional effect or force underlines how the instrument is regarded as subordinate to the will of the ruler.

As discussed in Chapter 5, Saudi Arabia's constitution is the Quran and the *Sunna*, and the country's Basic Law is a subordinate or supplementary document. The Basic Law does, however, spell out some of the key issues of governance, including the succession mechanism, which, it would appear, the family intends should have constitutional status. Al-Fahad provides an interesting perspective of the Basic Law, which he describes as:

> . . . unabashedly honest, promoting no rights that will not be protected, promising no elections, and not conceding the principle of accountable governance in any direct way. Indeed, the Saudi Basic Law signifies, if anything, a qualified rejection of many of the standard notions of constitutionalism in terms of rights and freedoms, while ratifying a powerful executive circumscribed only by historical practices and Islamic ideas of governance.[50]

In the other states of the area, the constitutions enjoy more conventional status. With the notable exception of Kuwait, however, none of these constitutions could be said to possess greater substantive power than the Saudi Basic Law and may lack the blunt honesty to which Al-Fahad refers.

The constitutions of these countries reflect, to a great extent, their tribal and Islamic origins. The Saudi Basic Law, for example, in its treatment of succession, decrees in Article 5(b) that future rulers of the country shall be drawn from the ibn Saud family, but also that the most upright among them shall become King. Determining who is most fit or upright is, of course, a highly subjective and political judgement and, in practice, has been resolved by resorting to seniority. This is in part a compromise designed to minimise family infighting. It is also consistent, however, with the Arabs' respect for seniority and the prominent status given to older people.[51] The creation of the Allegiance Committee in October 2006, was ostensibly intended to regularise the Saudi succession process, and it reflects some of these considerations. A royal decree announced the establishment of the Allegiance Committee, which, according to Article 1, comprises:

1) Sons of King Abd Al-Aziz Al-Saud, the founder of the Kingdom of Saudi Arabia;
2) Grandsons of King Abd Al-Aziz whose fathers are deceased, incapacitated (as determined by a medical report) or otherwise unwilling to assume the throne. Members appointed by the King must be capable and known for their integrity.
3) A son of the King and a son of the Crown Prince, both to be appointed by the King. They should be capable and known for their integrity. If a vacancy arises on the Allegiance Committee, the King will appoint a new member in accordance with Sections 2 and 3 of this Article.

The Committee's establishment has probably created a situation whereby the influence of the Sudayiri Seven will be countered by the formal incorporation of some of the less powerful or involved descendants of ibn Saud into the selection process. One observer suggests the measure was specifically directed at Prince Nayef, one of the Sudayiri Seven.[52] The Committee structure also underscores the ambivalent attitude of the royal family to the basis on which succession should proceed. While acknowledging the provisions of the Basic Law, the Committee introduces a process of election into the procedure. Unlike the Basic Law, however, the Allegiance Committee also gives some recognition to the past practice of basing succession on seniority:

> The Allegiance Committee will be chaired by the eldest son of King Abd Al-Aziz, with the second oldest brother as his deputy. In case neither is available, it will be chaired by the eldest grandson of King Abd Al-Aziz. (Article 15)

The other Gulf states emphasise the hereditary nature of their rule but have adopted different paths to that goal. Kuwait's constitution describes the country as an hereditary emirate with succession to the leadership limited to the descendants of Mubarak the Great (Article 4(1)). Furthermore, the emir is required to declare his heir apparent within a year of his accession (Article 4(2)). Oman describes itself as an hereditary sultanate based on the male descendants of Sayyed Turki bin Said bin Sultan and gives a Royal Family Council responsibility for determining the succession. Qatar's provisions require the successor to be a male from the family, introducing primogeniture with the requirement that the successor be one of the ruler's sons (Article 8).

In determining what might be driving Gulf leaders in the development of their constitutions, it is important to note that the constitutions are all based on edicts imposed from above. Even the Qatari constitution, which was ostensibly introduced to liberalise the Qatari political and social systems and which was praised in the West as a great step towards democracy, was presented to the citizenry by the Emir without public debate. There was no suggestion that proposals for change might be entertained. The constitution has numerous democratic features and purports to promote the participation of Qatari citizens in the political life of the country. To that end, it was subject to a plebiscite in 2003. The constitution also, however, contains provisions, such as the following, that limit the democracy on offer:

> Personal freedom shall be guaranteed and no person may be arrested, detained, searched, neither may his freedom of residence and mobility be restricted save under the provisions of the law; (Article 36)

As Herb notes, the constitution was not the result of public pressure, but was an indication of the emir's desire to strengthen his control and to limit the potential for future challenges. The ruler's actions are not likely to weaken his or his family's dominant position for the foreseeable future.[53] The rulers of these countries have instead maintained effective control over the contents and direction of their constitutions. A reading of these constitutions and a monitoring of the actions of the regimes themselves reinforce the idea that the constitutions all have one overriding objective: regime survival and consolidation. The rulers are using their constitutions to help take their regimes from informal, personal structures to governmental systems that are capable of dealing with the increasingly complex environment in which they find themselves. The Gulf regimes' objectives appear to involve limiting the involvement of their populations in the political life of their countries, keeping external criticism at bay and anticipating the growth of any demands for participation or transparency. This is done, in part, by ensuring that family members occupy the key political, economic and commercial posts in their countries. They also seek to create an atmosphere in which criticism of the government is regarded as un-Islamic, because challenging a ruler is widely regarded as unacceptable, disloyal and pointless and potentially a sin under Islam. This approach is most apparent in the Saudi Basic Law, which states in Article 6 that:

> Citizens are to pay allegiance to the King in accordance with the holy Quran and the tradition of the Prophet, in submission and obedience, in times of ease and difficulty, fortune and adversity.

The secret of their success

Family-based succession practices appear to have contributed greatly to the ability of the Gulf monarchies to maintain stability (although the ability to distribute some of the proceeds of the oil sector may also have helped). The philosophy and the structure of these regimes are clearly authoritarian and, for a range of reasons, the governments are becoming increasingly remote from their populations. Some analysts argue that the regimes of the Gulf are little better than parodies of the traditional Arab ruling system.[54] Unlike traditional tribal societies, which relied to a large degree on consultation and consensus, however, the monarchies of the Arabian Peninsula have adapted many modern features to the structure of their regimes. These include the pervasiveness of the secret police (*mukhabarat*), the resort to censorship and extensive social regulation, the arbitrary nature of the law and the ruling families' exemption from the reach of the law, often broadly defined to include individuals who are remote from power, such as clients of members of the ruling families.

Nevertheless, the family-based monarchies retain a considerable degree of affinity to their origins and remain understandable or familiar to the average citizen and accessible to important elements of society. A number of the rulers of the countries of the Gulf were born in times when traditional ways were still a part of their lives. Even young Emiratis, for example, may have spent significant parts of their lives in the traditional way. Many of these people still expect certain aspects of the old ways to apply, such as access to a tribal sheikh's or ruler's *majlis*. These expectations continue to bind ruled and ruler alike. Right to the end of his life, Sheikh Zayed of the United Arab Emirates held regular *majlis* for the population. On those occasions, despite the growing numbers involved and the increased complexity of issues considered, Zayed behaved in the traditional way. Emirati citizens would regularly ask him direct if he would help them in their dealings with government or neighbours. Zayed's responses tended to be arbitrary, with little concern for existing law or for possible precedent, but with attention to matters of tribal balance and loyalty as well as a sense of justice or fairness for the individual concerned.

In Saudi Arabia, the practice of holding the traditional *majlis* was inevitably affected by the murder of King Feisal in 1975. Security became a concern and with that, the creation of a barrier between the ruler and the ruled was formed. Nevertheless, some of the principles of the practice linger. Long notes the continued importance of consultation among those whose opinions count. From the consultation is derived the idea of consensus (*ijma*), to which all involved in the consultation are bound. This does not equate to the Western idea of democracy, but this consultative form of government, combined with the centrality of the Quran in the constitutional structure, does impose significant limits on a ruler's power.[55]

Unlike the situation in Jordan and Morocco, the elite of the Gulf states is largely confined to the royal families. There are, of course, many wealthy families outside the royal families, especially in Kuwait, but they lack power and are dependent on the goodwill of the ruling family. One person interviewed for this research explained how his grandfather had been a major commercial force in Qatar but had been inadvertently drawn into a regime succession struggle in the 1960s. The grandfather found himself on the side of the branch of the family that initially gained the throne but over time lost power to another branch. The grandfather's mistake was not forgotten or forgiven and the family was subjected to extensive discrimination, which continues to today.

Another important element in the success of Gulf regimes is that members of the region's royal families see personal benefits in the maintenance of the system and contribute directly to its survival. As noted above, princes and sheikhs regularly occupy vital positions in their countries' political, commercial and social structures. As such, they might not rise to be King but they, nonetheless, often have important roles to play in policy development and stand to gain considerable material benefits. This system, which seeks to draw in members of the ruling family to consolidate their loyalty, is more in line with Arab tradition. An implication that might be drawn from this idea is that the power networks based on family relationships are more reliable and durable than those based simply on self-interest, as in Jordan or Morocco. There is less reliance by the regime on people outside the family and loyalty is more diffusely directed at the family as a whole than at one individual, the king.

It is also possible that the family-based system continues to survive because the states of the Arabian Peninsula, while not confronting the fundamental challenge posed by the role of Israel in the lives of Jordanians, still face considerable challenges on the domestic and external fronts. There is the long-standing perception of Iran as the regional hegemon and a threat to their security. There are also the concerns directly posed by Iraq to Kuwait and Saudi Arabia and to the other littoral states to lesser extent. The location of these states in the centre of the Middle East's oil sector guarantees that they will be the focus of Western and others' strategic concerns. Their place on the front line of the Arab-Persian confrontation also ensures extensive support for their stability and, therefore, for the survival of the different regimes.

A final factor behind the survival of the family-based monarchies is, as suggested above, that the states of the Arabian Peninsula are able to exploit the great wealth they have secured from their oil resources to buy the loyalty of their populations. The size of the wealth is out of all proportion to the wealth to which people of the region were historically accustomed, but the practice of distributing largess to secure loyalty is not unusual. Tribal sheikhs have traditionally maintained the loyalty of their followers by leading the tribes on raids for booty or by distributing wealth that had been secured more peacefully around their tribes. Gause suggests that it is a combination of the strategic importance and the great wealth of the countries of the Arabian Peninsula rather than the domestic characteristics of the political systems that they are developing that has enabled them to survive.[56]

It is, however, possible that the type of government that dominates the Arabian Peninsula does so because it is well suited to the requirements of the time. That includes nation building and the need to bring very conservative people along with that task. Attempts to impose revolutionary change, as was seen in Yemen, Syria and Iraq, were confronted by the reality of the conservatism of their populations and the undeveloped nature of the societies and economies involved. A regime with greater sympathy for the traditions of its people and with more limited ambitions of change is more likely to gain the people's support and loyalty.

This chapter has divided the monarchies of the Arab world into two categories based on whether their succession is organised according to primogeniture or family-based consensus. They have been examined on the basis of the issues raised in previous chapters, namely tribalism, leadership approach and the place of constitutions in political systems. These are all relatively successful regimes, despite their considerable vulnerabilities to domestic and external challenges. They are also relatively young states under ruling families whose experience of the modern political system is limited. The families are busy consolidating their hold on power and seeking to perpetuate their situation.

The concept of a constitutional structure is one of the new aspects of the modern political system with which the ruling Arab families are coming to terms. They have recognised in the constitutional approach one means of contributing to their longevity, including their ability to determine the succession process. The Arab monarchies have taken different paths to the goal of constitutional consolidation. The United Arab Emirates has developed a republican monarchy. Oman has introduced into its constitution a succession process that seems destined to provoke uncertainty among the population and infighting within the ruling family. Kuwait has, largely by force of circumstances rather than by choice, adopted an approach which gives outsiders a much greater role in key issues, including succession.

What does emerge and what is important from the point of view of this book is that common to all approaches to succession is a strong focus on family, tribe and on a direct handover of power from father to son. This was a feature from the early days of the Saudi dynasty and there are signs that the interest in primogeniture has not vanished. The cases of Hassan to Mohammed in Morocco, Hussein to Abdallah in Jordan and Zayed to Khalifa in Abu Dhabi have all reflected a succession process based on primogeniture. This is, to an extent, a curious inclination on the part of Arab monarchs, who have such close sympathies with tribal attitudes, which have served to constrain the ambitions of Arab leaders over time.

Given the problems facing republican regimes, it is not inconceivable that the monarchic model may become the dominant feature of Arab political systems. Almost all Arab countries have experienced monarchic rule,[57] although not all those experiences have been successful. Nevertheless, to the extent that the tribal tradition is conducive to a monarchical system, it is possible that the model might be attractive to republican regimes seeking to consolidate their rule in the future.

The Arab monarchies do, however, face major problems in the future. The new leaders start with certain advantages, including their wealth, education and external connections. They do, in many cases, however, lack the experience and the humility of leaders like Sheikh Zayed of the United Arab Emirates, whose willingness to listen to the people and whose understanding of their interests engendered great personal loyalty. The problems to confront the new leaders are of fundamental importance. Family and regime loyalty will become increasingly difficult to maintain in the face of the huge growth of the number of people claiming membership of the ruling family and the inevitable divergence of interests among family members. As Anderson suggests:

> The monarchies, because they have (fairly) clear procedures for succession, seem best equipped to meet the immediate challenges of change . . . Still, the monarchies face the more fundamental dilemma of creating a twenty-first century rationale for monarchy itself. . . . It all adds up to the continued personalization of politics and a lack of political institutionalisation. Initially, then, politics in the next generation will continue to amplify the importance of the personal temperaments of rulers.[58]

The strength of the forces driving the constitutional structures of monarchic governments, including arrangements for succession, gains added significance when one examines the way in which the predilection for dynastic rule has spread across most Arab political systems and has gained expression in Arab republics. This is the issue to be considered in Chapter 7.

7 Hybrids

Monarchic republics of the Arab world

> This was Cromwell's tragedy. Republicanism deprived him of a crown, and by so doing, it also deprived him of a legitimate base upon which to perpetuate his rule.[1]

The phenomenon of Arab republican leaders seeking to perpetuate their families' hold on power through the process of dynastic presidential succession is one of the most significant developments in modern Arab political history. This phenomenon is not unique to the Arab world. In Cuba, for example, Fidel Castro was replaced by his brother Raul. Argentina has seen family-based transitions of presidential power involving the Perons and the Kirchners. The Egyptian columnist, Mohammed Abu Al-Hadid, went so far as to suggest that the practice existed in the United States as well, noting in 2000 that 'one of the leading candidates in the presidential elections is the son of ex-president George Bush'.[2] (He might well have also considered the examples of the Roosevelts, the Kennedys and the Clintons in this context.) Mustafa Al Feki suggests in the Egyptian journal, *Al Ahram Weekly*, that 'Arab republics assume an Asian quality when it comes to succession', noting similar experiences in India, Bangladesh, Sri Lanka and the Philippines.[3] What is unique about the Arab situation is that the phenomenon appears to be widespread throughout the republics of the region. The attraction of dynastic rule in these republics is being played out as a counterpoint to the Arab monarchies, where succession is overtly and constitutionally determined on the basis of family rule. Reflecting this irony, Arab commentators have developed the neologism *jumlaka*. '*Jumlaka*' is a compression of the Arabic words '*jumhuriya*', meaning 'republic', and '*mamlaka*', meaning 'monarchy', to describe the development.

The inclination to dynastic rule in republican systems in the Arab world has been detected in a number of countries. Iraq, Syria, Egypt, Libya, Yemen and Lebanon are the most frequently mentioned. The only practicing example so far is Syria, which is discussed in detail below. In Iraq, Saddam Hussein was understood to have chosen first his older son, Uday, and then a younger son, Qusay, as his successor before the American invasion in 2003.[4] In Libya, Colonel Qaddafi is believed to have decided that his son, Saif Al Islam, will succeed him.[5] Yemen's President, Ali Abdallah Saleh, is understood to be preparing his son, Ahmad, to replace him in time for the next presidential elections in 2013.[6] Egypt's President

Mubarak appears to be positioning his son, Gamal, to replace him.[7] In Lebanon, the murder of former Prime Minister Rafiq Hariri highlighted the long-established dynastic nature of Lebanese politics when his role was taken over by his son, Saad.[8]

In these cases, the chosen sons of the presidents have been given the opportunity to develop their skills and build up their political bases through appointment to significant positions in the state power structure. In Iraq, before the American invasion, Uday Hussein was prominent in a number of political organisations and his brother, Qusay, had a dominant role in the security services. Qaddafi's son, Saif Al Islam, has been prominent in a number of important Libyan foreign policy initiatives as well as in helping his father to deal with domestic challenges from Islamic groups and the Revolutionary Committees. In Yemen, Ahmad Saleh controls some of the major security forces in the country, while Gamal Mubarak is playing an increasingly prominent role at the political, economic and foreign policy levels. While not politically active until the murder of his father, Saad Hariri had for some time been a major force in his father's business interests.

The following examines a number of republics that highlight the attraction of republican leaders to a dynastic system of government. To an extent, the leaders considered are consistent with Weber's categories of leadership, namely charismatic, bureaucratic and traditional (see Chapter 1). The republican leaders, specifically the fathers, Hafez Al Assad, Hosni Mubarak, Ali Saleh, Saddam Hussein and Muammar Qaddafi, represent Weber's charismatic leaders. Each one has gained legitimacy through the state-building process and has seen himself as being above the law. Lacking this heroic background, the sons must attempt to draw on the reflected glory of their fathers, but they are also seeking more rule-based sources of legitimacy – Weber's bureaucratic leadership. Underpinning these characteristics, however, is the persistence of tradition in the Arab world, what Weber describes as traditional leadership. The tenacity of the tradition forces the sons of charismatic leaders to adapt their pursuit of rule-based legitimacy to accommodate the family and the tribe as a basis of their people's loyalty. It is inevitable that there are considerable variations in this pattern across the different regimes. On one hand, the countries' historical experiences have been different and their social structures show considerable diversity. On the other hand, the republics also have much in common. All have been occupied by foreign powers and most have been exposed to some degree of lingering foreign influence. Egypt, Syria, Libya, Yemen and Iraq all experienced monarchic rule.

While reliance on traditional dynastic practices is widespread, there are exceptions to this pattern among Arab republics. The Palestinian Authority, for example, has so far not displayed any tendency towards dynastic rule, despite its clan-influenced political system. Many of the same succession issues bedevilling the other republics confront the Palestinian leadership. A number of factors, however, including the relative dominance of the old Fateh leadership and the emergence of Hamas, have delayed the emergence of dynastic pressures.[9] Tunisia is also not generally mentioned as a possible case of *jumlaka*. As noted earlier, however, the Tunisian President, ben Ali, has moved family members into significant positions of power throughout the Tunisian political and economic systems. Moreover, the close involvement of the regime in the Tunisian business sector reinforces the broad concept of the urge to dynastic practices. In this respect Tunisia has many of the traits of the other Arab republics where the regime dominates and exploits the business sector.

One of the features that unite the five dynastically-inclined republics is the fact that they have all experienced long periods of rule by one individual. President Bourghiba ran Tunisia for 31 years and his successor, ben Ali, has been in power since 1987. Saddam Hussein was President of Iraq for 24 years. Hafez Al Assad ruled Syria for 29 years. President Mubarak of Egypt has been in power since 1981. Colonel Qaddafi has ruled Libya since 1969. President Saleh of Yemen has been in power since 1978 (see Appendix 3). In those Arab countries where the question of dynastic rule is not an issue (e.g Algeria, Sudan and Mauritania), individual leaders have been in power for shorter periods and are less well established.

It would appear that, superficially at least, there is a connection between the duration of a leader's period in office and his desire to perpetuate family rule. The longer an Arab ruler is in power, the more likely the issue of hereditary succession is to arise. Such a development might be predictable. Commonly, a new ruler in an Arab republic has had to set about consolidating his position by removing representatives of the old regime and replacing them with people he can trust. Central to this process is the appointment of loyalists to key government and security positions. Reflecting the importance of family and tribe in many Arab societies, these loyalists have regularly been drawn from the new ruler's family. Bellin describes entire branches of the Syrian military and security forces as being 'family affairs'.[10] Ali Saleh introduced family and tribal members into key positions when he gained power in Yemen and ben Ali increasingly followed a similar family-first policy after his seizure of power in Tunisia.[11] In so doing, the ruler creates a situation that is similar to that in monarchic regimes, where family rule is the practice. A core family elite is dependent on the survival of the ruler for its position and, more generally, because of its family membership, is committed to the survival of the regime as a whole. The core elite is supported by a clientalist network involving weaker branches of the family and a range of supporters outside the family network. This broader loyalty is then exploited to support the regime's survival beyond the life of the current ruler. Moreover, the longer the ruler is in power and his family is in a position of dominance, the more powerful and appealing the ambition to extend that position of dominance over generations becomes. Carapacio argues that the process of succession institutionalises the coalition of interests that have supported the regime over time and when personal rule 'becomes family rule, power monopolies endure or even solidify across generations'.[12]

A major challenge for these dynastic hopefuls is to ensure the compliance of the military and security services with their objectives. The armed forces have tended to be the agents of the regime's original seizure of power and often retain vestiges of the ideals that led to the seizure of power in the first place. As was seen in the early days of Syrian independence, the armed forces also retain the capacity to overthrow the new government if so inspired. The way the various regimes have approached this issue varies according to a range of factors, including history, the attitude of the various forces themselves and the ability of the regimes to develop alternate centres of power to limit the ambitions of the military and security forces. Some of these strategies are discussed below.

The appeal of dynasticism

Republican rulers are able to pursue dynastic succession because of the failure of the elites in those countries to develop sufficiently robust institutions and procedures that might regularise rule-based political procedures. In particular, the military coups, which characterised the early days of independence, were unable to establish legitimacy through constitutional and political means. In part this reflects the ongoing tension between traditional practices and modern, Western-inspired institutions and practices. Western structures, such as constitutions and parliaments, and liberal concepts, such as separation of powers and electoral competition, were introduced at the time of independence. Resistance to these influences from traditional elements which were attached to the dominant role of the family reasserted itself at independence. The result was ongoing tension between the modernist and traditionalist forces, which was resolved largely in favour of the traditionalists. Anderson argues that the result is that:

> From the Palestinian Authority to the Algerian democracy, from the Moroccan monarchy to the Syrian republic, the formal institutions of government are little more than facades behind which the rulers exercise enormous discretionary power, and within which citizens wield little influence.[13]

The Arab republics are arguably passing through a transitional phase to dynastic rule. Logically, in a republic, such a process faces some serious challenges, most of which have to do with the obvious task of achieving legitimacy for, and, therefore, acceptance of, the concept of dynastic succession itself. The regime's supporters, at least those outside the ruling elite, often continue to believe in the original reasons for its rise to power, including the ideal of republicanism. Such an ideal evidently precludes dynastic succession.

Over the history of the Arab republics, constitutions have been grandly announced and then regularly disregarded, especially where matters of regime security are concerned. In this respect the constitutions are examples of 'ornamental constitutions'.[14] Nevertheless, republican regimes are concerned with legitimacy and the constitutions and their provisions dealing with succession create certain difficulties for republican rulers seeking to legitimise their goal of dynastic succession. The very ideals that the regimes brought with them into power are often outlined in the countries' constitutions. Requirements that presidents achieve power by means of an electoral procedure, no matter how corrupted that might be, are difficult to brush aside completely and therefore contain the potential for the processes to be exploited by opponents, especially at times of regime weakness, such as during a succession. In Egypt, the constitution and the Constitutional Court have represented a major complication of President Mubarak's ability to hand over power to his son. Even in Syria, where respect for the constitution might be regarded as minimal, the regime still felt obliged to ensure that Bashar Al Assad's accession to the presidency was constitutionally correct. At the moment, republican regimes appear to be satisfied with pursuing their dynastic arrangements on an *ad hoc* basis at the time of each succession. This does, however, expose the arrangement to regular challenge and draws attention to the political sensitivity of the process. A dynastic succession procedure that is constitutionally valid would be easier to justify and defend. The problem for these regimes is how to develop a family-dominated arrangement that is compatible with the republican structures and traditions of their states.

While the idea of dynastic succession faces formidable obstacles, it has certain strengths as well. Some Egyptian writers commenting on the rise of Bashar Al Assad to the Syrian presidency suggest that such a step was necessary to maintain stability. The alternative was 'catastrophe' as it would have provoked the sort of unrest that characterised the Syrian republic in its early years.[15] This focus on the importance of domestic stability is a common theme throughout Arab political history and remains a concern among many Arabs, as repeatedly brought out in interviews conducted for this book. Carapico notes the stress on continuity on the part of Arab citizens but also on the part of outside powers, for whom stability is preferable to the pattern of military coups.[16]

There is also a widespread suspicion that the republican experiment is inconsistent with the Arab political tradition. Dynastic rule has the advantage of historical experience, especially among tribal groups, where the idea is well understood. Much has been written about the difficulties the Arab world encountered in accommodating an alien term denoting a concept of which it had no experience.[17] As noted above, all the countries where dynastic succession is an issue, except Lebanon, have had experience of monarchic rule.[18] Often those monarchic regimes were associated with independence from Ottoman or colonial domination, giving them a certain residual charismatic legitimacy among the public.

Another factor that might add to public support for or tolerance of a dynastic succession process is the perceived greater success of some of the Arab monarchies in pursuing economic and social development. As noted in Chapter 6, the monarchies are divided between rentier economies with the capacity to buy the support of their populations and oil-poor economies that have had to adopt other strategies to consolidate their power base. The same situation applies in the republican states, with Libya and Iraq able to apply their oil incomes to encourage support for their regimes and with Syria and Yemen lacking that capacity.[19]

Monarchies have tended to pursue modernisation in a relatively restrained way. They rely on traditional elements like tribes and Islam for support, and have pursued change within confines set by such conservative forces. The impact of change on society has been great but has not provoked the same degree of opposition that more deliberate attempts at social engineering might have provoked. By contrast, the Arab republics began with the ambitious and revolutionary goal of breaking from the past by re-ordering society through modernisation, socialism and industrialisation. This approach is reflected in their constitutions. The Algerian constitution, which is described in the Preamble as the 'concretisation of the people's genius, the reflection of their aspirations, the fruit of their determination and the product of deep social changes', is focused on promoting the achievements of the 1 November 1954 revolution and eliminating aspects of the *ancien régime* (Article 7). The Syrian constitution (Article 1(1)) presents the state as 'democratic, popular, socialist and sovereign' and the economy as a 'planned, socialist economy that seeks to end all forms of expropriation' (Article 13(1)).

These reform programmes disrupted traditional social and power arrangements, including the Ottoman-era landowning classes and the tribes. They did not, however, destroy the tribes. Qaddafi's launching in 1973 of his Third Universal Theory was an attempt to eradicate traditional ways of life and impose a new revolutionary ideology on his country. As with a number of the other republican revolutions, Qaddafi attempted to downplay the importance of Islam, declaring his state to be secular or at least to be a modernised version of Islam. Despite his best efforts, however, the traditional forces, drawing on Islam, persisted and frustrated Qaddafi's campaign. The Colonel was unable to institutionalise and legitimise his revolution or establish a basis upon which he could build lasting change.[20]

While the persistence of traditional attitudes and structures represented a significant brake on social and economic reform, they have also provided potential support for republican leaders seeking to instigate dynastic succession practices on the basis that this is, in effect, a reversion to the old way of doing things.

Syria: setting the trend

Syria provides the best and most clear-cut example of the hereditary principle at work in Arab republics. The succession of Bashar Al Assad to replace his father as President in 2000 was, according to some analysts, the least likely outcome of the death of Hafez Al Assad, although it was widely understood that this was Hafez' wish.[21] In the event, the transfer of power contained many similarities to the succession process followed in the Arab monarchies. Hafez Al Assad had decided some years before that he wanted to see his oldest son, Basil, succeed him. Basil, however, died before Hafez, who turned to Bashar as his heir, suggesting a pattern whereby, as with family-based monarchies, the line of succession extends beyond one individual in the family, staying in the immediate line of descent. As with the Jordanian experience, there was a brother with leadership ambitions who had to be dealt with. These steps and the exclusion of Hafez' brother, Rifa'at, reinforce the direct family nature of the process and the impression that family ties and the maintenance of established power structures rather than competency and experience were the essential criteria for leadership.

The legitimacy of Bashar's accession to power depended on his relationship with his father, not on military or political achievement. Much like the Saudi succession process, the group that supported or acquiesced in Bashar's accession to power was comprised mainly of members of the Al Assad family, the wider Kalbiya tribe to which the Assads belong and the Alawite community. This reflected Hafez Al Assad's dominance in the Syrian system. It also underlines the charismatic nature of that dominance. Hafez Al Assad paid lip-service to the institutions of state and to the ideas of democracy and the popular will. In the key areas on which his power was based, however, Assad relied upon the extended family. The armed forces, various security organisations, key ministries and the Ba`ath Party were controlled by members of his family, or at least by members of the Alawite community. The effect was to consolidate support for the regime and to isolate potential challengers.

Unlike the more planned succession process that might characterise a monarchy or the process that was envisaged for Basel, Bashar had little time to prepare for the presidency. He was put through a rushed training programme which was intended as an opportunity to build up experience of government and to develop support in key parts of the regime structure, especially the armed forces and the Ba`ath party. He was helped to install his own supporters throughout the state structure. These included his brother, Maher, the head of Presidential Guard, and his brother-in-law, Assef Shawqat, the head of military intelligence. At the same time, many senior members of the armed forces and security agencies, some of whom were among Hafez Al Assad's most loyal lieutenants, were forced by Hafez to retire to ensure that they did not complicate the new president's early years in power. This greatly strengthened Bashar's position as he set out to preserve his father's achievements and maintain the Alawi hold on power.[22]

Hafez' legacy, however, was only able to carry the new president so far and the resulting situation must still be regarded as transitional. The post-Hafez power elite is one in which Bashar Al Assad holds most of the levers of power, and he is growing in his ability to operate those levers effectively. Bashar is not, however, in the unrivalled position of power that his father enjoyed. Many of the people who came to power with Hafez Al Assad remain in powerful positions under the new president. These include several of Bashar's uncles and a cousin of his mother, who is from a rival Alawite family. The power elite also contains elements of the other communities in Syria, including the majority Sunni, as part of the regime's desire to accommodate the different elements that make up Syrian society. Both groups owe the new president very little, and there is a degree of stalemate in Syrian politics as a result. According to Glass, 'Divisions between the old guard and the reformers have paralysed the system'.[23] In this respect, Bashar's position contains parallels with Saudi Arabia, where the ruler's power is constrained by other members of the wider family power elite. Bashar was re-elected in a national referendum in 2007 and, while there is no suggestion that the result was anything but pre-determined, it may be a step towards a more secure hold on power for the President.

At the time of his assumption of power, the accession of Bashar was challenged from within and outside the core of the regime. Significant Sunni groups, including the Moslem Brotherhood, continue to resent the dominance of the Alawi, a minority and, in their eyes, an heretical, sect, although recent statements have tended to downplay the sectarian aspect of their opposition.[24] More serious perhaps is the risk of challenge from within the Alawi community, especially the Al Assad family itself. Several of Bashar's uncles, in particular, Rifa'at Al Assad, unsuccessfully challenged his rise to power and continue to question his legitimacy. Their challenge was directed at Bashar personally, not at the idea of continued Assad family rule or Alawi dominance. Rifa'at is now in exile and lacks a serious power base in the country, but he could serve as a focus for any discontent that might develop. Members of the old guard, who are not part of the Al Assad family, are understood to have expressed their reservations to Hafez about the idea of hereditary succession and could still challenge the succession if Bashar were to falter. Some members of the old guard appear to regard the succession as their gift, a gift that presumably could be taken back. Mustafa Tlas, the former Defence Minister, commented to the Egyptian newspaper *Al Ahram*:

> With Assad's death, we began to think that either I or Vice President 'Abd al-Halim Khaddam were worthy of filling the shoes of the dead president. However, in view of the fact that all of us were past seventy years of age, we were afraid of a situation in which every year we would have to change the country's leader, as had happened in the former Soviet Union. . . . We reached the conclusion that Bashar was indeed worthy of succeeding his father; after all, that had been the will of his father, Hafiz al-Assad, to whom Syria owes so much. After all, we were among his close friends. . . . Bashar is a young, promising leader, and he can rely on our support.[25]

The attitude of the Syrian elite is crucial as it determines the way the regime governs and handles key issues such as succession. The Alawi are a small minority in Syria. Many of them had advanced their interests through the armed forces in the colonial and post-colonial periods and through the Ba`ath Party. The regime established by Hafez Al Assad recognised from Syria's chaotic experience of the 1950s and 1960s that it would survive only by maintaining a united front in public. However, the pursuit of regime solidarity has impelled it towards a high degree of authoritarianism, an attitude justified by its policy of modernisation and also by the significant threats it has continually faced from domestic and external sources. Constitutionally a revolutionary regime (Preamble), the Syrian government tends to rule by the 'colour of law'.[26] The law, the constitution and the major institutions of Syrian governance exist as expressions of the ruler's wishes and have little meaning of their own. This attitude reflects Giorgio Agamben's state of exception, where the sovereign power is able to do anything to anyone, where law loses its context and where it is impossible to anticipate when and how it will be applied.

Examples of the regime regularly ignoring the provisions of its constitution in pursuit of political goals are noted in Chapter 5. The regime does not appear to regard itself as bound by the law when it comes to the daily process of governance. Moreover, for most Syrian citizens, the constitution contains little personal meaning for them, no safeguards for their personal rights. Rather it tends to be regarded as yet another device for controlling the population, for conveying and legitimising the wishes of the ruling group.

The constitution: more than window dressing

There are, however, contradictory indications that the regime's search for both domestic and international legitimacy has compelled it to seek a degree of legality and constitutionality for its policies. Like any regime, the Alawi rulers of Syria require, if not the support, the complicity or at least the acquiescence of significant proportions of the population, especially from among the Sunni majority. Bashar's relative weakness compared to his father and his non-revolutionary background demand that he base his legitimacy on more than armed force and charisma. This is achieved in three ways. The first way is to ensure that the Sunni community is kept reasonably satisfied. In part this involves having prominent Sunnis occupy important government and economic positions. The second way is to convince the population and the international community that the fall of the regime is unlikely. The third way is to create the impression among supporters and opponents alike that the regime is indeed legitimate. The constitution is an important device in this respect.

There is another important issue to consider when examining the significance of the Syrian constitution. For many politically alert citizens, the constitution has real meaning to the extent that it contains issues in which they genuinely believe. The Syrian constitution is an important declarative political instrument. It directly addresses some of the key political challenges that have faced the country since independence, especially the issues of Arab nationalism and Zionism (Preamble) and the problem of Syrian territory occupied by Israel and Turkey (Article 1).[27] These challenges are addressed at length in the Preamble of the constitution:

> The Arab masses did not regard independence as their goal and the end of their sacrifices, but as a means to consolidate their struggle, and as an advanced phase in their continuing battle against the forces of imperialism, Zionism and exploitation under the leadership of their patriotic and progressive forces in order to achieve the Arab nation's goals of unity, freedom and socialism.

Of great importance is the way in which the constitution deals with the role of the Ba`ath Party in Syria:

> The leading party in the society and the state is the Socialist Arab Ba`ath Party. It leads a patriotic and progressive front seeking to unify the resources of the people's masses and place them at the service of the Arab nation's goals (Article 8).

Hafez Al Assad and many of his contemporaries were committed members of the Ba`ath Party. It was also a means to power, to national unity across confessional divisions and to Arab modernity and unity in the face of the challenges of the day.[28] Many of these people who are still in positions of power expect to see the objectives and achievements of the Hafez regime honoured. Perthes describes a 'correctionist' trend in Syrian politics, which consists of people who want to see the continuation of measures (the 'corrective movement') begun by Hafez Al Assad in 1970 at the time of his coup. Members of this trend support continuity and identify with the system that has emerged out of the 1970 coup. These people still endorse the ideology of 1960s Ba`athist Arab nationalism.[29]

It is largely through the Ba`ath's central position that control of society and the armed forces in Syria is exercised. Bashar's supporters would, therefore, have been mindful of the importance of honouring expectations of members of the Ba`ath Party. The replacement of Hafez Al Assad would be done in a way that accorded with the constitution and Ba`ath Party rules.

Some of the major political comprises reached in the course of Hafez Al Assad's rise to power are contained in the Syrian constitution. These include an acknowledgement of the place of Islam in the society despite the Ba`ath Party's commitment to secularism: 'Islamic jurisprudence is a main source of legislation' (Article 3(2)). It also includes an acknowledgement of the central role of the armed forces in the 'corrective movement'. The armed forces' role involves not just the protection of the homeland, but the protection of the objectives spelt out in the constitution of unity and socialism (Article 11). As suggested in the discussion of Egypt, some of these compromises are delicately balanced and, in some cases, contested. The declarations in Article 1 that Syria is a socialist state, that the prominent role of the secular Ba`ath Party and that the specification that Islamic jurisprudence is 'a major source of legislation' highlight the sensitivity and inherent contradictions of some of the compromises contained. To ignore these arrangements by openly flaunting the constitution by, for example, defying constitutional requirements for the election of a president, would risk upsetting the compromises and provoking unrest. Perhaps with the horrors of the Moslem Brotherhood insurrection of the early 1980s in mind, Syria's leaders might see a degree of respect for the constitution as worthwhile if it contributes to the promotion of internal order.

The role of wives and mothers in the succession

As with most Arab countries, the role of women in the Syrian elite is clouded by traditional privacy. Hafez Al Assad actively promoted the liberation of women throughout his career. It became a major element of Ba`ath party doctrine and is enshrined in the country's constitution (Article 45). This policy appears, however, to have had a limited relevance as far as the ruling family is concerned. Hafez' wife, Anisah Makhlouf, remained out of public life throughout his presidency and her views on issues such as succession have never been made public. By contrast, it would appear that some younger female members of the Assad family have enjoyed greater freedom and have exercised considerable political influence. For example, Bashar's sister, Bushra, is reputed to have a significant interest in domestic politics and to have been a strong, behind-the-scenes influence on Hafez and Bashar. She is regarded as being a power in her own right, a part of the small ruling circle around the President. By contrast, Bashar's wife, Asma, plays an active and public semi-official role in a number of areas, including rural economic development and women's issues.[30] As a Sunni, Asma may also contribute to the regime's acceptability in the dominantly Sunni country.

The lack of visibility of the women of the Assad family hides another way in which they can exert an impact. In much the same way as the wives of the Saudi royal family become focal points around which members of the family align themselves, Hafez' widow, Anisah, personifies rivalries within the Alawi community and highlights a possible limitation on Bashar's power. Members of the Makhlouf family, in particular, Anisah's cousin, General Adnan Makhlouf, are in powerful positions throughout the system thanks to their family connections. Rivalry between the Makhlouf and Assad families goes back for generations[31] and any internal unrest could serve to advance Makhlouf ambitions and to ultimately weaken Bashar's hold on power.

The future of the inherited succession

Putting aside the possibility of a successful coup against Bashar, there are several measures that might be applied to determine the extent to which the Syrian regime genuinely has hereditary intentions. The first of these tests came at the end of Bashar's first presidential term in 2007. There was some speculation about whether Bashar would seek re-election, whether the ruling elite would allow him to do so and whether the population as a whole would tolerate a further continuation of family rule. In the event, there seems to have been no real challenge to Bashar's re-election from the Alawite elite. He achieved a predictably resounding vote in the election. From this, it may be assumed that Bashar is committed to ruling for the long term, but it will be necessary to wait for some years to be able to judge whether he intends to try to pass the presidency on to his son or perhaps to another member of the immediate family.

There are some significant obstacles to the extension of Assad rule. Lust-Okar considers the possibility of the regime developing genuine hereditary characteristics to be unlikely. She points out that, in addition to his evident skills as a political leader, Hafez Al Assad enjoyed legitimacy because of his role in the Ba`athist coup of 1963. She might have added his initiation of the corrective movement of 1970 and his ability generally to maintain stability through most of his years in power. Hafez was a classical charismatic leader. Bashar has been struggling to develop his own legitimacy and has been relying on his father's legacy.[32] This can be seen easily from the ubiquitous posters around Syria that depict Bashar with his father. This is also a feature of the Jordanian regime, but there, King Abdallah enjoys the legitimacy of his succession deriving from the institution of the monarchy as well as from his father's endorsement. Bashar lacks that institutional reinforcement and is involved in the transitional phase from charismatic to bureaucratic leadership. A further potential problem for Bashar is the possibility that some members of the regime might decide that they cannot maintain Alawite rule of Syria indefinitely. While the possibility is remote, should significant numbers of the Alawi leadership decide that it would be to their advantage to make peace with the Sunni majority, Bashar and his family would find it very difficult to maintain their dominance. The danger of such a development might be greater in the event of an agreement between Syria and Israel over the Golan Heights or a more general peace process between Israel and its neighbours. A reduction of tension between the two sides would weaken the regime's justification for maintaining emergency rule, for according a central place in the political process to the armed forces and for its refusal to allow genuinely competitive elections. Finally, Bashar is attempting, in Weber's terms, to routinise authority towards a law- or rules-based system. For Weber, such a step is likely to aggravate forces for instability, with new charismatic groups rising up against the emerging patrimonial structure of the formerly charismatic regime.[33]

Bashar has the advantage of incumbency and has so far survived intense international pressure to change his policies, especially from the United States and Israel. Indeed, that pressure may prove to be to his advantage to the extent that the external threat requires everyone to fall in behind the leader. Many Alawi officers believe that, for their personal and their sect's survival, Alawi power must be maintained at all costs. Allowing the embittered Sunni majority into power would, they fear, only invite retribution against the Alawi community.[34] This concern about retribution is reinforced by the constant, low-level (but often violent) expressions of opposition to Alawite rule in Syria and by the activities of Shi`a death squads in post-Saddam Iraq. Also to Bashar's advantage is the long-standing Arab acceptance of the idea of hereditary succession and of autocratic or authoritarian rule. As noted in the context of Jordan, the establishment of the Umayyad dynasty is discussed by people as if it was only yesterday. This is even more evident in Damascus, where the dynasty was based. Despite the best efforts of their successors, reminders of the Umayyads are plentiful throughout the country. The death of Muawiya, the first Umayyad Caliph, can be seen as the beginning of the move away from charismatic leadership to patrimonial, bureaucratic domination, a development that lends some credence to Bashar's position. Bashar certainly appears to welcome the opportunity to identify himself and his regime with the Umayyads.

A major challenge for Bashar, should he seek to perpetuate his family's dominance of Syria, is to develop a longer-term strategy to incorporate his family's succession into the Syrian political process, to regularise the process and to give it an institutional legitimacy that it currently lacks. The current *ad hoc* arrangement is open to challenge every time the president dies and will expose the regime to political challenge from within its ranks and from outside, thereby raising the possibility of political instability. A more secure process will have to be constitutionally logical and valid. One approach might be to amend the constitution to enable the president to nominate his successor. This would only require parliamentary endorsement. It is, moreover, effectively what happened in the transfer from Hafez to Bashar, and it builds on the precedent set by Muawiya. It is likely, however, to require a greater authority than Bashar appears able to exert at the moment.

The decision of Hafez Al Assad to secure the presidency of Syria for his son has provoked intense speculation about whether a precedent has been set, whether the dynastic course resolves any long-term problems and whether Syria and other Arab countries are embarked on a radical re-working of republican systems in the region. It would seem clear that there are certain powerful forces that might encourage such a development but, equally, it is evident that the project is a fragile one that has some formidable obstacles to overcome before it might be said to have succeeded. Among these is the desire of Syrian leaders to envelop their actions in the aura of constitutional legitimacy. In the long run, to establish a dynastic succession process it will be necessary for the process to be consistent with the country's constitution. It is now time to turn an example of the republics where dynastic rule is being talked about and where the constitution appears to be a significant obstacle: Egypt.

Egypt: the new pharaoh

Egypt is an important example because of its central position in the Arab world. Despite the pariah status it experienced for the period from Anwar Sadat's decision to reach an accommodation with Israel until the late 1980s, the country remains the most influential of Arab countries. It is the most populous and most politically, socially and economically sophisticated, so what happens in Egypt is of considerable importance to the rest of the region. Egypt is also, to a great extent, the international face of the Arab world. For these reasons, the barge-like process whereby Egypt's President Hosni Mubarak appears to be edging towards a dynastic transfer of power in favour of his son, Gamal, is of great relevance to what might happen elsewhere in the region. The President and his son have stated on numerous occasions that there is no plan to install Gamal as the next president. The elliptical nature of some of their comments, Gamal's diverse and highly political public activity[35] and the President's refusal to appoint a vice president continue, however, to provoke expectations that a dynastic transfer of power is planned.

The nature of the Egyptian regime makes this process of succession planning particularly interesting. The regime is authoritarian, based on the manipulation of democratic mechanisms, such as elections, to consolidate its hold on power. Force is also an important tool of political management and the security services enjoy wide powers, are ubiquitous and are willing to use brutal tactics against those who challenge the regime, including widespread use of torture.[36] Major provisions of the constitution are in limbo with the declaration of a state of emergency. From one perspective, the constitution is an irrelevance and, thanks to the state of emergency, offers no check to the powers of the president. As such, the regime's behaviour is consistent, along with Syria, with the description a 'state of exception'.

The most important feature of the Egyptian system is the centrality of the presidency. The arbitrary and capricious nature of the Egyptian system place the

President in Weber's charismatic category, with loyalty to the individual in power being the most important criterion for survival in the system. Promotion within public office does not rely on standard bureaucratic procedures, but on acceptance of the President as the supreme decision maker in all areas. This central position also bears some of the hallmarks of Weber's traditional category with the deep and widespread awareness of the Egyptian population of their Pharaonic and Islamic past. Both of these phases of Egyptian history accord importance to centralisation and a semi-divine leader.

Just as the history of the Umayyads is a constant presence in the Syrian and Jordanian political scenes, so the idea of monarchy has an important place in Egyptian thinking. While the monarchic model of more modern times is perhaps less prominent in people's thinking, largely because of the role of Nasser in its overthrow and associations with defeat in 1948, an older model appears to be alive in people's imagination. Mubarak is portrayed as the third longest-serving ruler of Egypt since the days of the Pharaohs. The media, especially the opposition media, regularly use terms from the Pharaonic age to portray Mubarak. His limited and ambiguous comments about the succession issue are, for example, described as Sphinx-like. He is often called the modern Pharaoh. This is a point raised by Perthes, who notes that many Egyptians speak about the Egyptian tradition as always featuring a centralist system headed by a ruler with divine or almost divine power. This leader embodies the country's unity, protects it externally and internally and guarantees the political stability that is so important in a society that has operated on the basis of predictability and routine for thousands of years.[37]

In contrast to Syria, there has been discussion in the media about the succession and about the possibility that the President will be replaced by Gamal. This debate has tended to wax and wane according to the electoral cycle, becoming more intent as elections approach. Accordingly, there was debate in the media in the months before the 2000 and the 2005 elections about Gamal's ambitions. This has resumed in preparation for the next round of elections in 2011. The debate has been largely contrived with government-controlled media attempting, in part using the Syrian example, to promote and justify the idea of hereditary succession in order to prepare the public and the military for the possibility. One newspaper columnist, for example, argued that Syria had no choice, if it was to avoid chaos, but to have 'this quiet and swift transfer of authority'.[38] The implication was that such an approach was also necessary in Egypt if chaos was to be avoided. Another argument put forward is that Gamal Mubarak has the necessary qualities to be President and should not be blocked just because he is the son of the ruling president. Importantly, the pro-government media has emphasised the determination of the President that the succession should follow the arrangements set out in Article 76 of the constitution.[39] These include the requirement that a nomination for the presidency be endorsed by at least 250 elected members of the People's Assembly, the Shura Council and councils at the governorate level and then subjected to a national election campaign.

The President's commitment has been greeted with a degree of scepticism by the government's opponents. For the opposition media the task of responding to the possibility of dynastic succession has been difficult as it is considered wise to avoid direct criticism of the President or of Gamal, especially in the Arabic-language media. Nevertheless, a number of prominent individuals, including Mohammed Hassenain Heikal and Saad Eddin Ibrahim, have felt sufficiently secure to argue publicly that Syria did not represent a precedent for Egypt and that the idea of hereditary succession had no place in Egyptian politics.[40]

Evidence of intent

As noted above, both the President and Gamal Mubarak have consistently denied their intention that Gamal should succeed to his father's position. Their denials are, however, greeted with some scepticism in Egypt. Gamal has given momentum to the speculation in the media with his active involvement in a wide range of political activities. His early public life was focused on economic issues, but over the past ten years or so he has worked to develop a political support base and has branched out into a range of issues, including foreign policy matters, especially Egypt's relations with the United States, Israel and Iraq. More generally, through his role in the General Secretariat of the National Democratic Party, Gamal has been working to establish his standing in the civilian elite. The impression gained is of someone developing his credentials to become Egypt's leader.

Perhaps the most significant or tangible basis for this scepticism is the President's refusal to appoint a Vice President since he himself succeeded to the presidency in 1981. The failure of Mubarak to appoint a Vice President has raised a debate about the role of the constitution in this area. In 2005, a number of amendments to the constitution were passed by referendum. Before those amendments were adopted, the constitution did not specifically state that the President must appoint a Vice-President, but it was possible to infer that requirement based on a reading of a number of articles. As a result of the amendments, the constitution is sympathetic to Mubarak's position. The only article dealing with the position of Vice President is Article 139:

> The President of the Republic *may* appoint one or more Vice-Presidents, define their jurisdiction and relieve them of their posts. The rules relating to the calling into account of the President of the Republic shall be applicable to the Vice-Presidents. (This writer's emphasis.)

Amended Article 82 states that:

> If on account of any temporary obstacle, the President is rendered unable to carry out his functions, he shall delegate his powers to the vice-president or the Prime Minister if there is no vice-president or, if available, he is unable to act in such capacity. The one who shall act on behalf of the President may not request any amendment to the Constitution or dissolve the People's Assembly or the Shura Council or to relieve the cabinet.

The words 'if there is no vice-president or, if available, he is unable to act in such capacity' reflect the changes introduced.

A common accusation levelled at the regime is that the Mubarak family is benefiting from the President's long term in power and that this is a significant motive driving their interest in the regime's long-term survival. Gamal's older brother, Ala'a, plays no political role. As a businessman, however, he is understood to be benefiting extensively from his father's connections. As with the other Arab political systems, the role of the female members of the Egyptian ruling house is obscure and not publicly discussed. There is, nevertheless, a widespread understanding that Gamal's mother, Suzanne Thabet Mubarak, is actively working to promote Gamal's ambitions.

One of the great appeals and strengths of the regime – and a theme common to all the countries examined in this research – is its promise of stability. The Preamble of the constitution refers to the 'sovereignty of law' as a way of avoiding civil strife and as a safety valve. Before the 2005 presidential elections an organisation was formed to promote Mubarak's re-election. The group, *Al Istimrar* (continuity), issued a communiqué in which it appealed to Mubarak:

> . . . to continue to present his candidacy for an additional term, in order to preserve the stability that is the basis for prosperity and advancement, and also in order to continue the process of freedom, democracy and the rule of law. [This is because] the time has come for all the world to hear the voice of the honourable sons of Egypt, who realise that Mubarak represents true stability in our country.[41]

The constitution

As outlined above, constitutionally, the process of presidential succession in Egypt is relatively clear. A referendum in May 2005 saw Article 76, which deals with the method of election of the president, amended to allow for direct, multi-candidate elections.[42] Previously, Parliament approved one candidate who was submitted to a plebiscite. The amendment allowed each registered political party to field a candidate for the September 2005 elections, but specified that, in future elections, a party would need to be licensed for at least five years and hold at least five per cent of the seats in the lower and upper houses of Parliament to get on the ballot. Independent candidates would need to withstand an extensive endorsement process.

The September 2005 elections were duly conducted under the new arrangements, and Mubarak won by a large majority. He and his supporters described the election as part of a continuing process of reform, within the framework of stability and security. His victory was, however, immediately condemned by his rivals, many of whom had boycotted the referendum, and by some observers who noted that his main opposition, the Moslem Brotherhood, was still banned and unable to submit a candidate. Critics protested that the amendment to the constitution meant that, given the government's permanent majority in the parliament, the chance of anyone not approved by the government being elected president was negligible. Importantly, in the context of the changes, the government did not repeal the state of emergency laws and used them energetically against its opponents, especially the Moslem Brotherhood.[43]

Despite the regime's cavalier attitude to the rule of law, at times the constitution and the law do play a significant part in the Egyptian political system, including in areas that bear on the issue of succession. Like the Syrian regime, the Egyptian government readily ignores the law when it suits it to do so and is arbitrary in its application of the law. Nevertheless, it rules through and in compliance with the law on a surprising number of occasions. Opponents of the regime are dealt with harshly, but the courts have from time to time displayed some independence in dealing with political issues.

The courts, especially the Constitutional Court, have for their part often issued findings that have embarrassed the government, underscoring a greater degree of independence than that permitted to similar courts in other countries of the region. An example is the case of Saad Eddin Ibrahim, an Egyptian democracy and human rights campaigner who was gaoled by the State Security Court in 2001 for accepting foreign funds without authorization, disseminating false information harmful to Egypt's interest and embezzlement. The judgement was widely criticised and eventually overturned by the High Court of Justice. Despite the highly political overtones of the exercise, the government eventually allowed due process to be followed and accepted the High Court's ultimate decision. Perhaps the Court's show of independence reflected the fact that Egypt has one of the longest histories of constitutional rule in the Arab world and also the tenuous nature of the balance of power in the country. It is, however, a precarious situation. Since the elections of 2005, the judiciary has been engaged in a struggle with the government over judicial independence.[44]

The opposition has been able to exploit the relative independence of the courts and of the political process to challenge a range of the government's electoral practices.[45] Conservative Islamist opponents of the regime's essentially secular orientation are using the courts to pursue their opposition to secularism and Westernisation. The government banned the Moslem Brotherhood (*Ikhwan Al Muslimeen*) from the electoral process through the amended constitution, but it has allowed Brotherhood members to stand for election as independents. In the 2005 elections, Ikhwan independents became the second largest group in Parliament. In such a context, the regime has been variously described as a 'multi-party autocracy' or as 'pluralist authoritarianism'.[46]

As with other countries in the region, the Egyptian constitution is the embodiment of the government's compromises and deals with the military, Islamic groups and business involving the Egyptian balance of power. Respect for that balance of power as expressed and guaranteed in the constitution is essential for stability. Attempts to change it or disregard it could cause the arrangement to unravel. This is important when looking at Gamal's prospects for gaining the presidency. Given the delicate balance of power and the important opposition he faces, Gamal would appear to be dependent on his father seeing out his term as President and then presenting the succession as orderly, legal and legitimate. A change of leadership in circumstances of crisis would be damaging to his prospects. In the lead up to the 2005 election, the leader of Egypt's Moslem Brotherhood, Mohammed Akef, told the media that he expected Gamal Mubarak to succeed his father as President, but that the process would take time and that Gamal would attempt to gain the position using constitutionally-mandated measures.[47] Akef was not endorsing the prospect. He and his party opposed the 2005 constitutional amendment, but he is reflecting a widespread attitude that the regime will do whatever it takes to have its way.

There are, however, numerous obstacles in the Mubarak's way. The 2005 elections were to have been an important step on the way to Gamal's goal, with many of his supporters elected to Parliament, thereby establishing a base for his next moves. In the event, instead of Gamal's new guard making gains, other candidates, many informally representing the Moslem Brotherhood or the old guard of the ruling National Democratic Party, achieved major gains. Many of the candidates who had been associated with Gamal's political progress failed to be elected or lost their seats. If his claim to the presidency is to be built on a solid parliamentary base, he may have to wait for another general election.

The late President Nasser may represent another obstacle to Mubarak's dynastic ambitions. Most Egyptians are too young to remember Nasser, but he has managed to cast his charisma and influence across the generations since his death. People still speak with admiration about Nasser, an attitude supported by opinion polling. A 2004 Zogby International poll of people in five Arab countries found Nasser to be the leader they most admired.[48] Given the importance in Egyptian history of the abolition of the monarchy in Nasser's revolution and his championship of Arab nationalism, anything with overtones of the monarchy might be difficult to sell.

A major issue confronting Gamal's ambitions is the role and attitude of the armed forces. From Nasser's coup in 1952 to the defeat of June 1967, the army could be said to have been intimately involved in the day-to-day government of Egypt. Sobelman suggests that the wording of Article 150 of the constitution – 'The President of the Republic shall be the Supreme Commander of the Armed Forces' – has led to the assumption that the president will always emerge from the ranks of the military or security network.[49] From the time of Mubarak's accession, however, the civilian arm of government has been gradually assuming greater control over the armed forces. Mubarak, for example, has removed senior and popular military leaders, such as Field Marshall Mohammed Abd Al-Halim Abu Ghazaleh, who might have challenged his control or sought to replace Mubarak when he goes. The replacements have often been men who are close to retirement and, therefore, do not offer a serious alternative to Gamal Mubarak. As a result, the army could be described as still exerting general supervision over developments and as providing a guarantee for the regime but with signs that its active involvement in the political process is slackening.[50]

Moreover, the amendment to Article 76 of the constitution noted above could be seen as further weakening the military's hold on power and as improving Gamal's opportunity to achieve the presidency through more conventional means. With direct election from a list of multiple candidates and the need for prior endorsement from a number of civilian bodies – the People's Assembly, the Shura Council and governorate councils – it is now likely that the election field will be dominated by non-military people. In such an environment, Gamal may be able to present himself as having won the election through his own efforts and merits, thereby adding to his claim to legitimacy.

Of course, the reality will be somewhat different as it is clear that the President has been working to facilitate his son's rise. In particular, in addition to his efforts to keep the military under control, he has been removing potential civilian rivals from positions where they might be able to challenge Gamal's ambitions. Just as Hafez Al Assad used an anti-corruption campaign to remove possible challengers to his son's accession to the presidency, so in Egypt, an anti-corruption campaign in 2000 coincided with Gamal's appointment to the General Secretariat of the ruling National Democratic Party, a campaign that saw a number of potential party rivals removed from the scene. In addition, over time, other prominent public figures have been moved out of the way, such as Amr Musa, the Foreign Minister who was promoted to head the Arab League.

Hosni Mubarak has worked hard for some years to establish links with the business community in Egypt and business leaders have been introduced into the regime's elite structure. According to Abdelnasser, prominent businessmen have become part of the second ring of Egypt's 'politically relevant elites', a development that adds to the impression that there is a transfer of power under way away from the military to civilian politicians.[51] Gamal has built on this and has secured significant support within the Egyptian business community. His enthusiasm for neo-liberal economic policies and his resistance to pressures from the Moslem Brotherhood have also helped to endear him and his ambitions among foreign business interests.

Libya: *sui generis*?

Libya represents another variation of the process of hereditary succession in an Arab republic. The process bears similarities with that of Syria and Egypt, but Libya has its own distinct characteristics, reflecting its history and the nature of the country's political structure. Under Colonel Qaddafi Libya is the closest an Arab regime might get to Weber's idea of the charismatic system. Qaddafi has ruled his country since he seized power in 1969. He has tried to do without the Western institutions of the post-colonial period that might impede his pursuit of his revolutionary ideas, including legal processes and civil liberties.[52] Qaddafi does not hold any formal office, except the crucial title of Highest Commander-in-Chief of the Armed Forces,[53] but his power is absolute and his legitimacy is solidly based, emanating as it does from his central role in the overthrow of the monarchy and in the subsequent political and economic life of the country. This is an example of legitimacy deriving from charismatic qualities rather than the colour of law. Numerous observers have concluded that Qaddafi is determined to pass power to one of his sons, Saif Al Islam.[54] As in Egypt, the prospect has been denied by both father and son, but the auguries are convincing, based largely on Saif's actions and the freedom and responsibility given to him by his father. Saif has become, in Ronen's words, 'ensconced at the summit of the Libyan political landscape'. He is:

> Focused on politics, and his initiatives are prominent in the state's political, diplomatic and public relations front – areas of activity that are closely connected and under the complete control of the state's apparatus.[55]

The constitution

Libya's constitutional structure is a maze of contradictions and confusions. The country had a formal, written constitution under the Sanusi monarchy from 1951 to 1969. This roughly followed the model of numerous other Arab constitutions of the day, reflecting European influence. With Qaddafi's coup, that constitution was abolished and a provisional instrument was adopted by proclamation of the Revolutionary Command Council 'to provide a basis for the organisation of the state during the phase of completion of the national and democratic revolution' (Preamble). This provisional constitution placed supreme authority in the Revolutionary Command Council (Article 18). Subsequently, there appears to have been no serious attempt to convert the provisional constitution into a permanent instrument. In 1977, a Declaration announcing the 'Establishment of the Authority of the People' was issued, which declared the Quran to be the constitution of the Libyan People's Socialist Arab Jamahiriya' (Article 2)[56] and handed all formal power to the people through the establishment of the Socialist People's Leadership Committees. These Committees are nominally extra-governmental organizations whose job it is to monitor adherence by government agencies and the general population to Qaddafi's ideas. As such, the Committees were created to augment Qaddafi's power but, over time, they began to show an inclination to go their own way and challenge the Colonel's demands.[57]

With the exception of the Leadership Committees, which do not appear in the 1977 Declaration but which do represent the country's supreme authority, the question of leadership is not addressed in the new constitutional arrangement. On this basis, it could be argued that the relevant article (Article 18) of the 1969 Provisional Constitution remains effective and that Qaddafi has effectively created a division between administrative government and the informal political leadership, which exercises real power.

The family's role

Even more than Gamal Mubarak, Saif Al Islam has been given every opportunity to establish himself in the Libyan political system and to gain experience in the intricacies of domestic politics and foreign relations. The effect of the constitutional structure and the administrative and political division is that, unlike the Syrian and Egyptian examples, Saif is not constrained by a need to channel his activities within a constitutional framework. He is able to concentrate on establishing his political power in the informal areas where real power resides and where few constraints apply.

Importantly, the promotion of Saif may have the added objective of reviving, re-orienting and even rescuing the regime. Many of Qaddafi's economic and social policies have generated widespread unrest and opposition. Concern about Qaddafi's policies has been boosted by Libya's less than impressive economic performance.[58] An Islamic resistance movement has gained ground since the 1970s, provoked in part by Qaddafi's attempts to transform Libyan society and to challenge some important tenets of conservative Islam. He has been the target of a number of assassination attempts. While Qaddafi appears to have the military and security forces well contained, the regime faces serious challenges from Islamic groups and from the People's Committees, with their new power.

In great need of a fresh political face to present to the outside world and a new approach to domestic problems in such difficult times, Qaddafi turned to Saif Al Islam, in whom he had complete trust and who had displayed considerable political skills. Saif was given great discretion to pursue his own policies in support of the regime. He has paid particular attention to Libya's international image, promoting human rights and the rule of law in the country.[59] He was prominent in the rescue of Western tourists captured by the Abu Sayef group in the Philippines in 2000 and was actively involved in resolving the case of the Bulgarian and Palestinian medical personnel who were accused of spreading HIV-Aids in Libya. He has been in the forefront of attempts to improve Libya's relations with the United States and France. In an article in *Middle East Policy*, Saif outlines his views on most of the major issues affecting Libyan foreign relations. The editor of the article, Milton Viorst, describes Saif as having been entrusted by his father with a series of important international negotiations and as a thoughtful and thorough representative of his country.[60]

Saif also has a particular view of the Libyan economy. Tariq Ali sees Saif as going in the direction of neo-liberalism:

> Does it also require a hereditary leadership? One of Qaddafi's sons, Saif al-Islam, is being groomed for the succession. Since he's a PhD student at the LSE and enamoured of the neoliberal West, there is little criticism here (Libya) of the proposed handover. Qaddafi, after all, is no longer the head of a 'rogue state' but a 'great statesman' (in the words of Jack Straw) and has received Blair in his tent. This helps to maintain the pretence that he's caved in to London, not Washington. It's so simple: Saif wants to privatise everything and turn Libya into a Gulf statelet.[61]

Saif's ambitions have been helped by improvements in the economy. After a long period of economic, political and social decline under United States' pressure and United Nations' sanctions, 1999 saw Libya begin its return to the international system. This produced an improvement in the country's fortunes, which have furthered the prospects for Saif's bid for power. Domestically, Saif still faces a long-term challenge of subduing the People's Committees and driving back the forces of Islamism on his father's behalf. Success in these areas will be central to Saif's prospects for succession. While there would appear to be no opposition with the capacity to block his rise to the top, were Saif to falter in these efforts, his progress towards the leadership would be hampered and opponents, including some from within the family, might be emboldened.

Like Syria and Egypt, Libya's political system is heavily influenced by Qaddafi's immediate family, by his extended family and by tribal networks. Saif appears to hold only one formal position, President of the Qaddafi International Foundation for Charity Associations, which has been used in a number of foreign policy initiatives. Other family members are established in central positions of power throughout the Libyan system. One of Qaddafi's sons is married to the daughter of the head of Libyan intelligence. His only daughter is understood to be politically influential, but she occupies no significant public position. Saif's other brother holds an advisory position, having been involved in a reputed coup attempt against Qaddafi. These family members are effectively involved at the edges of the regime. If they have political ambitions, they have been careful to contain them. Among the extended family, one of Qaddafi's nephews is commander of two of the country's most sensitive military regions. Another nephew is General-Coordinator of the Socialist People's Leadership Committees, from which position, according to Qaddafi, he will succeed as head of state.[62] Members of Qaddafi's second wife's family also occupy significant positions of trust throughout the country. Security operations are largely controlled by members of Qaddafi's tribe, the Qadadfa, or of tribes allied to the Qadadfa.

Assuming that the transition from father to son takes place, the nature of the regime to be run by Saif will be of interest. His public comments, so far, suggest a greater interest in and reliance on established and formal processes of governance. In an *Al Jazeera* interview, for example, he commented that the Libyan legal system was developing with the establishment of a basis for a legislative system backed by an independent judicial system. He claimed that the various people's courts established by his father were being wound down, that there was no longer any torture conducted, and that, in their place was a single, united judicial system in Libya.[63]

Yemen: tribal republic

Another country in the group of republics considering a dynastic handover of power is Yemen, where President Ali Abdallah Saleh has been in power since the unification of North and South Yemen in 1990.[64] Like the leaders of the other republics studied, Saleh's immediate and extended family has played an important part in helping him to maintain power. Like the Syrian case, the issue of Saleh's son's succession is not a topic of public conversation in Yemen. Journalists have been harassed and even gaoled for having raised the issue in public.[65]

Saleh's legitimacy is based on his central role in the unification of the two Yemens and on his subsequent efforts to provide stability to the country. He is, in

Weber's schema, another representative of the mixed charismatic-traditional type of leader. Saleh's highly personalised power rests on a range of measures, many of which are delicately balanced compromises and alliances with other powerful forces in the country. His task of maintaining control is particularly difficult, given that his regime lacks the economic and military resources to enforce his will in the way that the Syrian, Egyptian and Libyan regimes do. His response has been to arrange for the strategic placement of family members in vital military and political positions throughout the country. His oldest son and heir, Ahmed, is a colonel with control of the country's Special Forces and Republican Guards, upon whose loyalty and effectiveness the survival of the regime greatly depends. One half-brother is Commander of the Air Force and another is Chief of Staff of the General Command. Nephews occupy various senior positions in the army and the security forces. Various family members serve as governors in key districts. In addition, members of Saleh's sect, the Shiite Zaidis, and his tribe, the Sanhan, play an important part in maintaining the regime.

The intricacy of this political structure reflects the complexity of Yemeni society. Traditionally, it is a deeply divided country, reflecting often expedient alliances based on tribal, social, religious and political ties.[66] Over the past decade, the divisions appear to have moved slightly and hardened, with the potential to disturb the balances on which Saleh holds power. Lingering discontent in the south of the country is hardening into resistance to the central government. Tribes that have not benefited from the government's largesse have taken to arms against the government in several persistent uprisings. In addition, political Islam has emerged as a serious threat to regime stability. Complicating matters has been a deterioration in Yemen's economic performance with reserves of oil, which in 2007 contributed about 85 per cent of Yemen's export income and 33 per cent of GDP, declining dramatically. It is in this context that Ali Abdallah Saleh is thought to be attempting to position Ahmed as his successor. As with the other republican examples discussed, it is likely that to have any chance of success, Saleh will have to ensure that the succession is seen as legitimate by adhering to constitutional law as it relates to succession.

The constitution

Yemen's constitution was adopted by referendum in 1991, following the unification of North and South. It has subsequently been amended in 1994 and 2001 to fit Saleh's dynastic ambitions. Among the amendments to the original constitution is the change to Article 112 (formerly Article 111), which extended the presidential term from five to seven years and limited a president to two terms. Ahmed is in his mid-thirties, which makes him too young to run for the presidency,[67] but he will be of age when the next elections are held in 2013.

Scepticism about the regime's commitment to the rule of law is sharpened by the section in the constitution dealing with the judiciary and, in particular, the Supreme Judicial Council (Articles 147–52). The concept of separation of powers runs throughout the constitution, and Article 147 specifically states that 'The judiciary authority is an autonomous authority in its judicial, financial and administrative aspects . . .' The Council's role is to ensure that aspects of the judiciary dealing with appointment, promotion and dismissal are conducted according to the law. The Council is also responsible for the development and approval of the judicial budget. The Council is, however, chaired by the President with the assistance of the Minister of Justice and the Deputy Minister of Justice. The other members are judicial, though all are direct or indirect presidential appointments. It is hard to see how such an arrangement can be compatible with judicial independence and with the rule of law more generally. Phillips argues that the regime's commitment to the rule of law has actually declined over time as the political system has become more centralised.[68]

Nevertheless, as with the constitutions of other Arab countries, the Yemeni constitution exerts a degree of influence over the government and the ambitions of the President, given the political compromises that are contained in it. The limitation to two terms for a president and the adoption of Shari`a law as 'the source of all legislation' (Article 3) represent attempts by Saleh to mollify Islamic and tribal hostility to the regime. The President is bound to not stray too far from those provisions if he is to hold his coalition together. It is likely that Saleh and Ahmed will follow the example expected from Egypt of ensuring that Ahmed's path to the presidency follows all the constitutional markers.

President-in-waiting?

Ahmed has many advantages on his side, including the powerful positions he holds. His control of key security forces gives him a solid power base from which to build his claim. He has been a member of the House of Representatives since 1997, which puts him in a good position to ensure he has the endorsement of the ten per cent of the members of the House that is required by the constitution for candidates to the presidency (Article 107(e)). Saleh's decision to continue for another term gives Ahmed time to consolidate his power and to develop these advantages.

Ahmed's path to the presidency may appear inexorable. In a volatile country like Yemen, however, it is unlikely to be smooth. As noted above, some of the established relationships and alliances upon which Saleh has relied in order to maintain power have begun to show signs of stress. For example, in early 2006, Abdallah Al Ahmar, the leader of the main opposition party in Parliament and the paramount sheikh of one of the major tribal confederations of the country, announced that he was leaving Yemen 'to Ali Abdallah Saleh and his sons' and indicated that the alliance with Saleh, which has survived for 30 years, was close to collapse.[69] Al Ahmar ultimately remained in the country and continued to play an important role in the opposition to Saleh. His opposition was, however, a highly structured arrangement which was based on an understanding between his family and that of Saleh and which contributed to stability in the country. His death in early 2008 underlined the importance to the President of maintaining the understanding with Al Ahmar's successors. The armed forces also pose something of a challenge for the future. While Saleh has so far managed to control the armed forces and security agencies, Islamic militants are understood to have infiltrated their ranks. A transfer of power from Saleh to Ahmed might provide an opportunity for such groups to act against the regime. Observers note dissent building in the face of the increasingly serious economic problems of the country. Unless dramatic improvements in the economy can be achieved, some commentators consider that the dissent could build to the point where it threatens the regime.[70]

Perhaps a greater danger for Ahmed's ambitions is to be found in his own shortcomings. Ahmed appears not to have been a success during a period he spent at Sandhurst and he has had a mixed record in the various jobs entrusted to him by his father. This has included some visible roles, including responsibility for dealing with the tribes' practice of kidnapping foreign visitors for ransom. If Ahmed is unable to learn from his experiences, his shortcomings could make it very difficult for the President to proceed with Ahmed as his successor. The tough world of Yemeni politics is unlikely to tolerate an ineffectual president for long and other members of Saleh's family, some of whom are understood to have their own presidential ambitions, could be expected to remove Ahmed before outsiders could destroy the family's hold on power. As it stands, one of Saleh's half-brothers, Mohsen Al Ahmar, the military commander of the northern and western districts, is understood to have opposed Ahmed's rise to power. On the other hand, there appears to be little political interest in an open contest for the leadership. When, in early 2006, Ali Abdallah Saleh announced his decision not to run again for the presidency, there was consternation in the ruling party. According to Novak, the ruling party in the Parliament 'expressed sheer panic' at the thought of Saleh withdrawing. Given that an alternative candidate did not appear achievable through democratic means, the party was faced by a prospect of members of Saleh's family 'fighting it out to become the next nominee'. Fortunately for the party, Saleh allowed himself to be drafted again.[71]

The four republics examined in this chapter reflect certain common characteristics. They involve long-standing rulers, whose families have been closely involved in their maintenance of power and have become committed to the perpetuation of their hold on power. They also involve a broader elite that supports the status quo as a way of ensuring the domestic distribution of power and resources to which they are committed. The rulers enjoy legitimacy reflecting Weber's military form of charisma, the status of the military hero that has been a major factor in their ability to hold onto power. For these charismatic rulers, their countries' constitutions have been intended as means of consolidating their power, of spelling out the rules of the game and, potentially, as means for legitimising the succession of their sons to the highest level.

These rulers have been operating in dangerous and divided societies, which have, in the case of Egypt, proven fatal to a leader who did not have a sufficient hold on power. All have been confronted by formidable opposition and have been willing to employ maximum force to suppress that opposition. They have, however, also enjoyed a degree of support or at least acquiescence among the bulk of their populations, who are more interested in stability and security than in access to political power. There would appear, also, to be a potential willingness among the general population of the four countries concerned to tolerate dynastic succession for the same reasons of security and stability. The rulers are attempting build on that tolerance to prepare their sons' accession through Weber's ritual or magical procedure: election.

There are, however, many obstacles for the various inheritances of power. As Weber notes, the specifically personal basis of charismatic authority is removed by the death of the leader and the transient nature of the charismatic leader's effect focuses attention on the political issue of the succession. Much will depend on the successor's political skills as he attempts to develop his own basis for legitimacy. This is unlikely to conform to Weber's charismatic form, given that the new leaders are coming to power at a time of relative stability. Instead they will have to rely on the traditional and bureaucratic claims to legitimacy. The travails of Bashar Al Assad are a good indicator of how difficult this process will be for all the presidential hopefuls.

Despite the best efforts of the ruler and the abilities of his son, the passing of an established republican ruler will always generate uncertainty in the Arab world. It will also encourage opponents of the regime to exploit this uncertainty to push for change. The established leaders of Syria, Egypt, Libya and Yemen have attempted to give their sons the best possible chances of resisting the challenges that are to come. They have done this by giving them opportunities to develop their political skills and to establish their own power bases within the system. The sons, for their part, have made their own use of the family and tribal networks upon which their fathers built their power. The sons have also attempted to make their constitutions work for their ambitions. With the exception of Saif Al Islam in Libya, the other contenders appear to be attempting to ensure that their climb to the top is consistent with the requirements of their countries' constitutions. This is part of Weber's routinisation of authority. Gamal Mubarak and Ahmed Saleh will probably seek to secure approval of their parliaments and the endorsement of their dominant parties. Success, however, will not resolve the fundamental and logical problem of how a dynastic structure can be explained and justified in the constitution of a republic. The new generation of rulers could attempt to convert their political systems into monarchies, where the problem does not arise. This would, however, be a major break with the historical ideologies of their societies and would require great authority to succeed. It is to be doubted that a ruler lacking charismatic qualities would be able to succeed in such an objective. The alternative would appear to be a continued *ad hoc* arrangement whereby the ruler spends much of his time attempting to prepare for his son's succession but which would always be open to criticism and challenge.

8 Tradition versus change

The challenge of dynasticism in the Arab political tradition

> A major weakness of the Arab states . . . is their origins as Western inventions, which is sometimes resented as alien, while at the same time people are obsessed with the unrealized potential of these states. Consequently, they have faced repeated challenges by sub- and supra-state groups and ideologies, ranging from tribes to pan-Islamic ideologies. Although the Middle Eastern states have survived these challenges, the logic of stateness has not been fully internalized.[1]

The Arab world is home to a distinct and sophisticated political tradition that is coming to terms with the huge degree of political, economic and social change that has swept through the region since the demise of the Ottoman Empire. This book has examined one aspect of this tradition, namely the widespread phenomenon of dynastic succession in Arab political systems. Increasingly, the process of political succession is being played out in the context of the growing importance of national constitutions and governments' attempts to embody succession in those instruments. Succession is a major concern for both republican and monarchic forms of government and the issue raises a number of significant areas of common ground that underlie the two types of system. A starting premise is that, as in political systems elsewhere, political succession in the Arab world is ultimately a political act and, while subject to intense public speculation, is decided largely along informal lines behind closed doors. A distinctive feature of the Arab system is, however, that the groups making the decisions about who is to rule tend to regard the issue as a family matter. There is a limited connection to or input from the populations of the various countries. Normally, popular input is limited to the opportunity to endorse the decisions, either in the traditional tribal manner according to the Saudi Basic Law or by means of a tightly scripted election as occurs in countries like Syria and Egypt.

The Arab political tradition

It became evident in researching this book that the Arab political tradition comprises two distinct and competing characteristics that operate on the ways in which Arabs conduct their politics. One characteristic is that of adaptability and a willingness to accept influences from outsiders. This characteristic was apparent from the early days of Islam and the ongoing contacts with Byzantium. This demanded an approach to running an extensive, multi-national and multi-religious empire which was more predictable, cohesive and long term than the Arabs' traditional form of governance could provide. Traditional tribalism was well suited for small nomadic communities in difficult environments, where effective leadership was an essential element in the ability of tribes to survive. In such an environment, tribes blended democratic elements with authoritarianism in their approach to governance. The resulting system was, however, too personal and simply not sophisticated enough to provide the basis for a political system in an advanced society.

Tribal traditions were also directly challenged by concepts introduced by Islam. Islam was a truly revolutionary force in the Arab world and inspired great changes in the ways Arabs approached their place in the world. At the same time, Islam was itself deeply influenced by the tribal milieu in which it developed, and in some respects it reinforced some of the characteristics of the old world. Crucially, the Prophet Mohammed did not provide clear guidance to those who came after him in a number of key political areas, in particular, the process of political succession and nature of leadership. In the early days after the death of the Prophet, the Arabs fell back on their traditional practices. Over time and in the face of evident weaknesses in their own tribe-based approaches, Arabs drew upon Persian and other models for methods of meeting the increasingly complex challenges facing the Islamic empire. This was the beginning of a long period of borrowing and adaptation, accentuated by the lengthy period of foreign rule over the Arab world. As a result, a combination of tribal, authoritarian Persian and Islamic practices and theory emerged as the dominant basis for political practice in Arab societies.

A major feature of these foreign borrowings was their authoritarianism and dynasticism, as well as their lack of enthusiasm for constitutional and law-based methods of government. Instead, the emphasis was on charismatic and traditional bases of legitimacy. A challenge to this approach came in the forms of the most recent influences to bear on the Arab political tradition, namely, Western ideals of liberal democracy and the rule of law. In some ways, these are the first truly alien influences to make their mark on the region and they have introduced concepts and practices, such as secularism and party politics, that have no historic roots in the region. Many Arabs responded enthusiastically to this new influence, seeing in Western political ideas and structures solutions to some of the huge challenges facing the region since the end of the Ottoman Empire. These influences have become a lasting feature of the region's landscape, albeit, significantly altered to reflect the different circumstances of the Arab world compared to the West.

While part of the Arab response to outside influences has been adaptation and assimilation, another response has been a reversion to traditional features of the political system. This second characteristic of the Arab political tradition highlights the conservatism of the people of the region and reflects a yearning for an idealised, simpler past under the Prophet and the Rightly-Guided Caliphs. While having little basis in reality, this image exerts a great attraction to more conservative and marginalised elements in Arab societies and influences their political behaviour. An important outcome of this approach is the persistence of tribal and, in particular, family loyalties and attitudes as guides to social and, especially, political behaviour. It is striking the way that, regardless of whether people are of the modernising, adaptive school or are more conservatively inclined, major issues, such as political succession, will be deeply influenced by considerations of the traditional reliance on family and tribe. With this in mind, this book examined a number of aspects of the Arab political system as it relates to family and tribal attitudes, leadership and legitimacy, succession and the role of constitutions.

Family loyalties and the political process

A fundamental element of the Arab political tradition that emerged from this review is that family loyalties and attitudes, ultimately derived from the tribal past, permeate Arab societies and are major factors behind the impulse towards dynastic political succession. This is an important feature of the broad sweep of Arab politics, but one that has been challenged by the more modern interest in class-based and economic explanations for political behaviour. Moreover, many analysts maintain that urbanisation and the great power of the modern state in the Middle East have destroyed the traditional tribal way of life and with it, the power of the tribes. While it may generally be true that the tribalism of today bears few practical resemblances to what it was less than one hundred years ago, there is considerable evidence that many of the values and attitudes of tribalism still possess a considerable hold on the people of the Arab world, especially, but not only, at times of national weakness or stress. Examples of family and tribal attitudes and loyalties influencing national politics have been drawn from countries as diverse as Morocco, Libya and Iraq. These examples demonstrate that it is not so much the material power of a tribe that is important, although the tribes still have the capacity to exercise considerable force if the circumstances are conducive. Rather it is the persistence of tribal and especially family loyalties and attitudes that is a key to the understanding of the dynastic impulse and the nature of Arab political behaviour. It is clear that these loyalties and attitudes inherited from the tribal past represent much of the glue that holds together the various Arab regimes and provides the impulse that drives Arab rulers to seek to have their sons replace them in power.

Much of the analysis has a historical focus. This is because, while people in other political systems are inclined to dwell on past glories, for Arabs their history remains an important, even a defining, part of the modern political process. The experience of generations under foreign rule, the importance of tribal traditions and the centrality of the framework established by the Prophet Mohammed mean that Arabs often look to the past for inspiration, guidance and, importantly, solutions to modern problems. Even those regimes that have attempted widespread social and economic modernisation since independence and have been willing to adopt ideas and structures from the West have felt the need to make resort to their past. For example, the Egyptian constitution makes frequent direct and indirect reference to the future and the country's objectives, but it also recalls its past:

> We, the people of Egypt, who have been toiling on this glorious land since the dawn of history and civilization (Preamble).

For Arabs, there is the added complication of intense external pressures, which seek to influence the way they deal with basic political challenges. As Carl Brown notes, this influence has been more pervasive and penetrating in the Middle East than in any other region of the world.[2] Again, in the face of this penetration, the instinctive reaction of many people in the region has been to fall back on the past, trying to find comfort and a reaffirmation of their identity in the apparent certainties of history.

Throughout all this turmoil, attitudes derived from the tribal ethos have remained potent influences on the way Arabs look at the world around them, including their political systems. The most important of these is the desire to promote the family and the view that the family remains, amongst all the uncertainty, the one source of reliable support and the main focus of loyalty. This attitude exerts a major influence on the way Arab leaders approach their roles today.

Leadership and legitimacy

The strong emphasis on charismatic and traditional forms of leadership in the Arab world has led to a focus on the personal legitimacy of the people in power.[3] As noted in Chapters 1 and 3, a common view of Arab leaders is that they are tyrannical autocrats who lack legitimacy. Salem, for example, described the nationalist republics as suffering from 'a lingering crisis of legitimacy . . . that has helped make them among the most repressive in the region and in the world'.[4] In examining some of these claims, it was found that while some Arab regimes certainly deserve such criticism, Arab regimes in general enjoy a greater level of legitimacy than their critics acknowledge. It is clear that without this legitimacy even the most despotic regime would not survive.

Arab regimes are able to appeal to tradition and family loyalty to enhance their legitimacy because, to a great extent, the reliance on family and tribe makes sense to the general population and is consistent with society's expectations. The understanding and acceptance by Arab societies of the intimate involvement of family in many forms of political, social and economic life help to create a manageable environment in which regimes can operate. This attitude has important implications for both leadership practices and the question of political succession.

The focus of Arab leaders on security and their reliance on their family and tribal support systems can be interpreted as evidence of the potentially fragile nature of their regimes. And there is no question that Arab regimes are vulnerable to violent acts of opposition. Many, if not most, Arab leaders have been the target of assassination attempts and most governments endure substantial domestic unrest. This evident vulnerability should not, however, be taken as a sign that Arab leaders lack legitimacy. Arab rulers have displayed great tenacity over the past 30 or so years, a factor that cannot be attributed solely to the efficiency and ruthlessness of their security systems. There are numerous other factors contributing to their survival, indeed, the very success of Arab regimes in maintaining their hold on power has contributed to the degree of legitimacy they enjoy. The complex networks of alliances and clientalist relationships that the regimes have established mean that significant sectors of Arab societies outside the dominant families and tribes still have vested interests in the survival of the regimes. The regimes have also gained considerable public acceptance for their provision of stability and predictability. In such an environment it is possible for people to adapt and accommodate to the rules, such as they are. Together, these factors have given Arab regimes a critical mass of public support.

At the same time, the longevity of Arab leaders and the public's acquiescence should not necessarily be taken as an indication of absolute legitimacy and a willingness on the part of their people to accept whatever a regime might choose to do. Arab politics are too complex for such a convenient correlation. The rulers of the Arab world operate in an unsettled, contested environment. Despite what appears to be majority tolerance of the existing arrangements, there is a fundamental rejection of some of the basic ordering principles of the state by significant elements of society. As such, legitimacy is likely always to be a volatile attribute, a problem aggravated by the degree of change through which the Arab world has passed since the fall of the Ottoman Empire.[5] Under such conditions, Arab leaders have regularly fallen back on appeals to tradition as a way of softening the impact of change. Alternatively, they have turned to traditional bases of support, which ultimately means reliance on the control of force and politics by the family and the tribe. The result is a precarious legitimacy, but one that has now endured over several generations. It would seem clear that these regimes are not going to fade away or be easily removed.

Succession

It is clear that, despite the dissatisfaction with the various governments in place and the pressure for reform, succession based on the family and the tribe is accepted to a significant degree throughout the Arab world. This is true at the level of the power elites themselves, but it is also true among the general population. Moreover, succession based on primogeniture appears to have a strong, instinctive appeal to many of those in power. This support results, in part, from the underlying importance of family at many levels of public activity in the Arab world. Family or dynastic succession is a common feature of business in all countries of the Arab world. It is hardly surprising that this attitude should also apply to the political sector, where sovereign power has come to be seen as part of a family's entitlement and something that should be closely held within the family group.

The analysis of Arabs' handling of political succession suggests a failure or a reluctance to allow Western-style institutionalised mechanisms to develop in a way which would allow them to play a major role in the handling of key issues of regime maintenance. Instead, as in their approach to leadership, Arab monarchs and presidents have increasingly relied on practices based in traditional forms of government to deal with succession. The region's monarchies have been reasonably successful at providing a plausible framework for succession. In large part, this is because their approach to governance draws extensively from traditional tribal practices and exploits traditional family loyalties, elements which generally have support in their societies. This urge towards dynastic rule is, however, also apparent among the republics, where most leaders are intent on passing on power to their own family members.

It would appear that, superficially at least, there is a connection between the duration of a leader's period in office and his attempts to perpetuate family rule. The longer an Arab republican ruler survives in power, the more likely the issue of hereditary succession is to arise. This is largely because the longer the ruler is in power, the more opportunities his family has to establish and consolidate control over the key instruments of political and economic power. This in turn breeds expectations of continued control within the ruling family and in the community at large.

While the dynastic impulse is dominant throughout the Arab world, it should be remembered that there is also opposition to the practice. Tribal and Islamic approaches are ambiguous about the handling of succession and they can be interpreted as constraints on the ability of Arab rulers to dispose of the leadership as they choose. Much of the opposition to dynastic practices is represented by largely conservative elements who base their arguments on tribal and Islamic precedent. There are also significant forces inspired by Western models that are pressing for electoral and constitutional reform as part of a campaign for greater democracy in the region.

Given the tenacity of the dynastic principle in the Arab region, it is possible to make some forecasts about directions Arab systems might take in response to domestic and external pressures for change. In the modern context, the succession process is obviously tied up with regime type. While similarities between the republican and monarchic systems have been stressed throughout this book, the fact remains that there are fundamental logical, political and constitutional problems with the existence of a formal ruling dynasty within a republican system. By contrast, the greater logic of the monarchic systems with regard to succession works to support their succession arrangements. The challenge for the republican systems will be to assimilate their powerful impulses to establish family rule in their countries with the constitutional arrangements in place.

Constitutions

To a great extent, Arab nations are states of exception which have little appreciation of the rule of law. Despite a history of constitution making and the great tradition and depth of Islamic jurisprudence, constitutions in the Arab world lack the political and ideological status and relevance that they enjoy in other parts of the world, especially in the West. The examination of Arab regimes' attitudes to those provisions in Arab constitutions that deal with political succession demonstrate a ready willingness among Arab leaders to ignore, distort or casually amend the documents should they present obstacles to their political objectives. At the same time, there is evidence that constitutions do have relevance, especially as they relate to the strategies of Arab regimes that are seeking to explain and legitimise their dynastic ambitions. The region's written constitutions and legislative frameworks have come to represent important ways of regularising, systematising and legitimising the practice of succession, especially as Arab governments diversify their mechanisms of control beyond military force. Rather than depend heavily on force, Arab ruling groups have begun to employ constitutional and other measures as a way of consolidating their dominant positions and to establish sets of rules for government within that dominance. Their expectation is that the development of constitutions will relieve or divert some of the pressure for change and add to the legitimacy of their rule. Based on experience in other parts of the world and on a few tentative signs in the Arab region itself, however, these instruments have the potential to play a role which goes beyond that expected by their designers in Arab political processes.

The rule of law is likely to remain a vulnerable concept in the Arab world for the foreseeable future, but constitutions could increasingly assume a role in creating legal limits on the power of the ruling regimes. As regimes seek to formalise their position of dominance, they have incorporated into their constitutions some of the important political compromises and concessions they have made to other power centres. The constitutions have, as a result, become methods of developing and maintaining societal understandings and political compromises, of expressing and guaranteeing delicate balances of power and allocations of spoils and of providing frameworks for political action. The ability of political groups to hold these regimes to their commitments could, over time, lead to the constitutions developing a life of their own and playing a significant role in the political life of these societies. They could serve to establish limits beyond which governments and their opponents will hesitate to go. This role of constitutions could extend to the facilitation of change in the political process towards more accessible and responsive governments.

Importantly, while the significance of the compromises made by the current regimes may not be fully apparent at the present, their longer-term implications might be considerable. Arab constitutions are largely intended to promote the dominance of the ruling houses in the region. This does not mean that constitutional monarchy or constitutional republicanism is unlikely. The desire of Elizabeth Tudor and Charles II to preserve their families' dominant positions in English political life was no less than the desire of ruling families in Arab republics and monarchies to achieve the same end. In the case of England, however, deals struck led eventually, if unpredictably, to the development of firm constitutional controls on the powers of the head of state. As Thompson notes in his discussion of eighteenth-century English legal development:

> . . . we have seen the law being devised and employed, directly and instrumentally, in the imposition of class power. . . . Eighteenth-century law was more substantial than that. Over and above its pliant, instrumental functions it existed in its own right, as ideology; as an ideology which not only served, in most respects, but which also legitimised class power. . . . And the rulers were, in serious senses, whether willingly or unwillingly, the prisoners of their own rhetoric; they played the games of power according to rules which suited them, but they could not break those rules or the whole game would be thrown away.[6]

There are many forces in play in the Arab world that are pushing in a similar direction. The constitutional challenge for Arab monarchic and republican rulers is to find a survival formula that will enjoy real legitimacy and will endure across generations. In the short term, this will require some thoughtful and far-sighted strategies by the new leaders in the region.

Signs that some of the aspiring leaders are looking at new ways of establishing and consolidating their power have emerged. The original divisions and weaknesses in their societies that have characterised the region since independence persist, and these will continue to challenge modernising activities. In particular, the negative aspects of the family ethos, the suspicion of outsiders, the ambiguous attitudes to the state as a focus of loyalty and the importance of clientalist networks in regime maintenance will work against attempts to place family rule within more broadly structured, rule-based arrangements.

Arab monarchies of the future

In looking at Arab monarchies, it is possible to divide them into two categories based on whether their succession is organised according to a form of primogeniture or a family-based consensus. The monarchies were reviewed in terms of their nature from the perspective of the issues raised in earlier chapters, namely tribalism, leadership approach and the place of their constitutions in their political systems. The monarchies analysed are relatively successful regimes, despite their ongoing vulnerability to domestic and external challenges. Most are also relatively young states with limited experience of a sophisticated political system. The ruling families in these monarchies are all intent on consolidating and perpetuating their hold on power, and they are turning to constitutions to help them to this end.

The concept of a constitutional structure is one of the aspects of the modern political system with which the ruling families are coming to terms. Some aspects of constitutions are hardly consistent with the objectives of family-based monarchies, but the regimes have identified in the constitutional framework one means of contributing to their longevity, including their ability to legitimise the succession process. The Arab monarchies have taken different paths to this goal of constitutional consolidation of their succession arrangements. The United Arab Emirates has developed a republican monarchy. Oman relies on a family council, a process that relies on a council consisting of members of the ruling family.

Kuwait has, more by force of circumstances than by choice, developed in the direction of a constitutional monarchy, with people outside the ruling family playing a much greater role in key royal family issues, including succession.

What emerges from this review and what is important from the perspective of this analysis is that a strong focus on family, tribe and a direct handover of power from father to son is common to all approaches to succession. This was a feature in the early days of the Saudi dynasty, and there is evidence that the interest in primogeniture there has not vanished. The successions from Hassan to Mohammed in Morocco, Hussein to Abdallah in Jordan and Zayed to Khalifa in Abu Dhabi have all reflected a process based on primogeniture. At first glance, this is a surprising inclination on the part of Arab monarchs, who have sought to present themselves as sympathetic to tribal attitudes and concerns. It is also difficult to accommodate the dynastic impulse with some of the major schools of Islamic political thought. Regardless of the inconsistencies, however, Arab monarchs have not been willing to be diverted from their goals by ideas and practices that might have served to constrain their ambitions over time.

Arab monarchies could face major problems in the future as established rulers leave the scene. Their successors start with considerable advantages, including a system created by their fathers, their established political structures and networks, their wealth, their education and their external connections. The future monarchs, however, lack the experience and, potentially, the understanding of leaders like Jordan's King Hussein, whose toughness, closeness to the people and understanding of their concerns engendered great personal loyalty. This is a criticism directed specifically at King Abdallah of Jordan and King Mohammed of Morocco, who are seen as lacking a human touch and are inclined to unnecessary ruthlessness. Significant problems may rise to confront the new leaders of the family-based regimes. Family and regime loyalty will become increasingly difficult to maintain in the face of the huge growth in the numbers of ruling family members, and the inevitable divergence of interests that will develop as the ruling groups grow larger. Some problems are perhaps even more fundamental. Will the monarchic form of government be able to adapt to the changing political environment to the extent that it retains its relevance and its hold on the loyalty of its populations?

Arab republics: what lies ahead?

The four republics examined reflect a range of common features which bear on their approach to succession. They involve long-standing rulers, whose families have been closely involved in their maintenance of power and have become committed to the survival of their families' hold on power. They also involve the co-option of a broader elite that supports the status quo as a way of ensuring the domestic distribution of power and resources to which they are committed. The rulers have tended to enjoy legitimacy consistent with Weber's ideas of charisma drawn from military prowess, and this has been a major factor in their ability to hold onto power. For these charismatic rulers, their countries' constitutions were initially used to assist in mobilising their populations for the social and economic transformations they had planned. Gradually, they have developed more conservative goals, focusing on the consolidation of their power, especially through family and tribal networks. The constitutions have also been exploited as a means for legitimising the succession of the sons of rulers to the highest office.

Despite the logical incongruity of such a situation in republics and the difficulty in systematising such an approach, republican regimes appear determined to maintain family rule. If they are to succeed in doing so, they will need to find some form of constitutional justification for their arrangements. The current process in republics of *ad hoc* transfers of power leaves too much to fate and exposes those regimes to periods of particular vulnerability. Of course, monarchies also face uncertainty and instability during the succession process, as was made clear in Chapter 6, but at least their mechanisms and procedures, if not the individuals concerned, are generally accepted as legitimate. The need to regularise and systematise the practice, therefore, represents a challenge to all Arab republican governments.

These republican rulers have been operating in dangerous, divided societies, which have in some cases proven fatal to leaders who did not have a sufficient hold on power. All have been confronted by formidable opposition and have had to be willing to employ force to suppress that opposition. They have, however, also enjoyed a degree of support or, at least, acquiescence among the bulk of their populations, who are more interested in stability and security than in access to political power. There would appear, also, to be a potential willingness among the general population of the four countries concerned to tolerate dynastic succession for the same reasons of security and stability. The current rulers are attempting to build on that tolerance to prepare their sons' accession through a merging of two of Weber's forms of legitimacy, which are traditional and legal, that is, through constitutionally-based endorsement of dynastic succession. The way the traditional element of legitimacy is preserved is through the election process, which effectively involves voters being asked to endorse a family-based succession in an uncontested election. This process is quite distinct from the electoral process as understood in the West, but it reflects the Arabs' historic experience by turning the elections into something akin to the traditional pledge of allegiance (*bay'a*) that tribal members would offer to their new leader on his accession. Weber's legal form of authority is introduced through the constitutional regularisation of this distinct electoral process.

There are, however, many obstacles facing the various approaches to the transmission of power. As Weber notes, the specifically personal basis of charismatic authority is removed by the death of the leader. The transient nature of the charismatic leader's effect focuses attention on the political issue of the succession.[7] Much will depend on the successor's political skills as he attempts to develop his own basis for legitimacy and on his predecessor's effectiveness in preparing for the succession. The basis for a new ruler's authority cannot be the same as his predecessor's. He must rely on the traditional and legal forms, given his lack of a significant military background. The travails of Bashar Al Assad are a good indicator of how difficult this process will be for all presidential hopefuls.

Despite the best efforts of the ruler and the abilities of his son, the passing of an established ruler will always generate uncertainty. It will also encourage opponents of the regime to exploit this uncertainty in order to push for change. The leaders of Syria, Egypt, Libya and Yemen have attempted to give their sons the best possible chances of resisting the challenges that are to come by providing them with opportunities to develop their political skills and to establish their own power bases within the system. The sons, for their part, have made their own use of the family and tribal networks upon which their fathers had built their power. The sons have attempted to make their constitutions work for their ambitions. The various contenders appear to be attempting to ensure that their climb to the top is consistent with the requirements of their countries' constitutions. This is consistent with Weber's 'routinisation' of authority, where rules play a major part in political management. Gamal Mubarak and Ahmed Saleh will probably seek to secure the endorsement of their dominant parties, the approval of their parliaments and public acknowledgement by means of a controlled election. The exception is Saif Al Islam in Libya, where the constitution, to the extent that it could be said to exist, provides little guidance on what power and legitimacy might be based.

Successful transfers of power, however, will not resolve the fundamental and logical problem of how a dynastic structure can be explained and justified in the constitution of a republic. It is not clear how republican governments might address the incongruity of their desire for dynastic rule and the logical difficulty posed by an hereditary republic over the long term. Western political ideologies have not proven to be particularly durable over the years since independence. Western institutions remain, but their original intent has been hollowed out in order to provide a framework in which Arab leaders can pursue their own interests. Given the problems facing republican regimes, it is not inconceivable that the monarchic model may become the dominant feature of Arab political systems. Almost all Arab countries have experienced monarchic rule, although not all those experiences have been successful.[8] Nevertheless, to the extent that the tribal tradition is conducive to a monarchical system, it is possible that the model might be attractive to ruling families in republican regimes seeking to consolidate their rule in the future. The path to such an outcome might be found in the impact of the Arabs' past on the remnants of Western control, much as Arab monarchies have resorted to tradition to sustain their power.

Political change: substance or a mirage?

The demands of the modern world, the dramatic growth of the populations of Arab countries and their struggling economies, coupled with the increasingly difficult task of controlling the people of the region, have led to demands for political reform and modernisation. Arab regimes have recognised that they must respond to these demands and that they must become more sophisticated in their approach to governance if they are to maintain and consolidate their hold on power.

Importantly, the course taken in this direction by republican and monarchic regimes is to rely more on political processes than their traditional base of the power of the military. This involves maintaining power over all arms of the military and security forces but reducing the ability of those groups to coalesce against the regime by reducing their funding and dividing these groups among themselves. They are then able to pursue legitimacy through elections and the political process more generally, in a way that tends to preclude members of the military from playing a political role. This is a significant change in the way Arab political systems are run, but it should be noted that the change is occurring in a manner consistent with the Arab tradition rather than the liberal democratic ideals favoured by the West. Increasingly, they are turning to the mechanisms of state, including the rule of law, or at least the colour of law, not to transfer power to the people, but to consolidate their positions. This is, in part, a necessary response to both changing security and economic circumstances and pressure from outside. Importantly, it is also a sign of greater confidence among Arab leaders in the stability of their systems.

Appendix 1

Definition of some terms used

aya – a verse or sub-division of a Sura in the Quran.
asabiya – a key feature of Arab relationships; small group solidarity based on blood relationships. Described by ibn Khaldoun as more important in Arab political culture than elements such as royal authority and religious merit.
bay'a – contract, homage, election; an oath of allegiance.
caliph – Deputy of (the Prophet of) God or successor to Mohammed. The leader of the Sunni Moslem community (also Khalifa).
Companions – the close and contemporary followers of Mohammed.
dajal – deceit, pretending to be other than you are.
fiqh – Islamic jurisprudence, legal theory.
hadar – city dweller.
Hadith – traditions of the teachings and examples of the Prophet Mohammed, which are not contained in the Quran. Great numbers are recorded, many of which are not regarded as authentic. Hadith form the basis of the Sunna.
hayaat – committee.
ijma' – agreement or unanimity; consensus (of legal authorities).
ijtihad – independent judgement; the reaching of a decision based on general principles.
imam – the leader of the Moslem community. For Shi`a Moslems, the term specifically denotes the descendents of the Prophet Mohammed, through his daughter, Fatima, and her husband, Ali ibn Abi Talib, who the Shi`a regard as the true rulers of the Moslem community.
jahiliya – the age of ignorance before the teaching of Mohammed.
jumhuriya – republic.
Majlis al Shura – Consultative Council.
mamlaka – monarchy.
mulk – Rule. Can be applied to kingdom or dynasty.
Mu'maneen – The Faithful.
nasihat al-muluk – Counsel for Kings.
patrimonialism – a form of government centred on family structures and highlighting the authority of the father. Max Weber used the term to describe how government can become a projection of the family, involving traditional norms and treating the various arms of government as instruments of personal control.

primogeniture – the largely European concept of the right to inheritance of the first born. In the political context it relates to the idea that leadership of a political unit should follow immediate family lines, possibly based on the oldest son (agnatic primogeniture).

qabila – a term for tribe.

Quraysh – the tribe of Mohammed.

qawm – another term for tribe.

Rashidun – Rightly Guided; the four caliphs who immediately followed the Prophet Mohammed; Abu Bakr Al-Siddiq, Omar ibn Al-Khattab, Othman ibn Affan and Ali ibn Abi Talib. They were from among the Prophet's Companions and were regarded as representing the high point of Islamic political life.

Shari`a – the body of Islamic law derived from the Quran and the Sunna, including the Hadith.

sheikh – old man, headman of a tribe, a religious leader.

Shi`a – followers of Ali bin Ali Talib; the Partisans of Ali; revere a number of Imams who were descendant from Ali. The minority group in Islam who can be found in many Arab states around the Arabian/Persian Gulf. The majority in Iran and Bahrain. The three main branches of Shi`a thought are the Zaidities, Isma'ili and the Imamites.

shura – consultation.

sunna – the habits and religious practices of the Prophet Mohammed, which were recorded for posterity and serve as the ideal Islamic norm.

Sunni – the people of the Sunna. The majority sect in Islam.

sura – the basic division of the Quran below chapters or books.

tribalism – the range of loyalties and attitudes based on family, clan, tribe and tribal confederation.

ulema – learned men; the guardians of the religious and legal traditions of Islam.

Umma – a community, generally identified with the Islamic community or Arab community.

Appendix 2

Formal constitutional status: members of the Arab League

	Enacted	Nature	Basis	Amendment
Algeria	1996	Republic	Direct election	Presidential.
Bahrain	2002	Monarchy Constitutional	Hereditary Primogeniture	Royal/ Parliamentary.
Comoros	1996	Republic By island	Direct election renewable	Presidential/ Parliamentary.
Djibouti	1992	Republic	Direct election One re-election	Presidential/ Parliamentary.**
Egypt	1980	Republic	Direct election.	
Iraq	2004	Republic	Appointed.	
Jordan	1952	Monarchy	Hereditary. Primogeniture.	
Kuwait	1962	Emirate	Hereditary. By Emir.	
Lebanon	1926	Republic	Elected by parliament.	
Libya	1992	Republic	Appointed by RCC.*	
Mauritania	1991	Republic	Direct election.	
Morocco	1996	Monarchy Constitutional	Hereditary. Primogeniture.	
Oman	1996	Sultanate	Hereditary.* Ruling family Council.	
Palestine	2003	Republic	Direct election.***	
Qatar	2003	Emirate	Hereditary. By Emir/family council.	
Saudi Arabia	1992	Monarchy	Hereditary.* Most fit by king in Allegiance Council.	
Somalia	1995	Republic	Direct election.***	
Sudan	1998	Republic	Direct election.	
Syria	1973	Republic	Direct election.	
Tunisia	1991	Republic	Direct election.	
UAE	1996	Federal Republic	Elected by Supreme Council.	
Yemen	1991	Republic	Direct election after parliamentary approval.	

* Constitution is the Quran
** Constitutional court/council
*** Provisional or draft status.

Appendix 3

Long-standing leaders: terms of office

President Bourghiba of Tunisia	1956 to 1987 – 31 years.
King Hassan of Morocco	1961 to 1999 – 38 years.
President Hussein of Iraq	1979 to 2003 – 24 years.
King Hussein of Jordan	1953 to 1999 – 46 years.
President Assad of Syria	1971 to 2000 – 29 years.
President Zayed of UAE	1972 to 2004 – 32 years.
(Ruler of Abu Dhabi)	1966 to 2004 – 38 years
Apart from Bourghiba and Saddam Hussein, these rulers have been succeeded by their sons.	
President Mubarak of Egypt	in power since 1981.
Colonel Qaddafi of Libya	in power since 1969.
Sultan Qaboos of Oman	in power since 1970.
President Saleh of Yemen	in power since 1978.
President Zine El Abidine ben Ali of Tunisia	in power since 1987.

Appendix 4

The constitution of Medina[1]

1. This is a document from Mohammed the Prophet, governing relations between the Believers i.e. Moslems of Quraysh and Yathrib and those who followed them and worked hard with them. They form one nation – Umma.
2. The Quraysh Mohajireen will continue to pay blood money, according to their present custom.
3. In case of war with any body they will redeem their prisoners with kindness and justice common among Believers. (Not according to pre-Islamic nations where the rich and the poor were treated differently).
4. The Bani Awf will decide the blood money, within themselves, according to their existing custom.
5. In case of war with anybody all parties other than Moslems will redeem their prisoners with kindness and justice according to practice among Believers and not in accordance with pre-Islamic notions.
6. The Bani Saeeda, the Bani Harith, the Bani Jusham and the Bani Najjar will be governed on the lines of the above (principles).
7. The Bani Amr, Bani Awf, Bani Al-Nabeet, and Bani Al-Aws will be governed in the same manner.
8. Believers will not fail to redeem their prisoners they will pay blood money on their behalf. It will be a common responsibility of the Umma and not of the family of the prisoners to pay blood money.
9. A Believer will not make the freedman of another Believer as his ally against the wishes of the other Believers.
10. The Believers, who fear Allah, will oppose the rebellious elements and those that encourage injustice or sin, or enmity or corruption among Believers.
11. If anyone is guilty of any such act all the Believers will oppose him even if he be the son of any one of them.
12. A Believer will not kill another Believer, for the sake of an unbeliever. (i.e. even though the unbeliever is his close relative).
13. No Believer will help an unbeliever against a Believer.
14. Protection (when given) in the Name of Allah will be common. The weakest among Believers may give protection (in the Name of Allah) and it will be binding on all Believers.
15. Believers are all friends to each other to the exclusion of all others.

16. Those Jews who follow the Believers will be helped and will be treated with equality. (Social, legal and economic equality is promised to all loyal citizens of the State).
17. No Jew will be wronged for being a Jew.
18. The enemies of the Jews who follow us will not be helped.
19. The peace of the Believers (of the State of Medina) cannot be divided. (It is either peace or war for all. It cannot be that a part of the population is at war with the outsiders and a part is at peace).
20. No separate peace will be made by anyone in Medina when Believers are fighting in the Path of Allah.
21. Conditions of peace and war and the accompanying ease or hardships must be fair and equitable to all citizens alike.
22. When going out on expeditions a rider must take his fellow member of the Army-share his ride.
23. The Believers must avenge the blood of one another when fighting in the Path of Allah. (This clause was to remind those in front of whom there may be less severe fighting that the cause was common to all. This also meant that although each battle appeared a separate entity it was in fact a part of the War, which affected all Moslems equally.)
24. The Believers (because they fear Allah) are better in showing steadfastness and as a result receive guidance from Allah in this respect. Others must also aspire to come up to the same standard of steadfastness.
25. No unbeliever will be permitted to take the property of the Quraysh (the enemy) under his protection. Enemy property must be surrendered to the State.
26. No unbeliever will intervene in favour of a Quraysh (because the Quraysh having declared war are the enemy).
27. If any unbeliever kills a Believer, without good cause, he shall be killed in return, unless the next of kin are satisfied (as it creates law and order problems and weakens the defence of the State). All Believers shall be against such a wrong-doer. No Believer will be allowed to shelter such a man.
28. When you differ on anything (regarding this Document) the matter shall be referred to Allah and Mohammed.
29. The Jews will contribute towards the war when fighting alongside the Believers.
30. The Jews of Bani Awf will be treated as one community with the Believers. The Jews have their religion. This will also apply to their freedmen. The exception will be those who act unjustly and sinfully. By so doing they wrong themselves and their families.
31. The same applies to Jews of Bani Al-Najjar, Bani Al Harith, Bani Saeeda, Bani Jusham, Bani Al Aws, Thaalba, and the Jaffna, (a clan of the Bani Thaalba) and the Bani Al Shutayba.
32. Loyalty gives protection against treachery. (Loyal people are protected by their friends against treachery. As long as a person remains loyal to the State he is not likely to succumb to the ideas of being treacherous. He protects himself against weakness.)

33. The freedmen of Thaalba will be afforded the same status as Thaalba themselves. This status is for fair dealings and full justice as a right and equal responsibility for military service.
34. Those in alliance with the Jews will be given the same treatment as the Jews.
35. No one (no tribe which is party to the Pact) shall go to war except with the permission of Mohammed. If any wrong has been done to any person or party it may be avenged.
36. Any one who kills another without warning (there being no just cause for it) amounts to his slaying himself and his household, unless the killing was done due to a wrong being done to him.
37. The Jews must bear their own expenses (in War) and the Moslems bear their expenses.
38. If anyone attacks anyone who is a party to this Pact the other must come to his help.
39. They (parties to this Pact) must seek mutual advice and consultation.
40. Loyalty gives protection against treachery. Those who avoid mutual consultation do so because of lack of sincerity and loyalty.
41. A man will not be made liable for misdeeds of his ally.
42. Anyone (any individual or party) who is wronged must be helped.
43. The Jews must pay (for war) with the Moslems. (This clause appears to be for occasions when Jews are not taking part in the war. Clause 37 deals with occasions when they are taking part in war.)
44. Yathrib will be Sanctuary for the people of this Pact.
45. A stranger (individual) who has been given protection (by anyone party to this Pact) will be treated as his host (who has given him protection) while (he is) doing no harm and is not committing any crime. Those given protection but indulging in anti-state activities will be liable to punishment.
46. A woman will be given protection only with the consent of her family (Guardian). (A good precaution to avoid inter-tribal conflicts.)
47. In case of any dispute or controversy, which may result in trouble the matter must be referred to Allah and Mohammed. The Prophet of Allah will accept anything in this document, which is for (bringing about) piety and goodness.
48. Quraysh and their allies will not be given protection.
49. The parties to this Pact are bound to help each other in the event of an attack on Yathrib.
50. If they (the parties to the Pact other than the Moslems) are called upon to make and maintain peace (within the State) they must do so. If a similar demand (of making and maintaining peace) is made on the Moslems, it must be carried out, except when the Moslems are already engaged in a war in the Path of Allah. (So that no secret ally of the enemy can aid the enemy by calling upon Moslems to end hostilities under this clause.)
51. Everyone (individual) will have his share (of treatment) in accordance with what party he belongs to. Individuals must benefit or suffer for the good or bad deed of the group they belong to. Without such a rule party affiliations and discipline cannot be maintained.

52. The Jews of al-Aws, including their freedmen, have the same standing, as other parties to the Pact, as long as they are loyal to the Pact. Loyalty is a protection against treachery.
53. Anyone who acts loyally or otherwise does it for his own good (or loss).
54. Allah approves this Document.
55. This document will not (be employed to) protect one who is unjust or commits a crime (against other parties of the Pact).
56. Whether an individual goes out to fight (in accordance with the terms of this Pact) or remains in his home, he will be safe unless he has committed a crime or is a sinner (i.e. no one will be punished in his individual capacity for not having gone out to fight in accordance with the terms of this Pact).
57. Allah is the Protector of the good people and those who fear Allah, and Mohammed is the Messenger of Allah (He guarantees protection for those who are good and fear Allah).

Appendix 5

Power maps

Figure A5.1 Mapping Power: Jordanian Politically Relevant Elites, 2002.[1] From *Arab Elites: Negotiating the Politics of Change* edited by Volker Perthes. Copyright © 2004 by Lynne Rienner Publishers, Inc. Used with permission of the publisher.

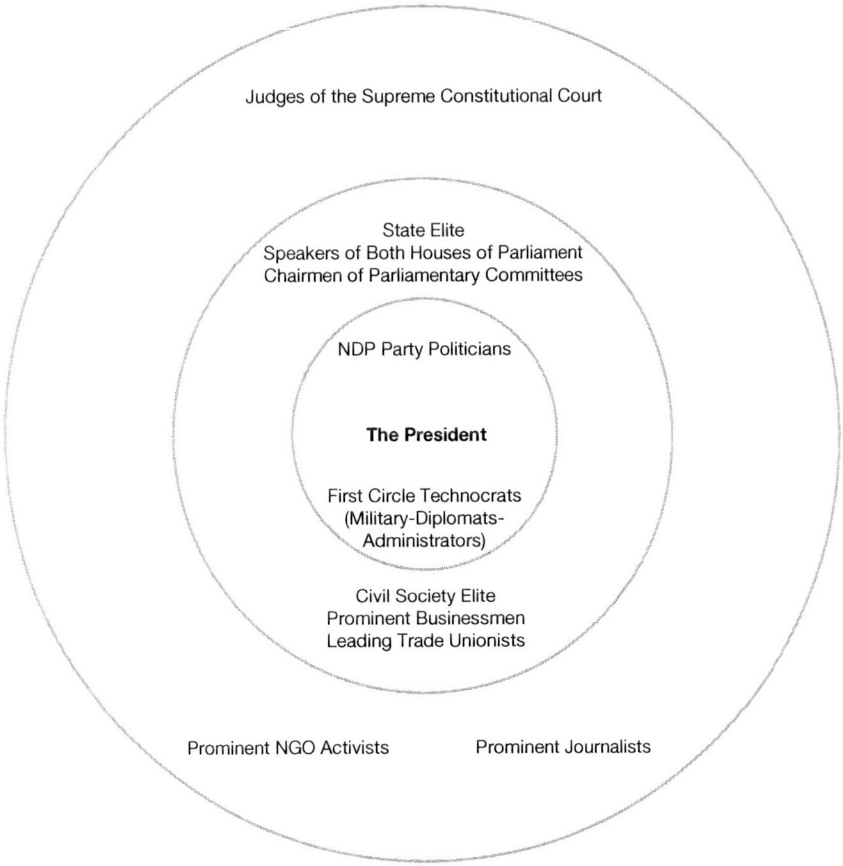

Figure A5.2 Egypt's Politically Relevant Elites, 2002.[2] From *Arab Elites: Negotiating the Politics of Change* edited by Volker Perthes. Copyright © 2004 by Lynne Rienner Publishers, Inc. Used with permission of the publisher.

Appendix 6

Letter from Hussein to Hassan[1]

This is the letter sent to Prince Hassan by King Hussein of Jordan during his illness, transferring succession from his brother, Prince Hassan, to his son, Prince Abdallah.
25 January, 1999

My Dear Brother,
Your Royal Highness Prince Hassan,
May God protect you,

I am sending you Arab Hashemite greetings with affection and appreciation.

More than thirty years ago, I entrusted you with the position of crown prince, and you have accomplished the task entrusted to you with diligence, enthusiasm and resolve that knows no fatigue or failure. You have been a brother and a supporter standing by my side in difficult times shouldering with me a great deal of responsibilities on the domestic and sometimes external fronts.

When I entrusted you with this mission, it was my response to your desire and it was my appreciation of your capabilities. I was satisfied because what good we aim to achieve with God's blessing is for Jordan and for all its people and their future generations.

I entrusted you with the post of crown prince and I was, with the will of God, responsible for that decision at the time, at a time when the eldest son of the King had not reached the age defined by the Constitution to allow him to assume responsibility in case the King had died by the will of God.

At that time, a dark atmosphere was affecting the whole nation because dangers, rumours and speculation were rife concerning the imminent end of Jordan, a country with a mission, principles and morals, and a true affiliation to the nation.

At the time, we were forced to introduce an amendment to Article 28 of the Constitution so that a brother of the King could assume the post of the Crown Prince. I chose you for the post with the blessings and approval of my brother, His Royal Highness Prince Mohammad. You have been privileged to hold that post despite the fact that your brother Mohammad was older than you. My dear brother Mohammad displayed understanding and altruism.

At the time my decision concerning succession to the throne was not subject to any personal or emotional considerations but rather was a national one. It was a decision stemming from my feeling of responsibility and the need to place the national interests and the country's stability and survival above all considerations and interests. My objective was to perform my duty towards my people and nation, to seek God's blessing and peace of mind, and to achieve stability and reassure all Jordanians about the future. This requires cohesion and national unity by God's grace after going through all kinds of experiences and ordeals.

We have sought to be transparent in all our affairs and we were keen on modernisation and reforms in all matters that lead to progress and success and in an atmosphere of democracy.

It was during my first trip abroad for medical treatment when cancerous cells were discovered in my left ureter, which was removed in addition to my left kidney. The suffering I felt at the time was a reason for my deep insight into the past and the present, as I was carrying the Holy Quran when I moved from one therapy session to another. God's words served as my spiritual and mental nourishment. I had reached a point when I concluded that the long trip had exhausted me physically and I felt my agility was not like before and that there were boundaries, which, if crossed, would take their toll on my resistance.

I was left with my mind and memory intact, thank God, and I was looking forward to doing whatever I could towards serving the nation and its future and the coming generations until the last breath of my life.

To achieve that, I returned home deciding to abdicate the throne in your favour despite the differences between us at times. My small family was offended by slandering and falsehoods, and I refer here to my wife and children. When I heard this most of the time, I attributed it to the tendency towards rivalry among those who pretend to be faithful to you and who attribute to you anything good in whatever you do. I have failed over the years in my advice to you and our family to stop asking the media to focus on persons instead of focusing on content and on those who we should celebrate, such as graduates and creative people.

We have overlooked all these matters because when I returned, I was accorded a great reception by my Jordanian family on that eternal day, which left an indelible impression on me. The Jordanian family has overwhelmed me with its noble feelings that strengthened my resolve and determination to do the impossible to help Jordan achieve peace, following in the footsteps of Egypt and after our Palestinian brothers assumed their responsibilities towards achieving that goal, because this is a right which they exercise with their own will. We support their cause and the Palestinian leadership with all our might.

The commencement of the peace process came at a time when Jordan was under siege and the doors were closed. It came at a time when it was believed that the country had come to a standstill.

Through the peace process, we secured the restoration of occupied Jordanian territory and we found the solution for the water problem and our full share of water was returned to us. We are still searching and cooperating with all parties to secure the needs of the nation and its future generations, and we continue our efforts towards developing our agriculture and industry. We are trying to achieve peace and we are exploiting all our influence to support our Palestinian brothers, helping them regain their rights on their land and establish their own state on their national soil. We are trying to achieve the objective of all people seeking a just peace in this region. We stand strongly against any tendency towards destruction and death and against the use of weapons of mass destruction. We demand that the whole world stand united against any party seeking destruction or backing terrorism, wherever they might be.

After a thorough examination, it is clear to me that the situation has become extremely dangerous and is a source of constant concern to the world in view of the capability and ease of developing weapons and the access to expertise to make those weapons and use them. Perhaps biological weapons are the most dangerous of all, because they reintroduce to the world certain diseases that have already become extinct, like smallpox.

Production of vaccines against the disease has stopped, and the effects of these vaccines end after a time if not used. In addition, there are doubts revolving around the effect of any remaining quantities of the vaccine. The most dangerous aspects of this disease is that its symptoms do not appear immediately, and the carrier of the disease can easily transmit it to those with whom he has contact.

In the present time of fast communication, such disease can move with an amazing speed around the world, ending the lives of all people without discrimination.

In addition, the world is witnessing material greed, which can cause great damage to the earth's environment unless sound measures are taken. It has to be pointed out that cancer is an outcome of that situation. For example, skin cancer has been proven to be a result of holes in the ozone layer. No doubt other forms of cancer result from environmental pollution in the atmosphere, in addition to smoking. What is more dangerous is that such an atmosphere leads towards drastic changes in the world, like changes in the climate and in rainfall. Such an atmosphere also can cause devastating floods and is behind fires that destroy tropical forests and pollute the waters of rivers, lakes and seas.

Returning to the peace process, I appreciate what you have done to make it succeed, and I should admit it was not an easy job. You have helped me in selecting competitive Jordanians who are loyal to their country and capable of working and defending its rights under all conditions. For that I am grateful and I appreciate what you have done.

Some people may question the reason behind keeping certain officials in their positions. My answer is they are the elite of this nation and they have risen to the occasion with the courage and true affiliation to the country and great affection towards serving their homeland, whether civilian or military personalities, technicians or experts.

After my first trip abroad for treatment we entered the peace process and we exerted all efforts towards making it a success. We embarked on this mission armed with our strong belief in God, our belief that we are all the descendants of Abraham and our belief in the futility of wars and tragedies that befall people.

We were oriented towards construction and doing good, and we have always sought to persuade the world that peace cannot be achieved without justice and that the world should deal with the Arabs on an equal footing so that the inhabitants of this region can protect their interests. We have called on the world to start a serious and objective dialogue in order to lay down the new principles for actual cooperation, free of selfishness and free of the desire to place petty interests above major ones. We welcome any one who is committed to contributing to a law governing bilateral or collective dealings among the people of the world to join us. Those who go astray must be held accountable for their actions, because the world should not be monopolised by groups seeking to tamper with the fate of mankind at will.

As for our Hashemite situation, I remember I spoke about that at a big meeting for officers and officials at the conference hall at Al Hussein Medical City. I stressed the formation of a family council to take care of those who are worthy of belonging to the family of the Prophet Mohammed, peace be upon him, and the house of the Prophet.

I have lived through many experiences and I noticed at an early age how some climbers climb onto the branch to ruin the relation between brothers and between father and son, and I swore to myself that this would not happen here in my lifetime. But surely, this has become the objective of every declared or hidden enemy, and all of those have used all means at their disposal to weaken confidence between leadership and people, but they have not succeeded.

Their plan at this stage, together with those who want to destroy Jordan, was to instigate infighting in the ranks of the leadership after they failed to dismantle the base, and they find in my being alive an impediment to all their designs, forgetting that Al Hussein has lived only to gain the blessings of God, to have a clear conscience and to achieve the best for all his people, regardless of their origins, who cooperate in holding the banner high and carrying the message of Jordan with their heads held high, not bowing except before God.

Until that time, I was determined to hand the first responsibility to you, but after you, I envisioned a role for the family council in which to ensure the unity of the Hashemite Family so that when the time came for you to choose your successor, the family would have a great role in naming the most suitable successor, in accordance with the benevolent traditions of Islam.

The most important traits to which young men should aspire are mutual respect, frankness, the fortitude to reject malice and a quest for knowledge, starting with the honour of serving in the Jordan Armed Forces, the Arab Army, to be a model for young people and to earn the honour that they deserve for their abilities and capabilities.

I envisioned that the Council would include all Hashemite Jordanians, including yourself, Prince Raad Bin Zayed Bin Hussein, Prince Zayed Bin Shaker and Prince Ali Bin Nayif, and that all of them would rise to the level expected of them, believing in the importance of their duty and under the threat of punishment for departing from the rules and from a consensus that would achieve the objective and light the right path for future generations and show respect for the country's laws and love for all people, without any injustice or malice. I aspired that the Hashemites would deal with all people as they would wish people to deal with them, removed from envy or greed, refraining from mobilising people against people's own interests, without dividing them into followers of this or that and destroying the edifice of Jordanian society in a way that would fulfil the interest of the country's enemies.

We differed over [the Council] because your opinion was that it should be achieved only when you were at the helm. I placed between your two hands a few papers that I wrote myself. I did not show them to anyone. They consisted of the main tenets of my proposal, and when I received your comments on them, the response did not reflect the spirit of my proposal, nor did they meet the needs of the times.

We have differed, and we still do, over the succession, and who would succeed you. You were completely opposed to this until the time you would have assumed the Throne and decided who would have been your successor.

All the princes and princesses are my children and the grandchildren are mine too. You and your sister were the closest to me within the family. Your sons and daughters are like my own children; Abdullah, Faisal, Ali, Hamza and Hashem.

Hamza, may God give him long life, has been envied since childhood because he was close to me, and because he wanted to know all matters large and small, and all details of the history of his family. He wanted to know about the struggle of his brothers and of his countrymen. I have been touched by his devotion to his country and by his integrity and magnanimity as he stayed beside me, not moving unless I forced him from time to time to carry out some duty on occasions that did not exceed the fingers on one hand. That is how Hamza Ben Al Hussein spent his holiday, between his studies at Harrow and his admission to the military academy at Sandhurst, after my insistence. I order him now, as his father and leader, to continue his studies there without any interruption until he finishes, by God's grace.

As for his brothers and sisters, they have both visited me, leaving behind them on many occasions their families and children for extended periods of time. These visits pleased me, but at the same time made me worried about those who they left behind. Of my family, at the forefront were my brother Mohammad and my sister Basma, who visited me and donated marrow that matches my own. You also volunteered to donate marrow except that yours did not match mine.

As for Noor, she brought happiness to me and cared for me during my illness, with the utmost loving affection. She, the Jordanian, who belongs to this country with every fibre of her being, holds her head high in the defence and service of this country's interest. She is the mother who devotes all her efforts to her family. We have grown together in soul and mind, and she has had to endure a great deal of hardship to ensure that I was being attended to. And she, like me, also endured much anxiety and many shocks, but always placed her faith in God and hid her tears behind smiles. She also has not escaped the attempts of criticism. Why not? [Because there are] climbers who want to reach for the summit, and when the fever was getting high some people thought it was their chance.

I have intervened from my sickbed to prevent meddling in the affairs of the Arab Army. This meddling seemed to be meant to settle scores and included retiring efficient officers known for their allegiance and whose history and bright records are beyond reproach. At the forefront were the Field Marshal and the Chairman of the Joint Chiefs of Staff, who was envied because of a house. I am the one who paid for the house. I have collected the money in instalments over years until it was built modestly. Its costs in no way approach the estimates made by many. That was because of his loyalty and his integrity and because we wanted to give him something commensurate with his rank and position, especially that he receives his counterparts from all over the world.

Some people are asking did others receive the same care? The answer is yes. From the meek to the mighty, wherever it was possible to do so.

Perhaps it was wrong at times, but the support of those who deserve it is one of my greatest responsibilities, and [I do] not do it for personal gain. Excelling students and needy patients benefited.

And then, there is another question. Where is all this coming from? The answer is I have raised [funds] for my country and my people to ensure their progress and to ensure that they lead dignified lives, through continuous development. All [those funds] went to the objective of national self-reliance and to the treasury.

On the personal level, that was God-given; the result of many brothers in Arab and Muslim nations who were very magnanimous towards me, knowing my situation and sufferings over the years. They have helped me pay my debts and helped me also to spend on those who serve their country. I thank them and I am grateful to them for their magnanimity.

All of this has given me many sleepless nights while I was on my sickbed, on top of my personal suffering. What made me sleepless for the first time in my life is that I was asking myself, why is there insistence on change in the Army since we know the need for reform and development and the Chairman and myself were busy all the time providing our army with all available experience, local and international. I have used my authority as Supreme Commander of the armed forces to stop any action that would have led to the fragmentation and politicisation of the Army. We have ensured that service in the Army would achieve all our ambitions in its continuous development on the strongest basis as a shield for the country and as our pride.

The same applies to the transfer of efficient ambassadors without reason except the reason of age, although, those ambassadors represent the king, the state and the country. That's why I returned to the homeland: to rectify matters as soon as possible and to assume my duties towards future generations.

I have found that after all these years, during which circumstances and conditions have changed both in our region and at the national level, by God's grace, we have achieved a high level of credibility, confidence and international recognition, all of which call on us to continue the tireless and sincere work to provide the chance for young people to serve their country and enrich our march with new vision and new experience. All of this requires us to take great care of our affairs and look at the future with objectivity and far-sightedness.

I have received your letter in which you place the matter of succession between my hands and in which you express your readiness to hear my decision concerning that matter. I thank you for that.

I have found that to take a decision, I must refer to the original Constitutional rule, where I find that all conditions that originally dictated the exception have passed, and that, therefore, His Royal Highness Prince Abdullah would, in such a case, immediately assume all duties and responsibilities as the Crown Prince of the Hashemite Kingdom of Jordan.

I thank you, Your Royal Highness, my dear brother, and express my deepest appreciation to you for all the sincere efforts that you have exerted during the past three decades. I thank you for all your achievements in the fields of development, education, intellectual discourse, science and environmental affairs through your overseeing of many programmes at our national institutions. I value in you the spirit of true and genuine brotherhood towards myself, expressed in your generous letter, which I also feel towards you. This reflects what should ever be the case within our Hashemite Family and which should always be a pillar of the Hashemite Family of love and affection, a family which embodies a feeling responsibility and understanding towards new developments and circumstances of a new era and regards these developments with a great deal of awareness and the ability to deal with them objectivity and with selflessness.

I am sure that you are receiving this decision of mine with self-content, and with the spirit of a member of the one united Hashemite team. I am sure that you will be relieved of all the psychological and familial pressures. Jordan and the world at large will be your world in which there are so many of issues in many fields that need your knowledge, expertise and deep intellect, and concerns worthy of your tireless efforts and that, by God's grace, will be supported by us. You will always stay close to me as a brother, an intellectual and a man of principle.

May God bless you,

Al Hussein
January 25, 1999,
Shawwal 8, 1419

Notes

Introduction

1 Maria R. Menocal, *The Ornament of the World* (New York: Back Bay Books, 2002), p. 19.
2 Frederic Volpi, 'Pseudo-democracy in the Muslim world', *Third World Quarterly*, vol. 25 issue 6 (2004), p. 1070.
3 See for example, Glen E. Perry, 'The Arab democracy deficit: the case of Egypt', *Arab Studies Quarterly*, vol. 26 no. 2 (spring, 2004), pp. 91–107.
4 W. Montgomery Watt, *Islamic Political Thought* (Edinburgh: Edinburgh University Press, 1999), p. 121.
5 Morocco, Algeria, Tunisia, Libya, Egypt, Palestine, Lebanon, Syria, Jordan, Iraq, Yemen, Saudi Arabia, Kuwait, Bahrain, Qatar, the United Arab Emirates and Oman.
6 The transfer of political power through members of the immediate family. See Appendix 1.
7 Seymour M., Lipset, *Political Man* (London: Heinemann, 1969), p. 45.
8 W. Montgomery Watt, op. cit., pp. 120–21.
9 Antony Black, *The History of Islamic Political Thought* (Edinburgh: Edinburgh University Press, 2001), p. 18.
10 Antony Black, ibid., p. 350.
11 R. Tapper, 'Anthropologists, historians and tribespeople on tribe and state formation in the Middle East', p. 70, in Philip S. Khoury, and Joseph Kostiner, *Tribes and State Formation in the Middle East* (Berkeley: University of California Press, 1990), pp. 48–73.

1 The Arab political tradition

1 Abdallah Rashid, 'Long Live Dictatorship', *Al Ittihad*, Abu Dhabi (29 June 2003) cited in *Middle East Media Research Institute*, no. 536 (10 July 2003), available online: http://www.memri.org/bin/articles.cgi?Page=subjects&Area=reform&ID=SP53603. (Accessed 29 May 2009).
2 The World Bank, 'Better Governance for Development in the Middle East and North Africa', Washington, DC (2003), p. 8 available online: http://worldbank.org/92HM CDTM60. (Accessed 29 May 2009) and United Nations Development Programme, *First Arab Human Development Report* (New York: United Nations, 2002), available online: http://hdr.undp.org/reports/view_reports.cfm?year=0&country=0&region=R1&type=0&theme=0&launched=0. (Accessed 29 May 2008).
3 Arab League home page available online: http://www.arableagueonline.org/arableague/english/level2_en.jsp?next=0&level_id=11&x=22&y=10.
4 L. Carl Brown, *International Politics and the Middle East* (Princeton: Princeton University Press, 1984), pp. 4–5.

5 Ian Lustick, 'The absence of Middle Eastern great powers: political 'backwardness' in historical perspective', *International Organization*, vol. 51 issue 4 (1997), pp. 653–83.
6 United Nations Development Programme, op. cit., pp. 27–28.
7 World Values Survey, available online: http://wvs.isr.umich.edu/ and Zogby International, available online: http://www.zogby.com/ and Pew Research Centre, *Pew Global Attitudes Surveys,* available online: http://pewglobal.org/.
8 Samuel P. Huntington, *The Third Wave: Democratisation in the late Twentieth Century* (Norman: University of Oklahoma Press, 1991), p. 114.
9 Bernard Lewis, 'Islam and liberal democracy: a historical overview', *The Atlantic Monthly,* vol. 271 no. 2 (February, 1993), available online: http://www.theatlantic.com/issues/93feb/lewis.htm. (Accessed 8 June 2006).
10 Abdallah Rashid, 'Long Live Dictatorship', *Al Ittihad*, Abu Dhabi (29 June 2003) cited in *Middle East Media Research Institute*, no. 536 (10 July 2003), available online: http://www.memri.org/bin/articles.cgi?Page=subjects&Area=reform&ID=SP53603. (Accessed 29 May 2009).
11 Rami G. Khouri, 'Kuwait's election and the freezing of Arab politics', *Common Ground News Service* (9 September 2003), available online: http://www.dailystar.com.lb/article.asp?edition_ID=1&article_ID=67591&categ_id=5. (Accessed 9 September 2003).
12 The body of laws derived from the Quran, the Sunna and the *Hadith*.
13 Amos Asa-El, 'Middle Israel: Let Hamas Rule', *The Jerusalem Post*, (13 August 2001).
14 Michael C. Hudson, *Arab Politics: the Search for Legitimacy* (New Haven: Yale University Press, 1977), p. 395.
15 Jeane Kirkpatrick, 'Dictatorship and Double Standards', *Commentary*, New York, vol. 68 part 5 (November 1979), p. 44.
16 J. E. Peterson, 'The Nature of Succession in the Gulf', *The Middle East Journal*, vol. 55 issue 4 (autumn, 2001), p. 581.
17 J. E. Peterson, 'Succession in the States of the Gulf Cooperation Council', *The Washington Quarterly,* vol. 24 no. 4 (autumn, 2001), p. 185.
18 Marina Ottaway, op. cit., p. 12.
19 Salafism is an interpretation of Sunni Islam dating back to the ninth century – under the name of Ahl al-*Hadith*. Its central features were combined in the teachings of a fourteenth-century scholar, Ibn Taymiyya (d. 1328). Ibn Taymiyya was willing to condemn as heretics Moslems who did not share his views. He declared that war against Moslem rulers who did not apply the *Shari`a* permissible. Ibn Taymiyya's teachings were adopted by a movement in central Arabia in the eighteenth century. Widely known as Wahhabis, its adherents call themselves the believers in the oneness of God (*Muwahhidun*).
20 Chibli Mallat, 'From Islamic to Middle Eastern Law: A Restatement of the Field (Part 1)', *The American Journal of Comparative Law,* vol. 51 (autumn 2003), p. 700.
21 The range of loyalties and attitudes based on family, clan, tribe and tribal confederation.
22 A survey conducted in Jordan, Morocco, Lebanon, Saudi Arabia, Egypt and the United Arab Emirates in July 2004 found that former Egyptian President Gamal Abdel Nasser was the most admired political figure in the region. Given Nasser's close identification with Arab nationalism, the finding would suggest that the wave of Islamic fundamentalism washing over the Arab world has not swept away Arab nationalism as a force. Also Jim Lobe, 'Losing Arab Hearts and Minds: It's the Policy Stupid', *Inter Press Service* (23 July 2004), available online: http://www.aaiusa.org/press-room/628/aainew072304. (Accessed 2 June 2009).
23 Solidarity based on blood relationships (*Asabiya*).
24 Elie Kedourie, op. cit., pp. 266–67.
25 Lisa Anderson, 'Political Decay in the Arab World', *Middle Eastern Lectures*, no. 4, The Moshe Dayan Centre for Middle Eastern and African Studies, Tel Aviv University

(2001), pp. 9–10, available online: http://www.dayan.org/mel/anderson.pdf. (Accessed 18 October 2004).

26 George R. Elton, *England under the Tudors* (London: Methuen & Co. Ltd., 1963), pp. 462–64 and David L. Keir, *The Constitutional History of Modern Britain* (London: Adam and Charles Black, 1964), pp. 266–67.

27 Ami Ayalon, 'Semantics and the modern history of non-European societies: Arab 'republics' as a case study', *The Historical Journal*, vol. 28 issue 4 (December, 1985), pp. 829–30.

28 Mahdi Zahraa, 'Characteristic features of Islamic law: perceptions and misconceptions', *Arab Law Quarterly*, vol. 15 no. 2 (2000), p. 189.

29 Egyptian Government, Egyptian Constitution, 1971 (amended 2005), Government Services Portal, available online: http://www.egypt.gov.eg/english/laws/Constitution/default.aspx. (Accessed 29 May 2009).

30 Toby Dodge and Richard Higgott, *Globalization and the Middle East* (London: Royal Institute of International Affairs, 2002), pp. 197–98.

31 David E. Long, 'The role of the extended family in Saudi Arabia', *Saudi-American Forum* (10 March 2003), available online: www.saudi-american-forum.org/Newsletters/SAF_09.pdf. (Accessed 24 August 2006).

2 Competing influences: tribalism, Islam and outsiders in the Arab world

1 Antony Black, *The History of Islamic Political Thought* (Edinburgh: Edinburgh University Press, 2001), p. 309.

2 M. Moncef Khaddar, 'Beyond colonialism and nationalism', *Arab Studies Quarterly*, vol. 24 no. 4 (autumn, 2002), p. 84.

3 Antony Black, *op. cit.*, p. 350.

4 Max Weber, *The Theory of Social and Economic Organisation*, (trans.) A. M. Henderson and T. Parsons (The Free Press, 1964) and Brian S. Turner *Weber and Islam* (London: Routledge and Kegan Paul, 1974).

5 Ibn Khaldun, *The Muqaddimah: an Introduction to History*, (trans.) F. Rosenthal, N. J. Dawood (ed.) (Princeton and Oxford: Bollingen Series, Princeton University Press, 2005), pp. 96–103.

6 Patricia Springborg, 'Politics, primordialism and orientalism: Marx, Aristotle and the myth of gemeinschaft', *The American Political Science Review*, vol. 80 no. 1 (March, 1986), p. 187.

7 Amatzia Baram, 'Neo-tribalism in Iraq: Saddam Hussein's tribal policies 1991–96', *International Journal of Middle East Studies*, vol. 29 no. 1 (February, 1997), p. 18.

8 Albert Hourani, 'Tribes and states in Islamic history', in Philip S. Khoury and Joseph Kostiner (eds.), *Tribes and State Formation in the Middle East* (Berkeley: University of California Press, 1990), pp. 303–4.

9 Cited in Lisa Anderson, 'Tribe and State: Libyan anomalies' in Philip S. Khoury and Joseph Kostiner. (eds.), ibid., p. 299.

10 Paul McGeough, 'Fatal collision with tradition', *The Sydney Morning Herald* (30 July 2004), available online: http://www.smh.com.au/articles/2004/07/29/1091080376624.html. (Accessed 21 December 2006), Paul McGeough, 'Share power or lose control, Iraq warned', *The Sydney Morning Herald* (22 July 2008), available online: http://www.smh.com.au/articles/2004/07/21/1090089220981.html. (Accessed 21 December 2006), and F, Biedermann, 'Iraq's X-factor: the tribes', *Salon.com* (26 March 2003), available online: http://dir.salon.com/story/news/feature/2003/03/26/tribes/index.html. (Accessed 8 December 2006).

11 Gertrude Bell, *The Desert and the Sown* (London: Virago, 1985) and Jacques Berque, 'Du nouveau sur les Bani Hilal?', *Studia Islamica*, vol. 36 (1972) pp. 99–111.

12 The caliphs Abu Bakr Al-Siddiq, Omar ibn Al-Khattab, Othman ibn Affan and Ali ibn Abi Talib.

13 A community. Regularly used to refer to the community of Moslems. See Appendix 1 for terms used.
14 Jonathan P. Berkey, *The Formation of Islam* (Cambridge: Cambridge University Press, 2003), p. 71.
15 Basam Tibi, 'The simultaneity of the unsimultaneous: old tribes and imposed nation-states in the modern Middle East', in Philip S. Khoury and Joseph Kostiner, op. cit., p. 140.
16 Hanna Batatu, 'Iraq's underground Shi`a movements: characteristics, causes and prospects', *Middle East Journal*, vol. 35 4 (autumn, 1981), p. 583 and Mamoun Fandy, 'Tribe vs Islam: the post-colonial Arab state and the democratic imperative', *Middle East Policy Council Journal*, vol. III, no. 48 (1994), accessible online: http://www.mepc.org/journal/9406_fandy.asp. (Accessed 5 December 2006).
17 Amatzia Baram, op. cit., p. 1.
18 J. Kalb, 'The Amish, David Koresh and a Newer World Order', quoted in R. J. Antonio, 'After postmodernism; reactionary tribalism', *The American Journal of Sociology*, July vol. 106 no. 1 (2000), p. 55.
19 David Ronfeldt, 'Today's wars are less about ideas than extreme tribalism', *Christian Science Monitor* (27 March 2006), available online: http://www.csmonitor.com/2006/0327/p09s01-coop.html. (Accessed 4 December 2006).
20 Elham M. Manea, 'Yemen, the tribe and the state', paper presented to International Colloquium on *Islam and Social Change,* University of Lausanne (10–11 October 1996), available online: http://www.al-bab.com/yemen/soc/manea1.htm. (Accessed 4 December 2006).
21 As'ad Abukhalil, 'Change and democratisation in the Arab world: the role of political parties', *Third World Quarterly*, vol, 18 no. 1 (1997), p. 160.
22 Marc Bloch, *Feudal Society, Vol. 1: The Growth of Ties of Dependence*, (trans.) L. A. Manyon, (London: Routledge & Kegan Paul, 1971) and A. N. Poliak, *Feudalism in Egypt, Syria, Palestine and the Lebanon: 1250–1900*, Royal Asiatic Society (1939) pp. 1–87.
23 Marc Bloch, op. cit., pp. 123–24.
24 Brian S. Turner, *Weber and Islam* (London and Boston: Routledge & Kegan Paul, 1974), p. 100.
25 See for example, Craig R. Black, 'Deterring Libya: the strategic culture of Muammar Qaddafi', *The Counter-proliferation Papers*, Future Warfare Series No. 8, *US Air University* (October 2000), p. 14, available online: http://www.au.af.mil/au/awc/awcgate/cpc-pubs/black.pdf. (Accessed 5 December 2006) and C. H. Moore, 'The northeastern triangle: Libya, Egypt and the Sudan', *Annals of the American Academy of Political and Social Science*, vol. 489 (January 1987), p. 30.
26 P., Claude, 'Washington puts trust in Iraq's tribal system', *Le Monde* reported in *Guardian Weekly* (17–23 September 2004), p. 20.
27 Amatzia Baram, op. cit.
28 Lisa Anderson, op. cit., p. 297.
29 Fahed T. Al-Thakeb, 'The Arab family and modernity: evidence from Kuwait', *Current Anthropology*, vol. 26 no. 5 (December 1985), p. 577.
30 Suad Joseph, 'Connectivity and patriarchy among urban working-class Arab families in Lebanon', *Ethos*, vol. 21 no. 4 (December, 1993), pp. 452–84.
31 Laurie Ferguson, *The Journalist and Islam*, conference run by Macquarie University, University of Technology, Sydney, and Australian Research Council, Sydney, 7–8 December, 2006.
32 L. Massignon, 'Cartes de repartition des kabyles dans la region parisienne', *Opera Minora*, Beirut, vol. 3 (1963), pp. 569–74 cited in Albert Hourani, 'Tribes and states in Islamic history', in Philip S. Khoury and Joseph Kostiner (eds.), op. cit., p. 305.
33 Amatzia Baram, op. cit., p. 13.

34 As'ad Abukhalil, op. cit., p. 153.
35 D. W. Brinkerhoff, and A. A. Goldsmith, *Clientalism, Patrimonialism and Democratic Governance: An Overview and Framework for Assessment and Planning*, (Cambridge, USA: Abt Associates Inc., December 2002), pp. 10–11.
36 James T. Quinlivan, 'Coup-proofing: Its Practice and Consequences in the Middle East', *International Security,* vol. 24 no. 2 (autumn, 1999), p. 135.
37 Basam Tibi, op. cit., p. 142.
38 N. Pelham, 'King of Jordan "feared being upstaged" by his half-brother', London, *Financial Times* (30 November 2004).
39 S. Kettering, 'The historical development of political clientelism', *Journal of Interdisciplinary History,* vol. 18 no, 3 (1988), p. 427.
40 Martha N. Kessler, 'Inheriting Syria: Bashar's trial by Fire', *Middle East Policy*, vol. 12 no. 3 (autumn, 2005), pp. 173–76. Also Eyal Zisser, 'The succession struggle in Damascus', *Middle East Quarterly* (September 1995), available at: http://www.meforum.org/article/264. (Accessed 10 September 2006).
41 Jonathan P. Berkey, op. cit., pp. 67 and 71.
42 Laith Kubba, 'Recognising pluralism', *Journal of Democracy*, Vol. 7 (2), 1996. p. 86. Richard Tapper, 'Anthropologists, historians, and tribes people on tribe and state formation in the Middle East', in P. S. Khoury and J. Kostiner, op cit., p. 71.
43 Individuals of the first generation of followers of the Prophet. Regarded as important sources of genuine *Hadith*s.
44 Barnaby Rogerson, *The Heirs of the Prophet* (London: Abacus, 2006), p. 47.
45 Bernard Lewis, *The Middle East* (London: Phoenix Giant, 1998), p. 64.
46 N. J. Coulson, *A History of Islamic Law* (Edinburgh: Edinburgh University Press, 1972), p. 133.
47 Samir Al-Khalil, *The Republic of Fear: the Politics of Modern Iraq* (Berkeley: University of California Press, 1989), p. 97. Al-Khalil claims that Stalinism was the model that Ba`athism sought to emulate.
48 W. Montgomery Watt, *Islamic Political Thought* (Edinburgh: Edinburgh University Press, 1999), p. 79.
49 Brian S. Turner, op. cit., p. 83.
50 Brian S. Turner, op. cit., pp. 79–80.
51 Antony Black, op. cit., p. 65.
52 Antony Black, op. cit., pp. 2, 92 and 112.
53 Antony Black, op. cit., p. 52.
54 John Gray, Al *Qaeda and What it Means to be Modern* (London: Faber and Faber, 2003), pp. 75–79. Such objectives include the removal of American forces from Saudi Arabia and the liberation of Jerusalem.
55 George Antonius, *The Arab Awakening* (London: Hamish Hamilton, 1961), Chapter III.
56 Saed A. Arjomand, 'Islam, political change and globalisation', *Thesis Eleven*, no. 76 (February 2004), pp. 14.

3 The just prince: leadership and legitimacy in the Arab world

1 Mohammed ibn Zafar Al Siqilli, *Sulwan Al Muta' fi Udwan Al Atba* (Consolation for the Ruler who is Unloved by his Subjects), cited in Joseph A. Kechichian and R. Hrair Dekmejian (eds.), *The Just Prince*, (London: Saqi Books, 2003), p. 13.
2 Mohamed Talbi, 'A record of failure', *Journal of Democracy*, vol. 11 no. 3 (July 2006), p. 66.
3 Monte Palmer, *The Politics of the Middle East* (Ifasca: Illinois: F. E. Peacock Publishers, 2002), p. 14.
4 Karen Kramer, 'Arab political pacts: an unlikely scenario', *Journal for Democracy*, vol. 17 no. 4 (October 2006).

5 H. Lasswell, *Politics: Who gets What, When and How*, (New York: Meridien Books, 1958).
6 Lawrence E. Walsh, *Final Report of the Independent Counsel for Iran-Contra Matters*, United States Court of Appeal for District of Columbia. Concluding Observations, vol. 1 (4 August 1993), pp. 561–67. Walsh described Iran-Contra as 'the product of two foreign policy directives by President Reagan which skirted the law' and the result of 'the desire of persons in high office to pursue controversial policies and goals even when the pursuit of those policies and goals was inhibited or restricted by executive orders, statutes or the constitutional system of checks and balances.' Also American Bar Association, *Task Force on Presidential Signing Statements and the Separation of powers Doctrine*, Washington DC (July 24 2006) available online: http://www.abanet.org/op/signingstatements/aba_final_signing_statements_recommendation-report_7-24-06.pdf. (Accessed 30 July 2006). This report describes G. W. Bush's practice in this area as unconstitutional and contrary to the separation of powers doctrine.
7 Glen E. Perry, 'The Arab democracy deficit: the case of Egypt', *Arab Studies Quarterly*, spring, vol. 26 no. 2 (2004), p. 99.
8 Patrick Seale, *Asad: the Struggle for the Middle East* (Berkeley: University of California Press, 1995), p. 333.
9 Max Weber, *The Theory of Social and Economic Organisation*, (trans.) A. M. Henderson, and T. Parsons (New York: The Free Press, 1964), p. 347.
10 Seymour M. Lipset, *Political Man* (London: Heinemann, 1969), p. 70.
11 Robert D. Putnam, *The Beliefs of Politicians* (New Haven and London: Yale University Press, 1973), p. 238 and Jean Blondel, *Comparative Government* (Sydney: Philip Allen, 1990), pp. 284–86.
12 Joseph A. Kechichian and R. Hrair Dekmejian op. cit., and Antony Black, *The History of Islamic Political Thought* (Edinburgh: Edinburgh University Press, 2001), pp. 108–44.
13 The dominant tribe of Mecca, which acquired a central place in the early Islamic political system.
14 W. Montgomery Watt, *Islamic Political Thought* (Edinburgh: Edinburgh University Press, 1999), p. 40.
15 Brian S. Turner, *Weber and Islam* (London: Routledge & Kegan Paul, 1974), p. 85.
16 W. Montgomery Watt, *Muhammad at Mecca* (Oxford: Clarendon Press, 1953), p. 1.
17 Baram has written about 'neo-tribalism' in Amatzia Baram, 'Neo-tribalism in Iraq: Saddam Hussein's tribal policies 1991–96', *International Journal of Middle East Studies*, vol. 29 no. 1 (February 1997), pp. 1–31.
18 T. E. Lawrence, *Seven Pillars of Wisdom* (London: Jonathan Cape, 1935), p. 68.
19 Qays were from northern Arabia and supported the Abbasid movement. The Yemen were from south Arabia and underpinned Umayyad rule. See P. K. Hitti, *A History of the Arabs* (Basingstoke: Palgrave, 2002), pp. 280–81.
20 H. A. R. Gibb, *Studies on the Civilisation of Islam* (London: Routledge and Kegan Paul, 1969), p. 84.
21 N. J. Coulson, *A History of Islamic Law* (Edinburgh: Edinburgh University Press, 1972).
22 Tafseer Comparison. Available online: http://www.tafseercomparison.org/study4.asp?TitleText=Study%204:%20Verse%204:59. (Accessed 26 September 2006).
23 Michael C. Hudson, *Arab Politics* (New Haven: Yale University Press, 1977), p. 2.
24 Volker Perthes, 'The political economy of the Syrian succession', *Survival*, vol. 43 no. 1 (spring, 2001), p. 146.
25 Patrick, Seale, op. cit., p. 340.
26 Lived 397–430AD. Bishop of Hippo and a philosopher and theologian of central importance.
27 Brian Tierney, *Religion, Law and the Growth of Constitutional Thought, 1150–1650* (Cambridge: Cambridge University Press, 1982), pp. 29–30.

28 Ibn Khaldun, *The Muqaddimah*, N. J. Dawood (ed.) (Princeton: Princeton University Press, 2005), pp. 136–37.
29 Bernard Lewis, 'Islam and liberal democracy: a historical overview', *Journal of Democracy*, vol. 7 no. 2 (April 1996), p. 55.
30 The subject of a major twelfth-century work by Mohammed ibn Zafar al Siqilli, *Sulwan al Muta fi Udwan al Atba,* see reference (1) above.
31 Martin E. Spencer, 'Weber on legitimate norms and authority', *The British Journal of Sociology*, vol. 21 no. 2 (June 1970), p. 126.
32 Paul Salem, *Bitter Legacy: Ideology and Politics in the Arab World* (Syracuse: Syracuse University Press, New York, 1994), p. 27.
33 Simon Bromley, *Rethinking Middle East Politics* (Cambridge: Polity Press, 1994), pp. 103–5.
34 This view is not without its critics, but it is one formed by the writer over many years in the region. For support for this view see Jafar P. Al-Askari, *A Soldier's Story* (London: Arabian Publishing, 2003). Al-Askari's support for the Ottomans was only undermined by the excesses of Abdul Hamid and, later, the Young Turks. Also William R. Polk, *Understanding Iraq* (London: I. B. Tauris, 2005), pp. 103–4. For a different perspective see George Antonius, *The Arab Awakening* (London: Hamish Hamilton, 1961), p. 33.
35 R. Pillai, T. A. Scandura and E. A Williams, 'Leadership and organizational justice: similarities and differences across cultures', *Journal of International Business Studies*, vol. 30 no. 4 (1999), p. 775.
36 M. Barnett, 'Institutions, roles and disorder: the case of the Arab states system', *International Studies Quarterly*, vol. 37 no. 3 (September, 1993), pp. 271–96.
37 Samir Al-Khalil, *The Republic of Fear: the Politics of Modern Iraq* (Berkeley: University of California Press, 1989), pp. 113–14.
38 Patrick, Seale, op. cit., p. 338.
39 Abu Hamid Al Ghazali, quoted in H. A. R. Gibb, op. cit., pp. 142–43.
40 H. B. Sharabi, *Nationalism and Revolution in the Arab World* (Princeton: D. van Nostrand Co., Inc, 1966), p. 90.
41 Brian S. Turner, op. cit., p. 25.
42 Martin E. Spencer, op. cit., p. 125.
43 Patrick, Seale, op. cit., p. 338.
44 W. Montgomery Watt, op. cit., p. 76.
45 Matti Dogan and Dominic Pelassy, *How to Compare Nations* (New Jersey: Chatham House, 1990), p. 21.
46 Sultan bin Zayed Al Nahayan, cited in Joseph A. Kechichian and R. Hrair Dekmejian (eds.), op cit., p. 20.
47 Alan Richards and John Waterbury, *A Political Economy of the Middle East* (Boulder: Westview Press, 1996), p. 311.
48 James T. Quinlivan, 'Coup-proofing: Its Practice and Consequences in the Middle East', *International Security,* vol. 24 no. 2 (autumn, 1999), p. 131.
49 Ray Takyeh, 'Qadhafi's Libya and the prospect of Islamic succession', *Middle East Policy*, vol. VII no. 2 (February 2000), p. 159.
50 D. Rueschemeyer, E. H. Stephens and J. D. Stephens, *Capitalist Development and Democracy* (Chicago: University of Chicago Press, 1992), cited in Ali R. Abootalebi, 'Civil society, democracy and the Middle East', *Middle East Review of International Affairs*, vol. 2 no. 3 (September 1998), p. 49.
51 Brian S. Turner, op. cit., p. 23.
52 Paul Salem, op. cit., p. 262.
53 Merger of Egypt and Syria, 1958–61.
54 Brian S. Turner, op. cit., p. 80.
55 Abdelsalam M. Maghraoui, 'Depoliticisation in Morocco', *Journal of Democracy*, vol. 13 no. 4 (October 2002), p. 30.

56 Gaetano Mosca, *The Ruling Class* (New York: McGraw-Hill, 1939), p. 53.
57 Phoebe A. Marr, 'The Political Elite in Iraq' in *Political Elites in the Middle East*, Chapter V (Washington, DC: American Enterprise Institute for Public Policy Research, 1975), p. 109.
58 Gaetano Mosca, op. cit., p. 404. Mosca identified two levels of elite: one politically powerful, the other acting more as a link to the rest of society.

4 Family first: Arab succession and dynasticism

1 Antony Black, *The History of Islamic Political Thought* (Edinburgh: Edinburgh University Press, 2001), p. 351.
2 Eyal Zisser, 'The succession struggle in Damascus, *Middle East Quarterly*, vol. II no. 3 (September 1995). Available online: http://www.meforum.org/article/264. (Accessed 10 September 2006).
3 Monte Palmer, *The Politics of the Middle East* (Itasca: F. E. Peacock, 2002). pp. 284–85.
4 Nutting describes the response to Nasser's resignation as 'a spontaneous outburst of public feeling . . . was to astonish even the most cynical of foreign observers'. Anthony Nutting, *Nasser* (London: Constable, 1972), p. 425.
5 Steven Runciman, *The Fall of Constantinople* (Cambridge: CUP, 1969), Chapter 1, Philip Hitti, *History of the Arabs* (Basingstoke: Palgrave, 2002), p. 674, Sydney N. Fisher, *The Middle East: a History*, (London: Routledge & Kegan Paul, 1971), pp. 182–84 and 200–204.
6 W. Ullman, *Medieval Political Thought* (Harmondsworth: Penguin, 1975), p. 85.
7 Louis J. Cantori, in L. J. Cantori *et al.*, 'Political succession in the Middle East', *Middle East Policy*, vol. 9 no. 2 (September 2002), p. 105.
8 Richard K. Betts and S. P. Huntington, 'Dead dictators and rioting mobs; does the demise of authoritarian rulers lead to political instability?' *International Security*, vol. 10 no. 3 (winter, 1985–86), p. 136.
9 Martin E. Spencer, 'Weber on legitimate norms and authority', *The British Journal of Sociology*, vol. 21 no. 2 (June 1970), p. 125.
10 Described by Black as a 'turn in power'. Antony Black, op. cit., pp. 50–51.
11 Antony Black, op. cit. (2001), p. 351.
12 Geoffrey R. Elton, *Tudor England* (London: Methuen & Co. Ltd., 1963), pp. 202, 213, 269.
13 D. L. Keir, *The Constitutional History of Modern Britain* (London: Adam & Charles Black, 1964), p. 8.
14 In Australia, where the leadership selection process is widely endorsed, the legitimacy of the process whereby in 1975 the Governor General replaced the Prime Minister, Gough Whitlam, with the opposition leader, Malcolm Fraser, was questioned by a significant portion of the electorate and was only partially resolved by resort to the ballot box.
15 George M., Trevelyan, *England under the Stuarts* (London: Folio Society, 1996), p. 91.
16 W. Montgomery Watt, *Islamic Political Thought* (Edinburgh: Edinburgh University Press, 1999), pp. 34 and 38.
17 N. J. Coulson, *A History of Islamic Law* (Edinburgh: Edinburgh University Press, 1972), p. 103.
18 S. Zerhouni, 'Morocco: reconciling continuity and change', in Volker Perthes (ed.), *Arab Elites: Negotiating the Politics of Change* (Boulder: Lynne Rienner, 2004), pp. 72–74.
19 Phoebe A. Marr, 'The Political Elite in Iraq' in *Political elites in the Middle East*, Chapter V, (Washington, DC, American Enterprise Institute for Public Policy Research, 1975), p. 109.

20 Philip Hitti, *op. cit.* (2002), p. 178.
21 Michael C. Hudson, *Arab Politics: the Search for Legitimacy* (New Haven: Yale University Press, 1977), p. 19.
22 Max Weber, *Ancient Judaism,* (trans.) Hans H. Gerth and Don Martindale (New York: Free Press, 1967), p. 11.
23 W. Montgomery Watt, op. cit. (1999), p. 35.
24 The re-election of Bashar to the presidency in May, 2007, was officially described in Syria as 'renewing the pledge of allegiance' (*tajdeed al bay'a*).
25 J. E. Peterson, 'Succession in the States of the Gulf Cooperation Council', *The Washington Quarterly* (autumn, 2001), p. 174.
26 K. Al-Dakhil, 'Abdallah streamlines Saudi succession plans but limits the power to chose', *saudidebate.com* (25 October 2006). Available online: http://www.islamdaily.net/EN/Contents.aspx?AID=4968. (Accessed 25 October 2006).
27 Gulf News, 'RAK Ruler appoints Crown Prince', *WAM/Gulf News* (15 June, 2003), available online: http://archive.gulfnews.com/articles/03/06/15/90260.html. (Accessed 20 June 2003), and 'UAE prince outed, army sent in', *The Tribune* (16 June 2003), available online: http://www.tribuneindia.com/2003/20030616/world.htm#5. (Accessed 20 June 2003).
28 Barnaby Rogerson, *The Heirs of the Prophet* (London: Abacus, 2006), pp. 80–120.
29 Michael C. Hudson, op. cit., (1977), p. 32.
30 Lisa Anderson, 'Arab democracy: dismal prospects', *World Policy Journal,* vol. 18 no. 3 (autumn, 2001), pp. 53–56.
31 Richard K. Betts and Samuel P. Huntington, op. cit., pp. 192–120.
32 Lisa Anderson, op. cit. (2001), pp. 53–56.
33 Mehmet Demir, 'Human rights briefing', *Middle East Report* No. 163, (March–April, 1990), p. 38.
34 Kamal Salibi, *The Modern History of Jordan* (London: I. B. Tauris, 1993), p. 203.
35 Kantorowicz describes primogeniture as the practice whereby England and France recognised that the succession to the throne was the birthright of the eldest son. On the death of the monarch the son became the king automatically. E. H. Kantorowicz, *The King's Two Bodies: a Study in Mediaeval Political Theology* (Princeton: Princeton University Press, 1970), p. 330.
36 W. Montgomery Watt, op. cit. (1999), p. 35.
37 Michael Herb, *All in the Family* (Albany: State University of New York Press, 1999), pp. 237–38.
38 Jean-Jacques Rousseau, *The Social Contract,* (trans.) M. Cranston (Penguin, 1968), p. 120.
39 When a sultan succeeded to the throne he would kill all his brothers by strangulation. (The largest killing took place on the succession of Mehmed III, when 16 brothers were killed and buried with their father.) In anticipation of Sulaiman the Magnificent's death in 1559, his sons engaged in a series of battles for the succession, in part, provoked by this method of resolving succession disputes.
40 Joseph A. Kechichian, *Succession in Saudi Arabia* (New York: Palgrave, 2001), pp. 175–79.
41 Joseph A. Kechichian, op. cit. (2001), pp. 95–96.
42 Lebanon is something of an exception to this rule, insofar as elections are markedly less predictable that those held in other Arab countries. Even in Lebanon, however, power is controlled by a relatively small group of individuals.
43 Charles Tripp, *A History of Iraq* (Cambridge: Cambridge University Press, 2002), pp. 169–70.
44 Sheila Carapico, 'Successions, transitions, coups and revolutions', in L. J. Cantori *et al.*, 'Political Succession in the Middle East', *Middle East Policy*, vol. 9 no. 3 (September 2002), pp. 109–10.

45 A. Shefa, 'Towards the September 7 presidential elections in Egypt', *Middle East Media Research Institute*, Enquiry and Analysis Series, No. 237 (2 September 2005), available online: http://memri.org/bin/articles.cgi?Page=archives&Area=ia&ID=IA23705. (Accessed 21 January 2006).
46 A., Drysdale, 'The succession question in Syria', *The Middle East Journal*, vol. 39 no. 2 (spring, 1985), pp. 246–57.
47 Robert D. Putnam, *The Beliefs of Politicians* (New Haven and London: Yale University Press, 1973), p. 238.
48 Numerous writers highlight this factor in regime survival, for example, K. H. Vickers, *England in the Later Middle Ages* (London: Methuen & Co., 1950), p. 225 and Francis Fukuyama, *The End of History and the Last Man* (London: Penguin, 1992), pp. 15–16 and Ian Kershaw, *Hitler: 1936–1945: Nemesis* (Penguin Books, 2000), pp. 698–700 and Isaac Deutscher, *Stalin* (Penguin Books, 1970), p. 614.
49 Mark Tessler, 'Arab and Muslim political attitudes: stereotypes and evidence from survey research', *International Studies Perspectives*, vol. 4 (2003), p. 177.
50 Antony Black, op. cit. (2001), pp. 314–18.
51 See, for example, the writing of Al Jihaz (776–868/9), in Antony Black, op. cit. (2001), pp. 25–27.
52 Suad Joseph, 'Connectivity and patriarchy among urban working-class Arab families in Lebanon', *Ethos*, vol. 21 no. 4 (December 1993), p. 478.
53 Toby Dodge, and Richard Higgott, *Globalization and the Middle East* (London: Royal Institute of International Affairs, 2002), pp. 197–98.
54 Edward Walker, cited in C. Giacomo, 'Will the son succeed the father as Egypt's president?' *Reuters Arab News* (June 2003), available online: http://www.aljazeerah.info/News%20archives/2003%20News%20archives/June%202003%20News/30n/Will%. (Accessed June 2003).
55 S. H. Gotowicki, *The Role of the Egyptian Military in Domestic Society* (Leavenworth: National Defence University, 1997), available online: http://fmso.leavenworth.army.mil/documents/egypt/egypt.htm. (Accessed 16 September 2006).
56 Andrzej Kapiszewski, 'Democratising the Arab States', *Krakowskie Studia Miedzynarodowe*, (2004), p. 115.
57 BBC, 'Rumsfeld rejects 'cleric-led' rule', *BBC News* (25 April 2003), available online: http://news.bbc.co.uk/2/hi/middle_east/2975333.stm. (Accessed 25 April 2003).

5 Constitutionalism and constitutions: the challenge of succession

1 Walter Bagehot, *The English Constitution* (London and Glasgow: Collins Fontana, 1968), p. 83.
2 Brian S. Turner, *Weber and Islam* (London: Routledge & Kegan Paul, 1974), pp. 23 and 24.
3 A. H. Al-Fahad, 'Ornamental constitutionalism: the Saudi Basic Law of Governance', *The Yale Journal of International Law,* vol. 30 no. 2 (2005), p. 395 and Nathan J. Brown, *Constitutions in a Non-constitutional World* (Albany: State University of New York Press, 2002), p. xiii.
4 S.E. Finer (ed.), *Five Constitutions* (Sussex: Harvester Press, 1979).
5 T. E. Baker, 'Constitutional theory in a nutshell', *William and Mary Bill of Rights Journal,* vol. 13 no. 57, (2004), p. 72.
6 L. A. Powe, *The Warren Court and American Politics* (Cambridge, Mass.: Belknap Press, Harvard University Press, 2001), p. 494.
7 Amendment of the Australian constitution requires approval by the majority of all electors voting and by a majority of all electors voting in at least four states. The French constitution can be amended by a majority of three fifths of both houses of the parliament meeting together. Article 89, available online: http://www.oefre.unibe.ch/law/icl/fr00000_.html.

8 G. S. Mahler, *Comparative Politics* (New Jersey: Prentice Hall, 2000), p. 25.
9 R. M. Unger, *Law in Modern Society* (New York: The Free Press, 1976), pp. 60 and 61.
10 The Australian constitution was largely intended to address the rivalries of the different colonies at the time of federation and to give expression to the compromise over protection and free trade.
11 I. D. Duchacek, *Power Maps: Comparative Politics of Constitutions* (Santa Barbara: California, Clio Press, 1973).
12 Nathan J. Brown, op. cit., pp. 3–7.
13 J. Graham and E. C. Marques, 'Understanding Constitutions: A Roadmap for Communities', *Institute on Governance* (Ottawa: October 2000), p. 4, available online: http://www.iog.ca. (Accessed 21 May 2009) and B. Li, 'What is Constitutionalism?' *Perspectives*, vol. 1 no. 6, (June 2000), p. 2.
14 B. Ackerman, 'The rise of world constitutionalism', *Virginia Law Review*, vol. 83 no. 4, (1997), p. 772.
15 B. Li, op. cit., p. 1.
16 R. M. Unger, op. cit., pp. 163 and 164.
17 D. J. Manning, *Liberalism* (London: J. M. Dent & Sons, 1976), pp. 77–78.
18 Isaiah Berlin, *Four Essays on Liberty*, London: Oxford University Press, 1975), pp. 121–31.
19 Howard Nenner, *By Color of Law* (Chicago: University of Chicago Press, 1997), p. 83.
20 Unless otherwise stated, constitutional texts referred to are taken from the website *International Constitutional Law*, A. Tschentscher (ed.), available online: http://www.oefre.unibe.ch/law/icl/.
21 For a discussion of the Constitution of Medina, see, for example, W. M. Watt, *Islamic Political Thought* (Edinburgh: Edinburgh University Press, 1999), pp. 5–6 and 130–34.
22 M. A. M. Khan, 'The Compact of Medina: A Constitutional Theory of the Islamic State', *Mirror International* (New York: Greenpoint, 30 May 2001).
23 D. Smock, *Islam and Democracy*, Washington, DC: United States Institute of Peace, Special Report No. 93 (September 2002), p. 5.
24 C. Mallat, 'From Islamic to Middle Eastern Law: A Restatement of the Field (Part 1)', *The American Journal of Comparative Law*, vol. 51 (2003), pp. 699–750.
25 H. A. R. Gibb, *Studies on the Civilisation of Islam* (London: Routledge & Kegan Paul, 1969), p. 200.
26 N. J. Coulson, *A History of Islamic Law* (Edinburgh: Edinburgh University Press, 1972), p. 2.
27 E. Cham, *Politics and Society in Contemporary France (1789–1971)* (London: George G. Harrap, 1972), p. 53. The French Constitutional Charter was promulgated by Louis XVIII soon after the restoration and, while establishing certain civil rights common with those in other parts of Europe, it also (in Articles 13–19) enhanced the power of the monarch: 'La personne du Roi est inviolable et sacree. Ses ministres sont responsable. Au Roi seul appartient la puissance executive.' (Art. 13). See also E. Lefebvre, *The Belgian Constitution of 1831: The Citizen Burger*, Discussion Paper, 4/97, Zentrum fur Europaische Rechtspolitik, (1997), and F. H. Hinsley, *The New Cambridge Modern History: Vol. XI: Material Progress and World-Wide Problems: 1870–1898* (Cambridge: Cambridge University Press, 1979), pp. 276–78. Bismarck's 1871 constitution was clearly monarchic and intended to block the aspirations of liberals.
28 Sami Zubaida, *Law and Power in the Islamic World* (London: I. B. Tauris, 2005), p.137.
29 *Ottoman Constitution, 1876*, Article 3, Bilkent University, available online: www.bilkent.edu.tr/~genckaya/documents1.html. (Accessed 13 May 2006).
30 *Ottoman Constitution, 1909*, Bo#abgaziçi University, Art. 3, available online: http://www.anayasa.gen.tr/1909amendment.htm. (Accessed 13 May 2006).
31 Given Palestine's unresolved status, its constitution is regarded as provisional.

32 William B. Quandt, *Saudi Arabia in the 1980s* (Washington: The Brookings Institution, 1981), p. 7 and Joseph A. Kechichian, *Succession in Saudi Arabia* (New York: Palgrave, 2001), p. 1 and A. H. Al Fahad, op. cit., pp. 381–82.
33 Beings, usually wicked, who tempt believers. According to the Quran, Allah created man from clay, angles from light and ginns from smokeless fire – Sura 55, Aya 17.
34 Antony Black, *The History of Islamic Political Thought* (Edinburgh: Edinburgh University Press, 2001), p. 229.
35 T. E. Masoud, 'The Arabs and Islam: the troubled search for legitimacy', *Daedalus* vol. 128 no. 2, (Boston: spring, 1999), pp. 137–38.
36 J. B. Alterman, 'The False Promise of Arab Liberals', *Policy Review On-line*, No. 125 (June/July 2004) Available online: http://www.policyreview.org/jun04/alterman.html. (Accessed 21 December 2005).
37 Articles 8, 9 and 13–23.
38 Nathan J. Brown, op cit., p. xiv.
39 UNDP, *Arab Human Development Report* (New York: United Nations, 2003), pp. 133–45.
40 For example, in 1980, Saudi per capita GDP was USD30,000. In 2004 it was around USD8,000.
41 King Feisal of Saudi Arabia was assassinated in 1975 while holding a traditional *majlis*.
42 On the role of Islam, for example, Yemen – Articles 1 and 2, Oman – Article 2, Bahrain – Article 6. On Arabism, see, for example, Lebanon – Preamble, Kuwait – Article 1, Jordan – Article 1.
43 A. A. Saif, *Constitutionalism in the Arab Gulf States* (Dubai: Gulf Research Centre, 2004), p. 20.
44 Antony Black, op cit., p. 157.
45 Independent judgement or the working out of a decision from general principles.
46 Learned men, guardians of Islam's religious and legal traditions.
47 *Bay'a* implicitly expresses a set of mutual pledges between ruler and ruled that bears some similarity to Rousseau's Social Contract.
48 Ikhwanweb, 'Muslim Brotherhood Initiatives For Reform in Egypt,' (29 March 2006). Available online: http://www.muslimbrotherhood.co.uk/Home.asp?zPage=Systems&System=PressR&Press=Show&Lang=E&ID=4162. (Accessed 15 August 2009).
49 Nathan J. Brown, op cit.
50 U. Thaysen, 'A new constitution for a new Germany?' *German Studies Review*, vol. 16 no. 2 (May 1993), p. 302.
51 The state of emergency legislation is regularly renewed by the government. Reports of violations under the emergency laws are commonplace. For example, Michael Slackman, 'Melee in Cairo reveals stress in Government', *The New York Times* (28 April 2006). Renewal is usually justified by domestic threats to the government. Human Rights Watch describes it as 'Egypt's emergency without end', *Human Rights News*, New York, 25 February, 2003. Available online: http://hrw.org/press/2003/02/egypt022503.htm. (Accessed 4 April 2007). According to the United States State Department, 'The constitution prohibits arbitrary arrest and detention; however, during the year, police and security forces conducted large-scale arrests and detained hundreds of individuals without charge under the Emergency Law. . . . The government continued to use the Emergency Law under the official state of emergency to try non-security cases in the emergency courts and to restrict many other basic rights.' *Country Report on Human Rights Practices, Egypt* (6 March 2007), available online: http://www.state.gov/p/nea/ci/81997.htm. (Accessed 4 April 2007).
52 Amnesty International, 'Syria: Time to make human rights a reality in Syria', *AI Index*: MDE 24/06/2005, Public News Service no. 211 (4 August 2005), available online: http://www.amnestyusa.org/countries/syria/document.do?id=80256DD400782B848

0257053005 B6443. (Accessed 21 April 2006). Also ibid., 'United States of America: Below the radar: Secret flights to torture and 'disappearance', *AI Index*: AMR 51/051/2006 (5 April 2006), available online: http://web.amnesty.org/library/Index/ENGAMR510512006. (Accessed 21 April 2006).

53 D. Schenker, 'Jordan and the Islamicists: Unfinished business', *Washington Institute for Near East Policy*, Peacewatch, no. 334 (27 June 2001), available online: http://www.washingtoninstitute.org/templateC05.php?CID=2025. (Accessed 21 April 2006).

54 Neil Macfarquhar, 'Heavy Hand of the Secret Police Impeding Reform in Arab World', *New York Times* (14 November 2005). Available online: http://www.nytimes.com/2005/11/14/international/middleeast/14jordan.html?ex =1289624400&en=f1e197fd717a8eb5&ei=5088&partner=rssnyt&emc=rss. (Accessed 14 November 2005).

55 For example, R. Bronson, 'Syria: Hanging Together or Hanging Separately', *The Washington Quarterly* (autumn, 2000), p. 96.

56 Howard Nenner, op cit., p. 65.

57 L. E. Walsh, *Final Report of the Independent Counsel for Iran-Contra Matters*, US Court of Appeal for District of Columbia, Vol. I, Concluding Observations (4 August 1993), pp. 561–67, available online: http://www.fas.org/irp/offdocs/walsh/. (Accessed 9 May 2006) and J. Nichols, 'The Rule of Law versus the Rule of Chaney', *The Nation* (23 February 2006), available online: http://www.thenation.com/. (Accessed 9 May 2006).

58 American Bar Association, 'Task Force on Presidential Signing Statements and the Separation of Powers Doctrine' (July 2006), available online: http://www.abanet.org/op/signingstatements/aba_final_signing_statements_recommendation-report_7-24-06.pdf. (Accessed 18 February 2008).

59 Antony Black, op. cit., pp. 143–44.

60 E. I. J. Rosenthal, *Political Thought in Medieval Islam* (Cambridge: Cambridge University Press, 1958), p. 131.

61 Michael Herb, 'Parliaments in the Gulf Monarchies: A Long Way from Democracy', *Daily Star* (4 December 2004). Available at Tharwa Net-Watch: http://www.tharwaproject.com/English/Main-Sec/NetWatch/NW_12_6_04/Herb.htm. (Accessed 20 December 2004).

62 A. Garfinkle, 'The new missionaries', *Prospect* (April 2003), pp. 22–24.

63 Vali Nasr, 'The rise of Muslim democracy', *Journal of Democracy*, vol. 16 no. 2 (April 2005), p. 14.

64 Jacques Berque, *Egypt: Imperialism and Revolution* (New York: Praeger Publishers, 1972), pp. 109, 365 and 443.

65 Marina Ottaway, 'Democracy and Constituencies in the Arab World', *Carnegie Papers*, no. 48 (July 2004), p. 11, available online: http://www.carnegieendowment.org/files/CP48.Ottaway.final.pdf.

66 A. Khalaf, 'Rules of succession and political participation in the GCC states', in A. Khalaf and G. Luciani (eds.), *Constitutional Reform and Political Participation in the Gulf* (Dubai: Gulf Research Centre, 2006), p. 45.

67 A. H. Khalaf, 'Why has Qatar gone constitutional?', *Daily Star*, 18 July 2002, available online: http://www.lebanonwire.com/0207/02071820DS.asp. (Accessed 30 August 2004).

68 Harold J. Berman, *Law and Revolution*, (Cambridge, Mass.: Harvard University Press, 1983), p. 4.

69 W. M. Watt, *The Influence of Islam on Medieval Europe (Islamic Surveys)* (Edinburgh: Edinburgh University Press, 1972), p. 84.

70 The nature of the relationship of the state to Arab society and the centralising process is discussed in some detail in Sami Zubaida, op. cit., pp. 121–81.

71 Sami Zubaida, op. cit., pp. 136–38.

72 Al-Fahad, op. cit., p. 392.

73 D. L. Keir, op. cit., p. 8.

74 D. L. Keir, op. cit., pp. 249–55.

75 Alexis de Tocqueville, 'L'ancien regime et la revolution', p. 205, quoted by J. Elster, 'Tocqueville on 1789: preconditions, precipitants and triggers', in C. B. Welch, (ed.), *The Cambridge Companion to Tocqueville* (Cambridge: Cambridge University Press, 2006), pp. 75–76.

76 M. A. Tétreault, 'Three Emirs and a Tale of Two Transitions,' *Middle East Report Online* (10 February 10 2006). Available online: http://www.merip.org/mero/mero021006.html. (Accessed 17 March 2006).

77 Howard Nenner, op. cit., pp. 32 and 34.

78 G. Agamben, *State of Exception*, (trans.) K. Attell, (Chicago: University of Chicago Press, 2004).

79 Lisa Anderson, 'Political Decay in the Arab World', *the Moshe Dayan Centre for Middle Eastern and African Studies*, (Middle Eastern Lectures, no. 4, Tel Aviv University, 2001), p. 10, available online: http://www.dayan.org/mel/anderson.pdf. (Accessed 21 November 2006).

6 Back to the future: Arab monarchies

1 Abd Al-Rahman ibn Khaldun, *The Muqaddimah*, abridged edition, N. J. Dawood (ed.), Franz Rosenthal (trans.), (Princeton: Princeton University Press, 2005), p. 47.

2 Antony Black, *The History of Islamic Political Thought* (Edinburgh: Edinburgh University Press, 2001), p. 51.

3 Michael Herb, *All in the Family* (Albany: State University of New York Press, 1999.), p. 8.

4 Michael Herb, ibid., p. 9.

5 Lisa Anderson, 'Political Decay in the Arab World', *Middle Eastern Lectures*, no. 4, The Moshe Dayan Centre for Middle Eastern and African Studies, Tel Aviv University (2001), p. 8, available online: http://www.dayan.org/mel/anderson.pdf. (Accessed 23 April 2006).

6 P. Aarts and G. Nonneman (eds.), *Saudi Arabia in the Balance: Political Economy, Society, Foreign Affairs* (London/New York: Hurst and Company, New York University Press, 2005) – final chapter. Also L. Anderson, 'Dynasts and Nationalists: Why Monarchies Survive', in *Middle East Monarchies*, Joseph Kostiner (ed.) (London: Lynne Rienner, 2000), pp. 66–67.

7 Michael Herb. op. cit., p. 1.

8 Sami Zubaida, *Law and Power in the Islamic World* (London: I. B. Tauris, 2005), pp. 154–55.

9 J. Adams, 'The rule of the father: patriarchy and patrimonialism in early modern Europe', in C. Camic, P. S. Gorski and D. M. Trubek (eds.), *Max Weber's Economy and Society: a Critical Companion* (Stanford, CA: Stanford University Press, 2005), pp. 242–43.

10 For example, Rachel Bronson, 'Syria: hanging together or hanging separately', *The Washington Quarterly,* vol. 23 no. 4, (autumn, 2000), pp. 91–105.

11 David Fromkin, *A Peace to End All Peace* (London: Phoenix Press, 2000), p. 93.

12 Sydney N. Fisher, *The Middle East: A History* (London: Routledge & Kegan Paul, 1971), p. 381.

13 Jordan has had two monarchs named Abdallah. Where necessary in terms of context, the kings will be described as Abdallah I and Abdallah II.

14 They are from the Hejaz along the west coast of the Arabian Peninsula.

15 J. Nevo, 'Changing identities in Jordan', *Israel Affairs*, vol. 9 no. 3 (spring, 2003), p. 189.

16 Abdallah ibn Al Hussein, *My Memoirs Completed* (London: Longman, 1978), p. vii.

17 Peter Snow, *Hussein: A Biography* (New York: Robert B. Luce, 1972), p. 22.

18 Raymond Hinnebusch, *The International Politics of the Middle East* (Manchester: Manchester University Press, 2003), p. 194.
19 R. Ryan and J. Schwedler, 'Return to democratisation or a new hybrid regime: The 2003 elections in Jordan', *Middle East Policy*, vol. 11 no. 2 (summer, 2004), p. 3.
20 William Beeman, 'Chalabi's Return – After Fallout with US, Former Iraqi Exile Plays All Sides', *Pacific News Service* (New America Media, 8 November 2005), available online: http://news.pacificnews.org/news/view_article.html?article_id=5207 5943cedbf2d83f3298b5c9cde0b5. (Accessed 8 November 2005).
21 This is not a uniquely Arab characteristic. As soon as the French had captured Damascus from Arab forces in 1920, the French General, Gouraud, went to the tomb of Saladin, kicked it and announced, 'Awake Saladin, we have returned. My presence here consecrates the victory of the Cross over the Crescent'. The British General Allenby expressed similar sentiments when he arrived in Jerusalem in 1917.
22 Martin Asser, 'Jordan's succession saga', *BBC World*: Middle East (6 February 1999), available online: http://news.bbc.co.uk/1/hi/world/middle_east/272678.stm. (Accessed 21 August 2006).
23 Nicolas Pelham, 'King of Jordan 'feared being upstaged' by his half-brother', *Financial Times* (London, 30 November 2004), available online: http://www.ft.com/cms/s/0/ 552273c2-4276-11d9–8e3c-00000e2511c8.html. (Accessed 22 May 2009).
24 Appendix 10 – Letter to Hassan by King Hussein, transferring succession from Hassan to Abdallah (25 January 1999), available online: www.kinghussein.gov.jo/ 99-jan25.html. (Accessed 15 May 2005).
25 C. R. Ryan, 'Political liberalization and monarchical succession in Jordan', *Israel Affairs*, vol. 9 no. 3 (spring, 2003), p. 133.
26 Martin Asser, op. cit..
27 Peter Snow, op. cit., pp. 95 and 206.
28 Nicolas Pelham, op. cit..
29 Michael Herb, op. cit., pp. 237–38.
30 K. Salibi, *The Modern History of Jordan* (London: I. B. Tauris, 1993), p. 169.
31 On Talal's accession to the throne, his younger brother, Nayef, contemplated a coup but could not assemble sufficient support. Talal's abdication was managed through the establishment by the family of a Throne Council with the capacity to exercise the king's powers and by the decision of the Prime Minister, Abu Al-Huda, to seek Talal's deposition through parliament. P. Robins, *A History of Jordan* (Cambridge: Cambridge University Press, 2004), pp. 75–78 and 81–82.
32 A. Susser, 'Succession success', *The New Republic* (22 February 1999), p. 17.
33 Appendix 6 – Mapping Power, Andre Bank and Oliver Schlumberger, 'Jordan: between regime survival and economic reform', in Volker Perthes (ed.), *Arab Elites: Negotiating the Politics of Change* (London: Lynne Rienner, 2004), p. 46.
34 Article 340 of the Penal Code exonerates anyone who kills for family honour. The government has attempted on a number of occasions to reverse this law, but it has been blocked by the lower house of parliament.
35 S. Zerhouni, 'Morocco: Reconciling Continuity and Change', in Volker Perthes (ed.), op. cit., pp. 61 and 69.
36 Michael Herb, op. cit., p. 222.
37 Bahrain is excluded from the consideration as it is constitutionally an 'hereditary constitutional monarchy' and based on primogeniture. Bahrain National Charter, Article 1(b).
38 Mohammed Al-Fahim, *From Rags to Riches: A Story of Abu Dhabi* (London: Centre of Arab Studies, 1995), Chapter 6.
39 Joseph A. Kechichian, *Succession in Saudi Arabia* (New York: Palgrave, 2001), p. 1. Also A. H. Al-Fahad, 'Ornamental constitutionalism: the Saudi Basic Law of Governance', *The Yale Journal of International Law*, vol. 30 no. 2 (2005), pp. 381–82.

40 Joseph A. Kechichian, op. cit., pp. 95–96.
41 M. S. Doran, 'The Saudi Paradox', *Foreign Affairs*, vol. 83 no. 1 (January/February, 2004), pp. 35–51.
42 Nimrod Raphaeli, 'The succession in Kuwait: the triumph of constitutional order over tribal norms', *Middle East Media Research Institute,* Enquiry and Analysis Series, No. 263 (2 February 2006), available online: http://www.memri.org/bin/articles.cgi?Page=archives&Area=ia&ID=IA26306. (Accessed 24 May 2006).
43 Anthony Cordesman, *Saudi Arabia Enters the Twenty-First Century: III. Politics and Internal Stability* (Washington, Centre for Strategic and International Studies, 30 October 2002), p. 13.
44 Also known as 'patrilineal primogeniture' – inheritance based to seniority of birth among the sons of a monarch.
45 A. H. Al Fahad, 'Ornamental constitutionalism: the Saudi Basic Law of Governance', *Yale Journal of International Law,* vol. 30 no. 2 (2005), p. 389.
46 Joseph A. Kechichian, op. cit., pp. 5 and 36.
47 Joseph A. Kechichian, op. cit., p. 26.
48 Cynthia Nelson, 'Public and private politics: women in the Middle Eastern world', *American Ethnologist*, vol. 1 no. 3 (August 1974), p. 558.
49 On 8 May 2009 Human Rights Watch reported the detention of a member of the United Arab Emirates royal family, Sheikh Issa bin Zayed al Nahayan, in connection with the videotaped torture of an Afghan grain dealer. The action, if Human Rights Watch is correct, would have been taken after intense external pressure on the government.
50 A. H. Al-Fahad, op. cit., p. 376.
51 The term 'sheikh', which is widely used in the region as a term of respect, carries a number of meanings, including tribe or family leader, old man and traditional or religious scholar.
52 H. Miles, 'Saudi king loses power to choose his successor', *The Daily Telegraph*, London (10 February 2007) available online: http://www.telegraph.co.uk/news/main.jhtml%3Bjsessionid%3DYOSGXL4RS4BVXQFIQMFCFGGAVCBQYIV0?xml=/news/2007/02/10/wsaudi10.xml. (Accessed 14 February 2007).
53 Michael Herb, op. cit., p. 178.
54 For example, William B. Quandt, 'The Middle East on the brink: prospects for change in the 21st century', speech given at University of Virginia, September 1995, available online: http://www.people.virginia.edu/~wbq8f/MEITALK.htm. (Accessed 20 June 2003). Also Lisa Anderson, 'Absolutism and the resilience of monarchy in the Middle East', *Political Science Quarterly*, vol. 6 no. 1 (1991).
55 David E. Long, 'The role of the extended family in Saudi Arabia', *Saudi-American Forum* (10 March 2003), p. 4, available online: www.saudi-american-forum.org/Newsletters/SAF_09.pdf. (Accessed 29 June 2007).
56 F. G. Gause III, 'The persistence of monarchy in the Arabian Peninsula: a comparative analysis', in Joseph Kostiner (ed.), op. cit., p. 168.
57 Algeria, Lebanon and Tunisia are the main exceptions in the Arab heartland.
58 Lisa Anderson, op. cit. pp. 8–9.

7 Hybrids: monarchic republics of the Arab world

1 Howard Nenner, *By Color of Law* (Chicago: University of Chicago Press, 1977), p. 124.
2 Mohammed A. Al-Hadid, 'Succession from fathers' rule to their sons is common', *Al Gumhuriya*, Cairo, (15 June 2000). Quoted in Yotam Feldner, 'Egypt's Succession, Part I: Will Egypt Follow Syria's Precedent?', *Middle East Media Research Institute* (24 July 2000). Available online: http://www.memri.org/bin/articles.cgi?Page=archives&Area=ia&ID=IA3100. (Accessed 23 August 2006).

3 Mustafa Al Feki, 'Content over form', *Al Ahram Weekly*, issue 711 (7–13 0ctober 2004), available online: http://weekly.ahram.org.eg/2004/711/op2.htm. (Accessed 28 October 2006).
4 BBC, 'Saddam's rival sons', *BBC News* (22 July 2003), available online: http://news.bbc.co.uk/2/hi/middle_east/2236137.stm. (Accessed 6 September 2006).
5 Yehudit Ronen, 'Libya's rising star: Saif Al Islam and succession', *Middle East Policy*, vol. XII no. 3 (autumn, 2005), p. 142.
6 G. D. Johnsen, 'Saleh's road to re-election', *Middle East Report On-line,* 13 January 2006, available online: http://www.merip.org/mero/mero011306.html. (Accessed 20 January 2006).
7 Yotam Feldner, op. cit..
8 BBC, 'Saad Hariri: novice political heir', *BBC News* (2005), available online: http://news.bbc.co.uk/2/hi/middle_east/4110398.stm. (Accessed 6 September 2006).
9 L. Martin, 'Arafat's duelling dilemmas: succession and the peace process', *Middle East Review of International Affairs*, vol. 6 no.1 (March 2002), pp. 60–71.
10 E. Bellin, 'Coercive Institutions and Coercive Leaders', in M. P. Posusney, and M. P. Angrist (eds.), *Authoritarianism in the Middle East* (Boulder and London: Lynne Rienner, 2005), p. 33.
11 Steffen Erdle, 'Tunisia: Economic transformation and political restoration', in Volker Perthes (ed.), *Arab Elites: Negotiating the Politics of Change* (Boulder and London: Lynne Rienner, 2004), pp. 214–15.
12 Sheila Carapico, 'Successions, transitions, coups and revolutions', in L. J. Cantori, *et al.*, 'Political Succession in the Middle East', *Middle East Policy*, vol. 9 no. 3 (September 2002), p. 109.
13 Lisa Anderson, 'Political decay in the Arab world', *Middle Eastern Lectures*, number 4, *The Moshe Dayan Centre for Middle Eastern and African Studies*, Tel Aviv University, (2001), p. 10, available online: http://www.dayan.org/mel/anderson.pdf. (Accessed 17 January 2005).
14 A. H. Al-Fahad, 'Ornamental constitutionalism: the Saudi Basic Law of Governance', *The Yale Journal of International Law*, vol. 30 no. 2 (2005), pp. 375–96.
15 Between 1949 and 1962 Syria experienced eight coups. Between September 1961, and September 1962, there were three coups.
16 Sheila Carapico, op. cit., p. 109.
17 Ami Ayalon, 'Semantics and the modern history of non-European societies: Arab 'republics' as a case study', *The Historical Journal*, vol. 28 no. 4 (December 1985), pp. 821–34.
18 While Syria's experience was limited, the perceived betrayal of the monarchy by France and Britain had a lasting impact. Tabitha Petran, *Syria* (London: Ernest Benn, 1972), pp. 59–60.
19 Syria and Yemen have oil reserves, but these are less significant features of their economies than is the case in Iraq or Libya. In January 2007, Syria had reserves of 2.5 billion barrels and Yemen had 3 billion. By contrast, Iraq had 115 billion barrels and Libya had 39 billion. *Oil and Gas Journal*, vol. 104 no. 47 (18 December, 2006), available online: http://www.ogj.com/currentissue/index.cfm?p=7&v=104&i=47. (Accessed 13 November 2007).
20 Ray Takeyh, 'Qadhafi's Libya and the prospect of Islamic succession', *Middle East Policy*, vol. VII no. 2 (February 2000), p. 157.
21 Glen E. Robinson, 'Elite cohesion, regime succession and political instability in Syria', *Middle East Policy*, vol. 5 no. 4 (January 1998), p. 176.
22 Rachel Bronson, 'Syria: Hanging together or hanging separately', *The Washington Quarterly* (autumn, 2000), pp. 97–98. Among the people removed in the preparations for Bashar's accession were Hikmat Shihabi, Chief of Staff, Ali Duba, head of intelligence, Mohammed Khuli, head of the Air Force, Adnan Makhluf, head of the

Republican Guard and Ali Haydar, head of the Special Forces. Their replacement by people loyal to Bashar was a crucial step in preparing the way.

23 Charles Glass, 'Is Syria Next?' *London Review of Books*, vol. 25 no. 14 (24 July 2003), pp. 1–3.

24 J. Brandon, 'In exile, opposition groups unite against Damascus', *Christian Science Monitor* (1 November 2005), available online: http://www.csmonitor.com/2005/1101/p07s02-wome.html. (Accessed 10 September 2006).

25 Cited in E., Zisser, 'Does Bashar al-Assad Rule Syria?', *Middle East Quarterly,* (winter, 2003), available online: http://www.meforum.org/article/517. (Accessed 9 September 2006).

26 Howard Nenner, op. cit..

27 After World War I, the Sanjak of Alexandretta became part of the French Mandate of Syria. The area comprised Turks, Sunni Arabs and large numbers of Alawites. In 1939, France ceded the Sanjak to Turkey, a decision that has never been accepted by Syria.

28 Patrick Seale, *Asad: the Struggle for the Middle East* (Berkeley: University of California Press, 1995), pp. 30–36 and 61.

29 Volker Perthes, 'The political economy of the Syrian succession', *Survival*, vol. 43 issue 1 (spring, 2001), p. 147.

30 Michael Slackman and K. Zoepf, 'Chief Syrian suspect is at centre of power', *New York Times* (6 November 2005), available online: http://www.iht.com/articles/2005/11/02/news/syria.php. (Accessed 9 September 2006).

31 Patrick Seale, op. cit., pp. 55–56.

32 Ellen Lust-Okar, 'Bashar Al-Assad's rise to the presidency', in L. J. Cantori *et al.*, op. cit., p. 114.

33 Brian S. Turner, *Religion, Law and the Growth of Constitutional Thought, 1150–1650* (Cambridge: Cambridge University Press, 1982), p. 24. Weber's expectation is consistent with de Tocqueville's comment that the most dangerous time for a regime is when it attempts reform.

34 Glen E. Robinson, op. cit., p. 171.

35 Jeremy Drummond and Roula Khalaf, 'Mubarak's son rules out succession', London, *Financial Times* (24 April 2001), p. 12: 'He seems to be a candidate for something.'

36 Committee on Torture, 'Conclusions and recommendations of the Committee against Torture: Egypt'. *United Nations*, New York, 23/12/2002. CAT/C/CR/29/4D (5.b, c).

37 Volker Perthes, 'Pharaoh Re-elected', *SWP Comments*, No. 39, Berlin, German Institute for International and Security Affairs (September 2005).

38 Muhammad Abu Al-Hadid in *Al-Gumhuriya*, cited in Feldner, Y., "Egypt's succession, Part 1: Will Egypt follow Syria's precedent?" *Middle East Media Research Institute*, Enquiry and Analysis Series, no. 31 (24 July 2000), available online: http://www. memri.org/bin/articles.cgi?Page=archives&Area=ia&ID=IA3100. (Accessed 5 September 2006).

39 The Egyptian constitution was amended in key areas, including the succession, in a referendum in 2005. References to the constitution are from 'Egypt's Government Services Portal: http://www.egypt.gov.eg/english/laws/Constitution/default.aspx.

40 Yotam Feldner, op. cit., Part I.

41 Cited in Shefa, A., 'Towards the September 7 Presidential elections in Egypt', *Middle East Media Research Institute*, Enquiry and Analysis Series, No. 237 (2 September 2005), available online: http://memri.org/bin/articles.cgi?page=archives&Area=ia&ID=IA23705. (Accessed 21 January 2006).

42 A. Hamzawy, 'Egypt: Creating a new political reality', *Arab Reform Bulletin*, vol. 3 no. 5 (June 2005), available online: http://www.carnegieendowment.org/publications/index.cfm?fa=view&id=17049&prog=zgp&proj=zdrl,zme#creating. (Accessed 26 June 2005).

43 I. El Amrani, 'Controlled reform in Egypt: neither reformist nor controlled', *Middle East Report On-line* (15 December 2005), available online: http://www.merip.org/mero/mero121505.html. (Accessed 15 December 2005).
44 Too much should not be made of the courts' power. The newspaper, *Al Shaab*, was closed by the government in 2000 and, despite 13 court decisions that it should be allowed to resume publication, it remains closed.
45 Ami Ayalon, 'Egypt's quest for cultural orientation', The Moshe Dayan Centre for Middle Eastern and African Studies – section headed 'Courtrooms as a battleground', available online: http://www.tau.ac.il/dayancenter/D&A-Egypt-ami.htm. (Accessed 27 May 2005).
46 A. Abdalla, *Egypt before and after September 11, 2001*, Deutsches Orient-Institut im Deutsches Ubersee-Institut, DOI Focus No. 9 (March 2003), p. 28. Also Volker Perthes, 'Pharaoh Re-elected', op. cit., p. 2.
47 *Al Jazeera*, 'Egypt's Islamists see Gamal president', 18 January 2005, available online: http://english.aljazeera.net/NR/exeres/4BC753F9–263D-4D95–85B5–5D6ACD9339DB.htm. (Accessed 19 January 2005).
48 D. Linzer, 'Poll Shows Growing Arab Rancour at US', *Washington Post* (23 July 2004), p. A 26.
49 D. Sobelman, 'Gamal Mubarak, President of Egypt?', *Middle East Quarterly*, vol. 8 no. 2 (spring, 2001), p. 35.
50 S. H. Gotowicki, *The role of the Egyptian military in domestic society*, National Defence University (1997), available online: http://fmso.leavenworth.army.mil/document/egypt/egypt.htm. (Accessed 16 September 2006).
51 Gamal Abdelnasser, 'Egypt: succession politics', in Volker Perthes, op. cit., (2004), pp. 120–23.
52 Ray Takeyh, op. cit., p. 156.
53 H. Mattes, 'Challenges to security sector governance in the Middle East: the Libyan case', *Geneva Centre for the Democratic Control of the Armed Forces*, Working Paper No. 144 (August 2004), p. 7.
54 For example, Jason Brownlee, op. cit., in M. Posusney and M. Angrist (eds.), *op. cit.*, p. 56 and Y. Ronen, op. cit..
55 Yehudit Ronen, op. cit..
56 *Jamahiriya* is drawn from the word *jamahir* and connotes 'polity of the masses'. It is intended to mark a post-republican era – Ami Ayalon, op. cit. (1985), p. 834.
57 Yehudit Ronen, op. cit., p. 142.
58 Ray Takeyh, *op. cit.*, pp. 157–60.
59 Some of Saif's views, expressed on *Al Jazeera* television, are summarised in A. Dankowitz, 'Saif Al Islam Al Qaddafi's professed reform in Libya', *The Middle East Media Research Institute*, Enquiry and Analysis Series, No. 250, 11 November 2005, available online: http://www.memri.org/bin/articles.cgi?Page=archives&Area=ia&ID =IA25005. (Accessed 2 June 2009).
60 Saif Al-Islam, 'Libyan-American relations', M. Viorst (ed.), *Middle East Policy*, vol. 10 no. 1 (spring, 2003), p. 35.
61 Tariq Ali, 'Visit to Libya', *London Review of Books*, vol. 28 no. 5 (9 March 2006).
62 This is a position with no apparent power, the current incumbent having held the position since November 1992, without having made any appreciable impact on the country's political life.
63 A. Dankowitz, op. cit..
64 Before that, Saleh had been President of the Yemen Arab Republic (the North).
65 Brian Whitaker, 'Journalist arrested', *Middle East International*, issue 721 (18 March 2004).
66 Sarah Phillips, 'Cracks in the Yemeni system', *Middle East Report OnLine*, 28 July 2005, available online: http://www.merip.org/mero/mero072805.html. (Accessed 30 August 2005).

67 The president must be at least 40 years of age – Article 106 (a).
68 Sarah Phillips, 'Foreboding about the future in Yemen', *Middle East Report OnLine* (3 April 2006), available online: http://www.merip.org/mero/mero040306.html. (Accessed 27 May 2006).
69 Sarah Phillips, op. cit. (2006).
70 P. Kiernan, 'Surviving the odds', *The Middle East* (September, 1998), pp. 23–25.
71 J. Novak, 'Yemen's President Reneges on Democracy', *Worldpress.org* (28 June 2006), available online: http://www.worldpress.org/Mideast/2399.cfm. (Accessed 7 January 2007).

8 Tradition versus change: the challenge of dynasticism in the Arab political tradition

1 Meir Litvak (ed.), *Middle Eastern Societies and the West* (The Moshe Dayan Centre for Middle Eastern and African Studies, Tel Aviv University, 2006), pp. 21–22.
2 L. Carl Brown, *International Relations and the Middle East* (Princeton: Princeton University Press, 1984), p. 4.
3 Michael C. Hudson, *Arab Politics: the Search for Legitimacy* (New Haven: Yale University Press, 1977), pp. 18–20.
4 Paul Salem, *Bitter Legacy* (Syracuse: Syracuse University Press, 1994), p. 263.
5 Seymour M., Lipset, *Political Man* (London: Heinemann, 1969), p. 78: 'A crisis of legitimacy is a crisis of change'.
6 E. P. Thompson, *Whigs and Hunters* (London: Allen Lane, 1975), pp. 262 and 263.
7 Bryan S. Turner, *Weber and Islam* (London and Boston: Routledge & Kegan Paul, 1974), p. 79.
8 Algeria, Lebanon and Tunisia are the main exceptions in the Arab heartland. Syria's experience was short lived.

Appendix 4

1 *Constitution of Medina*, al-Islami, Khilafah al-'Alam (trans.) Not dated, available online: http://www.constitution.org/cons/medina/macharter.htm. (Accessed 28 November 2008).

Appendix 6

1 Hussein bin Talal, 'Letter to HRH Prince El Hassan', *The Cyber Library of Jordan – Hussein I.* 25 January 1999, available online: http://www.kinghussein.gov.jo/99-jan25.html. (Accessed 2 February 2006).

Bibliography

Aarts, P. and Nonneman, G. (eds.), *Saudi Arabia in the Balance Political Economy, Society, Foreign Affairs* (London/New York: New York University Press, 2005).

Abdalla, Ahmed, *Egypt before and after September 11, 2001*, Deutsches Orient-Institut im Deutsches Ubersee-Institut, DOI Focus No. 9, (March 2003), available online: http://www.mafhoum.com/press7/194P52.pdf. (Accessed 29 May 2008).

Abdallah ibn Hussein, *My Memoirs Completed* (London: Longmans, 1978).

Abdelnasser, Gamal, 'Egypt: succession politics', in Perthes, V., *Arab Elites: Negotiating the Politics of Change* (London: Lynne Rienner, 2004), pp. 117–39.

Abootalebi, Ali R., 'Civil Society, democracy and the Middle East', *Middle East Review of International Affairs*, vol. 2 no. 3 (September 1998), pp. 46–59.

Abukhalil, As'ad, 'Change and democratisation in the Arab world: the role of political parties', *Third World Quarterly*, vol. 18 issue 1 (1997), pp. 149–63.

Ackerman, B., 'The rise of world constitutionalism', *Virginia Law Review*, vol. 83 issue 4 (May 1997), pp. 771–97.

Adams, J., 'The Rule of the Father: Patriarchy and Patrimonialism in Early Modern Europe,' in Camic, C., Gorski, P. S. and Trubek D. M. (eds.) *Max Weber's Economy and Society: a Critical Companion* (Stanford, CA: Stanford University Press, 2005), pp. 237–66.

AfaqArabia, 'The Moslem Brotherhood Initiative for Reform' – translated from Arabic available online: http://www.afaqarabia.com/asp/Article.asp. (Accessed 6 January 2006).

El-Affendi, A., 'The elusive reformation', in Diamond, L., Plattner, M. F. and Brumberg, D. (eds.), *Islam and Democracy in the Middle East* (Baltimore: Johns Hopkins University Press, 2003), pp. 252–57.

Agamben, Giorgio, *State of Exception*, (trans.) Attell, Kevin, (Chicago: University of Chicago Press, 2004).

Ahmed, Akbar, 'Ibn Khaldun's Understanding of Civilisations and Dilemmas of Islam and the West Today', *Middle East Journal*, vol. 56 no. 1 (winter, 2002).

Ahrari, M. E., 'Political Succession in Saudi Arabia: Systemic Stability and Security Implications', *Comparative Strategy*, vol. 18 issue 1 (1999), pp. 13–29.

Al Jazeera., 'Egypt's Islamists see Gamal president' (18 January 2005) available online: http://english.aljazeera.net/NR/exeres/4BC753F9–263D–4D95–85B5–5D6ACD9339DB.htm. (Accessed 19 January 2005).

Albrecht, Holger and Schlumberger, Oliver, ' "Waiting for Godot": regime change without democratisation in the Middle East', *International Political Science Review*, vol. 25 no. 4 (2004), pp. 371–92.

Aldridge, James, *Cairo: Biography of a City* (London: Macmillan, 1970).

Alhajj, A. Juma, 'The political elite and the introduction of political participation in Oman', *Middle East Policy*, no. 3 (June 2000).

Ali, Tariq, 'Visit to Libya', *London Review of Books*, vol. 28 no. 5 (9 March 2006).

Alterman, Jon B., 'Egypt: Stable but for how long?', *The Washington Quarterly*, vol. 23 no. 4 (Autumn, 2000), pp. 107–18.

Alterman, Jon B., 'The False Promise of Arab Liberals', *Policy review On-line*, no. 125 (June/July 2004) available online: http://www.policyreview.org/jun04/alterman.html. (Accessed 21 December 2005).

American Bar Association, *Task Force on Presidential Signing Statements and the Separation of powers Doctrine*, Washington DC (July 24 2006) available online: http://www.abanet.org/op/signingstatements/aba_final_signing_statements_recommendation-report_7–24–06.pdf. (Accessed 30 July 2006).

Amnesty International, 'Syria, Time to make human rights a reality in Syria', *AI Index*: MDE 24/060/2005, Public News Service No: 211, (4 August 2005) available online: http://www.amnestyusa.org/countries/syria/document.do?id=80256DD400782B848 0257053005B6443. (Accessed 21 April 2006).

Amnesty International, 'United States of America: Below the radar: Secret flights to torture and "disappearance", *AI Index*: AMR 51/051/2006 (April 5 2006) available online: http://web.amnesty.org/library/Index/ENGAMR510512006. (Accessed 21 April 2006).

El Amrani, Issandr, 'Egypt: opening the constitutional debate', *Arab Reform Bulletin*, vol. 3 issue 2 (March 2005), available online: http://www.carnegieendowment.org/publications/index.cfm?fa=view&id=16643. (Accessed 9 August 2006).

El Amrani, Issandr, 'Controlled Reform in Egypt: Neither Reformist nor Controlled', *Middle East Report On-line* (December 15 2005) available online: http://www.merip.org/mero/mero121505.html. (Accessed 15 December 2005).

Anderson, Lisa, 'The state in the Middle East and North Africa', *Comparative Politics*, vol. 20 issue 1 (October 1987), pp. 1–18.

Anderson, Lisa, 'Tribe and State: Libyan anomalies', in Khoury, P. S. and Kostiner, J. (eds.), *Tribes and State Formation in the Middle East* (Berkeley: University of California Press, 1990), pp. 288–302.

Anderson, Lisa, 'Absolutism and the Resilience of Monarchy in the Middle East', *Political Science Quarterly*, vol. 106 no. 1, (1991), pp. 1–15.

Anderson, Lisa, 'Dynasts and Nationalists: Why Monarchies Survive', in Kostiner, J. (ed.), *Middle East Monarchies* (London: Lynne Rienner, 2000), pp. 53–69.

Anderson, Lisa, 'Arab democracy: dismal prospects', *World Policy Journal*, vol. 18 no. 3 (autumn, 2001), pp. 53–56.

Anderson, Lisa, 'Political Decay in the Arab World', *Middle Eastern Lectures*, no. 4 (2001), The Moshe Dayan Centre for Middle Eastern and African Studies, Tel Aviv University, available online: http://www.dayan.org/mel/anderson.pdf. (Accessed 18 October 2004).

Anderson, Perry, *Lineages of the Absolutist State* (London: Verso Books, 3rd Impression, 1986).

Andoni, L., 'King Abdallah: In his father's footsteps?', *Journal of Palestine Studies*, vol. XXIV no. 3 (spring, 2000) pp. 77–89.

Antonio, Robert J., 'After post-modernism: reactionary tribalism', *The American Journal of Sociology*, vol. 106 no. 1 (July 2000), pp. 40–87.

Antonius, George, *The Arab Awakening* (London: Hamish Hamilton, 1961).

Arabi, Oussama, 'Beyond power: neo-Shafi'ism or the Islamic constructive metaphor in Egypt's High Constitutional Court', *Arab Law Quarterly*, vol. 17 no. 4 (2002), pp. 323–54.

Arjomand, Said Amir, 'Islam, political change and globalisation', *Thesis Eleven*, no. 76 (February 2004), pp. 9–28.

Armstrong, Karen, *Islam: a Short History* (London: Phoenix Press, 2001).

Arnason, Johann P., 'Civilization and state formation in the Islamic context: re-reading ibn Khaldun', *Thesis Eleven*, no. 76 (February 2004), pp. 29–47.

Arnold, T. and Guillaume, A., (eds.), *The Legacy of Islam* (Oxford: Oxford University Press, 1968).

Asa-El, Amos, 'Middle Israel: Let Hamas Rule', *The Jerusalem Post*, (August 13 2001) available online: http://pqasb.pqarchiver.com/jpost/access/984373611.html?dids=984373611:984373611&FMT=ABS&FMTS=ABS:FT&date=Feb+3%2C+2006&author=AMOTZ+ASA-EL&pub=Jerusalem+Post&edition=&startpage=06&desc=Let+Hamas+rule. (Access 29 March 2009).

Ashford, Douglas E., 'Succession and social change in Tunisia', *International Journal of Middle East Studies*, vol. 4 issue 1 (January 1973), pp. 23–39.

Ashley, M., *England in the Seventeenth Century* (Harmondsworth: Pelican, 1965).

Al-Askari, Jafar Pasha, *A Soldier's Story* (London: Arabian Publishing, 2003).

Asser, Martin, 'Jordan's succession saga', *BBC World online* (January 6 1999) available online: http://news.bbc.co.uk/1/hi/world/middle_east/272678.stm. (Accessed 21 August 2006).

Avineri, Shlomo, 'Failed democratisation in the Arab world', *Dissent*, (autumn, 2002) available online: http://www.dissentmagazine.org/article/?article=556. (Accessed 27 April 2009), pp. 21–25.

Awad, Mohammed, 'The assimilation of nomads in Egypt', *Geographical Review*, vol. 44 no. 2 (April 1954), pp. 240–52.

Ayalon, Ami, 'Semantics and the modern history of non-European societies: Arab "republics" as a case study', *The Historical Journal*, vol. 28 issue 4 (December 1985), pp. 821–34.

Ayalon, Ami, 'Egypt's quest for cultural orientation', *The Moshe Dayan Centre for Middle Eastern and African Studies* (1999), available online: http://www.tau.ac.il/dayancenter/D&A-Egypt-ami.htm. (Accessed 27 May 2005).

Ayres, Ian and Macey, J. R., 'Institutional and evolutionary failure and economic development in the Middle East', *Yale Journal of International Law*, vol. 30 (2005), pp. 397–429.

Al Azmeh, Aziz (ed.), *Islamic Law: Social and Historical Contexts* (London: Routledge, 1988).

Bagehot, Walter, *The English Constitution* (London and Glasgow: Collins Fontana, 1968).

Baker, Thomas E., 'Constitutional theory in a nutshell', *William and Mary Bill of Rights Journal*, vol. 13 no. 57 (2004), pp. 57–172.

Balkin, Jack, M., 'What Brown teaches us about constitutional theory', *Virginia Law Review*, vol. 90 no. 6 (October 2004), pp. 1537–77.

Bank, A. and Schlumberger, O., 'Jordan: between regime survival and economic reform', in Perthes, V. (eds.), *Arab Elites: Negotiating the Politics of Change* (London, Lynne Rienner, 2004), pp. 35–61.

Baram, Amatzia, 'Neo-tribalism in Iraq: Saddam Hussein's tribal policies 1991–96', *International Journal of Middle East Studies*, vol. 29 issue 1 (February 1997), pp. 1–31.

Baram, Amatzia, 'The Iraqi Tribes and the Post-Saddam System', *The Brookings Institution*, (July 8 2003) available online: http://www.brookings.edu/views/op-ed/fellows/baram20030708.htm. (Accessed 2 December 2006).

Barnett, M., 'Institutions, roles and disorder: the case of the Arab states system', *International Studies Quarterly*, vol. 37, no. 3 (September 1993), pp. 271–96.

Baroudi, Sami E., 'The 2002 Arab Human Development Report: Implications for democracy', *Middle East Policy*, vol. XI, no. 1 (spring, 2004), pp. 132–41.

Batatu, Hanna, 'Some observations on the social roots of Syria's ruling military group and the causes for its dominance', *Middle East Journal*, vol. 35 issue 3 (1981), pp. 331–44.

Batatu, Hanna, 'Iraq's underground Shi`a movements: characteristics, causes and prospects', *Middle East Journal*, vol. 35 issue 4 (autumn, 1981), pp. 578–94.

Batatu, Hanna, *The Egyptian, Syrian and Iraqi Revolutions* (Washington, DC: Georgetown University Press, 1983).

BBC, 'Saddam's rival sons', *BBC News* (22 July 2003), available online: http://news.bbc.co.uk/2/hi/middle_east/2236137.stm. (Accessed 6 September 2006).

BBC, 'Rumsfeld rejects "cleric-led" rule', *BBC News* (25 April 2003), available online: http://news.bbc.co.uk/2/hi/middle_east/2975333.stm. (Accessed 25 April 2003).

BBC, 'Saad Hariri: novice political heir', *BBC News*, (20 June 2005), available online: http://news.bbc.co.uk/2/hi/middle_east/4110398.stm. (Accessed 6 September 2006).

Beeman, William, 'Chalabi's return – after fallout with US, former Iraqi exile plays all sides', *Pacific News Service* (8 November 2005), available online: http://news.pacificnews.org/news/view_article.html?article_id=52075943cedbf2d83f3298b5c9cde0b5. (Accessed 8 November 2005).

Bell, Gertrude, *The Desert and the Sown* (London: Virago, 1985).

Bellin, Eva, 'Coercive Institutions and Coercive Leaders', in Posusney, M.P. and Angrist, M.P. (eds.), *Authoritarianism in the Middle East* (Boulder and London: Lynne Rienner, 2005), pp. 21–41.

Berkey, Jonathan P., *The Formation of Islam* (Cambridge: Cambridge University Press, 2003).

Berlin, Isaiah, *Four Essays on Liberty* (London: Oxford University Press, 1975).

Berman, Harold J., *Law and Revolution* (Cambridge: Harvard University Press, 1983).

Bengio, Ofra, 'How does Saddam hold on?', *Foreign Affairs*, (July/August 2000) available online: http://www.foreignaffairs.org/20000701faessay64-p0/ofra-bengio/how-does-saddam-hold-on.html. (Accessed 15 March 2007).

Berque, Jacques, *Egypt: Imperialism and Revolution*, (trans.) Stewart, Jean (New York: Praeger Publishers, 1972).

Berque, Jacques, 'Du nouveau sur les Bani Hilal?', *Studia Islamica*, vol. 36 (1972), pp. 99–111.

Bertocchi, Graziella, 'The law of primogeniture and the transition from landed aristocracy to industrial democracy', *Journal of Economic Growth*, vol. 11 (2006), pp. 43–70.

Betts, Richard K. and Huntington, Samuel P., 'Dead dictators and rioting mobs; does the demise of authoritarian rulers lead to political instability?', *International Security*, vol. 10 no. 3 (winter, 1985–86), pp. 112–46.

Bhatia, Shyam, 'In the Middle East, the Sons Also Rise', *New Statesman* (February 12 1999).

Biedermann, F., 'Iraq's X-factor: the tribes', *Salon.com* (March 26 2003), available online: http://dir.salon.com/story/news/feature/2003/03/26/tribes/index.html. (Accessed 8 December 2006).

Bill, James A. and Springborg, Robert, *Politics in the Middle East* (New York: Addison Wesley Longman, 2000).

Birch, A. H., *Representative and Responsible Government* (London: George Allen and Unwin, 1966).

Black, Antony, *The History of Islamic Political Thought* (Edinburgh: Edinburgh University Press, 2001).

Black, Craig R., 'Deterring Libya: the Strategic Culture of Muammar Qaddafi', *USAF Counterproliferation Centre*, Air War College, Air University, Counterproliferation Paper No. 8, October 2000, available online: http://www.au.af.mil/au/awc/awcgate/cpc-pubs/black.pdf. (Accessed 5 December 2006).

Bloch, Marc, *Feudal Society, Vol. 1: The Growth of Ties of Dependence*, (trans.) Manyon, L. A. (London: Routledge & Kegan Paul, 1971).

Bloch, Marc, *Feudal Society, Vol. 2: The Growth of Ties of Dependence*, (trans.) Manyon, L. A. (London, Routledge & Kegan Paul, 1971).

Blondel, Jean, *Comparative Government* (Sydney: Philip Allen, 1990).

Bowles, Paul, 'Adam Smith and the "Natural Progress of Opulence"', *Economica*, vol. 53 no. 209 (February 1986), pp. 109–18.

Bradley, John R., 'Riyadh: a new front against US', *The Independent* (10 November 2003), available online: http://www.independent.co.uk/news/world/middle-east/riyadh-a-new-front-against-us-735183.html. (Accessed 15 August 2009).

Brandon, J., 'In exile, opposition groups unite against Damascus', *Christian Science Monitor* (1 November 2005), available online: http://www.csmonitor.com/2005/1101/p07s02-wome.html. (Accessed 10 September 2006).

Brett, Michael, 'The way of the peasant', *Bulletin of the School of Oriental and African Studies*, vol. 47 issue 1 (1984), pp. 44–56.

Brinkerhoff, D. W. and Goldsmith, A. A., *Clientelism, Patrimonialism and Democratic Governance: An Overview and Framework for Assessment and Planning* (Abt Associates Inc: Cambridge, USA, December 2002).

Bromley, Simon, *Rethinking Middle East Politics* (Cambridge: Polity Press, 1994).

Bronson, Rachel, 'Syria: Hanging Together or Hanging Separately', *The Washington Quarterly*, vol. 23 no. 4 (autumn, 2000), pp. 91–105.

Brown, L. Carl, *International Politics and the Middle East* (Princeton: Princeton University Press, 1984).

Brown, Nathan J., *Constitutions in a Non-constitutional World* (Albany State: University of New York Press, 2002).

Brownlee, Jason, 'The decline of pluralism in Mubarak's Egypt', *Journal of Democracy*, vol. 13 no. 4 (October 2002), pp. 6–32.

Brownlee, Jason, 'Political Crisis and Restabilisation' in Posusney, M. and Angrist, M. (eds.), *Authoritarianism in the Middle East*, (Boulder/London: Lynne Rienner, 2005), pp. 43–62.

Brumberg, Daniel, 'The trap of liberalized autocracy', *Journal of Democracy*, vol. 13 no. 4 (October 2002), pp. 56–58.

Brumberg, Daniel, 'Liberalisation versus democracy: understanding Arab political reform', *Carnegie Endowment for International Peace*, Democracy and Rule of Law Project, Working Papers, No. 37 (May 2003), available online: http://www.carnegieendowment.org/publications/index.cfm?fa=view&id=1250&prog=zgp&proj=zdrl,zme&zoom_highlight=Brumberg. (Accessed 1 June 2009).

Bulliet, Richard W., 'Twenty years of Islamic politics', *Middle East Journal*, vol. 53 no. 2 (spring, 1999), pp. 189–200.

Burgat, F., 'Yemen: between the Sana'a Declaration and the old formula of Arab Politics', *Arab Review Bulletin*, (March 2004), available online: http://www.carnegieendowment.org/publications/index.cfm?fa=view&id=1475&prog=zgp&proj=zdrl. (Accessed 17 August 2006).

Burman, Harold J., *Law and Revolution* (Cambridge: Harvard University Press, 1983).

Camic, C., Gorski, P. S. and Trubek D. M., (eds.), *Max Weber's Economy and Society: a Critical Companion*. (Stanford, CA: Stanford University Press, 2005).

Cantori, Louis J., Jacoby, Tim, Carapico, Sheila, Shehata, Samer, Lust-Okar, Ellen, Bargu-Hasturk, Banu, Robinson, Glenn, E. and Al-Kitbi, Ebtesam, 'Political Succession in the Middle East', *Middle East Policy*, vol. 9 no. 3 (September 2002), pp. 105–23.

Carapico, Sheila, 'Successions, transitions, coups and revolutions', in Cantori, L. J. *et al.*, 'Political Succession in the Middle East', *Middle East Policy*, vol. 9 no. 3 (September 2002), pp. 109–10.

Carol, Lucy, 'The Hanafi law of intestate succession: a simplified approach', *Modern Asian Studies*, vol. 17 no. 4 (1983), pp. 629–70.

Caton, Steven C., 'Power, persuasion and language: a critique of the segmentary model in the Middle East', *International Journal of Middle East Studies*, vol. 19 issue 1 (February 1987), pp. 77–101.

Centre for Arab and Middle Eastern Studies, 'Issues of Syrian Succession', American University of Beirut (September/ December 1999), available online: http://wwwlb.aub.edu.lb/~webcames/Arabdoc_syria.html. (Accessed 15 July 2006).

Cham, Eric, *Politics and Society in Contemporary France (1789–1971)* (London: George G. Harrap & Co. Ltd., 1972).

Clark, George, *Early Modern Europe* (London: Oxford University Press, 1963).

Claude, P., 'Washington puts trust in Iraq's tribal system', *Guardian Weekly* (17–23 September 2004), p. 20.

Collins, Carole, 'Imperialism and revolution in Libya', *MERIP Reports*, no. 27 (April 1974), pp. 3–22.

Committee Against Torture, 'Conclusions and recommendations of the Committee against Torture: Egypt'. *United Nations*, New York (23 December 2002). CAT/C/CR/29/4D (5. b, c).

Egyptian Government, Egyptian Constitution, 1971 (amended, 2005), Government Services Portal, available online: http://www.egypt.gov.eg/english/laws/Constitution/default.aspx. (Accessed 29 May 2009).

Constitution of the Hashemite Kingdom of Jordan, Library of King Hussein, available online: http://www.kinghussein.gov.jo/constitution_jo.html. (Accessed 7 January 2007).

Constitution of Medina, al-Islami, Khilafah al-'Alam (trans.) Not dated, available online: http://www.constitution.org/cons/medina/macharter.htm. (Accessed 28 November 2008).

Cordesman, Anthony, *Saudi Arabia Enters the Twenty-First Century: III. Politics and Internal Stability* (Washington: Centre for Strategic and International Studies, 2002).

Coulson, N. J., *A History of Islamic Law* (Edinburgh: Edinburgh University Press, 1972).

Council on Foreign Relations, 'Iraq: the role of tribes' (14 November 2003), available online: http://www.cfr.org/publication.html?id=7681. (Accessed 4 December 2006).

Crone, P. and Hinds, M., *God's Caliph* (Cambridge: Cambridge University Press, 1986).

Crone, Patricia, *Slaves on Horses* (Cambridge: Cambridge University Press, 2003).

Crystal, Jill, 'Authoritarian power and state formation in Ba`athist Syria: army, party and peasant', *World Politics*, vol. 46 no. 2 (January 1994), pp. 262–90.

Daechsel, Markus, 'Max Weber and Islam', *The Journal of Semitic Studies*, 2002, vol. 47 pp. 387–90 – review of Toby E. Huff, *Max Weber and Islam*, New Brunswick, Transaction Publishers, 1999.

Dahl, Robert A., *Modern Political Analysis* (New Jersey: Prentice-Hall, 1964).

Al-Dakhil, Khalid, 'Abdullah streamlines Saudi succession plans but limits the power to choose', *saudidebate.com* (25 October 2006), available online: http://www.islamdaily.net/EN/Contents.aspx?AID=4968. (Accessed 25 October 2006).
Dankowitz, A., 'Saif Al Islam Al Qaddafi's professed reform in Libya', *The Middle East Media Research Institute*, Enquiry and Analysis Series, no. 250 (11 November 2005), available online: http://memri.org/bin/articles.cgi?Page=archives&Area=ia&ID=IA25005. (Accessed 30 November 2005).
Dawisha, Adeed, 'Requiem for Arab Nationalism', *Middle East Quarterly*, volume X, no. 1 (winter, 2003), available online: http://www.meforum.org/article/518. (Accessed 2 December 2006).
Dawood, N. J. (trans.), *The Koran* (London: Penguin Classics, 1999).
Demir, Mehmet, 'Human rights briefing', *Middle East Report*, no. 163 (March–April 1990), pp. 38–39.
Deutscher, Isaac, *Stalin* (Penguin Books, 1970).
Diamond, Larry, 'Thinking about hybrid regimes', *Journal of Democracy*, vol. 13, no. 2 (April 2002), pp. 21–35.
Diamond, L., Plattner, M. F. and Brumberg, D., (eds.), *Islam and Democracy in the Middle East* (Baltimore: Johns Hopkins University Press, 2003).
Dicey, A. V., *Introduction to the Study of the Law of the Constitution.* (London: Macmillan & Co., 1915).
Dodd, Peter C., 'Family honour and the forces of change in Arab society', *International Journal of Middle East Studies*, vol. 4, issue 1 (January 1973), pp. 40–54.
Dodge, Toby and Higgott, Richard, *Globalization and the Middle East* (London: Royal Institute of International Affairs, 2002).
Dogan, Matti and Pelassy, Dominic, *How to Compare Nations*, 2nd ed. (New Jersey: Chatham House, 1990).
Doran, Michael Scott, 'The Saudi Paradox', *Foreign Affairs* (January/February 2004), available online: http://www.foreignaffairs.org/20040101faessay83105/michael-scott-doran/the-saudi-paradox.html. (Accessed 12 June 2004).
Drummond, Jeremy and Khalaf, Roula, 'Mubarak's son rules out succession' *Financial Times* (24 April 2001), p. 12.
Drysdale, A., 'The Succession Question in Syria', *The Middle East Journal*, vol. 39 no. 2 (spring, 1985).
Duchacek, I. D., *Power Maps: Comparative Politics of Constitutions* (Santa Barbara: California, Clio Press, 1973).
Dunn, M. C., 'The Coming Era of Leadership Change in the Arab World', *Middle East Policy*, vol. 5 no. 4 (January 1998), pp. 180–87.
The Economist, 'Syria: Bashar's world' vol. 355 (8175) (17 June 2000), pp. 24–26.
Eisenstadt, S. N., *Max Weber on Charisma and Institution Building* (Chicago: University of Chicago Press, 1968).
Elster, Jon, 'Tocqueville on 1789: preconditions, precipitants and triggers', in Welch, Cheryl. B. (ed.), *The Cambridge Companion to Tocqueville* (Cambridge: Cambridge University Press, 2006).
Elton, G. R., *England under the Tudors* (London: Methuen & Co. Ltd., 1963).
Enayat, Hamid, *Modern Islamic Political Thought* (London: I. B. Tauris, 2005).
Erdle, S., 'Tunisia: Economic transformation and political restoration', in Perthes, V. (ed.), *Arab Elites: Negotiating the Politics of Change* (Boulder & London: Lynne Rienner, 2004), pp. 207–36.

Esposito, John and Piscatori, James, P., 'Democratisation and Islam', *The Middle East Journal*, vol. 45, no. 3 (1991), pp. 427–40.

The Estimate, 'Bashar's challenges: the establishment and its discontents', vol. XI no. 8 (9 April 1999).

Fagnan, E. *Abou Youssouf Ya'koub – le Liver de l'impot foncier Libraire orientaliste* Paul Geuthner, 1921.

Al-Fahad, Abdulaziz H., 'Ornamental constitutionalism: the Saudi Basic Law of Governance', *The Yale Journal of International Law*, vol. 30, no. 2 (2005), pp. 375–96.

Al-Fahim, M., *From Rags to Riches: A Story of Abu Dhabi* (London: Centre of Arab Studies, 1995).

Fandy, Mamoun, 'Tribe vs. Islam: the post-colonial Arab state and the democratic imperative', *Middle East Policy Council Journal*, Vol. III, no. 48 (1994) available online: http://www.mepc.org/journal/9406_fandy.asp. (Accessed 5 December 2006).

Fathali, Omar, I. and Palmer, Monte, 'Opposition to change in rural Libya', *International Journal of Middle East Studies*, vol. 11 issue 2 (April 1980), pp. 247–61.

Fathi, S., 'Jordanian Survival Strategy: The election law as a "safety valve", *Middle Eastern Studies*, vol. 41 issue 6 (November 2005), pp. 889–98.

Al Feki, Mustafa, 'Content over form', *Al Ahram Weekly* issue 711 (7–13 0ctober 2004), available online: http://weekly.ahram.org.eg/2004/711/op2.htm. (Accessed 5 September 2006).

Feldner, Y., 'Egypt's succession, Part 1: Will Egypt follow Syria's precedent?' *Middle East Media Research Institute*, Enquiry and Analysis Series, no. 31 (24 July 2000), available online: http://www.memri.org/bin/articles.cgi?Page=archives&Area=ia&ID=IA3100. (Accessed 5 September 2006).

Feldner, Y., 'Egypt's succession, Part II: Does Gamal Mubarak have a chance?' *Middle East Media Research Institute*, Enquiry and Analysis Series, no. 32 (25 July 2000), available online: http://www.memri.org/bin/articles.cgi?Page=archives&Area=ia&ID =IA3200. (Accessed 5 September 2006).

Ferguson, Laurie, *The Journalist and Islam*, conference run by Macquarie University, University of Technology, Sydney, and Australian Research Council, Sydney (7–8 December 2006).

Finer, S.E. (ed.), *Five Constitutions* (Sussex: Harvester Press, 1979).

Fisher, Sydney N., *The Middle East: A History*, (London: Routledge & Kegan Paul, 1971).

Frisch, Hillel, 'Guns and butter in the Egyptian army', *Middle East Review of International Relations*, vol. 5 no. 2 (June 2001) available online: http://meria.idc.ac.il/journal/2001/issue2/jv5n2a1.html. (Accessed 11 January 2007).

Fromkin, David, *A Peace to End All Peace* (London: Phoenix Press, 2000).

Fukuyama, Francis, *The End of History and the Last Man* (London: Penguin, 1992).

Gambill, Gary C. and Abdelnour, Ziad K., 'Dossier: Rafiq Hariri: Prime Minister of Lebanon', *Middle East Intelligence Bulletin*, vol. 3 no. 7 (July 2001), available online: http://www.meib.org/articles/0107_ld1.htm. (Accessed 27 July 2006).

Gardner, David, 'Shadows Across the Thrones', *Financial Times*, London, (30 January 1999).

Garfinkle, A., 'The new missionaries', *Prospect* (April 2003).

Gause, F. Gregory III, 'Sovereignty, Statecraft and Stability in the Middle East', *Journal of International Affairs*, vol. 45 issue 2 (winter, 1992) pp. 441–69.

Gause, F. G. III, 'The persistence of monarchy in the Arabian Peninsula: a comparative analysis', in Kostiner, Joseph (ed.), *Middle East Monarchies*, (London: Lynne Rienner, 2000), pp. 167–86.

Gearon, Eamon, 'Yemen elections: better the president you know?', *The Middle East* (June 2006), pp. 12–13, available online: http://info.library.unsw.edu.au/cgi-bin/local/accessed/ej-accessed.cgi?url=http://gateway.proquest.com/openurl?res_id=xri%3Apqd& req_dat=xri%3Apqil%3Apq_clntid%3D&date=2006&rft_val_fmt=ori%3Afmt%3Akev%3Amtx%3Ajournal&issn=0305–0734&ctx_ver=Z39.88–2003&genre=article. (Accessed 19 October 2006).

Gellner, Ernest, 'Tribalism and state in the Middle East', in Khoury, Philip S. and Kostiner, Joseph (eds.), *Tribes and State Formation in the Middle East* (Berkeley: University of California Press, 1990).

El Ghobashy, Mona, 'Constitutional reform in Egypt', *Middle East Review* (spring, 2003), no. 226, available online: http://www.merip.org/mer/mer226/mer226.html. (Accessed 15 September 2006).

El Ghobashy, Mona, 'Egypt's paradoxical elections', *Middle East Report Online*, no. 238, (5 October 2006), available online: http://www.merip.org/mer/mer238/elghobashy.html. (Accessed 5 October 2006).

Giacomo, Carol, 'Will the son succeed the father as Egypt's president?' *Reuters Arab News* (June 2003), available online: http://www.aljazeerah.info/News%20archives/2003%20News%20archives/June%202003%20News/30n/Will%. (Accessed 30 June 2003).

Gibb, H. A. R., *Mohammedanism* (London: Oxford University Press, 1969).

Gibb, H. A. R., *Studies on the Civilisation of Islam* (London: Routledge and Kegan Paul, 1969).

Gillies, Paris, 'Breaking News – but whose?', *Le Monde-Guardian Weekly* (19 November 2004), p. 19.

Glass, Charles, 'Is Syria Next?', *London Review of Books*, vol. 25 no. 14 (2003), pp. 1–3.

Goodin, Robert, 'On constitutional Design', *ARENA Working Paper* series 97/26, Australian National University (15 October 1997).

Gotowicki, Stephen H., *The Role of the Egyptian Military in Domestic Society*, National Defence University (1997), available online: http://fmso.leavenworth.army.mil/documents/egypt/egypt.htm. (Accessed 16 September 2006).

Graham, J. and Marques, E. C., 'Understanding Constitutions: A Roadmap for Communities', *Institute on Governance*, Ottawa (October 2000), available online: http://www.iog.ca. (Accessed 27 July 2005).

Gray, John, *Al Qaeda and What it Means to be Modern* (London: Faber and Faber, 2003).

Gray, Matthew, 'Islam in the Iraqi and Afghan constitutions: a comparative perspective', *Journal of Global Change, Peace and Security* (February 2007), vol. 19 issue 1, pp. 17–31.

Gulf News, 'RAK Ruler appoints Crown Prince', *WAM/Gulf News* (15 June 2003), available online: http://archive.gulfnews.com/articles/03/06/15/90260.html. (Accessed 20 June 2003).

Gutas, Dimitri, 'The Study of Arabic Philosophy in the Twentieth Century, An Essay on the Historiography of Arabic Philosophy' *British Journal of Middle Eastern Studies*, vol. 29 no. 1 (2002), pp. 5–25.

Al-Hadid, Mohammed Abu, 'Succession from fathers' rule to their sons is common', *Al Gumhuriya*, Cairo (15 June 2000).

Halliday, Fred, *The Middle East in International Relations* (Cambridge: Cambridge University Press, 2005).

Hamzawy, A., 'Egypt: Creating a new political reality', *Arab Reform Bulletin* (June 2005), vol. 3 no. 5, available online: http://www.carnegieendowment.org/publications/

index.cfm?fa=view&id=17049&prog=zgp&proj=zdrl,zme#creating. (Accessed 26 June 2005).

Hassouna, Hussein A., 'Arab Democracy: The Hope' *World Policy Journal*, vol. 18 issue 3 (autumn, 2001), pp. 49–53.

Hawthorne, Amy, 'Political Reform in the Arab World: a New Ferment?', *Carnegie Papers*, Washington, no. 52 (October 2004) available online: http://www.carnegieendowment.org/files/CP_52%20Hawthorne.pdf. (Accessed 23 May 2007).

Heard-Bey, Frauke, 'The Gulf in the Twentieth Century' *Asian Affairs*, vol. XXXIII, part 1 (February 2002), pp. 3–17.

Heard-Bey, Frauke, 'The United Arab Emirates: statehood and nation-building in a traditional society', *The Middle East Journal*, vol. 59, issue 3 (summer, 2005), pp. 357–76.

Herb, Michael, *All in the Family* (Albany: State University of New York Press, 1999).

Herb, Michael, 'Parliaments in the Gulf Monarchies: A Long Way from Democracy', *The Daily Star*, Tharwa Net-Watch (December 4 2004), available online: http://www.tharwaproject.com/English/Main-Sec/NetWatch/NW_12_6_04/Herb.htm. (Accessed 20 December 2004).

Hinnebusch, Raymond A., 'Rural politics in Syria: a case study in the role of the countryside in the political development of Arab societies', *The Review of Politics*, vol. 44, no. 1 (January 1982), pp. 110–30.

Hinnebusch, Raymond A., *The International Politics of the Middle East* (Manchester: Manchester University Press, 2003).

Hinsley, F. H., *The New Cambridge Modern History: Vol. XI: Material Progress and World-Wide Problems: 1870–1898* (Cambridge: Cambridge University Press, 1979).

Hitti, Philip K., *Syria: a Short History* (London: Macmillan & Co. Ltd., 1959).

Hitti, Philip K., *History of the Arabs* (Basingstoke: Palgrave, 2002).

Hourani, Albert, 'Tribes and states in Islamic history', in Khoury, P. S. and Kostiner, J. (eds.), *Tribes and State Formation in the Middle East* (Berkeley: University of California Press, 1990), pp. 303–11.

Hudson, Michael C., *Arab Politics: the Search for Legitimacy* (New Haven, Yale University Press, 1977).

Hudson, Michael C., 'Democracy and Foreign Policy in the Arab World', *The Beirut Review*, The Lebanese Centre for Policy Studies, Beirut, no. 4 (autumn, 1992).

Human Rights Watch, 'Egypt's emergency without end', *Human Rights News*, New York (25 February 2003), available online: http://hrw.org/press/2003/02/egypt022503.htm. (Accessed 15 February 2007).

Huntington, Samuel P., *The Third Wave: Democratisation in the late Twentieth Century* (Norman: University of Oklahoma Press, 1991).

Huntington, Samuel P., *The Clash of Civilizations and the Remaking of World Order* (New York: Touchstone Books, 1998).

Hussein bin Talal, 'Letter to Hassan transferring succession from Hassan to Abdallah' (25 January 1999), available online: www.kinghussein.gov.jo/99-jan25.html. (Accessed 15 May 2005).

Ikhwanweb, 'Muslim Brotherhood Initiatives For Reform in Egypt,' (29 March 2006). Available online: http://www.muslimbrotherhood.co.uk/Home.asp?zPage=Systems&System=PressR&Press=Show&Lang=E&ID=4162. (Accessed 15 August 2009).

Imber, Colin, *Ebu's-su'ud: the Islamic Legal Tradition* (Stanford: Stanford University Press, 1997).

Inalcik, Halil, *The Ottoman Empire* (London: Phoenix Books, 2003).

Al-Islam, Saif, 'Libyan-American relations', Viorst, Milton *(ed.), Middle East Policy*, vol. 10 no. 1 (spring, 2003), pp. 35–45.

Johnsen, Gregory D., 'Saleh's Road to Re-election', *Middle East Report On-line* (13 January 2006), available online: http://www.merip.org/mero/mero011306.html. (Accessed 20 January 2006).

Johnsen, Gregory D., 'The election Yemen was supposed to have', *Middle East Report Online* (3 October 2006), available online: http://www.merip.org/mero/mero100306.html. (Accessed 5 October 2006).

Johnson, Thomas H., 'The prospects for post-conflict Afghanistan: a call of the sirens to the country's troubled past', *Strategic Insights*, vol. 2 (February 2006).

Joseph, Suad, 'Connectivity and patriarchy among urban working-class Arab families in Lebanon', *Ethos*, vol. 21 no. 4 (December 1993), pp. 452–84.

Kabasakal, H. and Bodur, M., 'Arabic cluster: a bridge between East and West', *Journal of World Business*, vol. 37 (2002), pp. 40–54.

Kalb, J., 'The Amish, David Koresh, and a Newer World Order', in Antonio, R. J., 'After postmodernism; reactionary tribalism', *The American Journal of Sociology*, vol. 106 no. 1 (July 2000).

Kantorowicz, Ernst H., *The King's Two Bodies: a Study in Mediaeval Political Theology*, (Princeton, New Jersey: Princeton University Press, 1970).

Kapiszewski, Andrzej, 'Democratising the Arab States' (Krakowskie: Studia Miedzynarodowe, 2004).

Katz, Mark, 'Assessing the Political Stability of Oman', *Middle East Review of International Affairs*, vol. 8 no. 3 (September 2004).

Kechichian, Joseph A., *Succession in Saudi Arabia* (New York: Palgrave, 2001).

Kechichian, Joseph A. and Dekmejian, R. Hrair, *The Just Prince: a Manual of Leadership* (London: Saqi, 2003).

Kechichian, Joseph A., 'Democratisation in Gulf Monarchies: A New Challenge to the GCC', *Middle East Policy*, vol. XI no. 4 (winter, 2004).

Kedourie, Elie, *The Chatham House Version* (Chicago: Ivan R. Dee, 1984).

Keefer, Philip and Vlaicu, Razvan, 'Democracy, Credibility and Clientelism', *World Bank*, Policy Research Working Paper No. 3472 (17 April 2006), available online: http://ssrn.com/abstract=609923. (Accessed 27 November 2006).

Keefer, Philip, 'Clientelism, credibility and the policy choices of young democracies', *World Bank*, Development Research Group, (September 2005), pp. 44, available online: http://www.qog.pol.gu.se/conferences/november2005/papers/Keefer.pdf. (Accessed 27 November 2006).

Keir, David L., *The Constitutional History of Modern Britain* (London: Adam and Charles Black, 1964).

Kershaw, Ian, *Hitler: 1936–1945: Nemesis* (Penguin Books, 2000).

Kessler, Martha N., 'Inheriting Syria: Bashar's trial by Fire', *Middle East Policy*, vol. 12 no. 3 (autumn, 2005), pp. 173–76.

Kettering, S., 'The historical development of political clientelism', *Journal of Interdisciplinary History*, vol. 18 no. 3 (1988), pp. 419–47.

Khaddar, M. Moncef, 'Beyond colonialism and nationalism', *Arab Studies Quarterly*, vol. 24, no. 4 (autumn, 2002), pp. 83–89.

Khadduri, M., 'The role of the military in Middle East politics', *The American Political Science Review*, vol. 47 issue 2 (June 1953), pp. 511–24.

Khalaf, Abd Al Isa, 'Political Reform in Bahrain: end of the road?', *Middle East International*, no. 719 (20 February 2004), pp. 26–29.

Khalaf, Abdulhadi, 'Why has Qatar gone constitutional?', *Daily Star*, (18 July 2002), available online: http://www.lebanonwire.com/0207/02071820DS.asp. (Accessed 15 March 2006).

Khalaf, Abdulhadi, 'Rules of succession and political participation in the GCC states', in Khalaf, Abdulhadi and Giacomo, Luciani (eds.), *Constitutional Reform and Political Participation in the Gulf* (Dubai: Gulf Research Centre, 2006), pp. 33–50.

Khalaf, Abdulhadi and Luciani, Giacomo (eds.), *Constitutional Reform and Political Participation in the Gulf* (Dubai, Gulf Research Centre, 2006).

Khalaf, Roula, 'Uneasy Shift to Political Liberalism', *Financial Times*, London (6 December 1999).

Khalaf, Samir and Shwayri, Emile, 'Family firms and industrial development: the Lebanese case', *Economic Development and Cultural Change*, vol. 15 issue 1 (October 1966), pp. 59–69.

Khaldun, Abd Al-Rahman ibn, *The Muqaddimah*, abridged edition, Dawood, N. J., (ed.), (trans.) Rosenthal, Franz (Princeton: Princeton University Press, 2005).

Al Khalidi, S., 'Jordan's king consolidates power', *The Age* (December 1 2004), available online: http://www.theage.com.au/news/World/Jordans-king-consolidates-power/2004/11/30/1101577482678.html?from=storylhs. (Accessed 21 August 2006).

Al-Khalil, Samir, *The Republic of Fear: the Politics of Modern Iraq* (Berkeley, CA: University of California Press, 1989).

Khan, M. A. M., 'The Compact of Medina: A Constitutional Theory of the Islamic State', *Mirror International*, Greenpoint, New York, (May 30 2001).

Khouri, Rami G., 'Kuwait's election and the freezing of Arab politics', *Common Ground News Service* (9 September 2003), available online: http://www.dailystar.com.lb/article.asp?edition_ID=1&article_ID=67591&categ_id=5. (Accessed 9 September 2003).

Khouri, Rami, G., 'Time to implement presidential term limits', *Agence Global* (August 4 2004), available online: http://www.agenceglobal.com/article.asp?id=199. (Accessed 4 August 2004).

Khouri, Rami G., 'Challenging the Catastrophic Cost of Rule by Colonels', *Agence Global* (17 May 2006), available online: http://www.agenceglobal.com/article.asp?id=911. (Accessed 17 May 2006).

Khoury, Philip S. and Kostiner, Joseph (eds.), *Tribes and State Formation in the Middle East* (Berkeley: University of California Press, 1990).

Kiernan, P., 'Surviving the odds', *The Middle East* (September 1998), pp. 23–25.

Kirkpatrick, Jeane, 'Dictatorship and Double Standards', *Commentary*, New York, vol. 68 part. 5 (November 1979), pp. 34–45.

Kline, Marlee, 'The Colour of Law: Ideological Representations of First Nations in Legal Discourse', *Social and Legal Studies*, vol. 3 no. 4 (1994), pp. 451–76.

Kolhatkar, Sonali and Ingalls, Jim, 'Giving democracy a bad name: Afghanistan's parliamentary elections', *Foreign Policy in Focus*, (September 16 2005), available online: http://www.fpif.org/fpiftxt/647. (Accessed 16 March 2007).

Kostiner, J., (ed.), *Middle East Monarchies* (London: Lynne Rienner, 2000).

Kramer, Karen, 'Arab political pacts: an unlikely scenario', *Journal for Democracy*, vol. 17 no. 4 (October 2006).

Kubba, Laith, 'Recognising pluralism', *Journal of Democracy*, vol. 7 no. 2 (1996), pp. 86–89.

Lambton, A. K. S., *State and Government in Medieval Islam: An Introduction to Islamic Political Thought: The Jurists* (Oxford: University Press, 1981).

Lasswell, H., *Politics: Who gets What, When and How* (New York: Meridien Books, 1958).

Lawrence, T. E., *Seven Pillars of Wisdom* (London: Jonathan Cape, 1935).

Lefebvre, Edwige, *The Belgian Constitution of 1831: The Citizen Burger*, Discussion Paper. 4, Zentrum fur Europaische Rechtspolitik (1997), available online: http://www.zerp.uni-bremen.de/deutsch/pdf/dp4_97.pdf. (Accessed 28 May 2009).

Lenczowoski, George, *Political Elites in the Middle East* (Washington, DC: American Enterprise Institute for Public Policy Research, 1975).

Leverett, F., *Inheriting Syria: Bashar's Trial by Fire* (Washington DC: The Brookings Institution Press, 2005).

Levitsky, Steven and Way, Lucan A., 'The rise of competitive authoritarianism', *Journal of Democracy*, vol. 13 no. 2 (April 2002), pp. 51–65.

Levitt, Matthew A., 'The political economy of Middle Eastern terrorism', *Middle East Review of International Relations*, vol. 6 no. 4 (December 2002), pp. 49–65.

Lewis, Bernard, *The Arabs in History* (London: Hutchinson's University Library, 1950).

Lewis, Bernard, 'Islam and liberal democracy: a historical overview', *The Atlantic Monthly*, vol. 271 no. 2 (February 1993), available online: http://www.theatlantic.com/issues/93feb/lewis.htm. (Accessed 8 June 2006).

Lewis, Bernard, 'The concept of an Islamic republic', *Die Welt des Islams*, New Series, vol. 4 no. 1 (1995), pp. 109.

Lewis, Bernard, 'Islam and liberal democracy: A historical overview', *The Journal of Democracy*, vol. 7 no. 2 (April 1996), pp. 52–63.

Lewis, Bernard, *The Middle East* (London: Phoenix Giant, 1998).

Lewis, Bernard, 'Monarchy in the Middle East', in Kostiner, J. (ed.), *Middle East Monarchies*, (London: Lynne Rienner, 2000).

Lewis, Bernard, 'On Liberty and Faith', *Jerusalem Post* (27 February 2003).

Li, B., 'What is Constitutionalism?', *Perspectives*, vol. 1 no. 6 (June 2000).

Linzer, D., 'Poll Shows Growing Arab Rancour at US', *Washington Post* (23 July 2004).

Lipset, Seymour M., *Political Man* (London: Heinemann, 1969).

Litvak, Meir (ed.), *Middle Eastern Societies and the West* (Tel Aviv University, The Moshe Dayan Centre for Middle Eastern and African Studies, 2006).

Lobe, Jim, 'Losing Arab Hearts and Minds: It's the Policy Stupid', *Inter Press Service* (23 July 2004), available online: http://www.aaiusa.org/press-room/628/aainew072304. (Accessed 2 June 2009).

Long, David E., 'The role of the extended family in Saudi Arabia', *Saudi-American Forum* (10 March 2003), available online: www.saudi-american-forum.org/Newsletters/SAF_09.pdf. (Accessed 24 August 2006).

Lucas, R. E., 'Monarchical Authoritarianism: Survival and Political Liberalisation in a Middle Eastern Regime Type', *International Journal of Middle East Studies*, vol. 36 (2004), pp. 103–19.

Lustick, Ian, 'The absence of Middle Eastern great powers: political "backwardness" in historical perspective', *International Organization*, vol. 51 issue 4 (1997), pp. 653–83.

Macfarquhar, Neil, 'Heavy Hand of the Secret Police Impeding Reform in Arab World', *New York Times* (14 November 2005), available online: http://www.nytimes.com/2005/11/14/international/middleeast/14jordan.html?ex=1289624400&en=f1e197fd717a8eb5&ei=5088&partner=rssnyt&emc=rss. (Accessed 14 November 2005).

Madelung, W., *The Succession to Mohammad: A Study of the Early Caliphate* (Cambridge: Cambridge University Press, 1998).

Madison, James, '*The Federalist Number 47*' in Madison, J., Hamilton, A. Jay, J., *The Federalist Papers*, The Avalon Project, Yale Law School (2008), available online: http://www.yale.edu/lawweb/avalon/federal/fed47.htm. (Accessed 29 May 2009).

Maghraoui, Abdelslam M., 'Depoliticisation in Morocco', *Journal of Democracy*, vol. 13 no. 4 (October 2002), pp. 24–32.

Mahler, Gregory S., *Comparative Politics: an Institutional and Cross-National Approach* (New Jersey, Prentice Hall, 2000).

Makdisi, John, 'Legal logic and equity in Islamic law', *American Journal of Comparative Law*, vol. 33 no. 1 (winter, 1985), pp. 63–92.

Mallat, Chibli, 'From Islamic to Middle Eastern Law: A Restatement of the Field (Part 1)', *The American Journal of Comparative Law*, vol. 51 (autumn, 2003), pp. 699–750.

Mallat, Chibli, 'From Islamic to Middle Eastern Law: A Restatement of the Field (Part 2)', *The American Journal of Comparative Law*, vol. 52 (2004), pp. 209–86.

Manea, Elham M., 'Yemen, the tribe and the state'. Paper presented to International Colloquium on Islam and Social Change at University of Lausanne (10–11 October 1996), available online: http://www.al-bab.com/yemen/soc/manea1.htm. (Accessed 4 December 2006).

Manning, D. J., *Liberalism* (London: J. M. Dent & Sons Ltd., 1976).

Mansfield, Peter, *The Arabs* (Harmondsworth: Penguin Books, 1978).

Marr, Phoebe A., 'The Political Elite in Iraq' in *Political Elites in the Middle East*, Chapter V (Washington, DC American Enterprise Institute for Public Policy Research,1975).

Marsh, David and Stoker, Gerry (eds.), *Theory and Methods in Political Science* (Basingstoke: Palgrave, 1995).

Martin, Lenore, 'Arafat's duelling dilemmas: succession and the peace process', *Middle East Review of International Affairs*, vol. 6 no. 1 (March 2002), pp. 60–71.

Masoud, T. E., 'The Arabs and Islam: the troubled search for legitimacy', *Daedalus*, Boston, vol. 128 no. 02 (spring, 1999), pp. 127–47.

Massignon, L., 'Cartes de repartition des kabyles dans la region parisienne', *Opera Minora*, Beirut, vol. 3 (1963), pp. 569–74 cited in Albert Hourani, 'Tribes and states in Islamic history', in Khoury Philip S. and Kostiner Joseph (eds.), *Tribes and State Formation in the Middle East* (Berkeley: University of California Press, 1990). op. cit., p. 305.

Mattes, H., 'Challenges to security sector governance in the Middle East: the Libyan case', *Geneva Centre for the Democratic Control of Armed Forces*, Working Paper No. 144 (August 2004).

McGeough, Paul, 'Share power or lose control, Iraq warned', *The Sydney Morning Herald*, (22 July 2004) available online: http://www.smh.com.au/articles/2004/07/21/1090089220981.html. (Accessed 22 July 2004).

McGeough, Paul, 'Fatal collision with tradition', *The Sydney Morning Herald*, (30 July 2004) available online: http://www.smh.com.au/articles/2004/07/29/1091080376624.html. (Acccessed 30 July 2004).

Menocal, Maria Rosa, *The Ornament of the World* (New York: Back Bay Books, 2002).

Mernissi, F., *The Forgotten Queens of Islam*, (trans.) Lakeland, M. (Minnesota: University of Minnesota Press, 1997).

Middle East Centre for Arab Studies, *A Selected Word List of Modern Literary Arabic* (Beirut: Khayats, 1969).

Miles, Hugh, 'Saudi king loses power to choose his successor', *The Daily Telegraph*, London (10 February 2007), available online: http://www.telegraph.co.uk/news/main.jhtml%3Bjsessionid%3DYOSGXL4RS4BVXQFIQMFCFGGAVCBQYIV0?xml=/news/2007/02/10/wsaudi10.xml. (Accessed 14 February 2007).

Moore, Clement H., 'The northeastern triangle: Libya, Egypt and the Sudan', *Annals of the American Academy of Political and Social Science*, vol. 489 (January, 1987), pp. 28–39.

Moore, Pete W. and Salloukh, Bassel, F., 'Struggles under authoritarianism: regimes, states and professional associations in the Arab world', *International Journal of Middle East Studies*, vol. 39 issue 1 (February 2007).

Mosca, Gaetano, *The Ruling Class*, (trans.) Kahn, H. D. (New York: McGraw-Hill, 1939).

Moubayed, Sami, 'Syria: reform balance sheet', *Arab Reform Bulletin* (March 2007), vol. 5 no. 2, available online: http://www.carnegieendowment.org/publications/index.cfm?fa=view&id=19064&prog=zgp&proj=zdrl,zme#moubayed. (Accessed 22 March 2007).

Nasr, Vali, 'The rise of Muslim democracy', *Journal of Democracy*, vol. 16 no. 2 (April 2005), pp. 13–27.

Nelson, Cynthia, 'Public and Private Politics: Women in the Middle Eastern World', *American Ethnologist*, vol. 1 issue 3 (August 1974), pp. 551–63.

Nelson, J. L., 'Go Away and Learn', *London Review of Books*, vol. 26 no. 8 (15 April 2004), pp. 23–25.

Nenner, Howard, *By Color of Law* (Chicago: University of Chicago Press, 1977).

Nevo, J., 'Changing identities in Jordan', *Israel Affairs*, vol. 9 issue 3 (spring, 2003), pp. 187–208.

Nichols, J., 'The Rule of Law versus the Rule of Chaney', *The Nation*, (23 February 2006), available online: http://www.thenation.com/. (Accessed 15 June 2006).

Nonneman, Gerd, 'Political reform in the Gulf monarchies: From liberalisation to democratisation? A comparative perspective,' *Sir William Luce Fellowship Paper*, No. 6, Durham Middle East Papers No. 80, Durham, University of Durham (June 2006), available online: http://eprints.dur.ac.uk/archive/00000222/. (Accessed 19 October 2006).

Norton, Augustus R. (ed.), *Civil Society in the Middle East* (Brill Academic Publishers), vols. 1, 1995, and 2, 2001.

Novak, Jane, 'Yemen's President Reneges on Democracy', *Worldpress.org* (28 June 2006), available online: http://www.worldpress.org/Mideast/2399.cfm. (Accessed 19 October 2006).

Noyon, Jennifer, *Islam, Politics and Pluralism* (London: Royal Institute of International Affairs, 2003).

Numani, S., *Umar*, (trans.) Khan, Z. A. (London: I. B. Tauris, 2004).

Nutting, Anthony, *Nasser* (London: Constable, 1972).

Oakshott, Michael, *On Human Conduct* (Oxford: Clarendon Press 1975).

Oil and Gas Journal, 'Special Report: Oil production, reserves increase slightly in 2006', vol. 104 issue 47 (18 December 2006).

Ottaway, Marina, 'Democratic Mirage in the Middle East', *Carnegie Papers*, Number 20 (October 2002), available online: http://www.carnegieendowment.org/files/Policybrief20.pdf. (Accessed 17 September 2005).

Ottaway, Marina, 'Democracy and Constituencies in the Arab World', *Carnegie Papers*, Number 48 (July 2004), available online: http://www.carnegieendowment.org/files/CP48.Ottaway.final.pdf. (Accessed September 2005).

Ottaway, Marina, 'Evaluating Middle East Reform', *Carnegie Papers*, Number 56 (February 2005), available online: http://www.carnegieendowment.org/files/CP56.Ottaway.FINAL.pdf .(Accessed September 2005).

Ottoman Constitution, 1876, Article 3, Bilkent University, available online: www.bilkent.edu.tr/~genckaya/documents1.html. (Accessed 13 May 2006).

Ottoman Constitution, 1909, Art. 3, Bo#abgaziçi University, available online: http://www.anayasa.gen.tr/1909amendment.htm. (Accessed 13 May 2006).

Owen, Roger, *State, Power and Politics in the Making of the Modern Middle East* (London: Routledge, 1992).

Palmer, Monte, *The Politics of the Middle East* (Ifasca: Illinois, F. E. Peacock Publishers, 2002).

Parolin, Gianluca Paolo, 'Generations of Gulf constitutions: paths and perspectives', in Khalaf, Abdulhadi and Luciani, Giacomo, (eds.), *Constitutional Reform and Political Participation in the Gulf* (Dubai: Gulf Research Centre, 2006), pp. 51–88.

Parry, Geraint, *Political Elites* (London: George Allen and Unwin, 1969).

Patai, R., *The Arab Mind* (Scribner, New York, 1973).

Pelham, N., 'King of Jordan "feared being upstaged" by his half-brother', London, *Financial Times* (30 November 2004).

Pellat, Charles, *Ibn-Al-Muqaffa* (Paris, Maisonneuve and Larose, 1976).

Perlmutter, Amos, 'The comparative analysis of military regimes', *World Politics*, vol. 33 no. 1 (October, 1980), pp. 96–120.

Perry, Glen, E., 'The Arab democracy deficit: the case of Egypt', *Arab Studies Quarterly*, vol. 26 no. 2 (spring, 2004), pp. 91–107.

Perthes, Volker, *The Political Economy of Syria under Assad* (London: I.B. Tauris, 1995).

Perthes, Volker, 'The Political Economy of the Syrian Succession', *Survival*, vol. 43 issue 1 (spring, 2001), pp. 143–54.

Perthes, Volker (ed.), *Arab Elites: Negotiating the Politics of Change*, (London: Lynne Rienner, 2004).

Perthes, Volker, 'Arab sons will frustrate the grandsons', Elite Change in the Arab World research project, German Institute for International and Security Affairs (31 December 2004), available online: http://www.swp-berlin.org/en/index.php?PHPSESSID=7da450ee7e5e0b2f12bb8597874559e5&active=home. (Accessed 15 March 2005).

Perthes, Volker, 'Pharaoh Re-elected', *SWP Comments*, No. 39, Berlin, German Institute for International and Security Affairs (September 2005).

Peterson, John E., 'Succession in the States of the Gulf Cooperation Council', *The Washington Quarterly*, vol. 24 no. 4 (autumn, 2001), pp. 173–86.

Peterson, John E., 'The Nature of Succession in the Gulf', *The Middle East Journal*, vol. 55 issue 4 (autumn, 2001), pp. 1–23.

Peterson, John E., 'The emergence of post-traditional Oman', Sir William Luce Fellowship Paper No. 5 (Durham, University of Durham, 30 September 2005), available online: http://eprints.dur.ac.uk/archive/00000139/. (Accessed 8 November 2006).

Petran, Tabitha, *Syria* (London: Ernest Benn, 1972).

Pew Research Centre, Pew Global Attitudes Surveys, available online: http://pewglobal.org/. (Accessed July 2006).

Phillips, Sarah, 'Cracks in the Yemeni system', *Middle East Report OnLine* (28 July 2005), available online: http://www.merip.org/mero/mero072805.html. (Accessed 30 August 2005).

Phillips, Sarah, 'Foreboding about the future in Yemen', *Middle East Report OnLine*, (3 April 2006), available online: http://www.merip.org/mero/mero040306.html. (Accessed 27 May 2006).

Pillai, R., Scandura, T. A. and Williams, E. A., 'Leadership and organizational justice: similarities and differences across cultures', *Journal of International Business Studies*, vol. 30 no. 4 (1999), pp. 762–79.

Poliak, A. N., *Feudalism in Egypt, Syria, Palestine and the Lebanon: 1250–1900* (London: The Royal Asiatic Society, 1939).

Polk, William R., *Understanding Iraq* (London: I. B. Tauris, 2005).

Posusney, M. P. and Angrist, M. P. (eds.), *Authoritarianism in the Middle East* (London: Lynne Rienner Publishers, 2005).

Powe, Lucas A., *The Warren Court and American Politics* (Cambridge Mass.: Belknap Press of Harvard University Press, 2001).

Pressfield, Steven, 'Why we will never see democracy in the Middle East', *ABC News* (11 September 2006), available online: http://abcnews.go.com/International/story?id=2384603&page=1. (Accessed 4 December 2006).

Putnam, Robert, D., *The Beliefs of Politicians* (New Haven and London: Yale University Press, 1973).

Quandt, William B., *Saudi Arabia in the 1980s* (Washington: The Brookings Institution, 1981).

Quandt, William B., 'The Middle East on the brink: prospects for change in the 21st century', speech given at University of Virginia (September 1995), available online: http://www.people.virginia.edu/~wbq8f/MEITALK.htm. (Accessed 20 June 2003).

Quandt, William B., 'Algeria's uneasy peace', *Journal of Democracy*, vol. 13 no. 4 (October 2002), pp. 15–23.

Quinlivan, James T., 'Coup-proofing: Its Practice and Consequences in the Middle East', *International Security*, vol. 24 no. 2 (autumn, 1999), pp. 131–65.

Ramadan, Said, *Islamic Law: its Scope and Equity* (London: Macmillan, 1961).

Raphaeli, N., 'The succession in Kuwait: the triumph of constitutional order over tribal norms', *Enquiry and Analysis Series*, Middle East Media Research Institute, No. 263 (2 February 2006), available online: http://memri.org/bin/articles.cgi?Page=archives&Area=ia&ID=IA26306. (Accessed 3 March 2006).

Rashid, Abdallah, 'Long Live Dictatorship', *Al Ittihad*, Abu Dhabi (29 June 2003), cited in *Middle East Media Research Institute*, no. 536 (10 July 2003), available online: http://www.memri.org/bin/articles.cgi?Page=subjects&Area=reform&ID=SP53603. (Accessed 15 August 2008).

Reuter, Timothy, 'Assembly Politics', *The Mediaeval World* (London: Routledge, 2001).

Richards, Alan and Waterbury, John, *A Political Economy of the Middle East* (Boulder: Westview Press, 1996).

Robins, Philip, *A History of Jordan* (Cambridge: Cambridge University Press, 2004).

Robinson, Glen E., 'Elite cohesion, regime succession and political instability in Syria', *Middle East Policy*, vol. 5 no. 4 (January 1998), pp. 159–79.

Robinson, Glen E., 'Palestine after Arafat', *The Washington Quarterly*, vol. 23 no. 4 (autumn, 2000), pp. 77–90.

Rogerson, Barnaby, *The Heirs of the Prophet Muhammad* (London: Abacus, 2006).

Ronen, Yehudit, 'Libya's rising star: Saif Al Islam and succession', *Middle East Policy*, vol. XII no. 3 (autumn, 2005), pp. 136–44.

Ronfeldt, David, 'Today's wars are less about ideas than extreme tribalism', *Christian Science Monitor* (27 March 2006), available online: http://www.csmonitor.com/2006/0327/p09s01-coop.html. (Accessed 4 December 2006).

Rosen, Richard, A., 'Constitutional process, constitutionalism and the Eritrean experience', *North Carolina Journal of International Law and Commercial Regulation*, vol. 24 (July 2001), pp. 263–304.

Rosenthal, E. I. J., *Political Thought in Medieval Islam: An Introductory Outline* (Cambridge: Cambridge University Press, 1958).

Rousseau, Jean J., *The Social Contract*, (trans.) Cranston, M., (Penguin Books, 1968).

Rustow, D. A., 'Succession in the Twentieth Century', *Journal of International Affairs*, vol. 18 issue 1 (1964), pp. 104–13.

Rubin, Uri, 'The "Constitution of Medina": some notes', *Studia Islamica*, No. 62 (1985), pp. 5–23.

Runciman, Steven, *The Fall of Constantinople*, (Cambridge: Cambridge University Press, 1969).

Ryan, C. R., 'Political liberalization & monarchical succession in Jordan' *Israel Affairs*, vol. 9 no. 3 (spring, 2003), pp. 129–40.

Ryan, C. R. and Schwedler, J., 'Return to democratisation or a new hybrid regime: The 2003 elections in Jordan', *Middle East Policy*, vol. 11, no. 2 (summer, 2004), pp. 138–52.

Sachs, Susan, 'Where brave constitutions are often window-dressing', *The New York Times* (9 March 2004), p. 14.

Sadiki, Larbi, 'Bin Ali's Tunisia: Democracy by Non-Democratic Means', *British Journal of Middle Eastern Studies*, vol. 29 no.1 (2002), pp. 57–78.

Sadowski, Yahya, 'Revolution, Reform or Regression? Arab Political Opinions', *The Brookings Review* (winter, 1990–91).

Sadowski, Yahya, 'The new Orientalism and the democracy debate', *Middle East Report*, no. 183, Political Islam (July–August 1993), pp. 14–40.

Saif, A. A., *What is Constitutionalism? Constitutionalism in the Arab Gulf States* (Dubai: Gulf Research Centre, December 2002).

Saif, A. A., *Constitutionalism in the Arab Gulf States* (Dubai: Gulf Research Centre, 2004).

Salem, Paul, *Bitter Legacy: Ideology and Politics in the Arab World* (Syracuse: Syracuse University Press, New York, 1994).

Salibi, Kamal, *The Modern History of Jordan* (London: I. B. Tauris, 1993).

Sarsar, Saliba, 'Quantifying Arab democracy', *Middle East Quarterly*, (summer, 2006), available online: http://www.meforum.org/article/970. (Accessed 17 January 2007).

Sartori, Giovanni, *The Theory of Democracy, Revisited* (New Jersey: Chatham House, 1987).

Schacht, Joseph, *Introduction to Islamic Law* (Leicester: Clarendon Books, 1983).

Schenker, David, 'Jordan and the Islamicists: Unfinished business', *Washington Institute for Near East Policy*, Peacewatch, No. 334, (27 June 2001), available online: http://www.washingtoninstitute.org/templateC05.php?CID=2025. (Accessed 15 January 2004).

Schmitt, Carl, *Political Theology: Four Chapters on the Concept of Sovereignty*, Schwab George (ed.), (Chicago: University Of Chicago Press, 2006).

Seale, Patrick, *Asad: the Struggle for the Middle East* (Berkeley: University of California Press, 1995).

Sharabi, H. B., *Nationalism and Revolution in the Arab World*, (Princeton: D. van Nostrand Co., Inc, 1966).

Shefa, A., 'Towards the September 7 presidential elections in Egypt', *Middle East Media Research Institute*, Enquiry and Analysis Series, No. 237 (2 September 2005), available online; http://memri.org/bin/articles.cgi?Page=archives&Area=ia&ID=IA23705. (Accessed 21 January 2006).

Shefa, A., 'Egyptian intellectuals assess Egypt's presidential elections', *Middle East Media Research Institute*, Enquiry and Analysis Series, No. 249 (9 November 2005), available online: http://memri.org/bin/articles.cgi?Page=archives&Area=ia&ID=IA24905. (Accessed 21 January 2006).

Shehata, Samir, 'Political Succession in Egypt', in Cantori, L. J., Jacoby, T., Carapico, S. and Shehata, S., 'Political Succession in the Middle East', *Middle East Policy*, vol. 9 no. 3 (September 2002), pp. 110–13.

Slackman, Michael, 'Melee in Cairo reveals stress in Government', *The New York Times* (28 April 2006), available online: http://www.nytimes.com/2006/04/28/world/middleeast/28egypt.html?ex=1303876800&en=ca1f4ff9f198d623&ei=5088&partner=rssnyt&emc=rss. (Accessed 28 April 2006).

Slackman, Michael, 'Under duress, Egypt's Islamist party still surges at polls', *New York Times* (28 November 2006), available online: http://select.nytimes.com/search/restricted/article?res=FB0616FF3F550C7B8EDDA80994DD404482. (Accessed 28 November 2006).

Slackman, M. and Zoepf, K., 'Chief Syrian suspect is at centre of power', *New York Times* (6 November 2005), available online: http://www.iht.com/articles/2005/11/02/news/syria.php. (Accessed 8 September 2006).

Smock, David, 'Islam and Democracy', United States Institute of Peace, Washington, DC, Special Report No. 93 (September 2002).

Snow, Peter, *Hussein: a Biography* (New York: Robert B. Luce, 1972).

Sobelman, D., 'Gamal Mubarak, President of Egypt?', *Middle East Quarterly*, vol. 8, no.2 (spring, 2001), pp. 31–41.

Spencer, Martin E., 'Weber on legitimate norms and authority', *The British Journal of Sociology*, vol. 21 no. 2, (June 1970), pp. 123–34.

Springborg, Patricia, 'Politics, primordialism and orientalism: Marx, Aristotle and the myth of gemeinschaft', *The American Political Science Review*, vol. 80 issue 1 (March 1986), pp. 185–211.

Springborg, Robert, 'Presidential Succession in Egypt: Praetorianism Diminished?', *London Middle East Institute*, (21 October 2004), available online: http://www.lmei.soas.ac.uk.ae. (Accessed 10 January 2005).

Stacher, Joshua, 'Egypt: a leap toward reform – or succession?', *Arab Reform Bulletin*, vol. 4 issue 8 (October 2006), available online: http://www.carnegieendowment.org/publications/index.cfm?fa=view&id=18782&prog=zgp&proj=zme. (Accessed 10 October 2006).

Sultan Bin Zayed Al Nahayan., introduction in Kechichian, J. A. & Dekmejian R. Hrair (eds.), *The Just Prince* (London: Saqi Books, 2003).

Susser, A., 'Succession success' *The New Republic* (22 February 1999), pp. 16–17.

Tafseer Comparison, 2004, available online: http://www.tafseercomparison.org/study4.asp?TitleText=Study%204:%20Verse%204:59. (Accessed 15 August 2009).

Taheri, Amir, 'Role of Islam in the Iraqi constitution', *Arab View* (13 April 2006), available online: http://www.arabview.com/articles.asp?article=384. (Accessed 16 August 2006).

Takyeh, Ray, 'Qadhafi's Libya and the Prospect of Islamic Succession', *Middle East Policy*, vol. VII no. 2 (2000), pp. 154–64.

Talal, Hussein bin, 'Letter to HRH Prince El Hassan', *The Cyber Library of Jordan – Hussein I*. 25 January, 1999, available online: http://www.kinghussein.gov.jo/99-jan25.html. (Accessed 2 February 2006).

Talbi, Mohamed, 'A record of failure', *Journal of Democracy*, vol. 11 no. 3 (July 2000), pp. 58–68.

Tapper, Richard, 'Anthropologists, historians, and tribespeople on tribe and state formation in the Middle East', in Khoury, Philip S. and Joseph Kostiner (eds.), *Tribes and State Formation in the Middle East* (Berkeley: University of California Press, 1990), pp. 48–73.

Tessler, Mark, 'Islam and democracy in the Middle East: the impact of religious orientations on attitudes toward democracy in four Arab countries', *Comparative Politics*, vol. 34 no. 3 (April 2002), pp. 337–54.

Tessler, Mark, 'Arab and Muslim political attitudes: stereotypes and evidence from survey research', *International Studies Perspectives*, no. 4, (2003), pp. 175–81.

Tétreault, M. A., 'Three Emirs and a tale of two transitions', *Middle East Report Online* (11 February 2006), available online: www.werip.org/mero/mero021006.html. (Accessed 19 October 2006).

Al-Thakeb, Fahed, T., 'The Arab family and modernity: evidence from Kuwait', *Current Anthropology*, vol. 26, no. 5 (December 1985), pp. 575–80.

Thaysen, Uwe, 'A new constitution for a new Germany?', *German Studies Review*, vol. 16, no. 2 (May 1993), pp. 299–310.

Thompson, Edward P., *Whigs and Hunters* (London: Allen Lane, 1975).

Tibi, Bassam, 'The simultaneity of the unsimultaneous: old tribes and imposed nation-states in the modern Middle East', in Khoury, P. S. and Joseph Kostiner (eds.), *Tribes and State Formation in the Middle East* (Berkeley: University of California Press, 1990), pp. 127–52.

Tierney, Brian, *Religion, Law and the Growth of Constitutional Thought, 1150–1650* (Cambridge: Cambridge University Press, 1982).

Titunik, R. F., 'Democracy, domination and legitimacy' in Camic, C. *et al.*, (eds.), *Max Weber's Economy and Society: a Critical Companion* (Stanford, CA: Stanford University Press, 2005).

Trevelyan, George M., *England under the Stuarts* (London: Folio Society, 1996).

Tribune, 'UAE prince ousted, army sent in', *The Tribune* (16 June 2003), available online: http://www.tribuneindia.com/2003/20030616/world.htm#5. (Accessed 20 June 2003).

Tripp, Charles, *A History of Iraq* (Cambridge: Cambridge University Press, 2002).

Tschentscher, A. (ed.), *International Constitutional Law*, last modified 7 September 2008, available online: http://www.oefre.unibe.ch/law/icl/. (Accessed 15 August 2009).

Turner, Brian S., *Religion, Law and the Growth of Constitutional Thought, 1150–1650* (Cambridge: Cambridge University Press, 1982).

Turner, Bryan S., *Weber and Islam* (London and Boston: Routledge & Kegan Paul, 1974).

Turner, Bryan S., 'The sociology of Islamic social structures', *Sociology*, vol. 33 no. 1 (February 1999), pp. 199–202.

Ullman, Walter, *Medieval Political Thought* (Harmondsworth: Penguin, 1975).

Unger, Roberto Mangabeira, *Law in Modern Society* (New York: The Free Press, 1976).

United Nations Development Programme, *First Arab Human Development Report*, New York, United Nations (2002), available online: http://hdr.undp.org/reports/view_reports.cfm?year=0&country=0&region=R1&type=0&theme=0&launched=0. (Accessed 27 August 2006).

United Nations Development Programme, *Arab Human Development Report*, New York, United Nations (2003), available online: http://hdr.undp.org/ reports/view_reports.cfm?year=0&country=0&region=R1&type=0&theme=0&launched=0. (Accessed 27 August 2006).

United Nations Development Programme, *Arab Human Development Report*, New York, United Nations (2004), available online: http://hdr.undp.org/reports/view_reports.cfm?year=0&country=0&region=R1&type=0&theme=0&launched=0. (Accessed 27 August 2007).

United Nations Development Programme, *Arab Human Development Report*, New York, United Nations (2005), available online: http://rbas.undp.org/ahdr2005.shtml. (Accessed 27 August 2007).

United States Department of State, *Country Report on Human Rights Practices, Egypt* (6 March 2007), available online: http://www.state.gov/p/nea/ci/81997.htm. (Accessed 4 April 2007).

United States Government, *National Security Strategy of the United States of America*, Washington, (September, 2002), available online: http://merln.ndu.edu/whitepapers/USnss2002.pdf. (Accessed 17 March 2006).

Vatikiotis, P., *Islam and Power* (London: Croom Helm, 1981).

Vickers, Kenneth H., *England in the Later Middle Ages* (London: Methuen & Co., 1950).

Vinogradov, Amal, 'The 1920 revolt in Iraq: the role of tribes in national politics', *International Journal of Middle East Studies*, vol. 3 issue 2 (April 1972), pp. 123–39.

Volpi, Frederic, 'Pseudo-democracy in the Muslim world', *Third World Quarterly*, vol. 25 issue 6 (2004), pp. 1061–78.

Walsh, L. E., *Final Report of the Independent Counsel for Iran-Contra Matters*, United States Court of Appeal for District of Columbia, vol. I, Concluding Observations (4 August 1993), pp. 561–67, available online: http://www.fas.org/irp/offdocs/walsh/. (Accessed 21 October 2006).

Waluchow, W., 'Constitutionalism', in Zalta, Edward N. (ed.), *The Stanford Encyclopaedia of Philosophy* (Spring 2004), available online: http://plato.stanford.edu/archives/spr2004/entries/constitutionalism/. (Accessed 12 March 2005).

Washington, H. A. (ed.), *The writings of Thomas Jefferson: being his autobiography, correspondence, reports, messages, addresses, and other writings, official and private* (New York: Taylor and Maury, 1853–54), available online: http://www.archive.org/details/writingsofthomas03jeff. (Accessed 26 May 2009).

Waterbury, John, *The Commander of the Faithful* (New York: Columbia University Press, 1970).

Watt, W. Montgomery, *Muhammad at Mecca* (Oxford: Clarendon Press, 1953).

Watt, W. Montgomery, *The Influence of Islam on Medieval Europe (Islamic Surveys)*, (Edinburgh: Edinburgh University Press, 1972).

Watt, W. Montgomery, *Islamic Political Thought* (Edinburgh: Edinburgh University Press, 1999).

Weber, Max, *The Theory of Social and Economic Organisation*, (trans.) Henderson A. M. and Parsons T., (New York: The Free Press, 1964).

Weber, Max, *Ancient Judaism*, (trans.) Hans H. Gerth and Don Martindale (New York: Free Press, 1967).

Weber, Max, *Economy and Society*, Roth, G. and Wittich, C. (eds.), (California: University of California Press, 1968).

Wehr, Hans, *A Dictionary of Modern Written Arabic*, Cowan, J. Milton (ed.) (London: George Allen and Unwin Ltd., 1971).

Welch, Catherine, Marschan-Piekkari, Rebecca and Penttinen, Heli, *Interviewing Elites in International Organisations: a Balancing Act for the Researcher* (3 February 2006), available online: http://www.uni-muenster.de/PeaCon/dgs-mills/mills-texte/The%20QualitativeInterview-InternationalBusinessResearch.htm. (Accessed 5 March 2006).

Whitaker, Brian, 'Hereditary republics in Arab states', *The Guardian* (28 August 2001).

Whitaker, Brian, 'Journalist arrested', *Middle East International*, issue 721 (18 March 2004).

World Bank, 'Better Governance for Development in the Middle East and North Africa', Washington, DC (2003), available online: http://worldbank.org/92HMCDTM60. (Accessed 29 May 2009).

World Values Survey, for example the 2005 survey. available online: http://www.world valuessurvey.org/. (Accessed 15 December 2006).

Wright, Robin, 'Two visions of reformation', *The Journal of Democracy*, vol. 72 no. 2 (April 1996), pp. 64–75.

Wright, Steven, 'Generational change and elite-driven reforms in the Kingdom of Bahrain', *Sir William Luce Fellowship Paper* No. 7, Durham Middle East Papers, No. 81 (June 2006), available online: http://eprints.dur.ac.uk/archive/00000221/01/wright.pdf. (Accessed September 2006).

Yamani, Mai, *Changed Identities* (London: Royal Institute of International Affairs, 2000).

Yousef, D. A., 'Predictors of decision-making styles in a non-Western country', *Leadership and Organisation Development Journal*, vol. 19 no. 7 (1998), pp. 366–73.

Zahraa, Mahdi, 'Characteristic features of Islamic law: perceptions and misconceptions', *Arab Law Quarterly*, vol. 15 no. 2 (2000), pp. 168–96.

Zaoual, Hassan, 'The Maghreb Experience: A Challenge to the Rational Myths of Economics', *Review of African Political Economy*, London (December 1999).

Zerhouni, Saloua, 'Morocco: Reconciling Continuity and Change', in Perthes, G. (ed.), *Arab Elites: Negotiating the Politics of Change* (London: Lynne Rienner, 2004), pp. 61–86.

Zisser, Eyal, 'The succession struggle in Damascus', *Middle East Quarterly*, vol. II no. 3 (September 1995), available online: http://www.meforum.org/article/264. (Accessed 10 September 2006).

Zisser, Eyal, 'Will Bashshar Al-Assad Rule?', *Middle East Quarterly*, vol. 7 no. 3 (September 2000), available online: http://www.meforum.org/article/69. (Accessed 10 September 2006).

Zisser, Eyal, 'Does Bashar al-Assad Rule Syria?', *Middle East Quarterly*, vol X no. 1 (winter, 2003), available online: http://www.meforum.org/article/517. (Accessed 9 September 2006).

Zubaida, Sami, *Islam, the People and the State* (London: I. B. Tauris, 2001).

Zubaida, Sami, *Law and Power in the Islamic World* (London: I. B. Tauris, 2005).

Zogby International, 'What Arabs Think: Values, Beliefs and Concerns', 19 November 2002, available online: http://www.zogby.com/search/ReadNews.cfm?ID=650. (Accessed 15 August 2009).

Zogby International, 'Unprecedented Middle East Poll Tackles Key Questions About Future Of Arab World', 9 November 2005, available online: http://www.zogby.com/search/ReadNews.cfm?ID=1042. (Accessed 15 August 2009).

Index